UNCOVERING ALIAS

AN UNOFFICIAL GUIDE

NIKKI STAFFORD AND ROBYN BURNETT

ECW PRESS

Published by ECW PRESS
2120 Queen Street East, Suite 200, Toronto, Ontario, Canada M4E 1E2

National Library of Canada Cataloguing in Publication

Stafford, Nikki, 1973-
Uncovering Alias : an unofficial guide / Nikki Stafford and Robyn Burnett.

ISBN 1-55022-653-3

1. Alias (Television program) I. Burnett, Robyn (Robyn S.) II. Title.

PN1992.77.A45S82 2004   791.45'72   C2004-902552-X

Colour section credits, in order: Avik Gilboa/WireImage.com, Christina Radish, Christina Radish,
Christina Radish, Christina Radish, Steve Grayson/WireImage.com, Steve Grayson/WireImage.com,
Christina Radish, Lester Cohen/WireImage.com, Christina Radish, Jim Smeal/WireImage.com, Christina
Radish, Christina Radish, Christina Radish, Christina Radish, Christina Radish

Cover and Text Design: Tania Craan
Typesetting: Gail Nina
Cover Photo: Sheryl Nields/Icon
Production: Mary Bowness
Printing: Tri-Graphic

The publication of *Uncovering Alias* has been generously supported by the Canada Council,
the Ontario Arts Council, and the Government of Canada through the
Book Publishing Industry Development Program. Canada

DISTRIBUTION

CANADA: Jaguar Book Group, 100 Armstrong Avenue, Georgetown, ON, L7G 5S4
UNITED STATES: Independent Publishers Group, 814 North Franklin Street,
Chicago, Illinois 60610

PRINTED AND BOUND IN CANADA

ECW PRESS
ecwpress.com

Table of Contents

The Anatomy of *Alias*

The Cast of *Alias*

Acknowledgments

Robyn:

I'd like to give a special thanks to the fans of *Alias* whose sites were incredibly informative and tons of fun. Thank you to Elisha at Jennifer Garner Fancube for your help with JG questions and to David at Project Alias for your enthusiasm. Thank you, Chris, for letting me dominate the television for a few months. Thanks, Mom and Jay, for getting me hooked on the show in the first place. Thanks to Jack and ECW for letting us pursue this book and for the constant support. An extra special thanks to Nikki for taking this journey with me and to Jen Hale for getting this project rolling.

Nikki:

Thanks so much to the fans of the show for making this book a reality, and for your dedication in following such a high quality series and keeping it on television. Thanks to Robert for putting up with me bogarting the television and disappearing constantly to work on this. Thanks to Jonathan and Fionna for your constant support throughout this project, to Sue for your encouragement and for reading early versions of the book, and to Jack David and everyone at ECW Press for your enthusiasm. And to Sebastian and Piquette for keeping me company throughout the process. Thanks so much to Robyn for making this book such a fun experience — I couldn't imagine working with anyone else on this. And finally, thanks to Jennifer Hale for all of your hard work and perseverance.

We'd like to dedicate this book to little Syd and the fans of *Alias*.

The Anatomy of Alias

Regarding J.J.

J.J. Abrams has been described as "the whole package in every respect." He can write, direct, produce, and even compose music. In many ways, he is the Sydney Bristow of the television production world: always active, always assuming a new persona, and definitely versatile. Not only does he push the envelope on a creative scale, but he's also good to work with, says Lloyd Braun, the chair of ABC's Entertainment Television Group: "He's just great to deal with day in and day out. It's very rare to have someone who's good at virtually every element of the business, but that's what J.J. is."

The son of television producer Gerald W. Abrams (*Nuremberg, Drop Dead Gorgeous*), Jeffrey Abrams was born in New York in 1966. After moving to Los Angeles, J.J. found inspiration in a day out with his grandfather. "Since I was a kid, I always knew I wanted to make movies and TV shows," he says. "My grandfather took me to the Universal Studios [California] tour and I just remember falling in love with the process of making movies. So I was interested in the idea of putting on a show." Before he was even 10 years old, he started to pester his father in the hopes of using dad's Super 8 camera to make his own movies. Eventually his father caved in, and Abrams has been filming ever since. It didn't start with the writing, however. As a child, he would draw pictures of shows that he wanted to create.

J.J.'s love of all things film continued through his teenage years, when he not only submitted films to the student festival circuit but actually won. While on the circuit he met up with Matt Reeves, who would eventually become the co-creator of the critically acclaimed series

Felicity. An article the *Los Angeles Times* ran on the work created by the two teenagers landed on the desk of Steven Spielberg. He offered them the chance to re-splice some of his short films for a possible television special. A few years later, after Abrams had graduated from college and sold a few scripts, he decided to approach Spielberg about a possible sequel to *Who Framed Roger Rabbit*. "I told him, 'You know, I spliced some movies of yours when I was a teenager.' And he said, 'I know.' The fact that he remembered freaked the hell out of me."

In the mid-1980s, while attending Sarah Lawrence College just north of New York City, Abrams discovered an appreciation for intelligent women. "[It] actually had an enormous impact. My mother is [also] a very strong woman; my wife [has] one of the most brilliant minds . . . I'm drawn to that," he claims. He would later take those qualities and imbue his television heroines with them. J.J. co-wrote his first comedic screenplay, *Taking Care of Business* starring Charles Grodin, while in college and sold it soon after graduating. While the film wasn't a huge box office success, it didn't hinder Abrams's career. He both wrote and co-produced his next film, *Regarding Henry* starring Harrison Ford. He also had a cameo in the film as a delivery boy. About this brief on-screen appearance J.J. jokes, "There are some things that should not be allowed to occur in nature, and one is me in the same frame with Harrison Ford."

J.J. followed with the films *Gone Fishin'*, *Forever Young* (which he also executive produced), and *Armageddon*, which hit theaters in 1998. Abrams admits to having bittersweet feelings about the action thriller: "[A]s someone who was an accredited writer on *Armageddon*, my one real question is, is that something you really want to publicize?" In between writing engagements he also found time to produce the films *The Pallbearer* and *The Suburbans*.

After *Armageddon* Abrams branched out into the world of television, which was not what he had expected to do. He thrived nonetheless: "I lucked into this incredible medium. The hours are brutal, the pressure's tremendous, and the need for material is insatiable. But it's so exciting to work with the same group of people on a long-term basis, and you're writing something you know is going to get shot. That just doesn't exist in features." It was a profitable move as well.

J.J. Abrams is one of a handful of talented young creators in television today.

With Matt Reeves, Abrams created *Felicity*, a romantic drama about a young college freshman in New York who is trying to figure out where life will take her. The Touchstone Television series was one of the first to really put the WB Network on the proverbial map. The critically acclaimed series won actress Keri Russell a Golden Globe for Best Actress in a Drama in 1998, the first year of the show (later, Jennifer Garner would achieve the same feat). The show was a popular one with the critics and launched the careers of actors Scott Speedman (*Underworld*, *Dark Blue*) and Scott Foley (who later married Garner). The Nielsen ratings dropped at the end of season 1, however, after the infamous "chopping of the locks," which left Keri Russell with a short, curly 'do. Still, Abrams was signed to a four-year deal, which then led to the creation of *Alias* three years later. He also continued moonlighting in film, writing, and producing the thriller *Joy Ride*.

It was while he was working on *Felicity* that Abrams came up with the concept for *Alias*. "It came about out of frustration in finding stories to write about on *Felicity* because there was no franchise, there was no crime or law or medicine or vampires or politics, there were no stories coming to our characters," he explains. "It was a show about very sweet, romantic characters going through their college lives, so it didn't really lend itself to high drama. And when you reach for high drama on a show like *Felicity*, you're accused of melodrama." So Abrams had a thought during a writing session: "I said, 'You know what would just rock? If Felicity was recruited by the CIA because then she'd have to go on these missions internationally and be in these incredibly high-stakes, life-and-death situations. She couldn't tell Ben. She couldn't tell Noel.'" The seed was planted and *Alias* was born.

Also inspired by the series *La Femme Nikita*, Abrams decided to take things a step further and explore the whole concept of family dysfunction in unusual circumstances. He says, "To me, it was about a young woman who was disenfranchised. She had no connection really to anyone, especially her mother and father. I was interested in seeing how this young woman, given that scenario, learns the truth about what she's doing and gets a perspective on herself and how lost she really is." Using the soundtrack from *Run Lola Run* for inspiration, Abrams wrote down the concept and pitched it to Touchstone at the end of 2000: "I wrote [a script], turned it in, and they said, 'Who do you want to direct it?' Without having thought it through very well, I said, 'Me,' and suddenly we were making the pilot." J.J. not only wrote, directed, and produced the first episode of *Alias*, but also created the show's techno theme song. "It blows my mind how much you can do with a handful of programs and a laptop computer," he quips.

Abrams has been influenced by so many different genres that he wanted to combine them to create something different. So for *Alias*, he mixed spy drama, comedy, romance, familial drama, science fiction, and the Hong Kong martial arts genres. He incorporated elements of *The Twilight Zone* and *thirtysomething*, as well as features of the spy shows *Mission: Impossible* and *The Avengers*. "When you write a pilot, you're building your dream space," J.J. says. "You want to populate that area with as many fun props as you can, so that when you're living in it for hopefully years, you're not bored." The show was not meant to be a literal interpretation; it was to have more of a comic book feel: "It's kind of a hyperreality that feels as compelling as something you might believe is actually happening right this second." His other goal was to take a B-genre concept and turn it into an A-list show through strong writing and commitment to the choices made. The *Alias* team has succeeded admirably. "It's escapist entertainment," J.J. says of the show, "but hopefully it's done well enough so people watching it don't feel it's a guilty pleasure, just simply a pleasure."

Abrams is a serial creator, constantly keeping himself busy by sketching, creating music on his keyboard, or molding clay. He even made a homemade chocolate bar for his wife one Valentine's Day. He's a big video game fan as well: "When I was younger, I was one of those people who would play Super Mario Brothers, back in the day when you couldn't save it, so you had to leave it on all day just so that you could come back to it instead of starting over. And then you come home and find out your roommate kicked the cord out of the socket. So I love games like that. For someone who was aspiring to be a writer — well, I don't know if I was ever aspiring to be a writer; I really wanted to be a movie director — it was an amazing way to exist in a world."

After the success of *Felicity*, J.J. Abrams developed a series for one of his *Felicity* actresses, Jennifer Garner.

You would think he has a full plate with *Alias*, but J.J. still has more projects on the go. He just signed an 18-month extension on his contract with Touchstone, which steps his production company, Bad Robot Television, up a notch. He has also hired Thom Sherman (senior VP of drama development at ABC) as his president. "I've secretly hoped the next phase of my career could be something like this, so I feel like I've just won the lottery," says Sherman. "J.J. is a monster talent, probably the smartest, most unique creative mind with whom I've worked, and he's also just a great person." Abrams was recently offered the chance to tackle writing the latest remake of *Superman*. J.J. put the pressure of re-creating this classic into perspective: "I'll do the best I can, then if the powers that be don't like it, I'm sure there will be a fiftieth writer. I think it's become one of the requirements of the WGA [Writers Guild of America], that at some point you have to be hired to write *Superman*. I'm excited about it, because I used to love Superman so much when I was a kid. My son goes to bed every night with a Superman shirt on. He's three and a half. I feel like I couldn't pass this up." While a new writer is now taking on the script, Abrams' version did get noticed.

He is also involved with two new series. The first, *Lost*, is about a group of castaways on a Pacific Island, and the second, *The Catch*, is a bounty hunter drama to star childhood friend and *Alias* alum Greg

Grunberg. J.J. may work with a multitude of genres, but whether the characters are off executing spy missions, attending college, or sweating it out in isolation, he always manages to make them three-dimensional. "Even though [the characters I write] might be at odds with someone, or damaged in some way, or not understood, the characters I tend to embrace are, deep down, good people," he says. So, is Abrams really the Renaissance man that everyone says he is? Perhaps, but he has a different viewpoint: "Anyone that's ever seen anything I've done certainly knows there's much I can't do. Doing *Alias* is the closest for me to working on student films, when I was a kid making movies . . . that's the best of all worlds, to do something where you feel almost closer to being a kid than you do an adult. Anything like that is a good thing."

There's no question regarding J.J. Abrams and his creative abilities: he is undoubtedly the complete package.

Spy Writing

Traditionally, television writers were poached from radio and the theater, but it has since become common for people to hop over to television from film, just as J.J. Abrams has done. There are obvious differences between the structure of television and film, one being that television writers commonly act as producers; as such, they have more control over their work than screenwriters. The hierarchy of the writing profession in the television industry, from bottom to top, works as follows: outside freelancers, who write speculative scripts for existing shows; readers; writers' assistants; staff writers; assistant producers, associate producers; then producers and, finally, executive producers. The latter are usually the creators of the show, or possibly the financial/business heads, and it is up to these individuals to run the ship. As writers move up the ranks on a television series, they will often receive a producer title, which shows their seniority in the group and brings with it supervisory responsibilities. It is not uncommon for executive producers to work on more than one series at once. The supervising producer is often the one who acts as head writer. There are also producers outside the writing department.

Executive producers can keep themselves involved simply with the business aspects of a series, or they can become involved more directly in the writing of the show — it depends on the individual. The concept of hiring a writer-producer for long-term contracts has become common, with one of the most notable situations being ABC's hiring of Steven Bochco in 1988 to underwrite the next 10 shows that he created. The creator of the hits *Hill Street Blues* and *L.A. Law*, Bochco followed this agreement with such shows as *Doogie Howser, MD* and NYPD *Blue*. He also had the freedom to become more experimental, generating the flop *Cop Rock*. J.J. Abrams has a similar deal with Touchstone Television.

So, who writes this marvelous mixed-breed show, *Alias*? "Some TV shows, it's pretty much six or seven individuals, writing individual episodes," says writer-producer Jesse Alexander. "Here, it's really collaborative, and I think that's important, because everybody brings a little something different to the table." The collaborative writing team has included J.J. Abrams (creator and executive producer), John Eisendrath (executive producer), Alex Kurtzman-Counter (executive producer as of 2003), Roberto Orci (executive producer as of 2003), Jesse Alexander (producer), Jeff Pinkner (producer), Daniel Arkin (co-producer), Vanessa Taylor (co-producer), J.R. "Rick" Orci, Debra J. Fisher (now with *The O.C.*), Sean Gerace, Crystal Nix Hines, Erica Messer, Monica Breen, Alison Schapker, Josh Appelbaum, André Nemec, Laurence Andries, R.P. Gaborno, and Christopher Hollier (for details on specific episodes, see the episode guide beginning on page 179).

Before the show could begin, the first thing Abrams had to do was assemble the best writing team for the task. "I was looking for an array of strengths and experiences that would add to the point of view of the writers' room. Some writers were stronger in terms of technical, high-concept invention. Others were more dramatic, character-based writers," he says. The room is run by writer John Eisendrath, whose job is to make sure that the stories are broken down properly. The interesting thing is that he had no genre experience before joining the show. "I always make fun of him now when he casually makes references to miniature electromagnetic pulse devices or something — things he *never* would have referred to only last year," Abrams said.

Alias writers maintain that the process they use is very collaborative. What exactly does that mean? There's the simple answer: "We all just basically get together and figure it out, and what's interesting is, as you do it, stories that you didn't think were gonna go anywhere just suddenly explode and other stories you're certain are gonna be great you can't figure out — they just die on the vine," says Abrams. John Eisendrath expands on that point: "It's not just people talking at each other, but it's people building on ideas. Somebody suggests something, someone doesn't agree with it but maybe thinks there's a piece of it that works, and we'll go in another direction with it. It's never been my experience that people, no matter how capable they are, can go off on their own and come up with something that will have their ideas as well thought out or stories as well formed as when they're 'subjected' to the group."

A former journalist and *Beverly Hills 90210* scribe, Eisendrath always appreciated that in those jobs he was constantly learning; working on *Alias* has allowed him to continue that learning process. The other writers on the team have come from diverse backgrounds, including the shows *Ally McBeal*, *Xena: Warrior Princess*, *Party of Five*, and *Profiler*, to name a few. The group assembled and the process began. The first objective was to expand the world that J.J. Abrams had created. "When you do the first year of a show, you're creating everything — nothing was there before . . . ," states Abrams. "Everything from the smallest detail to the largest macro view, everything is new."

Abrams came up with an unusual structural idea right at the start: why not implement the classic five-act cliffhanger structure to every episode of the show rather than simply the season finale? "Literally, the Writers Guild, I was told, might have problems with it, and the network was concerned that it might be confusing. But it was *so* against protocol, I just thought, *Screw it, it's what the show should be*, so we started doing it," Abrams recalls. "It's worked well sometimes and at other times I wish that we'd had some more satisfying material at the end of the show, either before or instead of a cliffhanger." This method follows that of the traditional serial shows, such as the classic *Batman* television series starring Adam West. The goal, however, is to make sure that there is some semblance of a conclusion to each episode so that the audience gets some satisfaction. For the writers, keeping that format is a different experience. "It's an amazing storytelling challenge, trying to keep the emotion up and keep the story consistent," says writer Jesse Alexander. Instead of separate entities, each episode links to the next, as though the entire season is just one long story.

The other unusual thing about *Alias* is that it does not have a bible for the writers to reference. Most of the show is brainstormed right there in the writers' room, allowing them to be spontaneous rather than locked into definite plans for a season. It is this flexibility that allows them to deal with issues that may arise. An extreme example is the tragedy of September 11, which led to some changes not only in the television schedule but in certain shows as well. For the *Alias* team, it meant returning to episode 4 (at the time they were working on 5 and 6) and taking out the reference to the World Trade Organization being a target for attack. On the whole, however, *Alias* does not reference real-life events; rather, it stretches into other realms, like science fiction, exploring such concepts as the prophetic Rambaldi artifacts. The flexibility comes into play in other areas as well. For example, when the character of Charlie wasn't serving the story anymore, he was written out. In another case, when the writers found out that the character of McKenas Cole was going to be played by Quentin Tarantino, they made sure to adjust the dialogue to fit the actor.

Instead of a full plan for the year, the writing team comes up with "tent poles" right at the start of the season. "We have crucial points [tent poles] in the season that we want to get to by certain episodes," says writer Rick (J.R.) Orci. "We'll map out each character's story arc broadly. A lot of times, we'll change it halfway through [the season]. . . . Then when we start to set the episode, all of the [staff] writers are in the conference room, and we outline the episode roughly, scene by scene." In season 1, one of those tent poles was that Sydney would discover the truth about her mother's KGB history by mid-season.

The writers' room sports a large board with color-coded cards that outline the major seasonal points. With this framework in place, the next step is to write each episode. One important goal is to keep *Alias*'s underlying theme intact: it's a show about a dysfunctional family in which all the members live in the world of espionage. All 10 writers, including Abrams, sit in the writers' room with the season all mapped out. At this point, they go through the season episode by episode. Taking a week to go over the details, the team usually begins with the character aspects of the story before delving into the action. After getting the general shape of an episode, the team goes through it more specifically, breaking it down into scenes on the infamous board. Once the episode beats are laid out on the board and the act breaks are strong enough, "John Eisendrath will cook up a great outline," explains writer and story editor Debra Fisher. From there, the writers take turns transforming the detailed outline into a full script. Sometimes a writer has the opportunity to contribute individual input into the script, but the major elements are preplanned.

There are other elements that need attention, however, and one of those is the story's technical aspects. That's where Rick Orci comes into the picture. Considered the Marshall of the writing team, Rick gets his ideas and information from *Popular Science* magazine, from conspiracy Web sites, and also from a Web site maintained by the Federation of American Scientists. The latter site helps with details on international agencies. As a consequence of his knowledge, Rick works on almost every script, though he adjusts his approach to the needs of his co-writers: "I work differently with everyone. Some writers will just write the mission and have a gadget and say in parentheses 'Tech,' and I'll just go back and fill it in for them, whereas some like me to help them brainstorm the mission and then help them write it. Some will write their own version of it and ask me to polish it up." Orci has even created a special Web site for the writers where he has compiled his research, allowing them to explore ideas themselves.

Rick Orci calls himself a "tech geek" and claims that fellow writer Jesse Alexander is also into the technical side of things. Coming up with Marshall's toy du jour and the language used to describe it might seem like a complete free-for-all, but the fact is that each item is based on theoretical possibilities. While the capabilities and functions of Marshall's gadgets may get exaggerated for the show, it doesn't mean they are not conceivable in science. "We've decided collectively to make up as little as possible," says writer Jeff Pinkner. When it comes to any information regarding aircraft, the writers turn to licensed pilot Jesse Alexander. Alexander also went to college with Abrams.

After a week or so, the writer assigned to the script delivers a draft to Abrams's office. At that point, J.J. goes through the script with the other departments, confirming its feasibility. This is where the collaboration continues, and once again, flexibility is important. In some cases, the locations chosen for a particular script are not possible to create, so adjustments need to be made. In other cases, there are issues with the time of day, and it is up to the production design team to come up with suggestions on how to make it work. The changes are made, and the script is set.

Alias has continually surprised critics and audiences by breaking away from conventional storytelling. "On the shows that I've been involved with before, there was always a policy that you can't just blow out all of your stories too quickly. You have to hold back, unravel things slowly," explains director and executive producer Ken Olin. "The thing that has been so incredible about *Alias* is just the opposite. It's like, we're just going to go for it. We're going to blow out as many stories as we can tell and do as much as we can do."

The episodes continue to be filled to the brim with a slew of elements, and with plot twist after plot twist. It would be easy to swamp the show with gimmicks, but the character stories still remain a priority. "The way we tell our character stories, we try to have our characters be as emotionally honest as they can be," says writer Jesse Alexander, adding, "It's odd, because in a spy show, where everybody has secrets, our characters are very emotionally honest with each other. That's something that J.J. pioneered in *Felicity* that we carried over into this show." It is this unique blend that makes *Alias* so compelling, and the writers have managed to embrace it fully. "Something that makes us different is that, sure, there's good guys and bad guys, but sometimes, within an episode, the bad guy, Arvin Sloane, you can end up feeling sorry for [him]. I don't know how many TV series blur those lines . . . ," claims writer Erica Messer.

The show has gone through major plot changes since the first season. "The second year of a show, in many ways the hardest year, is really about keeping [the story] alive and having it be something that evolves," says Abrams. And then came the amazing cliffhanger, which spun the show into a whole different direction. "It made us question not only what the characters were going through, but, working backwards, who the characters *were* to begin with, even if it meant re-examining who they were in a way that we might not have done just coming into a normal season three," explains Abrams.

One of the challenges the writers have had to deal with is that the complexity of the show makes it challenging for new viewers to glom on to it. As a consequence, they have made some adjustments as the seasons have progressed. "The good news and bad news about *Alias* is that you have to really watch it and go with it a couple of times before it grasps you or you grasp it," says Abrams. "It's not something that you immediately understand, like, 'Oh, it's about a young woman who's a lawyer in Boston.' There is a complexity to it. But the fun of the show is that there is ambiguity all around, and at the end of the day it's a show about a young woman who's just trying to live a normal life."

While some of the writers have changed since *Alias* began, it still keeps us guessing each week. Sydney Bristow not only captures the villains but captures the viewers, even if it takes her a few episodes. "She's your best friend who lives right next door, who is living a double life. I think that's really attractive to people," says Debra Fisher. As to what is going to happen next? J.J. Abrams reveals only this point: "We have in our heads the last beat of the series — whether it's three years from now or ten years from now, we have this last beat we really want to do. But every year, what we do is, we tell our story. . . . I always liken it to hiking in the fog: you see vaguely through the fog your destination. The closer you get, the clearer the paths become and the more you need to be flexible."

Until the season wraps, the writers will keep writing, moving along with the show and up the food chain. At present, writers Roberto Orci and Alex Kurtzman-Counter are developing their own project for Touchstone Television, which follows a woman working in the Secret Service, exploring how she balances her marriage and her career. Sound familiar? We'll soon find out. As for Sydney, she'll keep on kicking.

The Illusion of International Intrigue

Watching *Alias*, it is sometimes necessary to remind yourself that the actors are not in a Mexican courtyard, a Korean prison, or in downtown Paris. While stock footage is used for the sweeping shots of various international locales, imagination is required in order to create sets or find locations to serve as those countries (over 53 in total). Just as Sydney changes her appearance each week, thus creating a new alias, Southern California does the same thing, standing in for everything from Bali to Germany to Korea. In fact, the only time the crew left L.A. was to film an episode in Las Vegas, simply because re-creating Sin City was too expensive.

Furthermore, the action in the scripts is nothing if not ambitious. Director and executive producer Ken Olin explains: "We were trying to accomplish, day-to-day, the kinds of things that J.J. had written in *Armageddon*. First of all, we finally began to realize what was and was not possible. People jumping off buildings and shooting out windows is pretty major. Two years ago, [producer Sarah Caplan] and I would read the scripts and say to J.J., 'You can't do this.' But then we began to figure out how we could."

On board as a producer is Sarah Caplan, and Abrams couldn't be happier. "She has the impossible job of being handed scripts and fig-uring out how in the name of God to make them," says Abrams. Having worked with Abrams before on *Felicity*, Caplan welcomed the change *Alias* offered. She had also produced the psychic thriller tele-vision show *The Others*. She saw that the biggest challenge with *Alias* was that the crew would constantly be prepping for the show while shooting it. Once Caplan has a copy of an early draft of a script, she does an analysis to figure out the logistics regarding the necessary locations. Then, with the production design team, she gets to work on obtaining permits and discussing the art direction. As the pro-duction design team does its job, Sarah Caplan works with the director to determine his or her ideas about the script. She also works with the stunt group and effects teams. As she runs around sorting out details, she notes the changes that need to be made in the script and arranges for the adjustments. Together with the assistant director, she storyboards the episode and budgets it, adjusting the script continually as the work goes along.

The producers are reliant on location managers Mike Haro and Alison Taylor-Fletcher to find just the right spot to convert into the country of the week for production designer Scott Chambliss. As the production designer for *Alias*, Scott looks after how the world looks, both on external locations and on the soundstages. In season 1, Scott felt he needed to be much more precise in his location re-creations, but has relaxed a bit since then. He says, "Because it's so much about making a grand statement really fast, it was simpler for me to go after locations, architecture, and buildings that had some piece to them that the camera can spend two and a half seconds on and go, 'Okay, now we're in Afghanistan,' and build around that, knowing that if they turn the corner over there, they'll see the one-oh-one freeway."

Right at the start, Chambliss and his crew were on the lookout in Los Angeles for potential locations: "We hired a location photographer that I'd worked with before to go all over Los Angeles, photograph anything that was of any interest in helping us re-create international locations, and then I put books [of photos] together for [J.J. Abrams], and wrote suggestions — storyline things you could do with ways to shoot this place, none of which, of course, they ever used. But it was a way of developing a relationship . . ." After Chambliss gets each script, he begins discussions with the episode's director as well as producer Sarah Caplan to get a sense of the grand vision for the episode and whether it requires a location or the building of a set.

It wasn't just an international world that needed to be created, however. Chambliss and team decided to make the SD-6 headquarters very sleek, with advanced technology, while the CIA offices would feel more governmental, with a 1960s feel to them. When the set for SD-6 was designed and built, it not only created the illusion of being endless but was set up with different pockets so that it could be adjusted to the needs of the script. Meanwhile, Will's newspaper offices and the CIA offices were interchangeable in the first season for budgetary reasons. Creativity is key, and Abrams knows it. "[Production designer] Scott Chambliss is sort of the unsung hero of the show," he says. "In our show, everything is dependent on believing where you are." That includes believing in Sydney's personal world, in the world of the CIA, as well as in the idea of the existence of an organization such as SD-6. And that's on top of all the international locations that Sydney travels to. Whether it's shot in the studio or out somewhere in Burbank, each scene has to look real.

Working on location in Burbank isn't always permissible in the budget. "[With] this show, we average three to four days on location [per episode]. It's a matter of trying to find locations that will accommodate three full days of the script," states location manager Mike Haro. Once he's discussed the script with Chambliss, he'll begin by searching his location files or doing "cold scouting." Not all locations are exterior. Taking on the search for interior locations has benefits given that the soundstage is already overloaded with sets and it costs quite a bit to build new ones. In some cases, the locations used have come to light through word of mouth from other teams. In other cases, the same location is used more than once for entirely different purposes, which makes life much easier for the production design team. Some of the more common locations used include the Disney Ranch, Griffith Park, and the Terminal Annex post office, which has been used in six different instances so far. Thanks to the diverse architecture of Los Angeles, a multitude of cultures can be created.

The location managers work with their teams. "On the creative side, we work with the director and production designer in finding a location for every scene in the show that is going to be shot on location. We're [also] responsible for moving around a two hundred–person company literally every day," says Haro. The latter entails gaining the necessary permission to use the location; arranging for contracts and insurance; hiring police for crowd control; obtaining security and firefighters when necessary; arranging for parking for the trucks and the crew and, finally, doling out payments. There is also the task of working around timing limitations imposed on certain locations. For example, residential neighborhoods have set limits in some cases, requiring a crew to stop filming at 10 p.m. There are also union rules to be upheld, along with other regulations.

As stated earlier, the production design team plays a role in the episode development. During season 1, in the episode "The Reckoning," the script originally had Sydney retrieving something off a battleship. The episode did not have a stylized Sydney moment as most do, touching on the fun, sexy part of her character. Scott Chambliss was also having difficulty locating the ship, so he suggested shifting the scene to a stylish art gallery opening in London, which would have more of a sleek, cat-burglar look. Sure enough, that was what the sequence was changed to, and it worked. In many cases, the ideas that the writing team come up with are too big for a single episode. "So the biggest challenge for me in terms of providing a world for them to shoot in is actually being part of the process in wrangling it down to something that we can actually do," states Chambliss.

Because of the fast-paced nature of television, flexibility is more crucial than detail. As a consequence, Chambliss shifted his thinking for the second season: "Instead of being so literal in trying to capture the look of foreign countries or types of structures, I went very much more into creating mood or feeling or texture. It's not going off to fantasy-land, but just enough where they [the viewers] say, 'Oh, it's a dungeon,' or 'He's being held in a laboratory.'" As a result of looking outside the proverbial box, unusual locations have also become part of the *Alias* world. For example, an old post office has doubled as a hip, Danish-modern nightclub. Flexibility also plays an important role when problems arise. After the team got permission to use a colorful Mexican marketplace, things fell through two days before filming. According to Chambliss, the sets had been created and the stunts set up, "... so Mike [Haro] just started scouring through the Yellow Pages. . . . He looked specifically for places that advertised Mexican mariachi bands playing on the weekends, figuring that if they were out of our normal zone and they advertised, that they might be large venues. He found a brilliant one, way out below Vernon [California] that was indoor and outdoor, and it was so much better than the one we'd [planned to use] before. That's the adventure of the last-minute save that works wonderfully for the show, courtesy of our ingenious location manager."

And how does the work of the production design team affect the rest of the crew? Just ask director of photography, Michael Bonvillain: "Locations, I think, are key to the show — besides Jennifer, of course. Just the idea that she travels around so much is really important. If I get a great location, I'm happy as a clam."

Double Agent Disguise

One thing can be said for Sydney Bristow: no matter what trouble she's in each week, she *always* looks good. This feat is thanks, in large part, to head costume designer Laura Goldsmith, head hairstylist Michael Reitz, and head makeup artist Angela Nogara. Laura Goldsmith, whose first film work was in the Oscar-winning *Leaving Las Vegas*, sometimes has only 36 hours to pull together a costume for Jennifer Garner that will suit the episode. "She'll show me a scrap of fabric and a picture out of a magazine and she'll say, 'It's going to be something like this.' And then she'll go make it and come back and have eight of them! It needs to please me, it needs to please the viewers, and it usually needs to hide a harness and pads or something. Laura's just amazing!" says Garner.

In many cases, Laura isn't given any specific instructions for Sydney's outfit, with the exception that it has to be "stunning." J.J. Abrams admits, "When it's specified in the script what Sydney's wearing, she'll often come to us with better ideas. Laura is the one who says, 'Of these fifty, it's one of these three. What do you think?' I'll choose one and she'll say, 'What if we do this to it?' And suddenly it's the best thing you've ever seen."

Goldsmith isn't just costuming Garner, however. She's responsible for the whole cast of the show. That also includes the extras in the foreign locations and multiple copies of costumes for the stunt doubles. Like the other members of the *Alias* team, Laura is in constant motion. It's also very important to make sure the costumes are appropriate to the locale. "We usually reflect the climate we're in, the season we're in, the nightclub we're in, what country the nightclub is in to try and give it some kind of dash of wherever we are. Not as a cliché — like a beret in Paris or anything like that — but there are nuances we like to suggest so that you feel where you are," explains Goldsmith.

The cast of *Alias* gets together to promote the new series at a press conference in 2001.

Goldsmith came on board after the pilot episode. The pace of the show doesn't allow her to create elaborate sketches of possible costumes the way she would on a film set. Using Scott Chambliss' designs as a guide, she kept the SD-6 outfits very black and white, while the CIA costumes were more neutral in coloring, and the newspaper crew was dressed very casually, in denim and cords. As Sydney is a part of more than one world, her costumes have to reflect where she is in the story. To contrast Sydney's dark business suits in SD-6, Goldsmith kept her collegiate look very clean. Also, considering the elaborate nature of Sydney's "alias" costumes, Laura makes sure that Sydney wears simple, timeless clothing at home, such as a pair of jeans and a basic top. The spy clothing also has to adjust to the nature of the mission. "Usually, I'll get inspired by where we're going," says Goldsmith. "I'm always keeping my eyes open for stuff — zippered pants, something leather that might have a tactical, practical, and sexy look to it that I can kind of incorporate into different tactical looks every week."

From punk to pearls, Sydney has worn it all, although one of her more notable outfits was the blue rubber dress from season 1. For that, Goldsmith took Garner to the L.A. store Syren, which specializes in rubber and latex clothing and does custom design work for clients with . . . unusual needs. "They had to unlock the door to let me in and they locked the door behind me. And there are whips and there are chains . . . and I'm a nice girl from West Virginia and my eyes are like *this* big," remembers Garner. After dusting her body with baby powder, Garner needed the help of two people to get the dress on. It became one of the most famous outfits from the show and is an example of Goldsmith's ingenuity.

Another well-known outfit involved Cosabella lingerie — which Sydney modeled mid-air in a 747. In this instance, Goldsmith's instinct was in line with that of production designer Scott Chambliss. Unaware that she had chosen the same unique tomato red color that Chambliss had for the set, Goldsmith puts it down to either their being in sync or simple luck. In some cases the costume design requires research, but in other instances it's up to the imagination, as was the case for the outfits worn inside the Uzbekistani prison. And then there are the completely unexpected costumes. "Literally, we had to wrap a woman in C-4 explosives," says Goldsmith. "So we had to go online and figure out how to build a bomb, which was kind of scary, because you don't want anybody seeing that you've looked something like that up on your computer . . . !" Goldsmith has been nominated for Emmy Awards for her work, and she took home a Costume Designers Guild Award for Excellence in Contemporary Television in 2003.

Michael Reitz is the one responsible for the wild hair that Sydney sports each week, including the notorious red wig from the pilot episode. Reitz was waiting for Abrams to make a decision on what hair color he wanted for the wig. "When we were shooting the pilot at USC [the University of Southern California], this punk-rock girl walked by and he said, 'That's the color I want,'" Reitz recalls. "We talked her into letting us cut a piece of her hair. I took that hair to the wigmaker and we had it [Garner's wig] dyed." Considering Abrams got such inspiration from the film *Run Lola Run*, his choice was no great surprise.

Using Scott Chambliss's "look book," which provides different photos of individuals and places around the world, along with Goldsmith's own "look book," Reitz is able to come up with appropriate hair for each locale. It's important to make sure there is some variation as well. He also works closely with the two designers, as "they want an element of the set to be picked up in the clothes and the hair." Each wig is handmade and tailored specifically to Garner's head. Like Goldsmith, Reitz takes color swatches over to Abrams to get his input before proceeding. Even Jennifer Garner puts in her two cents' worth. In some cases Garner wears actual wigs, while in other cases she spends hours in the stylist's chair getting hair extensions put in. "Jen does all her business calls in my chair because she's there for so long," says Reitz.

Makeup artist Angela Nogara also finds *Alias* offers great freedom with regard to letting her imagination run wild. With Goldsmith and Reitz, Nogara takes part in discussing what Sydney's look will be each week. As Goldsmith must figure out how to make the costumes accommodate the show's action, Nogara has to adjust makeup to the specifics of the fighting in each episode. One of her initial roles involves "[breaking] down the script, figuring out who got beat up, who was bruised, who was beaten, who was disheveled, character by character." In terms of the way the process unfolds, it begins with the location scouts, then set design. Goldsmith is given the color palette, and then "we [Reitz and Nogara] would come in and talk about what kinds of clothes Sydney was wearing, what colors she'd have on, and then we would do our thing."

One thing is for sure: they do their "thing" extremely well.

Kick It in Gear

One of the elements that *Alias* is praised for is having a heroine who can climb walls, jump off buildings, defend herself against more than one enemy, and look like she knows exactly what she's doing. This is where stunt coordinator Jeff Habberstad comes into the picture. Having previously handled the stunts for the film *Spider-Man*, Habberstad claims that wire rigging was his specialty when he started with the show. With a feature film background, Jeff would also be able to make Abrams's cinematic vision a reality. *Alias* was his first television show. "I was fairly heavy-handed early in the series about trying to make it new and better and cool-looking," says Habberstad. He would meet up with the writing team and offer suggestions for possible stunts so that the writers could build a story around them. He acknowledges their efforts: "I've got to say that the writers have been real creative with how they've taken what I've suggested we can do and built it into a story that's not a way of building it in simply to do a stunt."

Jeff's first episode on *Alias* was the second of season 1, titled "So It Begins." Unlike the situation in many films, the wires and harnesses that were attached to Jennifer Garner did not need to be invisible in most cases. Sydney is a spy, after all, not a superhero. Garner is known for doing the majority of her own stunt work, including parachuting onto the back patio of a mansion and tearing off her diving gear to reveal a sexy outfit. In that particular instance, no computer-generated puppet was required: the stunt was real. There were some initial concerns about Jennifer doing a few of the more challenging stunts, but Habberstad's extensive knowledge of the mechanics behind each stunt put the crew at ease. In 2003, Jeff Habberstad won a creative Emmy Award for his work on the *Alias* episode "The Telling" (which tied with the show *Fastlane*). Jeff also works with special effects coordinators John Downey and Bruce Kuroyama, who organize such things as explosions, fires, or in the instance of "Almost Thirty Years," the flood sequence. They were the ones responsible for the sinking car in "Q & A," the stunt that has frightened Garner the most.

Aside from leaping off tall buildings, Sydney is required to do some serious fighting. Enter fight coordinator David Morizot. Blocking out new and exciting fight scenes on a continual basis can be rough, especially given the time constraints that come with television. "There are two arms, two legs, a head, and a certain number of moves that you can do as far as any fight is concerned," Morizot says. But the situation of *how* you do them is where you keep the freshness alive. I try to have one special move per fight." Fight coordination also requires flexibility, simply because situations such as location changes can arise and may not be conducive to the original sequence. Still, it helps that Jennifer

Garner is quick to learn. "Luckily I was a ballet dancer growing up, so I had pretty good aim with my kicks," she jokes.

Tech Toys

It just isn't an episode of *Alias* without Marshall explaining the latest high-tech gadget, which always comes in handy on the mission. As mentioned previously, it is up to writer-producer Jesse Alexander and writer Rick Orci to come up with these creations after extensive research using the Internet, books, and military magazines. The facts are a jumping-off point. "It's a combination of a desire for something to help the plot move along and then research as to what's really out there, and then we usually end up figuring a kind of a hybrid version — it's not exactly what's real, but it's not entirely unreal," says Abrams.

Once they have come up with the concept, the ball gets passed to prop master Chris Call and assistant prop master Chris Redmond. As with the writers and Abrams, it is important to Call and Redmond that there is a reality behind the fantasy prop. Having worked together on previous films such as *American Pie* and *Apt Pupil*, the team of Call and Redmond enjoy the fast-paced nature of *Alias* as well as the fact that they have substantial input on the design of the props and their usage. "One reason we got hired and why they like us is we're able to bring stuff to the table," says Call.

Before he gets to work, Call will talk with the writers to get an understanding of how the device works. Then it's his turn to do some research before coming up with a design. Using design magazines such as *Design Culture Now* and *I.D.* and tech journal *T3* for inspiration, sometimes he finds the solution right on the page: "I'll go in and sometimes scan a product right into my computer and start modifying it in Photoshop. Sometimes they have completely different applications than for what we're using it for, but we like the shape and the design." In other cases, Call will get to work sketching out what he thinks the device would look like, trying to break out of the conventional idea of what certain items are. "They wanted 'a bomb that stuck onto the side of the rafter to blow it up.' So that could be anything. I like to come up with something cool and something different," says Call. So the bomb ended up being a star-shaped device with a flip top. The prop team has created everything from lipstick-sized weapons to a rocket-powered luge. They are also responsible for creating the mystical Rambaldi artifacts.

Artist Andrea Dietrich is the woman behind the infamous Milo Rambaldi. An illustrator and storyboard artist for films, she also paints and works as a cinematographer. Having been recommended to the art department by producer Sarah Caplan, Dietrich was "initially hired to provide a madman's drawing for one of the early shows. I was then asked if I could do pen-and-ink — and thus the Rambaldi manuscripts began," she recalls. After meeting up with Call and Abrams, the three started studying different design reference books while getting a sense of Rambaldi's character. While Dietrich works on the paintings and pages of the manuscript, Call is involved with the objects, such as the notorious clock.

With less than a week to get two or three designs ready for each episode, Call is reliant on the prop house, Neotek. Neotek manufactures high-tech movie and television props and creates futuristic weapons and other devices. "They're the real magicians behind all this," claims Call. "The writers dream it up, we fine-tune it, and they actually make it happen. Then I bring it to the set, and Chris [Redmond] fixes it." "Fixing" refers to making final tweaks or changes to the prop in order to accommodate last-minute changes made by writers or the director. Alternatively, Call will head out to scour flea markets or rely on the company Sword and the Stone for the perfect prop. He will also go through the prop and drape department, modifying items to fit the show, such as the box holding the needles of fire that actor Quentin Tarantino used. Once a prop is ready, Chris Redmond explains it to the actor who is going to be using it. "There's frequently a makeup person applying makeup to [Jennifer Garner's] face while I'm showing her how the prop works in the next shot," he says. After the episode is shot, the props receive some touch-ups in post-production just to make them look that much cooler.

Modern technology and the film industry have an interesting relationship. In some cases, film inspires inventors and engineers. Take, for example, Dick Tracy's famous watch with the two-way screen: it inspired several real-life prototypes. Then, in 2002, William Shatner of *Star Trek* fame, with Chip Walter, came out with the book *Star Trek: I'm Working on That*, which looks at how the television industry has motivated scientists at prominent institutions across the U.S. to develop high-tech tools. In other cases, directors and producers will speak with futurists regarding the feasibility of their ideas in order to create plausible storylines and gadgets. And finally, it's not uncommon for producers to look to technological companies such as Sony in order to gain access to product prototypes or designs that may be in development. In the case of *Alias*, the team has also relied on CIA liaison Chase Brandon to get an idea of the government's technology. "Once they had a foundation of what our equipment and our capability — technologically speaking — looks like, that gave them, as writers, a reinforced license to go about creating their own stuff," says Brandon.

As for Abrams, he's a huge James Bond fan and loves the gadgets that Q created for 007. Add this film inspiration to the fact that his grandfather sold surplus electronics after World War II and it's no wonder that Abrams wanted to make the tech toys a big part of the show. J.J.'s grandfather taught him about the intricacies of the telephone when the youngster was only four years of age. Says J.J.: "I just loved gadgets, not just because I love what they did [but] I appreciated their insides. For me, clearly the character on our show — Marshall, who is a tech guy — he is clearly a nod to Q. There is so much fun [in] seeing what has he got this week."

Target in Sight . . .

The episode has been written. The set has been prepared. The actors know their lines. At this point, it's time to shoot the show. The actual filming includes the visual effects department, the director of photography, the cinematographer, and the director. As with production design, there is much work to be done before the cameras start rolling. To begin with, the lighting needs to be determined for each location, including the color design for the shot. Is it more blue in tone, or red? The idea was to keep Sydney's personal world warmer in its color tones, and to use longer lenses and less camera movement. SD-6 is another matter. Colder and gray, there are more rapid camera movements in that world to suggest a hectic place.

A lot of creativity is required during the shoot, considering not everything is exactly how we see it on-screen. In the season 1 episodes "Time Will Tell" and "Color-Blind," Sydney enters a 300-foot-deep cavern. The set itself was 12 feet by 12 feet. For the shots where Sydney is in the cave, the team went out on location to shoot at the Bronson Caves. The ladder fight in "Time Will Tell" was shot in the studio. Once those shots were combined with the image of the tall cavern, the illusion was complete. "Some people say, 'Where'd you go to shoot this?' The honest answer is: 'A very dinky, unimpressive little set that we augmented,'" explains visual effects supervisor Kevin Blank.

Alias's director of photography, Michael Bonvillain, has been involved with the show right from the very start. He agreed that the show shouldn't veer too much into the comic book fantasy world, but it shouldn't go for complete realism either. Keeping that concept in mind, the look became "heightened realism." Bonvillain's initial thought was to take five days per episode to shoot on location, then use the last three days to shoot on the soundstages at Disney. Unfortunately, due to budget cuts and the fall of Disney's stock after 9/11, spending that much to shoot on location was not possible. "We ended up shooting on the lot quite often, which is not my favorite place to shoot because it doesn't really look like Paris or any place except Disney. The hard part was keeping your enthusiasm and your standards while trying to keep things looking new," says Michael.

While they found themselves shooting on the lot more often than desired, Scott Chambliss and his production design team made a huge difference. Between Chambliss's team creating locations and the visual effects team adding in extra elements, ". . . [t]here's not a lot that you can't do, especially at night with a four-hundred millimeter lens," says Bonvillain. "So you put the Eiffel Tower in the background, shoot it long in sketchy lighting, and it looks like Paris. We don't stay on it long enough for you to tell."

. . . Adding Digital Enhancer . . .

Essentially, the visual effects team's job is to make the show look even better, and that is exactly what they do. The guy named Kevin Blank is the next link in the *Alias* chain. "Kevin Blank, who is a brilliant visual effects supervisor, often has to manufacture a matte painting with only a day's notice, in addition to an effect or stunt sequence," states J.J. Abrams. "As someone who has always been an effects fanatic — and anyone who watches the show knows how deeply my psychosis goes — it's really something that I put enormous importance on."

With his team, Blank is responsible for adding landmarks to skylines or adjusting certain shots to appear more appropriate to the locale of the episode. Blank is also part of the production coordination, determining the role of visual effects in each show. Shooting with a greenscreen is sometimes necessary, along with erasing certain elements in other shots. When Sydney parachutes down in Rio, Brazil, and the famous Christ the Redeemer statue is in the background, not only was a greenscreen used but a computer-generated version of Sydney was required as well. Blank also asked if Bonvillain could film the live-action element at dusk so that the lighting would be in sync with his sunset vision of the shot, and Bonvillain came through.

Using computer programs such as After Effects along with designating other tasks to freelance visual effects artists, the team plays a major role in helping to add those believable touches to the different locales. Not all the shots are stock photos, however. In some instances, the team actually uses camera footage from other locations, which is added to the shot they are working on; the two are match moved to make the shot seem like one rather than two joined together. For example, in "The Coup," a live-action shot of the Hong Kong subway was combined with the live-action shot taken on the Disney lot, thus making the final product much more realistic.

In the end, it's significantly cheaper to adjust the shots visually in post-production than to shoot in various locations. The consequence of this approach is that details make a huge difference. While the initial belief was that the visual effects on the show would primarily consist of matte paintings, that vision actually ended up growing more complicated by the second half of the first season. Additional special effects came to include adding in or removing details, such as trees in a courtyard. In a variation on this theme, the element is removed, the background is placed, and then the element is restored and adjusted to fit the background. In other cases, the background effects need to be colored to match the lighting in the scene. As the show has progressed, so has the need for visual effects. And yet, Blank insists that the visual effects have not taken over: "As a matter of fact, a lot of the visual effects are invisible to the audience, or they're not aware that visual effects are in play. We make use of stock photography and photographs, do a little digital manipulation, and place things we photograph in Los Angeles in other countries."

Alias is shot on film rather than digital video and is transferred to a D-5 high-definition format, which is a relatively new technology. The standard definition is D-1, and that is what most television screens will display, regardless of the way the footage is shot. Unfortunately, it is only the most expensive, high-definition screens that can display the detail. The high-definition format also means that the visual effects team has larger files to deal with, but for viewing in the long run, Blank prefers the D-5 standard. After all, *Alias* is constantly striving to break convention.

The Director's Report

With the whole team providing such a solid base, the director has the freedom to really work with the actors on the tip of the iceberg. J.J. Abrams keeps out of the director's way, but he does make sure that they have had a meeting to establish the tone of each episode. He'll also clarify the motivation for the scenes, but how the director chooses to go about eliciting performances from the actors is up to him or her. Each episode has a different director, which adds variety to the show, and some directors return for more than one go behind the camera. Ken Olin is one of those directors.

Both men agree that the performance of the actors is key. In the editing room, when Olin, Abrams, and the editors are making the final cut, performance is the one thing they are actually looking for when determining what sequence works out the best. "We have a crew that is so accomplished in terms of our abilities to realize these different sequences visually," says Olin. "It's always a thing of, 'What's the best performance?' and really trying to be true to that. Whatever the truth of the character's experience of the situation — *that's* always the biggest challenge."

The Sound of Sydney

"Music is more important to me than anything else," says J.J. Abrams. As a consequence, *Alias*'s creator has been very much involved with the music on the show, including composing the theme song. "People who know me say that I create TV shows to write the themes for them," he adds. Abrams decided he wanted a theme that felt like classic spy music, only with a techno twist. The problem was that composer Michael Giacchino had not yet been hired, and Abrams had only two days to come up with a theme song for the show. So, while working on the color corrections, Abrams pulled out his portable MIDI controller and his PowerBook and got to work composing.

Meanwhile, Giacchino was working on soundtracks to various video games for Dreamworks Interactive, a games division of the company owned in part by Steven Spielberg. Giacchino wrote the score for *The Lost World* game. Initially, the plan had been for the music to be synth-based; however, when Giacchino presented a demo theme to Spielberg and his team, Spielberg said, "'So, we're going to record those themes with a live orchestra, right?'" Giacchino remembers. "When he said that, the CEO of the games division started swearing. It's Steven Spielberg — are you going to say, 'No'? In his world, that's how the music is done." The music had to be recorded in Seattle and the budget was extended by $17,000, but the experience not only allowed him to show his talents — it changed his way of working. From that moment on he used live orchestras for the soundtracks to all his games.

J.J. Abrams first approached Giacchino through an e-mail after speaking with writer-producer Jesse Alexander, who is a huge video game fan. He had heard the score to the game *Medal of Honor*, which was released as a soundtrack as well. "[Alexander] went to J.J. with the soundtrack discs of the games I'd worked on and got him to listen to them," Giacchino says. "J.J. liked them, and I got this e-mail one night that said, 'Hi, my name is J.J. Abrams and I wrote *Armageddon*, *Regarding Henry*, and *Forever Young*, and I created *Felicity*. I want to know if you want to work with me.'" Surprised, Giacchino showed the e-mail to his wife, questioning its authenticity, but he replied and made his way to the *Alias* set to meet up with Abrams: "The first time I met J.J., they were still doing costume checks before shooting. I met Jennifer [Garner] that day, too. . . . It was probably a week before they started shooting the pilot. Then I didn't talk to J.J. until he was done shooting. When they edited it together, he called me and said, 'Hey, I want to send this over and see what you think.'" Giacchino loved it.

Abrams chose Michael because he was looking for someone with a similar sensibility toward music who could work with both a synthesizer and an orchestra, have a good instinct for what works, and fit in with the team he had assembled. "I knew that doing the score for *Alias* would require someone who was really flexible and fast, because music is so important to me," says J.J. Rather than create a conventional television score, the idea was to approach it cinematically. Abrams fought for a live orchestra for *Alias* and succeeded. Michael then set about coming up with a sound for the show. "J.J. loves techno and all that, but he also grew up listening to John Barry, John Williams, David Shire, and all these great film composers — all the same guys I grew up listening to," explains Giacchino. "I suggested that we should rely on more traditional film music in addition to the electronic stuff. He completely agreed, so we both had that in our minds from the very beginning."

With around 20 to 25 minutes of music to compose for each episode, Giacchino is kept busy. Each scene is musically tracked, making it more sophisticated. Michael sits down and watches each episode with J.J. so that Abrams can give him an idea of what kind of sound he is looking for each time. Giacchino has also been helpful to Abrams in an editing capacity. Knowing that the soundscape plays such a crucial role on the show, Michael has adjusted the music so that it fits specific situations and characters. For the higher action scenes he tends to add more electronica sounds, whereas for the more serious moments the orchestrated music plays a greater role. The main characters all have their own "sounds," and as other characters have emerged and grown, so has the music. Giacchino describes a few of the characters' themes: "Sydney's mom's theme is generally played on a cello, so usually a solo cello-type thing. [It has] an old Russian feel to it — it's kind of sad, and at the same time a mean type of theme. The theme for Jack [is played by] these low basses, which do this quick little motif. Sloane generally is represented with the bassoon, depending on what's going on in the scene." Sydney has a multitude of themes; which is used depends on what she is up to. With regard to the tempo of the music, Giacchino attempts to keep it anywhere from 100 to 140 beats per minute as a way of keeping consistent templates that the editors can use.

So how does Michael's job work? He receives a director's cut of an episode on a Wednesday, which helps him to determine what music is needed. The following day he is provided with the producer's cut of the episode, giving him an idea of the edit. He starts composing, knowing that by Saturday he will receive the final edit. There isn't a lot of time to get each episode done, but he has an idea of what J.J. is looking for, which makes the job easier. With the completed score, the orchestra records on the M Soundstage at Paramount Pictures with conductor Tim Simonek. When he's not working away on *Alias*, Michael writes orchestral pieces for the Southern California French Horn Ensemble.

As the show evolves, so does the music. Abrams continues to use contemporary songs at times, but he is extremely happy to have Giacchino on board: "Now, what he comes up with might not always be exactly how I saw it, but Michael approaches the music from a well-thought-out perspective. . . . The show is definitely better because of him."

Final Confession

The family that plays together stays together, and there is no doubt that those who belong to the *Alias* group have created a family. The actors are constantly talking about the closeness of the cast and crew, and in the case of this show, it's not just talk. "It's kind of amazing. We are very close. . . . I know you hear people say that all the time, but I've actually seen it," says Victor Garber. "The crew loves working on the show, even though we have to work really hard. There's nobody in the show that's difficult. We really have a great group. We — some cast members and I — even went on a weekend trip together and spent the weekend at an inn because we enjoy each other's company so much, and it was so cool." Yes, they really are that close, which makes their situation a rather ironic one considering just how tumultuous their relationships are on-screen.

A cohesive cast and crew is but one element of the show that is intertwined with many others. In essence, producing *Alias* is akin to creating a giant spider's web, where each thread is necessary for the creation of a strong final product. And what role does the audience have in all this?

"Come into my parlor," said the spider to the fly . . .

So It Begins . . .

It began one day in the *Felicity* writing room, and then ABC ordered a one-hour pilot after a pitch by Abrams. Given the tentative title *Alias* after *Spy Games* was rejected, the show was pegged as being along the same lines as the 1960s adventure-spy series *The Man from U.N.C.L.E.* with some *Mission: Impossible* and *La Femme Nikita* thrown in. The question was whether or not a show about a college student–spy would actually fly with audiences. While Abrams admitted that the premise for the show was actually quite silly, it was the idea of the story underneath that he held onto: a young woman dealing with her dysfunctional family, with the espionage element as a backdrop. It was the relationship complexities and emotional drama that Abrams wanted to explore — Sydney wasn't just an action hero. As a consequence, it was critical that the tone of the show remain consistent. "For it to work in a world of *Charlie's Angels* and *Austin Powers*, if the show was satire it would lower the stakes considerably. I also didn't want the show to be so self-serious that it became like you were laughing at it," says Abrams.

After a long audition process, Jennifer Garner was finally cast in the role of Agent Sydney Bristow. With her only major feature role being *Dude, Where's My Car?*, Garner was not the obvious choice, but the

One of the reasons the chemistry among all of the characters works so well on set is because the actors are such good friends off-camera.

production executives put aside their concerns at her anonymity and went with Abrams' instincts. Following her casting came that of Michael Vartan, Merrin Dungey, Bradley Cooper, Carl Lumbly, and theater veterans Ron Rifkin and Victor Garber. Greg Grunberg was cast in a recurring role, hopping over to *Alias* from the *Felicity* set.

All the cast members were intrigued by the quality of writing in the pilot episode. "Although you don't know exactly how long the show will be on, you know that there is a genius in charge of the ship. So I'm not afraid of any icebergs," says Michael Vartan. Ron Rifkin also found himself joining the group because of the script: "I had never seen anything like this before . . . it had a richness and intelligence to it that felt to me totally unique and original. It's such a good group. I mean, it's such a tribute to J.J. and the casting people that they put us all together." Carl Lumbly was attracted to how the show essentially offered many pieces of a puzzle and left it up to the viewer to put them all together. "I think we're also all enjoying the fact that we have a tight set that's also a respectful set," he maintains. "As actors, we understand the seriousness of the work at hand, and it's a joy to be on a set where everyone is doing the job, taking it seriously, having some fun, and working together to make this show as good as it can possibly be."

Abrams had already decided to break the structural writing rules. He had also decided to delay the theme song and credits until about 15 minutes into the show in order to pull viewers in and entice them to stay: "I love the feeling of watching a show and suddenly the credits come on and you realize, 'Oh my God, I've just gotten sucked into this world.'" It was Abrams's unique approach to the series that piqued director Ken Olin's interest. Initially Ken was offered the chance to direct the first episode following the pilot, which had greatly impressed him. "There was an energy to this: it wasn't so serious, yet there was room for it to be intimate. So I said, 'No, I don't want to direct the first episode.' To me, it was a completely no-win proposition after that pilot. The pilot is extraordinary and there was no way the show was being brought in on an eight-day schedule," says Olin. Abrams came back with the offer to bring Ken on board as a producer-director. It was too good to refuse, and Ken agreed. From the beginning Olin felt connected to J.J.'s vision, understanding the balance of humor and drama that he wanted to bring to the series.

While the tight, fast-paced schedule was a challenge for everyone, it didn't stop them from taking it on. The team's work ethic was about trusting instinct rather than second-guessing every decision. In August 2001, production began on the show and the pilot was picked up by the network. "The biggest surprise for me with *Alias* is that we even went from pilot to pickup. I did feel that *Alias* was a show that required a certain amount of attention from a viewer, and that's not something a lot of shows demand anymore," admits actor Carl Lumbly. "People have gotten used to seeing television that moves in a certain kind of way. You can miss two episodes and get right back into it."

While the crew was working hard at creating the series, two ABC network marketing executives, Alan Cohen and Michael Benson, were putting in a massive effort to sell the concept to the world. In the fall of 2001, 35 new shows would be airing, and they were doing everything they could to make sure *Alias* got noticed. Cohen, executive vice president of marketing , notes the importance of such a task: "In an era when there were three networks, [promotion] wasn't that important. You'd put on a show and people would find it. Now if you do that, your show gets lost. There's just too much clutter and competition out there." Having put much stock in *Alias*, ABC was banking on the show to be a hit for the network. As a consequence, the promotions for the show began in mid-May, and teaser television ads hit the airwaves with the hope that they would intrigue the viewers. Then the marketing team segmented the show in order to create different styles of advertisements that would appeal to different groups. It targeted the ABC daytime watchers with 30-second commercials focusing on Sydney's character and relationships. During *Monday Night Football* and *The Drew Carey Show*, commercials featured the action scenes, along with Garner in her sexy garb. *Alias* ads were everywhere, airing all hours of the day and night, and not just on ABC but on ESPN, ESPN2, Lifetime, and A&E. Radio advertisements bombarded the airwaves, and promotional posters hit the bus shelters. The *Alias* promoters also used what is called a "viral marketing" campaign, which entails leaking bits of information via the Internet. And then came the corporate sponsorship with Nokia, who took out ads in various magazines declaring itself the exclusive sponsor of the show. As a result, the premiere episode of *Alias* was commercial-free, with Nokia ads preceding and following the show. The idea was to make the opening big, which would draw the viewers in for more in later episodes.

All this promotion was resting on the shoulders of an unknown actress in a bright red wig. Jennifer Garner wasn't going to be unknown for long, however. "I feel challenged beyond what I can handle at all times. And I mean that in a good way," she says. "Shooting the fight scene in the garage [for the pilot] was the best day of my life, beyond a shadow of a doubt. It was the most fun I've ever had."

Season One:
Fall 2001–Spring 2002

My name is Sydney Bristow. Seven years ago I was recruited by a secret branch of the CIA called SD-6. I was sworn to secrecy but I couldn't keep it from my fiancé. And when the head of SD-6 found out, he had him killed. That's when I learned the truth: SD-6 is not part of the CIA. I'd been working for the very people I thought I was fighting against. So I went to the only place that could help me take them down. Now, I'm a double agent for the CIA, where my handler is a man named Michael Vaughn. Only one other person knows the truth about what I do: another double agent inside SD-6. Someone I hardly know . . . my father.

After the ratings dive of *Who Wants to Be a Millionaire*, ABC needed a hit show and *Alias* seemed to be the ticket. It was receiving a lot of buzz, thanks to the heavy promotion. That same year, the other shows scheduled to debut included *The Agency*, Steven Bochco's *Philly*, *Thieves* (co-starring Melissa George), *UC: Undercover*, *The Court*, and *24*. *Alias* was being identified as a cross between James Bond and *Felicity*, which left much to the imagination. It was a rough year for television in other ways, however. First of all, there was a threat of an actor/writer strike, which would stall television production. As a consequence, some of the larger-scale productions that were supposed to debut in the fall of 2001 were sealed before the Writers Guild of America contract expiration date in May and the Screen Actors Guild contract expiration in June. The second situation had a devastating impact on both the United States and the world at large.

The press screenings of *Alias* had been going very well, and the anticipation was growing. "We cannot wait to put this TV show on the air," said ABC executives. The show was scheduled to premiere on September 30, and the Nokia sponsorship was a great bonus. "As the television landscape becomes increasingly competitive, we are challenged to find new and inventive ways to make our programming stand out from the pack. This unique partnership with Nokia will help us do just that for *Alias*, and we applaud them for their belief and commitment to this compelling series," said the co-chair of ABC Entertainment Television, Stu

Bloomberg. Set to promote the company's new 3300 wireless phone series, ABC offered an interactive Web site and a contest in conjunction with Nokia, allowing site users the chance to win by participating in a code breaker sweepstakes. "Alias Alert" messages would be sent to those who registered through their mobile messaging. These messages would require the receiver to unscramble a phrase from the pilot episode. The correct responses would then be put in a draw, and two individuals would have the chance to win a spy wrist camera, a digital voice recorder, or an all-expenses-paid trip to the Covert Ops Spy Camp in Arizona. Another promotional bonus was that the show was filmed using high-definition television. Also, having a powerful female lead was an advantage for international sales. "A good rule of thumb for international buyers is more action. Action and female-oriented material travels best," stated Brian Frons, the head of acquisitions for SBS Broadcasting.

Even though it would be competing with the other two CIA shows, CBS's *The Agency* (which was officially endorsed by the CIA) and the innovative Fox show *24*, *Alias* was still unique in that it wasn't as completely realistic as the former or as dark as the latter. Seen as more "comic book" than the others, it still revolved around mainly the CIA, and for a change, the infamous agency was actually being portrayed in a positive light. Chase Brandon, a 25-year CIA operative and public-affairs liaison to Hollywood, was working with both *The Agency* and *Alias*. "[Historically, the CIA has] been imbued with these extraordinary Machiavellian conspiratorial capabilities," said Brandon. "To see our image changing for the outside world makes us feel better about ourselves internally. Even though the trend is toward making programs about the agency more realistic, there are in fact still writers and producers and directors who don't want to be confused by the facts." J.J. Abrams was quick to note that *Alias* was a dramatic story rather than a factual account of what happens inside the agency. "The truth can be inspiring and take you places, but I'm more interested in what I believe to be true and what works for the story than in doing a documentary on Langley procedure," he said.

It was this factor that made a difference after the terrorist attacks on the World Trade Center on September 11, 2001. The horrific events that occurred led to some necessary re-evaluation of a few of the upcoming pilots. For *Alias*, it meant changing a reference to the World Trade Organization being threatened with a bomb in episode 4. The writers then created a fictional group called the United Commerce Organization as a replacement. While *The Agency* made actual changes to the pilot episode and pulled references to Osama bin Laden, the Fox series 24 took out an exploding airplane from the show. The *Alias* pilot remained intact. "We're trying to be as responsible as we can be during this impossible tragedy to continue to do *Alias* as well as *Felicity*. The show is about this young woman who is herself a victim of violence, who's actually active in trying to effect change in not just her life, but for the good of the country. This was never intended to this extreme when I created the show, but I believe that there could be a kinship with her that people might feel because she is, in many ways, in the position that we're all in," noted Abrams. *Alias*'s nod to the comic book genre also helped the case to keep the show unaltered; while it deals with international espionage, the villains were not terrorists in the classic sense but rather very specific "bad guys."

The crew had concerns about whether or not the show would air as a consequence of the attacks. Two episodes of the show had already been filmed before the towers fell. It was a challenge for the crew to get back to work, remembers director of photography Michael Bonvillain. "We couldn't work; my crew was all crying. I remember thinking, There's no way this show is going to air, because it was too horrible an event." Abrams called up Disney, and one of the executives came down to speak to the cast and crew, reassuring them that the show would indeed air. It was still difficult to get back into the swing of things, however, because of the terrorist element. "A few weeks later we did an episode where we blew up a building, and there were people inside it. I said to J.J., 'I don't know how we can do this,' but as far as I can tell, nobody related to it or seemed to feel that it was in bad taste," says Bonvillain. Representatives from the Center for Media and Public Affairs in Washington, D.C., left the changes up to the networks. Media director Matthew Felling said, "News events can inspire TV dramas but never censor them. Quality content shouldn't give way to 'safe' content. Let the viewers be the judge." So, the premiere date for *Alias* remained the same: September 30.

Seen as having one of the best opening episodes in television history, the premiere episode won the highest ratings in its time slot, garnering 14.8 million viewers. What was surprising, however, was that the show didn't skew as young as the network had anticipated. The show received great praise from the critics, with *Entertainment Weekly* naming it the season's Best New Drama. Each week ended with a cliffhanger, requiring the audience to commit to the series. "For better or worse, we have developed certain signature moments in the show. What's nice about how we've been working is that we have storylines arced out for this year. It's not just an entertaining hour . . ." stated Abrams.

The show did receive some criticism from the Parents Television Council due to the violent nature in which Sydney's teeth were extracted in the pilot. But *Alias* wasn't the first show to be criticized for violence. Over the years, Fox was one of the trendsetters as the network allowed *The X-Files* more freedom in the violence department. Most networks stopped censoring their producers to the extreme that they had in the past. And yet, there were various explanations for the reason behind the increase in violence on television in 2001 compared with 2000 and 1999. Jamsheed Akrami, a communications professor at New Jersey's William Paterson University, stated that "Violence, as odd as it sounds, can have a sort of cathartic effect on people. When they are exposed to violence there is something of a vicarious element . . . [of] participation that could have a soothing effect on them. Media violence is . . . not real violence. Sometimes when people see that . . . they can project themselves as good guys, and whoever they don't approve of or dislike as the bad guys. [TV] can serve as a venue for venting out their frustrations."

The violence did not deter the viewers, however. Along with the television episodes, *Alias* was busy on the Web as well. "What's fun about this show and the site is that there's a detailed mythology to [*Alias*]. We're able to address things on the Web that we don't have time to address on the show. We have the official site, at ABC.com, which is going to be an entertaining wealth of information about *Alias*," said Abrams. The writers were also checking out the new fan sites popping up as a consequence of the show. "I think the *Alias* fan sites are amazing. . . . I skim them often. . . . I can't believe the work people put

CHRISTINA RADISH

into them. . . . We are always checking message boards to see how people react to things," revealed writer-producer Jesse Alexander. One thing that the fans seemed to rally against was the character of Will; they made their strong feelings known through the Internet and with many letters and e-mails of complaint to ABC. As a consequence of their concerns, the writers adjusted his story.

The ratings continued to impress, with *Alias* pulling in upward of 14.4 million viewers in early December, dominating the 18–49 adult viewer audience.

Jennifer Garner, as Sydney Bristow, has joined the ranks of tough but beautiful women on television.

As a consequence of its popularity, the successful series *The X-Files* was beginning to suffer. In January 2002, ABC announced that *Alias* had received a full-season order. "The cast and crew has been working beyond overtime to produce these episodes. We're all thrilled at the commitment ABC has made to *Alias* and can't wait to continue to exhaust ourselves," said Abrams. J.J. was still doing double time at this point, working on both *Alias* and *Felicity*.

Sydney Bristow joined the ranks of powerful female television heroines, which in *Alias*'s opening year included both Buffy and Willow in *Buffy the Vampire Slayer*, Max in *Dark Angel*, and the three witches of *Charmed*, just to name a few. Historically, tough women on TV had come packaged as Mrs. Peel in *The Avengers*, *Charlie's Angels*, *Cagney & Lacey*, *Wonder Woman*, *Xena: Warrior Princess*, Scully from *The X-Files*, and *La Femme Nikita*, for example. The ranks of strong female characters were growing with each year. In a way, Sydney is much like Buffy: all she wants is to be normal, and yet a part of her thrives on the life she lives. In between major missions and kung fu fighting, Sydney nurses childhood wounds and deals with her mounting vulnerability. She is extraordinary, and yet somehow seems ordinary . . . and she dresses well, too. Many credit the trend of strong, complex female characters to Joss Whedon's *Buffy the Vampire Slayer*. "I think *Buffy* legitimized [the genre] in a way that *Xena* didn't really get the opportunity to. I wanted to create a character I hadn't seen enough of in fiction, which was a girl who could really take care of herself and who went through a hero's journey," says Whedon. Abrams claims his inspiration came from Mrs. Peel of *The Avengers*: "I admire and enjoy *Buffy* immensely, but the thing about *Alias* that excited me was not about doing an action heroine, but rather telling the story of a woman estranged from her father, and whose mother was out there somewhere, missing. It was about someone going through a real crisis and trying to make her life work."

As *Alias* began to unfold, the actors reveled in the experience. "It's rare to get a series on the air and it's rarer for a series to stay on the air. And I thought, *If I did this, I could live with it*. It's very dimensional. It has a lot going on. It feels good to know that we're doing well and that our numbers are good. I never thought I'd say that phrase," said Victor Garber. Garber found himself suddenly getting into the action as the season progressed, which was a first for the actor. He admits, "I never thought I'd be wielding guns and climbing through elevator shafts." The new year brought some other interesting changes, such as the airing of *Alias* on both ABC and ABC Family (formally FOX Family), which was the start of the channel's switch to Disney programming. For the ABC Family network airings, however, the harsh language was deleted, making the show more "family friendly" even though the violent content remained.

Meanwhile, the award nominations were coming in. *Alias* was named Favorite New Television Drama for the 2001 People's Choice Awards, and Jennifer Garner accepted the statue. "If you have been working for a while, you get so used to being beaten down. To have a positive reaction, even if you believe in [your work] and love it, still makes you lose your breath," she said. Next came the Golden Globe nominations, including a nod for both Jennifer Garner (Best Actress in a Leading Role — Drama

Series) and Victor Garber (Best Actor in a Supporting Role — Drama Series). A first-time nominee, Garner suddenly found herself onstage accepting the award after beating out Lorraine Bracco, Amy Brenneman, Lauren Graham, Marg Helgenberger, Edie Falco, and Sela Ward. "I'm really glad I had that first glass of wine; I'm kind of regretting the second," she said as part of her speech.

While the show was receiving such accolades and critical acclaim, it was also dealing with mixed reviews that centered on the complicated nature of the series. British Sky Broadcasting was now showing *Alias* in the U.K., and Abrams addressed the concern that the complicated storyline would deter casual viewers from watching. Still, the ratings were rising, and ABC was receiving letters from more and more fans in support of the series. The show was also gaining celebrity viewers, including Quentin Tarantino and Steven Spielberg. Tarantino even became a guest star as former SD-6 agent McKenas Cole after Abrams discovered he was a fan of the series. Former James Bond actor Roger Moore stepped in as well, much to Abrams's great delight. The cast remained busy outside of filming, taking time to attend the Museum of Television and Radio's annual William S. Paley Television Festival in Los Angeles.

The Internet fans were growing as *Alias*-themed sites and posting boards continued to accumulate. The Random House children's division of Bantam Books had acquired the rights to write both an official companion to the series, titled *Alias: Declassified*, as well as *Alias: Recruited*, a fictional book that would be the first in a series of prequels to the show. Not only that, but *Alias* received 11 Emmy nominations in July 2002. Abrams remembers the moment: "I was thunderstruck. I got a call from my wife, who's in Maine. She was in the middle of nowhere, but she was online and had all the information before anyone. I sat up in bed and I couldn't believe it. It's amazing how fast you sit up when you hear the number eleven." Production started up again at the end of July, with the plan to create a 60-second theatrical trailer to be shown in movie theaters (before PG-13 and R-rated films) across North America.

And yet, while they were steady, the ratings were not as high as in the beginning; the first season ended with an average of 9.7 million viewers and ranked 65 out of 191 network television shows. Still, the presence of

Alias on the airwaves affected the classic series *The X-Files*, which was cancelled in 2002. While the ratings for the popular series had begun to drop once actor David Duchovny left, competing against the fast-paced world of Sydney Bristow was the final blow. Creator Chris Carter admitted that *Alias* played a key role in his decision to pull the series: "I was looking at this year's ratings, which were down from the season opener, and I felt we were counterprogrammed [by *Alias*]. It was kind of a strange beginning for us this year. We never had that before."

It was a final year for another show as well: *Felicity*. The good news was that *Alias* had received an early renewal by ABC a month before the network released its fall schedule, which was a rare move. The cliffhanger season ending had certainly packed a punch, and Abrams had a feel for some of the problems that had cropped up in the first season. "I felt that Will's character was going to be a stronger anchor for [Sydney's] normal life," he said. "What we found out pretty quickly is that his investigation — because we were ahead of him — frustrated people. We, on occasion, had him do some things that were perceived as stupid, because we knew he was playing with fire, even though it made sense from his point of view." With new ideas to explore, and a "mom" thrown into the mix, the cast and crew of *Alias* were getting revved up for work on season 2. "[*Alias* is] really a challenge to write for, and I think the last couple episodes [of the first season] were some of our best," claimed Jesse Alexander. "I think [the show] just got better [throughout the first season], and I think that's why the new season is going to be amazing. I think we have a much better handle on the show, and people who loved the show before are just gonna freak out."

Season Two:
Fall 2002–Spring 2003

"The second season was an easier year for us in some respects, just because the first season in the first few episodes we weren't quite crewed in the right way," says producer Sarah Caplan. "So it was hard for us to cope with everything. It was very difficult on production. By the second year we knew exactly what we needed to have in place in order to catch any fly balls that came our way."

For season 2, *Alias* was due to undergo some changes. First of all, the writing was going to receive an overhaul in an attempt to lure more viewers and boost the ratings. At the time, Abrams described the shift this way: "We'll still do some the way we did, but there will be a little bit less of the immediate life-and-death moments kind of cliffhanger, and the episodes will be satisfying in and of themselves. But there will always be something, a little nugget, to intrigue you to watch next week." There was some hope that *The X-Files* viewers would give *Alias* a try now that their show was off the air. Another notable change was the promotion of David Anders's Mr. Sark to a regular cast member.

The biggest change of all was the arrival of "Mom" in the shape of Swedish actress Lena Olin. "Mom is really the catalyst for all the stories this year," said Abrams. "She is clearly a manipulator, and the question is, how do you know when the liar is lying?" Lena Olin was at the top of the list for creator Abrams, even though Faye Dunaway was considered for the part as well. It certainly helped Olin that there was a strong resemblance between her and Garner. While there were some initial concerns about introducing a new member into an extremely close cast, Abrams felt that even if there were problems, "The mom is supposed to be an outsider anyway." Garner was very excited to have Olin join the team: "She's just such a *woman* and it's so cool. That's the element we need. . . . Our family is complete — our little twisted, dysfunctional, freaked-out, spy-happy family." It took five months to come up with a deal to get Olin on board, but in the end she signed on to appear in 16 out of 22 episodes. "I watched four shopping bags full of *Alias*," she recalls. "When I got offered the role I hadn't seen the show, so J.J. sent me four bags. I thought, *I can't go through this,* but I started and I was hooked. The acting is so good and the relationships were so interesting."

As for the rest of the season, the team had plans to bring on more new guest stars as well as have some from season 1 return. Milo Rambaldi was still going to be addressed, but Abrams claimed he would be handled a little differently this time around. "And to me, it's the part that keeps *Alias* unique, in that it's a spy genre show with a little bit of sci-fi thrown in for fun, which I love. It's an angle that I don't want to overdo, but I feel the sci-fi audience is so smart that a little bit actually goes a long way, and they don't need to be hit over the head with too much obvious stuff," he acknowledges. Also on the agenda outside of the show was *Alias* merchandising. Arcade Comics and Rob Liefeld were working on an *Alias* comic book that was to come out in December, while InkWorks trading cards, two 12-inch dolls, and a two-pack of 6-inch action figures would be hitting the store shelves.

The premiere episode was set to answer the majority of the questions presented in the season 1 finale. For example, how on earth does Vaughn get out of the hot water he's in? What's the story with Sydney's mom? What will happen to Will now that he's in the loop? In all cases, the cast, crew, and executives were happy with the new direction. "I will tell you that we have seen the first-episode script for *Alias*. This is going to drive some really provocative episodes this fall and certainly a big arc for the next season. I will promise you this is going to be the most interesting family on television this year," said Susan Lyne, the president of ABC Entertainment. The season itself would have a new family dynamic to deal with. "This year, more than ever, the inner lives of the characters [are key]," said Abrams. "There are secrets that Jack has; there are secrets that Mom has; there's a world that Sydney's trying to figure out. So what's really fun about the show, especially now, is that the missions are great, [but] we basically think, *What story can we tell that allows the emotional lives of the characters to come out?*"

The actors were relishing the new dynamic created with Olin's presence. The whole "divorced family" theme was now going to be played up, with two characters in a very contentious relationship and a daughter being tossed between them. "There are amazing moments that are entirely relatable, because it's about the kid feeling loyal to one parent, guilty about the other; hopeful about one parent, and copping to the other parent about that. There are these three people that have such baggage and agendas and concerns, and any dynamic between them — all of them being opposed to the other; two of them siding against the third; one of them defending the other for the first time; all three of them against a current enemy — any version of that is fascinating," said Abrams about the character development in season 2.

There were some questions, however, about the scheduling of the show. Even though *The X-Files* was no longer on the air, there were other shows to contend with on Sundays at 9 p.m.: *The Sopranos, Malcolm in the Middle, Angel,* and *Law & Order: Criminal Intent.* Furthermore, *Alias* was following *The Wonderful World of Disney,* which wasn't exactly in line with the spy series. The network was hoping that the mass-marketing launch — including the books, comics, action figures, DVD set, and the video game — along with the theatrical trailers would bring in the viewers. The ABC online game *Alias Underground* was also free for individuals to download, which was a television industry first. "We're always looking for innovative ways to increase awareness and tune-in, *Alias* is a signature show for our network, and *Alias Underground* is intended to complement on-air viewing while appealing to new audiences," said Mike Benson, senior vice president of marketing, advertising, and promotion. Ford and Nokia would be sponsoring the game, with both offering players the opportunity to win prizes.

There were also plans to broadcast a special episode following the Super Bowl in January. "It's going to be big and crazy and fun, and I'm sure I'll have to show more skin than I'm comfortable with, but that's a good reason to be in shape before Christmas," said Jennifer Garner. There was also the hope that the film *Daredevil,* co-starring Garner, would be a hit, thus indirectly offering *Alias* more exposure.

In September, Abrams sent a letter to the television critics on behalf of the show:

> *First of all, I don't know how you do your job. Come September you must get about 10,000 videotapes a week — how do you find time to watch them all? Seriously, I don't know how you do it. Therefore, it is with a pang of guilt that I send you yet another tape. If you happen to find the time to check out this first episode of* Alias' *second season, thank you in advance.*
>
> *Of special note: this episode features Lena Olin, who has joined the regular cast as Sydney Bristow's mother. I'd like to state, for the record, that Lena is of* NO RELATION TO OUR DIRECTOR, KEN OLIN.

As much as he'd like you to believe otherwise.

Thank you again for what you do. If you have any questions or comments or just want to drop by and watch us hang Jennifer Garner 200 feet in the air by a single, pencil-thin cable, please don't hesitate to call.
All the best,
J.J. Abrams

At the same time, Abrams was starting to receive flak from dedicated fans of *Superman*. The popular film site Ain't Cool News had begun bashing

Director Ken Olin, who is *not* related in any way to Lena Olin.

the first draft of the script that Abrams had created, which included a Krypton back story and references to Jimmy Olsen's sexuality. Harry Knowles, the site creator, even went so far as to suggest that angry fans show up at the *Alias: Declassified* book signing at the Los Angeles Barnes & Noble with the writer and cast in order to make their opinions known to Abrams. J.J. was not surprised by the backlash that came from the script, knowing that the fans are very passionate. He had experienced the intensity firsthand while visiting *Alias* Web sites in season 1. Abrams says, "I respect the fans and love to hear what they have to say. Unlike film, TV is an ongoing process. If you discover, oh gosh, they're not getting a storyline or a character isn't working, then you can make adjustments if you agree with them." With regard to Knowles' issues with the story of the man of steel, Abrams called him up personally to assuage his concerns, seeing as Knowles had not personally read the script, unlike Moriarty (Drew McWeeney), who wrote the review on Ain't Cool News. Knowles responded on the site by saying, "That J.J. is a *Superman* geek — he knows his stuff. Doesn't mean the movie won't suck, but it does mean there's a chance it might not." While Abrams is no longer attached to the film, he certainly has his hands full with other ventures.

Then it was time for the Emmys ceremony, and with its 11 nominations, *Alias*'s future looked bright. The show took home two Emmys, for Outstanding Cinematography for a Single-Camera Series (for the pilot episode, "Truth Be Told") and Outstanding Art Direction for a Single-Camera Series (for "Truth Be Told"). Garner, Garber, and Abrams got passed over. "When you watch the Emmys, the established shows tend to keep coming up," said Victor Garber in the aftermath. "That's why the win by [*The Shield* star] Michael Chiklis was such a wonderful surprise. . . . But for me, it's happened so many times, I'm used [to losing]. But if one more person had come up to me and said, 'Really, I think it's your year,' I would have just batted them."

Alias opened well with both the audience and the critics, beating out *Law & Order: Criminal Intent*, but after the Emmys the show still hadn't broken the top 20 mark, settling instead in the top 30 shows. The numbers kept falling, from 6.4 million viewers in September, to 5.6, then down to 5.4, while *Law & Order: Criminal Intent*'s numbers went up. And yet the show was still a favorite with the critics. "It weds both action and emotion. The show delivers on so many levels. There's a little bit of ABC, a little bit of WB in there," said Matt Roush, a critic for *TV Guide*. Some even questioned if it was the originality of the show that was the problem, seeing as it was so difficult to pigeonhole. The fact that *Alias* is not a self-contained show was also a possibility. It was also up against The WB Network's *Angel*, which could have been drawing female viewers away.

In October, the Academy of Television Arts & Sciences held a tribute to the show, with both Abrams and some of the cast in attendance. Everyone seemed optimistic, and Garber even showed off his comic talent. "One glass of Merlot, and 'spy daddy' is doing stand-up," said Jennifer Garner, laughing. Nonetheless, two days later, on October 29, there was some backlash when ABC decided at the last minute against showing a new episode of *Alias* after the World Series (it ran late) and instead aired a rerun. While this is a common practice, the issue was that ABC had been hyping new episodes of both *Alias* and *The Practice* all week only to change their plans last minute, leaving viewers disappointed.

Aside from that incident, however, there was no real understanding of why the show was not attracting more viewers. As a consequence, both Abrams and ABC began to really study what the issue could be. "We have to make the show more receptive to nonviewers. There is a feeling among people who have not watched the show that it's tough to break in," determined Lloyd Braun, ABC Entertainment chair. The other question was, was *Alias* just too intelligent for the viewers? Was the complexity of the family element combined with the intricate spy genre just too much? Why had *24*, another complicated series requiring faithful viewing, gone up in the ratings by 22 percent since the previous season while *Alias* had gone down by six percent? Was the promotional campaign not savvy or accurate enough? Or was it simply that *24*'s first DVD set came out so quickly after the show aired, causing more viewers to get hooked? Abrams worked overtime to deal with the issue; one strategy involved adding lengthy summaries at the beginning of each episode in order to explain what had happened in previous episodes.

The importance of getting an answer also stemmed from the fact that the show was so expensive to produce. Costing up to $1.7 million an episode, with a leading actress who was fast becoming an A-list star, the show's ratings had to improve in order to make the expenditure viable for the network. ABC argued the notion that the show was too expensive to produce. "[The] shows that are really expensive are shows that have gone through one cycle, and then have a chance to renegotiate their whole talent structure. I don't know whether it's expensive or not, but it's not expensive compared to *The West Wing* and some of those others," said Steve Sohmer, ABC's VP of marketing. Even with the problems, however, ABC had no intention of moving *Alias* from its Sunday night slot.

In December, *Alias* was featured on one of four 20-by-29-foot historic permanent posters to go up on display on the Disney Studio Lot, and the anticipation for the highly promoted post–Super Bowl XXXVII episode was rising. January 26, 2003, was the air date, and the network was pleased with the work created by the *Alias* cast and crew. "The episode that J.J. Abrams has written to air post–Super Bowl is a phenomenal hour of television, maybe the best hour of pure entertainment we've seen. This is a show that we have always believed deserved a bigger audience, and the Super Bowl will help introduce it to millions of new viewers," announced Susan Lyne, president of ABC Entertainment. The problem was, by the time the Super Bowl postgame analysis had ended, it was 11 p.m. Eastern Standard Time, which cut out a large group of potential viewers. "I was spitting blood. If I controlled it, I would have thrown *Alias* on during the third quarter," revealed ABC Entertainment chair Lloyd Braun. While *Alias* garnered its best ratings ever, with 17.4 million viewers tuning in, the episode generated the lowest post–Super Bowl numbers since 1987.

"Phase One" was phenomenal, beginning with Garner wearing the sexiest costume to date (lingerie, to be exact) and leading to the downfall of SD-6 — all sealed with a kiss. In one episode, Abrams completely changed the rules of the game: Sydney Bristow was no longer a double agent. The major antagonist organization had been overthrown. Francie II was revealed, and Vaughn and Sydney were free to be together. What had just happened? "In a way, this episode sort of breaks the dam and lets us do the stories that I, as a writer, have personally been dying to do, but have been unable to, given the structure of the premise and the paradigm of the show. This lets us go places that we've wanted to go for quite a while," confessed Abrams. Interestingly enough, it was the episode guest starring Ethan Hawke that was supposed to be aired post–Super Bowl. Abrams felt it was important that the episode in that time slot would allow new viewers to watch without feeling completely lost by the storylines.

One of the main reasons for the upheaval on the show was concern about the double-agent structure and its limitations. "If we did another story in which Sydney was almost found out, I was going to kill myself," stated Abrams.

"Phase One" acted as another pilot episode, allowing the writers to take the show in a totally different direction. It also meant more clarity for the viewers, claimed Abrams: "When you look at it and say, 'It's a show with good guys pretending to be bad guys, many of the bad guys are pretending that they're good guys, and quite a few of the bad guys don't even know that they're bad guys' — that's a difficult premise for anyone coming to the show from episode two on, because if you don't make it clear in every episode, they're going to be lost." The changes also gave the writers time to explore the characters rather than to focus solely on mission/countermission stories. One of those stories included the relationship between Sydney and Vaughn. "If I had another scene of Jennifer and Michael staring longingly at each other and not saying anything, I was going to lose my mind," said Abrams. "It was a relationship that we were not letting ourselves get that deep into, [and by moving it forward] it allows [Sydney] to experience as much joy and pleasure as heartache and stress and anxiety and fret. And unless you get her to that place, the relationship ends up existing forever in a somewhat sophomoric, juvenile place where we're not allowing it to deepen." The highly anticipated kiss was well earned, with both stars realizing the impact it would have on the audience. As a consequence, a little performance anxiety crept in for Michael Vartan: "She's kissing Leonardo DiCaprio, she's kissing Ben Affleck — she's doing all right. I just think, what a letdown it's going to be for her if she has to kiss me. If she calls me 'Ben' in our kissing scene, I'm going to flip."

"Phase One" led to the complete fall of SD-6, sending the show into a whole different direction. But, with SD-6 gone, another question was presented: What happens to archvillain Arvin Sloane? "J.J. and the writers were very careful when they told me," says Ron Rifkin. "J.J. told me what was happening before I read the script so I would know what was going on, and he said, 'This is a good thing for your character. Just understand: now you can go anywhere and do anything.' If I had not known that and saw that SD-6 was destructing, I suspect I would have been freaked out." The change in direction meant that Sloane would have more freedom, and that appealed to the writers.

It was also important to make the shift simply because the characters were beginning to look like incompetent spies. Either Sydney needed to be found out or SD-6 needed to be brought to a vulnerable point. It also didn't help that the longer Dixon and Marshall — two obviously intelligent agents — didn't realize that they were working for the enemy, the dumber they looked. So the decision was made. "Now . . . the doors are blown open. The guy who plays my partner, Carl Lumbly . . . he now has all this genius stuff to play: 'You've betrayed me all this time?' What does this mean to his marriage? What does this mean in his life?" said Jennifer Garner, obviously enthused about the possibilities the new storyline would open up. "[Also, Marshall] can be much more involved in the missions."

While there was some trepidation about bringing down the evil organization, in the end it wouldn't hinder the show. The stakes could remain high and Sydney could still find herself in danger, all while the plot became simplified. Internet fans were not pleased, concerned that the show would be compromised as a consequence of the change, but Ken Olin was quick to come to Abrams's defense, stating that the twists and turns would remain and the essence and intelligence of the show would not be lost. "I love the show so much that the last thing I would do is dumb it down," said Abrams. "There is a difference between dumbing it down and eliminating unnecessary confusion. Ultimately, the show is a mystery, and that's kind of the fun of it, but in a mystery, if you don't know who you are, it goes from being a mystery to being a mess. That, to me, is something we're going to be able to deal with."

With all these changes on the horizon, talks started regarding an *Alias* movie, although Garner was purportedly not comfortable with the idea of performing in a prequel to the show, feeling that she would be too old for the role. Abrams also had doubts: "[Discussions have] come up, and . . . it's an interesting idea. My agents have talked to me about it, and I know that they have talked to Disney about it, but it's nothing that is seriously being pursued," he said. "Given the fact that we try every week to do a movie version of the show, it's not clear to me what we would try to do that we aren't *already* trying to do." Even though a movie wasn't necessarily in the cards, Abrams was confident that season 3 was definitely in store for *Alias*, and the writers kept that in mind while finishing up season 2. And another perk for the show was the season 1 DVD release on September 2, 2003, which included a variety of special features, including an outtakes reel, behind-the-scenes footage, cast interviews, and more.

Through it all the cast kept themselves busy after hours with various charitable endeavors. Garner and Merrin Dungey partook in a series of public service announcements to air in February 2003; the ads created by ABC and the Advertising Council to celebrate Black History Month. Other shows participating in the announcements included NYPD *Blue*, *My Wife and Kids*, *The Practice*, *Less Than Perfect*, and *The View*. Meanwhile, Abrams continued with his involvement in the free downloadable game on the ABC site with writers Rick Orci and Jesse Alexander. "It's the computer gaming equivalent of Dickens's writing, where every month he would put out a new chapter in a story," Abrams said of *Alias Underground*. "We could have waited and released the whole game at once, but we thought, 'Wouldn't it be fun to release it a chunk at a time and get people involved as it goes?'" he explained. The game options included 10 missions, one of which was a training exercise. The goal was to get Sydney to collect Rambaldi artifacts while following her CIA and SD-6 orders, and in the end, she solves the mystery behind the collected artifacts. Abrams also pointed out that individuals didn't have to know anything about the series in order to enjoy the game.

In February, Acclaim Entertainment, Inc. made an agreement with Disney Interactive to produce a video game based on *Alias* for PlayStation 2 and Xbox. The game would also be released in the fall of 2003. In conjunction with the agreement with Disney, Acclaim also signed on cast members Jennifer Garner, Michael Vartan, Victor Garber, Ron Rifkin, Carl Lumbly, Kevin Weisman, and David Anders to bring their voices to the characters. J.J. Abrams and the writing team came on board as collaborators as well, enthusiastic about the project. "We'd been working on the show for two years, and we actually played video games for most of the time that we lived together, so for me a video game based on *Alias* is brilliant," said Abrams. "But it's only genuinely exciting because the game is actually fun to play. We've all played games based on TV shows and movies that . . . you know, shouldn't have gotten there. And the fact is — and this was important from the beginning — this is the game that *we* would all play, and that we're proud of, and that we felt was worthy of the show . . ."

While the ratings returned to their disappointing level after the Super

Bowl episode, the *Alias* team had achieved one major thing: an increase in male viewers, which was one of ABC's targets. Just before February sweeps, *Alias* ranked fourth in the 18–49 category, and hoped to attract more teenagers to the show as well as more males. It succeeded with the latter, with the post–Super Bowl audience. With prequel books on the shelves, a video game in the making, and a comic book that would introduce a new character before he arrived on the actual show, the team was hard at work marketing the series. Nokia was also working with ABC to create a specialized cell phone ring that mimicked *Alias*'s techno theme song. There was also the suggestion of giving the show a stronger, younger-skewing "lead-in" on Sundays for the third season.

The tone of the show shifted somewhat as well beginning with "Double Agent," guest starring Ethan Hawke. The episode opened with an eerily dark moment: a young female agent stands in a busy Berlin intersection wearing a vest packed with explosives and is forced to sing "Pop Goes the Weasel" before she is blown up. The rest of the show felt more familiar, as it explored the idea of altering a person's physical appearance by adjusting their DNA code. "Double Agent" placed fourth in the hour for overall audience, but it scored the highest numbers for season 2 in its regular time slot with 11.4 million viewers. Even though the ratings battle had yet to be won, *Alias* was guaranteed to be renewed for another season for two reasons: (1) ABC had spent an enormous amount of time and money on the show and (2) Abrams and the writing team could wrap up the story threads, if necessary.

Alias once again ended with a huge cliffhanger in "The Telling." "The way last year ended, I loved where we were going . . . and I feel like this year we have an even better ending," said Abrams about the season 2 finale. "If you're a longtime or a new fan of the show, I think it will blow your mind. It's that feeling I have of a giant secret that I just can't wait for everyone to see." And what a secret it was. Like "Phase One," "The Telling" felt as though Abrams and the *Alias* team had broken all the rules once again, leaving us wondering what could possibly happen next. The fans were still rooting for the show, with three *Alias* alumnae winning out in the *TV Guide* polls: 42.2 percent named Jennifer Garner the Most Beautiful Woman on television; 39 percent named Michael

Vartan the Best Looking Man; and Arvin Sloane topped them both with 55 percent naming him the Man You Love to Hate.

As expected, *Alias* was renewed for a third season. "From the beginning, the enthusiasm from the network has not wavered," said actor Carl Lumbly. "I think part of it has to be that we reach a critical demographic for them, the eighteen-to-forty-nine demographic. They also, I think, see the effort and realize that *Alias* is a journey worth taking. You have to take the journey to see where it leads, and ABC has made that commitment. So as much as I was surprised that we were ever picked up, I'm not surprised that we're coming back for a third season."

While the show was returning, there was some question as to whether or not actress Lena Olin would be back. "I couldn't be [a regular], because I live in New York. I'll see if we can work it out so that I can work a chunk of time [in Los Angeles, where the show is filmed]. There are two other [films] that I want to do that I want to fit in with the *Alias* schedule, and so I don't know how it's going to work out," she said. The other questionable returnees were Merrin Dungey and Bradley Cooper.

What would happen in the third season was anyone's guess. Once again it felt as though a new pilot was being created, with the rules all changing once more. Production on the third season began on July 22, 2003. "We're not double agents anymore," said Victor Garber. "SD-6 is gone, so we're CIA, and we're all trying to get the bad guys. We're trying to broaden the appeal for people just tuning in, so the show will be a little more straight-ahead. The first episode picks up two years later, so in a way it's a fresh start for everybody. But don't worry — it's still complicated."

Season Three:
Fall 2003–Spring 2004

The season-3 premiere came on the wave of the September 21 Emmy Awards, where *Alias* once again received 11 nominations. Jennifer Garner received a repeat nomination for Outstanding Lead Actress in a Drama Series, with both Bristow parents (Victor Garber and Lena Olin) receiving nods in the Supporting Actor and Actress category. The other nominations included Outstanding Art Direction and Cinematography for a Single-Camera Series (for "Phase One" and "Double Agent," respectively); Costumes ("Phase One"); Single-Camera Picture Editing ("Phase One"); Hairstyling ("The Counteragent"); and Sound Editing ("Phase One"). The series took home Emmys for Outstanding Stunt Coordination for "The Telling," and Outstanding Makeup (Non-Prosthetic) for "The Counteragent." In May of the same year, *Alias* was declared the Best Network Television series at the Saturn Awards, and Garner and Garber walked away with Best Actress and Best Supporting Actor wins.

On September 28, *Alias* returned to the small screen with fans waiting anxiously to understand what had happened to Sydney over a two-year period. With the extensive time gap, the writing team was able to completely shift the *Alias* world, giving viewers a fresh start once more. "It's one of the most exciting creative experiences I've had . . ." Abrams confessed with regard to season 3. "Imagine falling asleep and waking up twenty-four months in the future. There would be some pretty fundamental changes. What's fun about it is being able to say, OK, all the characters are pieces on the game board, and they've all rolled the dice and played quite a few turns, and now they're all much farther ahead than Sydney is, and in some cases it's shocking where they are and what's happened to them." (Interestingly enough, *24*, starring Kiefer Sutherland, moved its story forward three years for its season-3 premiere.) While Sydney's primary goal in season 1 involved taking down SD-6, that objective continued in season 2. Her latest goal included uncovering the dark mystery behind her disappearance and the actions that she took while living as Julia Thorne. There was also the villain du jour to contend with: the mysterious Covenant.

Once again the *Alias* world was being re-created, and yet the action and emotion were not compromised. In fact, the changes were quite shocking. Sloane a philanthropist? Jack in prison? Vaughn married to a sexy blond? "I'm the only guy who sort of doesn't change," said actor Greg Grunberg. "The only thing I've done in the two years is lose a few pounds. All of the other characters have gone through major changes,

So which Sark do you prefer, the longer-haired one from season 1 and 2 (left), or the buzz-cut bad boy of season 3 (right)?

good and bad." Even Mr. Sark had his own change: a new buzz-cut hairstyle. Some of the fans weren't pleased with the lack of blond locks, however. "J.J. has a history of cutting hair and losing ratings. So hopefully this won't happen," said Grunberg, in reference to the famous haircut disaster on *Felicity*. It didn't seem to be too much of a problem, however, as David Anders was invited to three different proms during the year! "I always say I have the Backstreet Boys contingent," said Anders. And Victor Garber was happy to see that Jack Bristow could finally start to explore his sense of humor: "I think he does have one and I think there are little hints every now and then that he has one, and hopefully there'll be more. Otherwise, I couldn't play him. Actually, [there is a scene] where he does actually make an ironic joke with Michael Vaughn on the plane and I'm so happy to see that."

There was also the addition of a new cast member to the fray: Mrs. "National Security Council Liaison" Vaughn, a.k.a. Lauren Reed, played by Australian actress Melissa George. Originally set to be a guest role like David Anders's Mr. Sark, things took a turn for the character of Lauren Reed when Melissa was asked to become a permanent member of the cast. "This is the first time we have played with a triangle on the show, but the thing about it is, I love Melissa's character," said Jennifer Garner. "I do not blame Vaughn at all for falling for her and Sydney respects Lauren, so it's not as if she is put there for the audience to hate. Everyone should be conflicted as to what the best resolution of this triangle should be." The new love interest for Vaughn created some major backlash from the fans. While Garner excused Vaughn, saying that Sydney had moved on from Danny's death in the same amount of time as Vaughn took to grieve Sydney, Michael Vartan did not receive the same understanding that had been extended to Jennifer Garner. "Girls were like, 'How *could* you?'" Vartan revealed. "It got to the point where I thought of having a T-shirt made that said: *The DNA matched!*"

The guest stars returned once more, starting with *Charlie's Angels: Full Throttle* bad guy Justin Theroux (who appeared with Melissa George in the David Lynch film *Mulholland Drive*) as a man who had a past with Julia Thorne. "Justin is the perfect actor to bring onto our show. You can't tell if he is charming or menacing," said Garner. "You know that he is sexy, but you don't know what his line is and what the nature of his relationship with Sydney is." Other guest actors in season 3 included Djimon Hounsou, David Cronenberg, Vivica A. Fox, David Carradine, Terry O'Quinn, and Pruitt Taylor Vince. Quentin Tarantino returned as McKenas Cole and Isabella Rossellini made an appearance as Katya, Syd's villainous aunt. "[Katya's] not intended to take the place of Irina. I like to have a woman, who is almost a maternal figure, on the show," said Abrams. The creator got his "guest star" wish fulfilled when Ricky Gervais of the award-winning British comedy series *The Office* came on board as an Irish bomber.

Bradley Cooper and Merrin Dungey returned as well, to the delight of fans. Will was "relocated" by Sydney as she searched for clues about her missing years, but he had also gone through his own identity change. "He's a foreman for a construction company. Big change. He's incognito. He's wearing the big boots. He's not sporting the flannel. He looks much different, though. He shaved his head for one thing. I'll say one thing — Will grows a pair," said Cooper. Merrin slipped into her bad girl role quite easily and now has a constant reminder of her *Alias* days: she presently plays guitar in her band, aptly named "Bad Francie." "We're using both of those actors in a way that is their best," said Abrams. "We're throwing them back into Sydney's life when it's at its most insane."

With all these changes, *Alias* was moving on a completely different track once more. The question was, would the fans follow? While the season premiere ratings were down from the season-2 premiere (at 7.5/10 from 8.5/12), they were above season 2's average rating of 6.43/8.96. The ratings dropped after the next few episodes of season 3, but eventually climbed back up with the episode "Prelude." *Alias* still had weight, however, beating out the WB show *Tarzan*, which was cancelled after eight episodes.

The backlash against Lauren Reed continued, however. Fans fought against the marriage from the start. "To generalize from the comments I've been hearing, from fellow critics and from my mailbag, I would say one constant has been the ambivalent-to-negative reaction to the character of Lauren and the actress playing her. It was inevitable that die-hard fans of the Syd-Vaughn relationship would be unforgiving toward her, and one of the more entertaining responses came from Patricia R., who in her rant suggested renaming the show *Days of Our Spies*," said *TV Guide* critic Matt Roush. Fans and critics alike also missed having Dixon in on the action. Thankfully, the writers had a "master plan," and Lauren's character took a new turn. And while Dixon still spent most of his time in the office, he did get back into the thick of things for a few episodes.

Outside the show, Jennifer got to work filming the CIA recruitment videos as a favor to the agency. "Women come up and say, 'I started working out because of you' or 'I learned this language.' Or a mom will say, 'My daughter and I watch your show together because your character is so honorable.' And that is just bitchin'," said Garner. The actress wasn't just inspiring potential agents, however. On Halloween, an unexpected event occurred in Washington, D.C., when two political legislative assistants caused a panic on Capitol Hill after bringing a plastic gun to work. The gun was actually part of a Halloween costume purchased at lunch, and it was to be the final touch to a Sydney Bristow costume. The gun was mistaken for a real revolver, which led to the House of Representatives coming to an emergency halt as a consequence (the first time that had happened since 9/11).

On the marketing front, the *Alias* video game went through a delay, but the prequel books kept coming out for the fans to enjoy. There was also lots of Web activity: the number of Web sites dedicated to *Alias* and chat forums grew, as did the amount of "fan fiction" being produced. What does the writing team think of fans exploring stories on their own? "We love it and we encourage it," says *Alias* writer J.R. Orci. "In a way, it's a form of making the show interactive. They've gone from being spectators to being creators. It creates a community where people give each other feedback and some people must go on to be published writers." The writing team is not allowed to read fan fiction for legal reasons, but the writers do take note of comments made in fan forums and letters they receive that critique the show. "[That's] one of the many great things about J.J., is that he does take the fans seriously," says actress Melissa George. "The fans are what makes something run or not in a way — they're very important."

While the mystery surrounding Sydney's disappearance could have been drawn out all season (much to the frustration of the viewers), the writing team came through with an episode at the midpoint that explained all. In the same vein as "Q & A" in season 1, "Full Disclosure" revealed to Sydney the events of the previous two years. "I feel, if you don't provide viewers with some concrete specifics, they start to get disinterested and feel, 'Oh, it's a lot of hot air, smoke and mirrors,' and not pay attention. You have to reward your fans," said Abrams of the approach. By positioning "Full Disclosure" mid-season, the writers were able to explore other storylines in more depth, including the infamous Rambaldi prophecies.

That May, *Alias* won the Saturn Award for Best Network Television Series, with Jennifer Garner winning Best Actress and Victor Garber winning Best Supporting Actor awards. Abrams had special action figures created for the cast as Christmas presents. The Wonderful World of Disney was scheduled to be moved from Sunday to Saturday, which could benefit *Alias* considering the Disney lead-in was mismatched with the action show. The second season of the show came out on DVD as well, just in time for the holidays. Then, in January, the Producers Guild of America announced the nominees for TV and movie producers of the year. J.J. Abrams, Ken Olin, John Eisendrath, and Sarah Caplan were all nominated for *Alias*, up against the producers of *The West Wing*, *24*, *Six Feet Under*, and CSI (*Six Feet Under* took the prize). Garner was nominated for Best Actress at the Screen Actors Guild Awards (but unfortunately lost to Frances Conroy of *Six Feet Under*). It seemed that 2004 was off to a good start, and even though the ratings hadn't been as strong as everyone had hoped, the show was still an ABC favorite. "We love that show. It's not going anywhere," said Susan Lyne, ABC's president.

As the season progressed, *Alias* started gaining a reputation as a sci-fi show. "As someone who is such an incredible fan of sci-fi, fantasy, and horror, to be looked at as a show in that genre was always my goal," said Abrams. And yet, he was clear that *Alias* wouldn't completely rely on the sci-fi elements. He wanted *Alias* to remain a mish-mash of various genres. The critics, however, were seeing major parallels between *Alias* and its Sunday-night sci-fi predecessor, *The X-Files*. As the Rambaldi prophecies became more integral to the plot, so did the science-fiction factor. How was the use of Sydney's eggs in the second coming of Rambaldi different from the alien conspiracies that Mulder and Scully had faced? Like *The X-Files*, the requirement for suspension of disbelief was growing with each episode. The essence of Rambaldi that was over 500 years old, Project "Black Hole," The Trust, The Passenger's brainwaves being predicted, green liquid independently forming a gelatinous mass of fluorescent ooze to create a battery for a sixteenth-century machine? It all made the lucid dreaming sequence with David Cronenberg seem almost . . . normal. "As we've been talking through ways to take the idea that we have for the end, there have been some ideas recently that are so extreme that if we actually dare to do some of these things, we'd have to be really careful that we don't cross the line," said Abrams, referring to the writers' dilemma. "Our audience is, for better or worse, really smart. Some of these ideas are so wild that how we execute them is ultimately as important as the ideas themselves."

Meanwhile, Abrams's project with Greg Grunberg, *The Catch*, was still in the works. While it was given the green light by ABC, development of show was pushed back to 2004–5 mid-season. Grunberg is set to remain on *Alias* for a bit longer. "I'd love to keep doing what I'm doing, but much more an integral part in the storylines instead of just being the guy who passes information along. What could be really cool is, in the way that Marshall is good with gadgets, I should be good at using magic or sleight of hand. That would be really funny," says Grunberg.

Abrams signed an 18-month extension with Touchstone TV for a high six-figure amount as his current deal was about to expire. "J.J. is without question one of the most amazing talents working in television today. I have been so fortunate to be associated with his many successes and look forward to riding his coattails in the future," said Stephen McPherson, the president of Touchstone TV. Abrams was also in the midst of turning his company, Bad Robot Television, into a full-fledged production company. In conjunction with *Alias* and *The Catch*, Abrams was also working on the pilot *Lost*. Coming out in fall 2004, *Lost* stars Matthew Fox (*Party of Five*), Dominic Monaghan (*The Lord of the Rings*), Ian Somerhalder (*Smallville*), and Daniel Dae Kim (*24*, *Angel*). It focuses on a group of plane-crash survivors trying to survive on a desert island.

Abrams was still devoted to *Alias*, however, and the plot twists continued, one of which was the revelation of Lauren's true colors. Right from the start there was conflict regarding the character and her relationship with Vaughn and it did not dissipate as the season progressed. What better way to deal with it than to change her spots? "We thought of Lauren working for the Covenant just like a woman having an affair," said writer Alison Schapker. "But it's still relatable, the idea of being lied to in a marriage." Going through with the change in Lauren's character allowed for more emotional tension with the characters as well as a new romantic alliance, this time involving a certain evil blond-haired young Brit *Alias* fans have come to know and love.

While the third season was airing, ABC was busy working at selling the syndicated rights to the series. TNT eventually purchased them for less than $200,000 per episode, which was a large drop from the initial price (just under $1 million per episode). It was also less than the price for such shows as *Without a Trace* (CBS) and *Law & Order* (NBC). While the fans will get a chance to revisit *Alias* episodes five nights a week starting in 2005 as a consequence of the deal, few networks were interested in purchasing the rights. This lack of interest might reflect the show's struggle with gaining "hit" status even though it has garnered critical acclaim. Another issue is the complex storyline, which has very few stand-alone episodes. There were high hopes that *Alias* would finally "break through," however, fueled by Jennifer Garner's being named the ShoWest "Female Star of Tomorrow" and her expanding movie career. "You are buying into a show that, positioned correctly, could become a cult favorite. It's likely at minimum to do credible numbers," said Katz Television VP and Director of Programming Bill Carroll.

The fans continued to support the series. First of all, an *Alias* convention was organized by Wolf Events in the U.K. for July 2 through 4, 2004, with David Anders, Merrin Dungey, and Bradley Cooper attending. Also in the works in 2004 was a series of *Alias* "marathons," with the proceeds going to the Juvenile Diabetes Research Foundation. Unlike classic marathon athletes, these participants in different U.S. cities would be sponsored not for running, but for watching a marathon of *Alias* episodes. Back on the *Alias* set, Jennifer Garner made one special fan's dream come true. Thanks to the Make-A-Wish Foundation, a young 15-year-old cancer patient named Rachel got to visit the cast of her favorite television series. Her whole family was invited on-set during a shoot, and once the filming was done, Garner greeted Rachel with a hug before they spent some quality time together.

In spring 2004, Garner was preparing for the opening of her film *13 Going on 30*. The film opened April 23 worldwide and grossed over $20 million on its opening weekend. Jennifer was quite pleased with the final product. "When I watched it, the thing that struck me the most is how much I'm smiling," she says. Her co-star, Mark Ruffalo, was impressed with the décor at the premiere, which included girls in Care Bear costumes handing out lollipops. "I've never been to so cute a premiere," he claims. "Usually the films I do, they don't even allow kids in." Apparently, Garner was particularly cute on-set as well. "Usually, [Garner would] sing some perversion of my name: 'Mark-us Ruffal-is,

Jennifer Garner arrives at the premiere of her successful film, *13 Going on 30*.

will you have some lunch with us?'" Ruffalo recalls. Jennifer enjoyed working with director Gary Winick so much that they decided to produce an independent film together. As a consequence, Garner formed her own production company, Vandalia Films (the original name of the state of West Virginia).

As the *Alias* season drew to a close, the writers disclosed that one of the main focuses for season 3 was the reveal that Arvin Sloane had had an affair with Irina Derevko while she was married to Jack. Throughout season 3, little hints kept coming out regarding Sydney's parentage. Initially the writers considered having a "closer" relationship develop between Sloane and Sydney, but they realized how it would damage the relationship dynamic between Jack and Syd. The problem was that they had invested so much time in the story of the "affair" — they needed another solution. Thus Nadia was born. Syd's half-sister, played by Argentinean actress Mia Maestro, only appeared in the final few episodes of season 3, but Maestro was hired to be a regular for season 4. "[Nadia] was potentially going to be a catatonic visionary. And then no one was really satisfied with that because it really limits what you can do with her," says writer Monica Breen. The writers had characters dropping references to this vague entity known as "The Passenger" for months, keeping all allusions as open-ended as possible to allow for a few different conclusions. As well as gaining a new cast member, the *Alias* writing team also picked up writer Jeffrey Bell. Having worked on *Angel* for three seasons and *The X-Files* before that, Bell signed on to *Alias* in April 2004 as a writer and co-executive producer and is a welcome addition to the group.

Before ABC announced in May that *Alias* would be returning for season 4, Garner revealed in April that the show was not going to be on the chopping block. "We are coming back for next year, which we are thrilled about," said Garner, "I don't know if it's been announced, but I'll be back. We hired new writers, we hired new cast members, so it's happening." While there were many changes happening behind the scenes, there were also changes on-screen, especially for Sydney. "Before, [in the first two seasons], she lived an isolated life, but she had a flip life that was with friends. She was involved in what they were doing, and they thought they were involved with what she was doing. I think this year has been about her isolation," Garner said about this shift in Syd's life. *Alias* certainly doesn't have an isolated audience, however. It can be seen in Argentina, Australia, France, Germany, Italy, Japan, Malaysia, the U.K., and the Philippines.

As for outside projects, Garner went from enjoying the success of *13 Going on 30* to once more donning the sexy outfit of superhero Elektra. The eponymous film, a spin-off of *Daredevil*, also stars Goran Visnjic (*ER*) and Terence Stamp (*The Limey*). Michael Vartan also had a new film on his plate: he is the love interest for Jennifer Lopez in *Monster-in-Law*. Before getting the role, however, Lopez had to approve of the actor. "She had just gotten off a plane from Miami and rushed from the L.A. airport to meet me. It was one of those situations where the director said I'd get the job [as long as] I didn't vomit on her shoes, because I was so nervous. But she made me feel so comfortable," said Vartan. Victor Garber was set to fill the shoes of Julius Caesar in the ABC miniseries *Empire*, also starring James Frain (*The Count of Monte Cristo*) as Brutus, Jonathan Cake (*The American Embassy*) as Tyrannus, Vincent Regan (*Troy*) as Marc Antony, and Fiona Shaw (*Harry Potter* films) as Fulvia.

Season 3 ended on May 23 with a great cliffhanger, leaving us to wonder about the fates of Lauren, Vaughn, Syd, Nadia, and even Jack. Once again, the characters revealed that they are not who they seem. On Tuesday, May 11, 2004, the official announcement was released: *Alias* would indeed be returning, only not in the fall as expected. Instead, season 4 of *Alias* would be premiering in January 2005. Part of the reason for this change was to alter the erratic scheduling the show received in season 3, which harmed its chances of garnering more viewers as well as keeping present ones. The second reason was to allow the network to air the series without any repeats in order to give the show real momentum. The strategy had worked well with such hit series as *The Sopranos* and *The Shield*, so ABC decided to use it for both *Alias* and *NYPD Blue*. *Alias* is a location-heavy show, making it difficult to film episodes back-to-back. The new scheduling allows for more time to shoot. "I think [Abrams] saw [Jennifer Garner] in *13 Going on 30*, and there was such joy and happiness in her face, I think we really want to get some of that infused back into the show, and we want to have a good running start to be able to do that," said ABC President of Primetime Entertainment Stephen McPherson.

The Internet fans, however, weren't all convinced that kicking off the season in January was the way to go, and they planned on mailing Stephen McPherson to tell him about it. "Operation: Dead Drop" was formed in the hopes of convincing executives to bring *Alias* back for the fall. The plan was for individuals to take brown paper bags, decorate or write on them, then mail them to the ABC executives on June 7 as a sign of support for the show. The site, SupportALIAS.com, was created to publicize the details of the mission.

The actors are still amazed at the dedication of the fans and appreciate their support. "People are very vocal about *Alias*. They feel very strongly about the show," says Victor Garber. "The people who watch it are fans and I find that wherever I go, someone would say, 'It's my favorite show on TV,' 'I never miss it,' and 'It's the only show we watch.' I mean, I get that a lot, so I think that's always a good sign. You know . . . they don't throw things at me." Jennifer Garner confesses that she is grateful to have *Alias* in her life: "It's just so nice to be on a show that you are really proud of because as an actor, especially in the beginning, you sometimes have to play parts that you don't really like because you have to work and you have to further your career. I've done some things that I wasn't necessarily so proud of, so to be on *Alias* and to just watch how great the show is every week is amazing."

As for J.J. Abrams, he is still very dedicated to making sure that *Alias* is the best show it can possibly be. "The attempt this year was to try to reset the world, and then shatter it," he said of season 3. "I believe that when you look back at *Alias* as a series, you'll see many different iterations of the show. And I think the fun in it for me is, I hope it's never so you'll tune in and you'll know exactly what you're going to get. It always feels like this is a very fluid, unexpected place."

Rambaldi prophecies? Spy family trees that continue to grow? Mysterious nemeses? No one is arguing, Mr. Abrams.

The Cast of Alias

Jennifer Garner *(Alias: Sydney Bristow)*

Enigmatic, versatile, and lethal, the character of Sydney Bristow is a chameleon both externally and internally. So how is it that a good girl from West Virginia, known for her "vulnerable-girl roles," ended up playing an emotionally scarred double agent? Says Jennifer Garner: "Sydney had a loneliness and desperation about her, and this desire to be normal. I'm not lonely and I am normal, but you connect with some roles more than others, and this one clicked the moment I got [the pilot script]. As crazy as some of the things that happen to Sydney are, J.J. makes them believable to me." Jennifer was no stranger to playing at being a spy; she used to do so as a kid, her favorite book being *Harriet the Spy*. "I probably read it 10 times," she says. "I talked my mom into buying me a little notebook like Harriet the Spy had. And I'd write down these things about my neighbors. 'Marge is wearing polka dots today. She has a poodle. Both start with *P*. Think about that.' I so truly wanted to be a spy."

Jennifer Anne Garner, a.k.a. Sydney Bristow, was born in Houston, Texas, on April 17, 1972. When Jennifer was three, the family moved to Charleston, West Virginia, population 53,000. There Jennifer grew up in a middle-class neighborhood with her older sister, Melissa, and her younger sister, Susannah. "[We] all have big ol' mouths. We had long, plain straight hair and wore no makeup. I was always happy to look like a Garner girl," she says. Her mother, Pat, was an English teacher at the local college, while her father, Bill, worked as a chemical engineer.

Even as a toddler, Jennifer was already beginning to crave the stage: "I so badly wanted to play Juliet before I even knew what acting was. In kindergarten, I named my hermit crab Juliet." She began taking ballet lessons at age three and continued with them for many years. "The one constant in my life that I did purely for love was ballet. That was because I had a great teacher who challenged me and insisted on discipline, but it was the only outlet for performing. I didn't realize what it was about — that I was so hungry to perform that I just danced all the time." Garner claims that even though she wasn't very good she stuck with it, citing her ballet teacher, Nina Denton Pasinetti, among her mentors growing up. Pasinetti claims Jennifer was very serious as a student, even crying when she failed to pull off certain moves. "I took my training seriously, even though I was not naturally gifted in that way," Jennifer remembers. "Some people would say that all that training was a waste of time, but as I see it, no knowledge or experience is ever wasted." Along with ballet, the three girls took piano lessons as well. The Garner household was a conservative one, keeping the girls away from things such as television, makeup, and jewelry, and the girls were very active in extracurricular activities and attended church on Sundays.

Eager to please, Jennifer gained the nickname "Puppy," as she claims she was seen as "kind of a tail waggin' kid." Being the middle child wasn't always easy for Garner. Melissa was a valedictorian and a champion majorette, and extremely talented at piano and in math. Susannah had the beauty, according to Jennifer, with large blue eyes and an ideal body. "I think I started performing to differentiate myself from them," says Garner. Jennifer's knack for performing extended beyond ballet, however. Her mother recalls that in fifth grade, Jennifer was the last performer in her elementary school talent show and was reciting a folk tale: "These kids had been sitting on the floor for an hour and a half, and they were restless and mean. But when she stood up, the gym got completely quiet. I thought, *This is not normal.* Because I wouldn't have been able to stand up there and quiet those kids down. She wore a pair of green overalls I'd made her, and if they showed the least bit of restlessness, she would drop one shoulder strap." She would also put on "Jennifer and Cary Shows" with her friend Elizabeth Cary, which included skits as well as performances of Garner's stories, which often were created on the spur of the moment.

Garner was not only a dancer but also a member of the swim team, and she played the E-flat alto saxophone with the George Washington Patriots Marching Band and got involved with community theater and musicals (yes, she can sing too!). By seventh grade she was performing in community musical productions. The household was always busy, even more so when there were foreign exchange students staying with the family. In the summers, the Garner family bonding continued when they all piled into a 23-foot sailboat for two weeks. The three girls would rotate their outfits in order to save money, and Garner ended up finding ways to earn some extra money in order to buy herself some new clothes. With her best friend, Carrie, Garner used her spare time to babysit, shovel snow, take care of the neighbors' pets, and at one point, the two even sold homemade ice cream. She also worked part time at Kelly's Men's Store in Charleston.

As if she wasn't busy enough, Garner also buried herself in books: "Initially, I wanted to be a poet and I wanted to be a librarian. When I was a little girl, I loved children's books. I wanted to be a children's book author, like Beverly Cleary or Laura Ingalls Wilder. And then as I got older, I was into all kinds of different things. My sister was very academic, and sometimes I'd think, *Oh, I want to copy her: I'll be a doctor or something.*" Garner's sister Susannah presently works as an accountant in Virginia, while Melissa works in marketing.

Jennifer sported a different alias in high school, wearing thick glasses and baggy clothes. She even wore a hoopskirt to the prom, which was not a fond memory for her, seeing as everyone else was far more "Sydney Bristow" in their fashion choices. The Garner girls were not allowed to pierce their ears or wear nail polish. That aside, Jennifer did date a popular football player for a while. "I wasn't popular, but I wasn't tragic, either," she jokes. She soon discovered the world of musical theater and became involved with Charleston Light Opera Guild shows both onstage and backstage, where she performed, built sets, and made costumes. And while she never had dreams about being a television star, she certainly was a fan of one in particular: Donny Osmond. She has been known to bug J.J. Abrams about having him guest star on *Alias*.

When Jennifer graduated high school in 1990, she moved to Ohio to

Jennifer Garner played saxophone at her high school, as seen in this 1991 yearbook photo. "I wasn't popular, but I wasn't tragic, either."

attend Denison University and study chemistry. She was quick to switch her major to theater, however. While she was in a sorority, Garner did not fall into the party scene but kept her driving focus to become an actress. Her professor Jon Farris claimed that Garner was his best student: "Not the most talented, but nobody knew how to work the way she knew how to work. We noticed that from the first week she was on campus. . . . She had a real aptitude for learning the craft of acting." Jennifer herself admits that while she wasn't "naturally talented, [I was] just really, really driven." Farris became her mentor, helping her to lose her strong West Virginia accent as well as teaching her all he could about the world of classical theater. "You couldn't drag me away from the drama department," she says.

In between academic years, Garner got actively involved in summer stock theater anywhere from Connecticut to Michigan: "I was an apprentice and built sets and made the costumes and sold tickets for three different summers of summer stock. I would occasionally perform, but that was so not the priority to me. Just being involved was what mattered." Her plan was to go on and become a regional theater actress and perform at Shakespeare festivals. At one point, she approached a veteran actress for some advice. "She told me to forget acting and go get a paralegal degree," Jennifer remembers. Fortunately, Garner shelved the advice and instead listened to her mother after graduating in 1994. "She said to me, 'Jennifer, go to New York to become an actress because that's what you really want to do.' I told her that that's not what normal people do after college, but she insisted."

In 1994, armed with her theater degree, Garner made her way to the Big Apple to visit some friends and ended up staying. Her first job (for $150 a week) was as an understudy in the Roundabout Theatre production of *A Month in the Country* starring none other than *Alias* villain Ron Rifkin. For nine months she slept on a futon on a woman's kitchen floor, paying $400 a month. "I would roll up pennies to take the subway to work in Times Square. I was broke, but I was happy." Even so, there were problems with her living situation, and Garner had to relocate. "I moved out finally in the middle of the night because I got scared — I mean, she followed me to auditions. She thought people were stalking her and nobody was." Jennifer soon moved into her own apartment with a roommate, Corinna. "For a month we sat on the floor and ate off a box because it was all we had. It was incredibly simple, but it was ours and we loved it."

At 22 years of age, Garner scored her first television role in New York, playing Melissa Gilbert's daughter in the Danielle Steele miniseries *Zoya*. She followed that performance with roles in the movie *Harvest of Fire* and on the television miniseries *Dead Man's Walk* as well as on *Law & Order*, *Swift Justice*, and *Spin City*. The roles weren't pouring in, however, which was a great source of frustration for Garner, especially when she would get down to the wire only to lose the part. When she wasn't acting or auditioning, Jennifer worked as a hostess/waitress at Isabella's, an Upper East Side establishment. "Now I see people around, like Steve Martin and Katie Couric, and they think they know me. But I'm like, 'That's because I seated you at table five every Wednesday.'"

At that point, Jennifer got involved with an investment banker and decided to follow him out west. "All of a sudden I was here and, of course, the guy went away," she says of the breakup.

When he moved to San Francisco, Jennifer stayed in L.A. and landed a major role in the Hallmark television movie *Rose Hill* in 1997. In the film, Garner falls for a dangerous cowboy. Next, Garner landed her first feature role in the film *Washington Square*, which she followed with *Deconstructing Harry* and *Mr. Magoo*. Also in 1997, Jennifer could be seen in *In Harm's Way* and *The Player* (on television). The following year, Garner had a role in the independent film *1999*, which focused on a group of young New York friends dealing with their personal issues at the end of the millennium.

Then came Garner's first shot at a television series: *Significant Others*, created by Amy Lippman and Christopher Keyser, the partnership behind the hit series *Party of Five*. Co-starring Eion Bailey (*Band of Brothers*) and Scott Bairstow (*Tuck Everlasting*), Garner completed the trio, playing Nell Glennon. On the show Jennifer played a nice but neurotic young woman who is unsure of what to do with her life and is caught in a love triangle with the two men. She enjoyed working with her co-stars and was disappointed to see the series cancelled.

In 1998, after a stint on *Fantasy Island*, Jennifer auditioned for a show that would change her life: *Felicity*. "J.J. made me audition five times for that. For a guest spot," she says. Garner was cast as Hannah Bibb, the musician girlfriend of Noel (Scott Foley), and she almost didn't take the part. But she did, ending up with two episodes under her belt and winning Scott Foley's heart. "I remember the very first day going home and telling my roommate, 'That's the girl I'm gonna marry,'" said Foley. While Garner was initially confused as to whether Scott's flirting was real or a consequence of the show, his gift of a huge bouquet of flowers after she finished shooting made things clear. The courtship was slow even though their characters had been kissing right off the bat. After many lovely dates, flowers, and a trip to Paris on New Year's Eve, Garner was hooked. Foley even quit smoking for her. A year later, with their beagle-boxer Maggie May and Maltese puppy Charlie Rose (and later, cat Wesley), Jennifer and Scott bought a house together.

While she was being romanced by Scott, Jennifer continued to work, appearing in the series *The Pretender* as well as reprising her role as Hannah on *Felicity*. In 1999, it seemed as though she had another shot to be a regular in a television series, playing Romy Sullivan in the Lippman-Keyser spin-off *Time of Your Life* starring Jennifer Love-Hewitt. The

J.J. Abrams with his two leading ladies — Keri Russell and Jennifer Garner.

character began as Daisy, a tarot-card-reading roommate for Love-Hewitt, but transformed into aspiring actress Romy. Alas, the series did not last. "There were a few roles along the way that I thought might be the one, but nothing came of them. Eventually, I came to terms with my situation and put more emphasis on being happy with my personal life. That helped me get through the long bouts of unemployment," says Garner.

Staying on the small screen, Garner was cast as a struggling dancer in the television movie *Aftershock: Earthquake in New York*, then played Ashton Kutcher's girlfriend in the big-screen comedy *Dude, Where's My Car?* While she claims the comedy was hard work, she still enjoyed herself. She and actress Marla Sokoloff played twins in the film, even though there was a nine-year age difference between them. Filming in Hawaii for the 2001 epic *Pearl Harbor* came next. After auditioning on the same day as 40 other women, Garner landed the role of Nurse Sandra, the "third" female lead in the male-dominated production. "I played one of five navy nurses and no one, absolutely no one, recognized me. I had curly hair and wore glasses. I was frumpy. But we shot in Hawaii, and I've come to the

CHRISTINA RADISH

Scott Foley and Jennifer Garner — they seemed made for each other, but unfortunately, the marriage wouldn't last.

conclusion that every West Virginia girl should have a few weeks in Hawaii." As the more serious member of the group, Garner's character is the one who has the most difficulty when the attack occurs. None of the actresses had been involved with such a large-scale action film before, which led to some tense moments on set. Tension was quickly alleviated, however, with the help of Madonna's album *The Immaculate Collection*. "We'd all gather at the makeup trailer ... and put on our Hawaiian grass skirts and coconut bras and dance around and make each other laugh." Garner remembers. She was pleased that the uss *West Virginia* received a positive nod in the film as well.

In September 2000, while out watching the sunset on the porch of their home in the San Fernando Valley, Scott proposed to Jennifer. They were married on October 19 in an intimate ceremony in their backyard. Shooting on *Felicity* was rescheduled in order to allow some of the cast and crew members to attend, including J.J. Abrams. While those who worked on the show were thrilled, the fans were still upset at Garner and Foley's union. Jennifer took the brunt of their wrath: "I'm hated on the Internet; I'm hated on the streets. People constantly come up to me and say, 'I hate Hannah.' And I say, 'Well, I married him, so I don't know what else to tell you.' At first I took it personally. Then I was like, *Jennifer, get over yourself.*" By no means a Hollywood "party" couple, Foley and Garner were quite happy with spending quiet nights in enjoying wine, cooking, and playing gin, as well as gardening and going on hiking excursions with their dogs. They also had the opportunity to work together on the independent film *Rennie's Landing* (now *Stealing Time*). Of her role Jennifer said, "I'm barely in *Rennie's Landing*. I just wanted to be involved and wanted to work with Scott again."

And then, in 2001, Jennifer proved the validity of the phrase "the third time's a charm." After J.J. Abrams came up with the idea for *Alias* during a writers' meeting for *Felicity*, his first thought for the lead was Jennifer: "[Jennifer] was always someone who I adored and loved working with, and she [had] this incredible potential that hadn't really been challenged yet. My wife was encouraging me to do something with Jennifer, believing Jennifer was going to be a huge star. I wrote *Alias* with her in the back of my mind. Obviously I didn't want to promise anything. In fact, I wasn't a hundred percent certain myself, having not seen her do this kind of thing before, if she could do it." Abrams told Garner about the role and what would be required, and Garner got to work. While she had no plans to do another pilot, Abrams's involvement changed everything. The problem was, Garner, in her own words, "hit like a girl. Scott was very encouraging, but he told me, 'If they ask you to throw a punch, you're sunk,' and I knew he was right." Opening the Yellow Pages, Garner found Master Yu, a martial arts teacher, and began training. "I went every day for over a month before my audition. I found it so hard physically that I would literally be in tears by the end of a workout. I stuck with it because the results were speaking for themselves. I knew I had to be very physical to get the role of Sydney, but once I got into it, I found the intense training quite sexy; the control and the focus and the power from within that you have to tap into. I just really connected with it." As part of her research she read books on MI-6, the British equivalent of the CIA.

When the time came to audition, Garner was called back five times.

Finally, the producers asked her if she could kick, allowing her to show off her new skills. Having earned a yellow belt, Garner not only had the physical skills for the role, but nailed the character. "Every time we did a scene, she just knocked it out of the park," says Abrams. Even so, the industry insiders were concerned about casting an unknown actress in the lead role. At the time, Jennifer was offered a role in a play, making the situation more immediate. Abrams remembers how it all came together: "I realized that she couldn't do the show if she did the play. So I called up the ABC execs and said, 'She's going to do this play. It would be a disaster if she does this play, because she's by far the best one we've got.' And they said, 'Then cast her.' So we did." Only Garner hadn't had a full screen test and Abrams began to worry that perhaps she couldn't pull it off. "We just cast her because we had to — it was an emergency. From that point on, what Jennifer did was remarkable. She committed herself so wholeheartedly. It was clear to me when it was the fight scene — halfway through, she was kicking the stunt man's ass. He had huge pads and everything and they were all soaked in sweat. If you look at the pilot, there's a huge dent in the side of the car that was caused by this gentleman throwing himself repeatedly into the car in the fight scene with her. Jennifer just clearly was the one."

Jennifer also impressed her co-stars with her skill. "My feeling when I read the script was that whoever played [Sydney] was going to have a lot resting on their shoulders and I just wondered when they introduced me to Jennifer whether she would have the strength to take on something so big. But within five minutes of reading with her, I found out that she is a hell of a lot stronger than she appears," says Victor Garber. Michael Vartan agrees that Garner seemed too sweet to play Sydney: "I thought, *There's no way this girl is going to be Agent Bristow,* 'cause . . . the part really read as a girl that had a little bit of a backbone and [it wasn't] until we started shooting and I saw the dailies [that I realized] what a great actress she is. She's a chameleon, being able to be so sweet in real life but to have this edge." Jennifer was equally in awe of her co-stars, including Ron Rifkin, whom she had worked with before. While shooting the pilot, she really got a sense of just how professional Rifkin could be: "After Danny's been killed, I grab Ron by his lapels. Well, his eyes would fill up with tears in the middle of every take and I was so blown away by how incredible he was, even though the camera was on me. At the end of the last take, he said, 'Jennifer, I didn't want to disturb you, but you were pulling my chest hairs. Could you maybe just grab the shirt?'"

Once she got the role, Jennifer's workouts intensified. She switched to personal trainer Valerie Waters and began a routine of cardio, strength training, and martial arts. Her stunt double, Dana Hee, was an Olympic gold medallist in martial arts, and while she performed some stunts, Garner did her fair share. "I do 95 percent of my own stunts. I shoot every one, and Dana Hee . . . shoots them as well. I'm trying to learn to act with my body the same way she does," Garner said. Abrams explains that he believes Jennifer's desire to do the majority of her stunts allows her to connect further with her character: "If anything, she's sometimes too enthusiastic. I don't think there's anything she hasn't wanted to do or done. There was a big explosion thing we wouldn't let her do. I'm sure she's still depressed about that."

To accompany her exercise regime, Garner eliminated flour and sugar from her diet, and Foley gave up cooking with butter. Her new schedule meant very early mornings as well, and sometimes that was a challenge. "I insist on six hours every night," she said. "One day last year I was really late for work. I was supposed to get up at four-thirty but woke up at seven-thirty. People were calling and calling, but we didn't hear the phone. When I woke up, I was hysterical, so Scott drove me to the set. That got me so keyed up about being late that sometimes now I wake up too early. I'll be in the shower thinking, *God, I am so tired today.* Then I'll get out and the clock will say two-fifteen! Now when I wake up, I quiz myself: Is it really time to get up? Did the alarm really go off?"

Garner was reluctant to call *Alias* her breakout role simply because she didn't know how the show would be received, but it ended up becoming just that. Suddenly, the image of Jennifer in her red wig was on billboards everywhere. "That red wig was before we started getting really great wigs. It really didn't fit my head. It was like a tight vice on my brain, but it did look cool," she recalled. Her husband was her biggest fan, asking people on the street if they had seen the pilot episode of his wife's show. Back at home in Charleston, Garner says her father "was thrilled by it more than anything I've ever done." When her mother, Pat, was asked about her reaction to the "dental" scene in the pilot, she said, "Well, I hate to see her tortured, but we've seen her raped, we've seen her killed, we've seen her abort, so what's a tooth?" Even

Jen with her parents, Pat and Bill, at the 2003 Emmy Awards, where she was nominated for Outstanding Lead Actress in a Drama Series.

though she enjoys *Alias*, her favorite among her daughter's projects is still the Hallmark film *Rose Hill*.

Alias offered emotion as well as action. With the action came the bruises, however. "I wear those like a badge of honor," Garner claimed. "I got out of the shower this morning, and I said, 'Scott, you want to see my bruises?' He said, 'Jen, I hate when you show me your bruises,' and I said, 'But you're the only one who can see them all!'" Thankfully, whenever Jennifer is tired of action, she has other options. "The best part is everything that exists in this world, that one thing isn't better than the other. If I'm tired of doing action sequences, I can have a beautiful dramatic scene with Victor, or if I'm exhausted after too many emotional scenes, there'll be a fun scene with Merrin and Bradley."

Between running lines, working out extensively, and shooting six days a week for 12- to 15-hour days, it's a wonder that Garner had any time for herself. She got the chance to watch Martha Stewart at four in the morning while she worked out on her elliptical trainer. In her spare time, she attended photo shoots and fight rehearsals, and for a while she prepared her meals for the week. To top it off, she'd even have the cast over for homemade goodies to watch the show. *Alias* really had become her life, and she claimed when she saw friends, she had to think of things to talk about other than the show. The violent world of Sydney Bristow was also creeping into Jennifer's life. She described one incident in particular: "I'm starting to have all these violent dreams. The other night the alarm went off in our house — the dog somehow set it off — and my husband, Scott, and I were creeping down the hall to make sure no one was in the house. He had a baseball bat, and I was behind him, and I was thinking, *What can I do first? Elbow? Knee to the crotch? Backspin hook kick?* So it's definitely bleeding over."

Alias was picked up for its full first season, and Jennifer became number one on *Seventeen* magazine's Ones to Watch list. Suddenly, Jennifer was in the limelight, attending premieres and award shows. "It traumatizes me every time I have to get dressed up for anything," she lamented. "I'm happiest in my black suit. I wore it to every premiere, and finally someone said, 'Jennifer, go out and buy yourself something new.' So now I'm learning to love nice fabrics. I'm getting better." The girl who was not allowed to wear makeup and pierce her ears (she still does not have pierced ears, and special earrings have been designed for her to wear for the show) was not only required to dress up off-screen, but had to don some interesting numbers on-screen as well. "I get embarrassed wearing the sexy outfits. Sydney's clothes are more va-va-voom than I'm used to. But it's fun to have permission to wear that stuff."

Sydney Bristow speaks over 17 different languages, and while Garner knows a little Spanish, she uses phonetic translations from Language.net in order to sound fluent. She also started learning sign language, which has helped her to communicate silently with her assistant on the set. She has fun playing a parodied "Action Girl" in order to warm up for her heavy action scenes. And as a self-confessed klutz, she somehow even manages to perform her stunts in high heels: "I'll be holding a gun up and running downstairs in heels and all I'm thinking about is just counting down the stairs, trying to just make it out alive."

The show continued to surprise and entertain, and Jennifer continued to commit to it completely. "She's the reason the show's working. There's a kind of sadness underneath Jennifer's incredibly jovial exterior — more an awareness of sadness in the world. She *gets* that, and in that way she's very close to Sydney," said Victor Garber. Guest star Quentin Tarantino recognized Garner's talent for both action and drama: "When I met her, I said, 'Just so you know, you're gonna work forever. You don't have to prove nothin' to nobody no more.'"

She certainly didn't have to prove anything to the media. She was making all sorts of "best of" lists, including "best arms" in *People* magazine's Best Body Parts competition and *Entertainment Weekly's* "IT Tough Babe," beating out vampire slayer Sarah Michelle Gellar. And then came the best of all: winning a Golden Globe for Best Actress in a Leading Role — Drama Series (for 2001). For Jennifer the evening was a bit of a blur: "I was in a total daze when I won. I was kind of dreaming. It was such a fun night. I didn't prepare a speech in case I won and then all of a sudden, I was in the car on the way there and got really nervous. Scott said, 'Well, do you want to talk about it?' and I said, 'No.' When we got there, my knees knocked in my chair under the table." She accepted her award with grace and humor, saying, "Man, I know I was good in *Dude, Where's My Car?*, but seriously. . . ." She had also garnered a new sex-symbol status. In April 2002, she was number one on *Maxim* magazine's 100 Sexiest Women list, which brought her great amusement. "To me it's just a crack-up. I go to work and remind the crew, 'Don't forget, I am *Maxim*'s sexiest woman of the year,' and they all laugh." That same year, Jennifer and Victor Garber were nominated for Emmy awards. "The Emmy nomination validates this whole year, a year in which I have grown so much," she said. Unfortunately, neither of them won, but the acknowledgement of *Alias* was still a triumph.

Alias wasn't the only thing on Garner's plate, however. She flew back to her alma mater in Ohio to give a speech as part of Denison University's Provost Alumni Scholar Series. She also took some time out in Charleston to help a fellow high-school friend, Corey Palumbo, who was running as the state legislative candidate, and shot a 30-second television spot on his behalf. And then came the big-screen offers, the first being a cameo role as a high-class call girl in the film *Catch Me If You Can*. A fan of *Alias*, director Steven Spielberg was impressed with the way Jennifer took on different personas each week. "The first time I saw Jennifer, I immediately said she would be the next superstar. I knew she was locked into [*Alias*] but I wondered if she would do this small role. She came in and worked for just one day and was simply remarkable," he said. Jennifer didn't mind the idea of working with Leonardo DiCaprio, either: "We kissed a whole lot. It was only uncomfortable for the first couple of minutes. Then you're just going for it, slobbering all over each other. . . . I went through a couple of tins of breath mints. It was magical."

Jennifer then jumped into the tight suit of comic book character Elektra in *Daredevil*, starring Ben Affleck. Avi Arad, the executive producer, wanted Garner right from the start, accommodating her busy schedule in order to book an audition. "[S]he asked if she could leave her cell phone on during the audition because her sister was in labor. That impressed me; it showed a warmth that we needed for this character," Avi said. Like her previous co-stars, Affleck was also surprised at how nice Jennifer actually was: "Jennifer's great, she's fabulous. She's actually better at [the fighting] than I am. She has had so much training from the *Alias* thing and she's a dancer, so she shames me every day." Jennifer beat out a handful of actresses for the role and donned the character's outfit with pride. "I wish I had read *Elektra* when I was younger," she said. "I think she's strong and cool and beautiful and smart. She'd be a good role model — until she turns into an assassin for hire and a hooker. But that's down the road. [In the movie] she's still pretty dignified." Her stunt double, Shauna Duggins (who replaced Dana Hee on *Alias*), encouraged Garner to push forward and try the stunts herself: "The audience wants to see her do it. The audience *needs* to see her do it." The fight scenes were a challenge, especially when going up against actor Colin Farrell (Bullseye). "I've never seen anyone more determined to kill me in his whole life. Colin was so into our fight scene; it's a good thing he smokes as much as he does, otherwise I don't know if I'd be sitting here . . . right now," said Jennifer. She had no concerns that the role, along with her *Alias* persona, would typecast her as an action star. Nor did she wonder which character would win in a fight: Elektra, who would fight dirtier. "[Sydney] is an optimist," Garner says, "and refuses to see the bad side. Whereas Elektra lives on the bad side and is fighting so hard to find an alternative, but [she] really doesn't feel a whole lot of hope."

The film brought more females into the audience than had been anticipated, and the romantic story between Elektra and Daredevil took the credit for the feat. Jennifer won the MTV Movie Award for Best

Jennifer kisses her MTV Movie Award for Best Female Breakthrough Performance, for her role as Elektra in *Daredevil*.

Female Breakthrough Performance. She also appeared on *Mad TV*, *Saturday Night Live*, and played herself on an episode of *The Simpsons*. Working on her first major feature film was easier thanks to Affleck, who offered her advice and acted as a mentor. Unfortunately, however, rumors that the two were romantically involved only put more strain on her marriage, even though they were unfounded. Jennifer was once again extremely busy and Scott was involved with his new comedy *A.U.S.A.*, allowing them very little time together.

She presented at the 2003 Academy Awards alongside Mickey Mouse but brought her childhood girlfriend Katie as her guest. Then came the news that Foley and Garner were separating. Scott admitted to having difficulties seeing his wife kissing other men on-screen as well as that their schedules were not conducive to spending time together. Jennifer said, "I get up while [Scott's] still sleeping. I come home and [Scott's] gone to bed. That's not the ideal schedule for a newlywed." Her fame was overwhelming for Foley. While the couple did their best to keep their marriage together, in the end it did not last. The two divorced in May 2003, citing irreconcilable differences. "I think people understood that we were just two normal people who really loved each other. I think they got that we're both pretty brokenhearted about it," said Garner.

Jennifer kept herself busy with her first comedic lead role in the feature film *13 Going on 30*. "[I]t's a comedy where nobody gets hurt or is on a wire, and you don't work all night, like, ever." In the same vein as the hit comedy *Big*, Jennifer's character goes into the closet during a party game, and when she comes out she's five days away from her 30th birthday. Not only did Garner's price tag go up for the film, but she also had director approval. Her enthusiasm for the role is obvious: "I'm so excited. I'm really nervous. But it feels closer to me character-wise than anything I have really played so far." Was it a challenge for her to play a 13-year-old? "Everyone in the *Alias* cast is like, 'Oh, yeah, this is a no-brainer. She's thirteen all right. She may be twelve.'" While working on a romantic comedy was a welcome change for Garner, director Gary Winick had to keep reminding her to lose her Sydney Bristow habits. "I would walk like I was creeping down a hall," she says.

Back in full swing on season 3 of *Alias*, Jennifer continued to give her all, signing on for seven seasons and gaining a pay raise. She began dating close friend and co-star Michael Vartan as well. Not only that, but Chase Brandon, a film industry consultant for the CIA (who has helped with *Alias*), approached the actress about appearing in the agency's new promotional recruitment video for university graduates. "We feel that Miss Garner, both in character as agent Sydney Bristow and as herself, embodies the intelligence, enthusiasm, and dedication that we're looking for. Our continuing efforts to enlist the best and the brightest would be admirably served by having her support," was his statement. Garner was only too happy to back the project: "It makes me feel so American!" She also has a standing invitation to visit the CIA, where apparently she has many fans.

In September 2003, Jennifer attended the Emmy Awards with her parents as a birthday gift to her father. This time Lena Olin was added to the list of nominees, putting the full Bristow family on the nomination card. Once again, however, all three actors were passed over. Garner was also nominated for another Golden Globe, but this time she lost out to Edie Falco. Still, Jennifer's enthusiasm for the work was far from waning. It was business as usual on the *Alias* set for season 3, but with a few new characters and a two-year gap added to the mix. Her energy was high, though the grips hid chocolate bars on the set — just in case. "She walks in at five a.m.; her hair is wet, her skin is perfect, and she looks like a warm, fresh spring day," says Michael Vartan. At around 6 a.m., she and Vartan get on the move on the studio lot — on their bicycles. Garner sports a pink one with a West Virginia license plate. "We ride around the lot and ring our bells and say good morning to everyone," she says. The work continues to be a challenge, but Garner is up for it. "We throw the gamut at her every day, and it doesn't matter whether it's a small emotional moment with a friend or a hugely devastating moment in her relationship with her father or if she's parachuting into a party in the south of France in a blond wig and slinky dress. No matter what we throw at Jennifer, what we get back every time is total commitment," says Abrams.

Jennifer's reputation for being a "nice girl" hasn't disappeared. As part of her many charitable efforts, she ran in a fundraiser for the

Jennifer, looking radiant at the premiere of *Daredevil*.

CHRISTINA RADISH

Elizabeth Glaser Pediatric AIDS Foundation, stood alongside Victor Garber in his fight to raise money for Pediatric Diabetes, and many directors will tell stories of critically ill children coming to visit her on the set. At present, Nike has created the Garner Girl sneaker, with proceeds going to charity. She has a new Labrador puppy, Martha (after Martha Stewart), a gift from the crew of *13 Going on 30* that she spends her time training in between acting and getting an occasional few hours of sleep. She even apologizes to reporters for wanting to keep her private life to herself. "We've always had the most fun working together, and he's one of my best friends," is her only comment on new beau Vartan. There is presently speculation that the couple has broken up due to the pressure of being in the media spotlight, but nothing has been confirmed.

In 2004 Garner stepped in as Gwyneth Paltrow's replacement in the film *Happy Endings*, and an *Elektra* film is in the works. In the former, Jennifer is once more playing a very different character. "It will be the grittiest role I've ever played," she admits. "[My assistant] kept saying, 'You really don't want to do this. You're smoking! And you show your boobs!' And I said, 'What, because I'm a good girl and I play a good girl? Of course I'll do those things. I can be bad.'" As for reprising her role as Elektra Natchios, Garner is quite happy to play the lethal lady again seeing as she collected so many comic books as research for the first film.

Until then, she will continue to battle terrorists on television. At some point, she would like to return to the stage: "I am hoping very much to go back to live theater. It's definitely what I started out doing; it's what I meant to do. This is all a happy accident and, hopefully, I'll get to go back." She likes to bake as a stress reliever, and continues to watch Martha Stewart religiously. She even appeared on an episode of Martha's show, talking Thanksgiving turkey. She loves to indulge in cheese and crackers, loves her female friends, and admits that she has no sense of direction. Though she used to hate having her photo taken, she's grown accustomed to it now and was front and center as she hosted the 2004 Academy Awards for Science and Technology. *Alias*, however, has provided her with more than just fame. "I feel like an apprentice to all these actors that I look up to and believe in and want to be like. Because I work with Carl I listen better in a scene than I used to; with Victor I'm more still; with Ron I'm more easy with my body movements. That's the gift the show has given me," she claims.

Whenever she gets the chance she loves to return to Charleston, and would love to see an episode take place in West Virginia: "It's the most beautiful place in the world. It's such an isolated community where you're not affected by cities and trends. I felt very protected and loved by the entire community, and I still do. I still go home and I go to the men's shop where I worked and I go to my church where I grew up and my friend's parents are still like my parents. It's the most important thing in my life that I grew up there." She was even acknowledged by the state itself. "The state [of West Virginia] read a declaration basically saying, 'She's our girl and we're proud of her.' My family got all dressed up and went to the Senate for it, and then they sent it to me. It's up in my house," she says.

At the end of the day, Jennifer Garner still stands by the fact that she was never hunting for stardom. All she wanted was to be able to perform: "It's never bothered me to have a smaller or bigger role. It didn't in college, where I'd sometimes audition for smaller roles because they can be more fun. When I studied acting in college, I wasn't the most talented person there — but I was the hungriest. It's about working and continuing to work." As for how it has changed her as a person? "I'm a normal Garner girl. I may be famous to the rest of the world, but I'm not to myself, and I'm not to my mom and to my friends."

THE GOOD GUYS

Victor Garber *(Alias: Jack Donahue Bristow)*

Steely-eyed Victor Garber may be poker-faced "Spy Daddy" Jack Bristow on *Alias*, but in reality he's a comedian at heart. "I think we should see a side to Jack where he secretly goes to a piano bar and sings show tunes on the weekend. Don't you think? Wouldn't that be good?" he asks. Born in London, Ontario, Canada, on March 16, 1949, Victor Joseph Garber's sole aspiration in life was to become an actor. Victor, his brother, and his sister all had a taste of the entertainment industry growing up: their mother was the host of her own television show for women, *At Home with Hope Garber*. She played a large part in his love for theater, driving him to the renowned Stratford Theatre Festival and making the two-and-a-half-hour trip to Toronto to catch shows at the O'Keefe Centre. One of those shows was the musical *West Side Story*; seeing it was a "seminal experience" for young Victor.

As a child he listened to as many Broadway musicals as possible. At age 10, he began performing in children's theater shows at the Grand Theatre in London, one of the productions being *The King and I*. He calls his experience working on a production of *Tom Sawyer* (which also included Canadian actress Kate Nelligan) as a turning point in his career. His ambition was so great that at 12 years of age he ventured to Stratford, Ontario, to audition for the part of Oedipus in the Stratford Festival's production of *Oedipus Rex*. While he was too young for the part, it didn't stop him from trying!

Another significant event occurred in Victor's life at the age of 12: he was diagnosed with juvenile diabetes. It was a crushing blow. "When I was a kid, there was no hope," he says. "You were told: this is your life. This is what you're going to be doing for the rest of your life. And that was kind of a hard thing to hear at twelve." Using his present *Alias* fame, Victor has become the spokesperson for the Juvenile Diabetes Research Foundation of Canada. He takes pride in knowing that Canadian researchers are at the forefront in the search for a cure for the disease. Victor asked co-star Jennifer Garner to film the spots with him: "Jennifer is a close friend and very supportive of me and the cause, having watched me struggle to manage the disease while dealing with the demands of a busy shooting schedule."

At 15, Victor enrolled in a summer acting workshop taking place at the University of Toronto's Hart House Theatre. It was the following year when he decided to quit attending London Central Secondary School. "[My parents] were nervous, but I left home when I was sixteen; I went off to be a singer." He continued with the Hart House acting troupe until 1967, when he joined up with Peter Mann, Laurie Hood, and Lee Harris to form a teen quartet called The Sugar Shoppe. Their

Victor Garber originally had aspirations of being a singer, before theater changed his life.

first song was the 1967 Centennial song "Canada" by Bobby Gimby. The band was a hit in Canada, and the group signed with Capitol Records in the U.S. The Sugar Shoppe went on to appear on both *The Tonight Show* and *The Ed Sullivan Show*. In the end, The Sugar Shoppe disbanded and Victor hooked up with another group.

While he was in Los Angeles performing, he saw a production of the hippie musical *Godspell*. "I sat there thinking, *I can do that.*" Once Victor returned to Toronto, he had the chance. Auditions were being held for *Godspell*, and after singing one of the show numbers for the audition, he was cast in the role of Jesus Christ. Also in the company were young actors Gilda Radner, Andrea Martin, Eugene Levy, Dave Thomas, and Martin Short, all of whom later made reputations for themselves as comedians. The musical director was Paul Shaffer of *Late Night with David Letterman* (now *Late Show with David Letterman*) fame. The show was performed in 1972 at the Royal Alexandra Theatre in Toronto. "That's when my life changed," Victor notes.

Director David Greene attended the opening of the Toronto production, not yet having cast the lead for his film version of *Godspell*. He took to the young actor immediately, finding his Jesus in Victor Garber. "I read in the paper: 'Yes, I think we've found a Jesus.' And it was *me*! It's absolutely true. I don't think I even had an agent," Garber recalls. Victor was about to make another move, this time to New York City. "My mother couldn't have been happier when I said I was moving to New York. My father wasn't so happy. He was a little more nervous." Victor found New York intimidating: "[T]he city really scared me. The density was daunting. I stayed at the Edison Hotel on Forty-Seventh Street and was afraid to leave my room. But then, after growing up listening to Broadway show albums, I saw *Hair* and said, '*This* is what I want to do.'"

Unfortunately, the film version of *Godspell* was overshadowed by Andrew Lloyd Webber's biblical musical *Jesus Christ Superstar* and didn't propel Victor into stardom in Hollywood. He didn't leave *Godspell* behind completely, however. Victor understudied the role of Jesus in the Broadway company of the musical, and on occasion he actually got to perform. Victor was still garnering roles, even though he had no formal training: "I became an actor by copying people. That's probably a blasphemous thing to say, but that's how I started. Fortunately, I had the ability to copy good actors. I saw what made something work onstage. If you're working with good actors, it's a lot easier to be good." His official Broadway debut was in Henrik Ibsen's *Ghosts* at the Roundabout Theater, and his performance won him a Theater World Award. He continued working onstage, learning as he went along. During a production of Molière's comedy *Tartuffe* in 1977, Victor only had one scene, but it was opposite actress Swoosie Kurtz. "In our big scene she'd say, 'No, don't move on that line.' I asked why. 'Because it's going to get a laugh.' I asked, 'How do you know?' She said, 'Trust me.' Swoosie taught me. I had no idea that it was a funny scene. At the first preview, I said my line and the audience fell over. That started my laugh addiction," Garber claims.

John Wood, the actor playing Tartuffe, was the lead in the new play *Deathtrap* by Ira Levin and wanted Garber to read for the part of Clifford Anderson. Not only did Victor land the part, but he received his first Tony nomination for his performance. He also learned an important lesson in attitude: "I'll never forget what Marian Seldes said one day when she came in for a Wednesday matinee of *Deathtrap*. I was dragging myself around, and Marian sort of sashayed into the theater, in mauve, smelling wonderful as she always did, and she said to me, 'Oh, my darling, we get to do it twice today.' And she did the role for five years. I thought to myself that day, *What does it take to shift my attitude to hers?*"

In 1985 Victor made his first foray into the land of prime-time television, starring in the short-lived CBC series *I Had Three Wives*. In the show Garber played an L.A. detective whose three wives helped him to solve his cases. The show did not last, which was no big surprise to Garber. Victor never strayed far from the stage, however. He took on a challenge with the autobiographical play *Wenceslas Square*, in which he found himself playing a variety of Czechoslovakian citizens. His experience with the play was not only one of his favorites, but he received both an Obie and Helen Hayes Award for his performance. He would also work with director Jerry Zaks in *Lend Me a Tenor*. That performance garnered him a second Tony nomination for his portrayal of the character Max, which was his last "younger" role.

While he was working on *Wenceslas Square*, another interesting opportunity arose: a chance to play the flamboyant pianist Liberace in a network television movie. "I had never played a leading role in a TV movie, and it was a director I had done *Godspell* with. Also, a lot of well-known actors had turned it down, and so I thought, *This is an impossible thing to do, so I'll try it*," Garber recalls. His longtime pal, actress Eileen Atkins, has a different memory of his decision: "Victor rang me and said, 'You won't believe how outrageous this is. They've asked me to play Liberace. As if I'm going to play that.' And I didn't say anything, but my head thought, *Actually, you'd make a rather good Liberace*. Later, Victor called me up and said, 'You're going to be so ashamed of me. I'm going to play Liberace because Ian McKellan said I wouldn't play it because I was being cowardly.'" So sure enough, Victor took on the role in *Liberace: Behind the Music*, finding inspiration in the elaborate sequined costumes.

Following *Liberace*, Garber had the opportunity to take on the role of another famous character: Ernest Hemingway in the Italian production of *The Legendary Life of Ernest Hemingway* for European TV. Victor claims that the director, José Sanchez, cast him in the role because his eyes were similar to the famous writer's. Victor portrayed Ernest from age 19 to 61. He also performed in such shows as *You Never Can Tell*, *Little Me* (for which he received another Tony nomination), *Arcadia*, *They're Playing Our Song*, *Noises Off*, and *The Devil's Disciple*. The latter, along with many of the plays Victor has been in, was performed in New York's famous Circle in the Square Theatre — namely, theater in the round. The challenge, of course, is trying to gauge the reaction of the people behind you. One of his favorite parts about the theater is that the atmosphere is so intimate — and yet that feature is not always a benefit. At one performance Garber remembers that ". . . there were these young girls sitting in the front row talking and pointing. And I wanted to stop the show and go over and say, 'Excuse me, do you know what this is doing to our performance?' But you just don't do that. So it's a real test of your concentration."

In 1990 Victor moved on to another stage musical, this time premiering the role of Anthony Hope in Stephen Sondheim's bloody musical *Sweeney Todd*, about a murderous barber. While Victor had not worked with Sondheim before, he was very familiar with Stephen's work. While touring with The Sugar Shoppe, Garber discovered Sondheim's musical *Anyone Can Whistle* and would sing along with his fellow bandmates. In fact, he credits his love of Sondheim for his wanting to be an actor. Working on *Sweeney Todd* was the start of a long-term relationship with Stephen Sondheim's work. Garber was involved with the Sondheim musical *Merrily We Roll Along* and originated the role of John Wilkes Booth in *Assassins*. *Assassins* didn't do terribly well, unfortunately. Neither did Garber's other show *Two Shakespearean Actors*, which had a limited run. In the wake of these two situations, Victor found himself questioning his career direction on the New York stage. His most recent Sondheim experience was in 1999, in the new musical *Wise Guys* with Nathan Lane. The two actors cleared their schedules only to find themselves out of work much sooner than expected. It was a disappointing experience for Garber. Even so, Victor's opinion of Sondheim has never wavered: "[W]hen you're in the room with Steve Sondheim and you hear for the first time a new song, and you just sort of dissolve in a puddle on the floor because it's so unbelievably great — that's one of the rare gifts that I've had in my life."

The opportunity to perform in the 1994 production of *Damn Yankees* was a thrill for Garber. Before he could hit the stage for the revival, however, Victor had to return home to Toronto for his father's funeral. "Even towards the end, when he had Alzheimer's, he would still crack jokes," Victor remembers. "And he could recall performing in a sketch, back when he was sixteen or seventeen. When the audience laughed, he realized that he was making them laugh. He said that it was the only time in his life that he really felt strong and fulfilled. I said to him, 'You have given me that.' It was so great to be able to tell him, and I could see that he heard me." Garber's "devilish" performance in 1994 brought him a fourth Tony nomination, but once again he was passed over. "I get nominated all the time, but I never win anything. I'm like [the] Susan Lucci [of the Tony awards]," he quipped.

Paul Schrader's 1992 thriller *Light Sleeper* was Victor's foray back into the Hollywood world of film. Following that came small roles in *Sleepless in Seattle* and *Exotica* and the opportunity to play Goldie Hawn's wealthy, sleazy ex-husband in *The First Wives Club*. He also guest starred on television shows such as *E.N.G.*, *The Outer Limits*, and *Frasier* (for which he received an Emmy nomination for his portrayal of Ferguson, the English butler) and performed in both American and Canadian television movies, including Alex Haley's *Queen*, *Dieppe* (for which he received a Gemini nomination), and Rogers and Hammerstein's *Cinderella*. It was the 1997 screen epic *Titanic*, however, that really brought Victor Garber to the forefront. Playing the doomed master shipbuilder Thomas Andrews, Victor brought a sensitivity to the supporting role that caught the attention of the audience.

After auditioning via videotape, Victor was working in a production of *Macbeth* in San Diego when he received the good news that he'd gotten the part. He met fellow Canadian and director James Cameron for the first time on set. Cameron's re-creation of the ship and its time touched the actor even though he was not required to get physical on the set of *Titanic*; in fact, he didn't even have to get wet. Cameron's amazing attention to detail, however, had its desired effect. Garber felt as though he had been transported into the past while working on the massive set: "I had a sudden ghostly feeling that this was exactly what it had been like. It was eerie." The shoot was five and a half months long for Victor, and not an easy one at that. "After three months I was going nuts," he says. "Each morning I'd look at the call sheets and actually cry. Not because they listed that day's potential hazards, like 'Beware of Drowning or Flying Objects,' but because my scenes would be tacked on at four p.m. — which I knew they'd never get to. Another day with nothing to do except read." At that point Garber would ring up David Warner and his other friends on set to play Scrabble and pass the time together. There were also rumors going around that *Titanic* would flop! It ended up becoming the top-grossing film of all time, which was overwhelming for Garber, who now had to deal with the unexpected fame: "It really was great to do something like [*Titanic*] and get noticed. But it's also strange. People look at me on the street. I mean, I'm glad I didn't end up on the cutting-room floor. Well, actually, I knew they couldn't cut me, since I'm the guy who says, 'The ship's sinking.'"

In the end, the experience put Garber on the map in Hollywood. Suddenly he was being offered better roles, including the chance to play Daddy Warbucks in the ABC Wonderful World of Disney version of the musical *Annie*. He returned to his Canadian roots to film a four-part television series called *Criminal Instincts* before taking a more biographical turn playing Sid Luft in the television movie *Life with Judy Garland: Me and My Shadows*. His performance earned him an Outstanding Supporting Actor in a Miniseries Emmy nod. Even though the role was more serious, Victor's comedic side surfaced. "He has a very funny sense of humor, which a lot of people don't realize," said producer John Ryan. Victor shifted from harassed husband to committing harassment in his next role as the sleazy lawyer in *Legally Blonde*. "I've played guys like this before," Victor said when the film was released. "They're arrogant wimps but they're more fun to play than the heroic good guys because they have these cracks in their makeup." Victor also had the opportunity to return to the stage, performing in the 1998 New York premiere of Yasmina Reza's hit play ART with Alan Alda and Alfred Molina.

It was Garber's theater skills that first caught J.J. Abrams's eye. He had seen the actor perform 20 years earlier in the farcical *Noises Off*. "I've been aware of his work onstage for years. What I love about Victor is he's done such incredible, varied material, and he's got a real facility for adapting to different genres — perfect for a show about a spy," said Abrams. J.J. approached Victor about auditioning for the role, which he did via closed-circuit television from New York. His abilities shone through the screen, landing Garber the role of double agent Sydney Bristow's father, Jack Bristow. J.J. Abrams had made his own impression on Garber when the actor read the pilot: "When I first read the script a few years ago I thought it was one of the best-written scripts I had ever read. The first thing I read was of my character on the phone talking to Sydney's fiancé. Though short, it was so beautifully written, and it made me laugh. I thought if I wanted to play a character, this would be it."

Even though Garber's first experience as a regular on a television series wasn't terribly positive, he had high hopes for *Alias*. "I knew I'd be OK if the show was on for five or six years because the writing was so good and the creative team was so strong," he says. "And then it just turned out to be that I was in love with everybody on the show. So it's turned out to be a miracle." Another thing that appeals to Victor about *Alias* is that the show requires audiences to pay attention to the details, making the series "intelligent" entertainment. It also helps that even though it's a spy show, the undercurrent involves complex relationships, which in Garber's case includes familial ties.

Jack Bristow is a man who leaves us wondering . . . is he good or is he bad? The reality is, there is no black-and-white answer. "The most sinister aspect of Jack is his detachment, his ability to distance himself from his feelings," says Garber. Yet he comes to the defense of his character when people call Jack Bristow a bad parent. He feels that everything Jack does is to protect his daughter, even if his methods aren't always the most admirable.

Also joining the cast was theater veteran Ron Rifkin, who lost out on the role of Jack Bristow when Garber took the part. As for what attracted Ron to the project, he says, "Actually, the thing that attracted me was Victor Garber." Victor's response? "Well. You know, that goes without saying." Friendly comic banter is apparently indicative of the *Alias* cast. It seems they just can't stop laughing. "Jennifer particularly is like a clown," claims Garber. "One day, we were doing a serious scene and fast-talking like we do and we could not stop laughing and the director had to stop the production. We had to go to our trailer and calm down and do it all again." Continual jokes about a "musical" episode of *Alias* keep them laughing, but knowing the unpredictability of the show, nothing would surprise Garber: "J.J. Abrams says his dream is to have Jack and Sydney stuck in a cabaret and the only way they can get out is by singing a song. Jennifer is a fantastic singer and David Anders, who plays Sark, well, he has a beautiful voice. So we could work on it."

Despite being the "older" actors on set, Garber and Rifkin had to keep up the same pace as the others . . . to start. "At first we were up at four-thirty every morning to train with the rest of them for the fight and action scenes and then we thought *No — we are too old to be getting up this early,* so we stopped doing it and obviously nobody had the heart to make us come back. Being older than the rest of them has to have some rewards," jokes Garber.

From the second season on, Jack Bristow left the office to get more physically involved with the missions. It was a new experience for Garber. "[They] joke about me in the writers' room by saying I don't want to do missions," he says. "Doing those fights and dealing with the physical aspects of it, particularly after you've been working fifteen hours, it can be really damaging, daunting. I'm a senior member of the company, so I look for the chair in the scene. I say to [director] Ken Olin, 'I think Jack should be sitting in this scene.'"

In 2002 Victor had the opportunity to work on the drama *Home Room* co-starring Erika Christensen, which looked at the aftermath of a shooting in a high school. That year Victor received another Outstanding Supporting Actor in a Drama Series Emmy nomination for his role as Jack Bristow after the second season of *Alias* (losing out to Joe Pantoliano in *The Sopranos*). Lena Olin and Jennifer Garner were also nominated. Victor won both a Golden Satellite Award and a Saturn Award for Best Supporting Actor in a Television Series. *Entertainment Weekly* named Victor Garber and Lena Olin the "Best Bad Parents" in 2002. With his steely gaze and his confident ability to spew out spy terms without hesitation, it's no wonder that Jack Bristow is a favorite. In fact, he has received great acclaim for his performance in all three seasons.

He has also had the opportunity to explore other roles, including Robert Foster in the Disney film *Tuck Everlasting* as well as Mayor Shinn in the television adaptation of the musical *The Music Man* starring Matthew Broderick. The latter allowed Garber to exercise his vocal chords once more. "I had so much fun doing *Music Man*; I had the best time. I'm ensconced in the spy world and on weekends I'm singing. . . . It's kind of schizophrenic and great. I feel very fortunate," he said of the experience. *The Music Man* had 13 million viewers the night it aired. Victor was also most recently cast in the lead part of Tevye in a television adaptation of *Fiddler on the Roof*. After convincing the original writers that he was the man for the part, the production was cancelled due to the 2003 war in Iraq, which made shooting in Prague too much of a risk. It was a great disappointment to Garber, who compared the appeal of the role with playing King Lear.

Victor Garber's fan base continues to grow, and as he does not own a computer (claiming they confuse him), he has not seen the many Web sites dedicated to both his character and himself. Victor's self-professed "hobby" is watching theater and spending time with friends over dinner. He has taught acting at HB Studios, and his two personal dreams are to move to Sag Harbor, U.S., and act in an English period film. He continues to live in New York and rents a home in Los Angeles while filming *Alias*. Even though he is enjoying the television process, theater remains his first love. "The stage is where I feel most comfortable, and I miss it all the time," he admits. "And when I go to see plays, I marvel at how people can do that. I've done it all my life, but I still find it mystical." He has no desire to take up the directing reins, however, preferring to remain an actor: "The greatest compliment I can receive as an actor is when people say to me, 'You just get better.' What else is there? But that's what I'm trying to do with my life: just get better. It's why I feel it's impossible to separate what you do from who you are."

As for what he'd like to see happen to Jack? "I honestly don't know. I just want to become an action figure."

Michael Vartan (Alias: Michael C. Vaughn)

As Agent Michael C. Vaughn, Michael Vartan has captured both criminals and the heart of Sydney Bristow. "Michael is so intense, very focused and contained. He can do these quiet, longing looks like no one else on the planet," says co-star Jennifer Garner. The audience has certainly come to appreciate Vaughn's longing looks as well, and yet, he did not grow up with the intention of being an actor. "I never thought about acting at all. In France, I lived in this little village, with cows and chickens on a farm. Showbiz to me was watching *Starsky and Hutch* reruns on French TV."

Michael Vartan was born on November 27, 1968, in Boulogne-Billancourt, Hauts-de-Seine, Île-de-France, to his American mother, Doris, and his Bulgarian-born father, Eddie. While Doris is an artist, Eddie is a musician. Michael's aunt is pop singer Sylvie Vartan; his uncle is Johnny Hallyday, France's answer to Elvis; and his cousin, David, followed in his parents' footsteps. Young Michael had no singing aspirations, however. Michael's family was soon split apart: "My parents got married, had me, and then got divorced practically the next day." Vartan stayed with his mother in California from age 5 to 11, then moved back to the small town of Fleury in France to be with his father.

Back in France, Michael spent lots of time with his cousin, David, where they were already starting to show signs of their future careers. "[W]e already were performing for our parents, who had to pay us ten francs [a little over a buck] to see us," Michael remembers. "And Julie, our friend, was dancing and singing. We were placing chairs and dividing the living room in two with a curtain. A small show in a way. We were also reviving some scenes of Louis de Funes in *La Folie des Grandeurs* or *La Grande Vadrouille*. Crazy!"

Michael and his cousin also shared a passion for motorbikes: "My cousin David was the one to get a bike first because he was older! But I caught up when my dad offered me a bike of the Italjet brand. It was extremely powerful and was making so much noise that neighbors from three miles away were complaining since it was so unbearable."

Living in a small town of 300 people was not a problem for Michael, who enjoyed the safety of it: "The most dangerous thing that could happen is that you might get stampeded by a herd of dairy cows." He spent much of his time playing soccer, and called his high school experience in Pontoise "gray and depressing." Very different from the American version, there were no organized sports for Vartan to participate in. Michael was not interested in finishing secondary school and did not have any aspirations to become a farmer. So at age 17, he gave his mother a call: "I thought, my mom's in California, what the hell am I doing here at seventeen? I conned my way to L.A., telling my mom I was coming here to go to art school." When he was 18, Vartan moved in with his mother and her new husband, writer Ian La Frenais.

Vartan was now stuck in California, whether he liked it or not, due to missing his recruitment date for the mandatory French military service. "I felt terrible, but there was no way I was going to go back and be arrested by the military police," he says. A shy, introverted teen, Michael called himself "the weird dysfunctional duckling of the family." Doris offered to pay for Michael to attend acting classes, believing them

Michael Vartan was born and raised in France before he moved to California at the age of 17.

to be an opportunity for her son to meet other people his age. Thinking it would be a way to meet girls, he agreed: "I never had a burning desire to be an actor, but I was curious to see what it was all about. I remember the first scene I had to do in acting class was Al Pacino from *Scarface*. I'm a nineteen-year-old kid from France, and I'm playing a Cuban drug dealer; it was pretty strange." The American dating scene was a different experience for Vartan as well. "In the village where I grew up, you'd go to a dance, kiss a girl, and that was it — she was your girlfriend," he says. "So when I started making out with a girl in a club in L.A., I thought, 'Here's my new girlfriend.' She had told me where she lived, and the next morning I showed up at her door with coffee and muffins. She was like, 'Dude, it's nine a.m. Go home.'"

In 1988 Vartan first appeared in a television documentary called *The History of the Black Leather Jacket*. A family friend had approached him about taking part in it: "I turned down the part, but then I learned they would pay me six hundred dollars a day — and I was theirs. I had no lines; I played a kid who was weak and scrawny and saved up to get a black leather jacket to change his self-image." After that project, Vartan was cast in a couple of French films: *Un homme et deux femmes* [Man and Two Women] and *Promenades d'été* [Summer Strolls]. In the latter, Michael was required to walk into a room and set down a toolbox, but Vartan's nervousness took over. "After about thirty takes, the director, who was French, said, 'Here, kid — maybe this will loosen you up a bit,' and he gave me a glass of champagne." Even so, Michael had made the decision to pursue acting seriously.

In his early 20s, Michael started his love affair with hockey, which continues to this day. He also had the opportunity to become a hockey player on-screen as well, for an episode of his step-father's television show *Spender*. "I've always ribbed him, 'When are you going to write something for a French-American hockey player with a tattoo on his left arm?'" Vartan says. "So he finally did, and I thought, *Fuck me; if I don't get this part I'm really crap!*" It was the role of French officer Jean/Massimo in the Traviani brothers' 1993 Italian epic *Fiorile* [Wild Flower] that brought Michael Vartan to the attention of the critics. "He's so hugely effective and so impossibly handsome it's hard to understand how he [has] avoided discovery by Hollywood," said critic Michael Medved at the time. Vartan's performance earned him a nomination for the French Caesar Award for Best Up-and-Coming Actor.

Things went quiet for awhile, with the exception of Vartan's small part in *To Wong Foo, Thanks for Everything, Julie Newmar*. Michael found himself killing time in the pool halls of Los Angeles: "My acting career was essentially going nowhere because I always seemed to be off playing pool when the auditions came up." Michael began to make some good money as his skills improved. "If you're good you can make a penny and if you suck, then you shouldn't be playing for money. It doesn't work like they've shown it in movies. . . . But you definitely meet some interesting characters. But . . . it became like a drug to me, so I had to step away from the pool halls," he says. Michael considered becoming a professional player for a time but changed his mind when he realized that his tutor, who ranked eighth in the world, didn't even have his own car. "It finally dawned on me there is no real future in being a professional pool player."

Even though he was struggling, Vartan did not want to use his family's fame to get work. Michael finally got back on track with the 1996 film *The Pallbearer*, starring Gwyneth Paltrow and David Schwimmer and produced by J.J. Abrams. It was Vartan's first major American film. He followed it with a lead in the romantic drama *Touch Me* and a major role in the critically acclaimed *The Myth of Fingerprints*. The latter was a great experience for Michael, and the film premiered at the Sundance festival in 1997. In November of that year he had a guest stint on *Friends* as Tom Selleck's optometrist son, Dr. Tim Burke. Next, Vartan appeared in the thriller *The Curve* as a college student whose desperation to attend Harvard has murderous consequences. "We were always goofing around on the set," he recalls. "So after each take the director would say, 'OK, Michael, now why don't you try giving me something I can use?'" At this point Vartan was engaged to actress Shannon Gleason, whom he had been with for ten years.

Then came the romantic Drew Barrymore film *Never Been Kissed*, Vartan's first starring role in a studio film. As the sensitive English literature teacher Sam Coulson, Vartan became a heartthrob overnight.

"Before I did *Never Been Kissed*, I got average attention from girls," he claims. "As soon as it came out, women were like, 'Oh my god!' It's not me, I assure you." Michael did not actually expect to get cast in the role ("I never really saw myself as an English literature teacher, since I don't understand what Shakespeare is saying — and now I'm teaching it?"); furthermore, he didn't enjoy the character simply because in his mind, "people like that don't exist." Working with Drew Barrymore, however, was a great treat for Vartan — as was kissing her. The film was released in 1999, the same year that Michael broke up with his fiancée.

His next projects were the independent romantic comedy *It Had to Be You* and an ABC comedy series entitled *The Guide*. About the show he had said, "I'm not at liberty to talk about the plot. I've got a shackle around my ankle that monitors every word I say. But I am the star, so ABC's really in trouble!" While the series didn't fly, Michael kept working, this time appearing in the Madonna feature *The Next Best Thing*, but not as "Mr. Nice Guy." How did it feel working with Madonna? "[I]t does hit you that this person is the most famous woman on earth, and I'm going to be kissing her. That was kind of scary."

Vartan played the lead in the film *Sand*, then jumped back to the small screen, taking on the famous character of Lancelot in the mini-series *The Mists of Avalon*. "There's a lot less focus on Arthur and Lancelot and fighting and the wars, and a lot more focus on the relationships of the people who lived in the fairy tale. And how screwed up all those people were, with everyone having sex with everyone else, brother having sex with sister . . . it was insane!" he said. His guest stint on *Friends* got him some recognition in the television business, which helped him land a two-episode role on *Ally McBeal* as the younger half of a father-son team both dating Ally at the same time. A few short months later, Vartan was auditioning for the role of Agent Michael C. Vaughn on *Alias*.

J.J. Abrams was familiar with Michael's work, having seen him in *The Pallbearer*. "They didn't really know what was going to happen with the character, as he was in the last scene of the pilot briefly," Vartan recalls. "But I read for J.J. [Abrams]. . . . Then they tested me on the usual rigmarole for the studio and the network, and I got the job." It was a huge coup for Michael, who didn't expect to get the part. "My friends and I always used to run around pretending to be undercover agents. Now I get to do all the things that guys fantasize about when they are boys: be a spy, go to faraway places with a pretty girl, save the day, use cool devices — and I'm getting paid for it! The best thing is, that unlike a real secret agent, I can't get hurt, which suits me even better." While Vartan was originally skeptical about joining a television series, he felt reassured by Kiefer Sutherland's words after working on the series *24*. "He realized that it was sometimes even more challenging than movies, and ultimately he's right," claims Michael. Abrams was happy to have Vartan join the cast: "[Michael Vartan] brings to *Alias* a warmth and sophistication that is so rare to find in someone who also happens to look like a movie star."

The character of CIA Agent Vaughn has a few things in common with Michael Vartan aside from the same first name (Vartan would have preferred something more exotic, like "Darius"). Both men's mothers share the same maiden name and the same birthday, and both were born in the same village in France. Michael relates to his character on a personal level as well: "[Vaughn's] a pretty simple character. What you see is what you get. He tries to do the right thing. He's a pretty decent fellow and there's no sort of strange things that are lurking in his psyche that might make him snap. And that's kind of how I see myself as well." Unlike Vaughn, however, Vartan is a bit of a clown — like many of his castmates — and can be found both cracking jokes and mimicking his mother, Doris.

While Vaughn spent more time in the office at the start of the series, he soon became active in the field, something that Vartan appreciated. While he films most of his stunts, there are certain things that Michael avoids: "I'm terrified of flying around in a helicopter, so if a scene calls for me to be hanging out of a helicopter at six thousand feet, I'd call for Tommy, my stunt double. He's funny, because a lot of the things they ask me to do really aren't that hard, [so] I end up doing them. He's like, 'Are you going to give me some work? Come on — I drove all the way from Bakersfield.'"

In addition to *Alias*, Michael can be seen in the creepy drama *One Hour Photo* starring Robin Williams. In the film, Vartan plays a cheating husband, and at one point is forced to pose naked with his mistress. It was the perversity of the scene that was more disconcerting to Vartan than the nudity, even with Robin Williams cracking jokes on set. Michael also keeps himself busy playing hockey two to three times a week. He's even started wearing a mask in order to avoid any unnecessary cuts or bruises that would have to be written into *Alias*. In conjunction with hockey, Michael plays tennis and golf, likes to bowl, and is a major New York Mets baseball fan. He admits that he would give up his acting career if it meant he could be a professional athlete.

A Renaissance man, Vartan also plays guitar and is an artist/painter. He's also addicted to eBay, and scours the site for sports memorabilia. He was caught by surprise, however, when his mother called to tell him that a clock sporting his image was being auctioned off. "I can't imagine what someone like Tom Cruise must have on eBay, so I think I'm getting off easy with just a clock," he jokes. With a diverse taste in music, this left-handed actor hates reading, is incredibly skilled at memorizing lines, is looking forward to getting some dogs, and "will put ketchup on anything. But it has to be Heinz."

Once seen as one of the industry's most eligible bachelors, Vartan has recently been pulled from the dating scene by co-star Jennifer Garner. The two keep their relationship very quiet. "It's interesting that Michael and Jennifer's dating coincides with a storyline where they're not together on the show," said J.J. Abrams. While there are rumors that the two actors have recently split up, nothing has been confirmed.

Life for Michael is good at the moment, and the actor knows it: "There have been times when I've been driving and I'll look up and there's the Hollywood sign and I'll think, *Wow, I made it — I'm a working actor in Hollywood!* I don't know how long it'll last for me, but so far, so good. But I always swore to myself that no matter what happened on this path I've chosen, I'd never take things too seriously. At the end of the day it's fun, a great escape — it's all about make-believe."

Carl Lumbly *(Alias: Marcus Dixon)*

Marcus Dixon is one of the good guys, and Carl Lumbly is no stranger to playing that role. And yet, Carl Lumbly became an actor by accident. Born to professional welder Carrol Egbert and Ida Braham Lumbly in

Montego Bay, Jamaica, on August 14, 1952, his father was a traditional man and a hard worker who discouraged an acting career right from the start. He kept Carl from the movies until he was a teenager, and believed that a stage career for his son meant putting on whiteface and entertaining with tap shoes. So, as a child, Carl learned whittling and woodworking from his father, who spent much of his time fixing things around the house and creating items that would be too expensive for the Lumblys to buy. For Carl, woodworking, or "construction" as his father called it, became a passion, and while other children preoccupied themselves with toys, Carl's time was spent with his wood, hammer, and nails.

Carl, his younger sister, Amy, and his parents ended up immigrating to the U.S. after his father befriended radio personality and *Minneapolis Star* columnist Cedric Adams while he was on vacation. He became their sponsor in Minneapolis, Minnesota, but the move was awkward for Carl's parents. His father never really managed to blend into the culture, while his mother spent most of her time in the house. "Once you stepped in the door [of our house], you were in Jamaica," says Lumbly. Unfortunately, during his freshman year of college, Carl had a nasty confrontation with his father. He immediately moved out and was estranged from his father for many years as a consequence.

Some might say that Carl's penchant for acting came out at an early age, when he would mimic his father's routine at suppertime, much to the pleasure of his sister. While attending South High School, Carl saw a couple of the high school shows but did not perform in any. His focus was on journalism when he first attended Macalester College in St. Paul, Minnesota. While Carl would veer away from this career, his sister, Amy, would go on to become a reporter for Channel 11, KARE-TV, and the E! Cable Network.

Carl performed in a couple of productions in college, but the possibility of acting didn't emerge until he was working as a freelance reporter for the Associated Press while also handling a job in public relations at 3M. He was assigned to write about a local improvisational workshop theater: Dudley Riggs's Brave New Workshop. When he arrived, he decided that auditioning for the group would add an

Carl Lumbly was born in Jamaica, and got his first big break as Detective Mark Petrie on *Cagney & Lacey*.

interesting angle to the story. Not only was he selected to join the improv group, but he stayed with them for two years. "What they were doing hadn't been written — it was happening right there. It was curious. It was like a writing form more than anything," he says.

Still writing freelance for the Associated Press, he decided to follow his girlfriend to San Francisco. There he saw an audition notice for two black actors, who were needed to perform in the South African political play *Sizwe Bansi is Dead* by Athol Fugard. Lumbly got one part, and the other young actor was none other than Danny Glover. The show took them to Los Angeles as part of a California Arts Council Tour, and they ended up working together on Fugard's *The Island* as well at the Eureka Theatre. The show went on tour and cemented a lifelong friendship between the actors. It also was a watershed moment for Lumbly, as it was this play that solidified his desire to act professionally.

Carl continued to perform onstage, branching out into television as well in episodes of *Emergency!*, *The Jeffersons*, and *Taxi*. He also made his film debut in *Escape from Alcatraz* in 1979. Then, in 1982, Lumbly received his first job as a series regular, playing Detective Mark Petrie on *Cagney & Lacey*. Lumbly was a mainstay on the series for the full run of six years. "He is an intense, wonderful actor, a sensitive man, who was always present for me when we worked. My only regret is that they didn't give us more scenes together," said actress Sharon Gless, who played the title role of Christine Cagney. Cast in the recurring role of Detective Petrie's wife was actress Vonetta McGee, who became Lumbly's real wife in May 1987. She also took on the role of Carl's wife in the 1990 film *To Sleep with Anger*, starring Danny Glover.

During his time as a series regular, Carl continued to perform onstage in plays such as *The Gospal at Colonus* and *A Midsummer Night's Dream*. His father came to see him in the former, the only play he saw his son perform in. "He told me he thought I was a good man," says Carl. As a result, Lumbly has been very particular about the roles he chooses, preferring the admirable types to the seedier characters. That hasn't always helped his career, however: "I'm told I'm uptight, I'm too priggish as an actor in the choices I'm willing to take. I had to style myself as an actor because I didn't know if I was a strong enough character to resist some of the roles I knew I didn't want my mom or dad to see. I worked so hard at that; I feel like I did it too well."

In the 1980s, Carl took roles in such films as *The Adventures of Buckaroo Banzai Across the 8th Dimension* and *Everybody's All American*, for which he received great praise for his performance. When *Cagney & Lacey* went off the air in 1988, Lumbly spent a year on the successful series *L.A. Law*. The short-lived series *Going to Extremes* allowed Carl to return to something familiar: Jamaica. The series followed medical students training in his homeland, but only aired three episodes. "It's like alchemy. You always know when you're onto something good, but you don't necessarily know up front what will serve as a hit. I never feel wildly disappointed, but also I'm never really prepared for it when it happens," he said about the cancellation.

Carl went on to receive superhero status when he took on the lead role of Dr. Miles Hawkins in *M.A.N.T.I.S.*, playing a paralyzed scientist who uses his special exoskeleton invention in order to fight crime. "I think that a lot of [sci-fi] is based on present science fact and kind of extrapolated into the future by people who are far-thinking. It's always fascinated me," Lumbly claims. "So maybe whenever I go in to audition for roles in these kinds of projects I give off a vibe of appreciating that kind of storytelling. I wanted that role [in *M.A.N.T.I.S.*]. Here was a flawed man who was trying to be noble and learned that he was more capable than he thought he was. That's a great place for an actor to start. *M.A.N.T.I.S.* was one of my favorite experiences, though I must now put *Alias* ahead of it." The 1994 television movie was turned into a series, but the latter did not last.

Carl kept busy, however, on both the stage and screen. He had roles in *Pacific Heights* and *How Stella Got Her Groove Back*. He ended up reprising his role as Mark Petrie in a reunion special of *Cagney & Lacey* and acting in television movies such as *Conspiracy: The Trial of the Chicago 8*, *Out of Darkness* and *The Wedding* opposite Halle Berry, just to name a few. "Some I have on my résumé; others I just hide my eyes and say, 'Hmmm, I think that was *Charles* Lumbly . . . only made that one film and then disappeared.' Those films still pop up on TV during late-night viewing and it can be quite painful," he says.

His work in *Nightjohn* and *On Promised Land* earned him Ace Award nominations, and he received a Best Actor nomination from the NAACP Image Awards for *Buffalo Soldiers*. He also took on the role of Mayor Christian Davidson in the 1996–97 series *EZ Streets*, which starred director-actor Ken Olin. The roles were constant. In 2000, Carl took on the role of Cuba Gooding Jr.'s father in *Men of Honor*. He also returned to the stage to perform in *Jitney* by August Wilson, and received great acclaim for his performance. "A lot of what has guided me in the past is the history of black men in this industry and the history of black men in this country. There's also the personal history with my father," says Lumbly.

And then came *Alias*. J.J. Abrams wanted Carl because he knew the veteran actor would bring a sense of dignity to the show. For Lumbly, the character of Dixon was the appeal: "Dixon is a man of the world and seemed to have all sorts of possibilities. I also found it intriguing to play a patriot. I am of a generation that came out of protest: the civil rights and anti–Vietnam War movements. In Dixon's case, he came out of that experience with a love for the possibilities of the country and the desire to defend it with everything, including his life." Interestingly enough, in the back story that Lumbly created for his character, Dixon was drafted and sent to Vietnam, which led to his desire to continue to serve his country.

Along with his enthusiasm for the character, Carl was also attracted to the show's cast: "We're a very tight group. I've been feeling like I'm a part of a theater company more so than I normally feel doing a television show. Many of us have done a lot of stage work, and there's a kind of admiration we have for one another's work. I feel like we're a team of Clydesdales: they run together well, pull effortlessly, and look pretty doing it." The cast have only good things to say about Lumbly as well. "[Sydney and Dixon's relationship is] one of my favorite relationships on the whole show, partially because I love Carl Lumbly so much. He's such a good friend and a partner in the way that Dixon is to Sydney," says Jennifer Garner. Victor Garber's answer is much shorter: "He's a god."

The character of Dixon has undergone major changes since the first season, both personally and professionally, leaving the audience wondering just where he will end up next. "The surprises are many and intriguing, but the joy of *Alias* is that it's this ongoing, endless puzzle. There are details that were given in the first season, details that appeared small at the time, but J.J. Abrams and the writers have a way of bringing these things back around and all of a sudden the details will have incredible significance," Lumbly says.

Even though *Alias* has been keeping him busy, Carl continues to work on other projects, including pal Danny Glover's directorial debut, *Just a Dream*. He also took on the role of The Father in the television remake of *Sounder*. Lumbly has lent his voice to the *Justice League* cartoon series as J'Onn J'Onzz, the Martian Manhunter, along with a few other series, including *The Wild Thornberrys*, and the recent *Alias* video game. His home country awarded him with the 2002 Doctor Bird Award (the equivalent of an Academy Award) for his acting work over the years. "It was a night which eclipsed any dream of recognition by Jamaica that I could ever have imagined," he says. "Yet I have always imagined the possibility that one day I could do something to be a positive force for Jamaica. I am not the 'greatest.' But the greatness of Jamaica runs through me, from my parents. It is that greatness of Jamaican spirit that has always guided me, like any prodigal son, back home."

When he's not working Carl is busy being a husband and father of 14-year-old Brandon and taking care of two dogs. His wife has not acted since 1998, but Lumbly would love to work with her again. Carl is presently working on a one-man show about abolitionist leader and author Frederick Douglass. While *Alias* is filming, Lumbly commutes from Los Angeles to his Berkeley home on the weekends, where he fixes up his house, just as his father once did. He continues with his woodworking, creating everything from bookshelves to decks; he's even built a sauna. "I don't live my life as an actor," says Lumbly. "There's no way to distinguish me from any of my neighbors here. I'm just the owner of a fixer-upper who is lucky enough to have a great family."

Kevin Weisman (Alias: Marshall J. Flinkman)

He's like this actor who does television work but not just television work sometimes it's onstage which is interesting because he's mostly known for his roles on television series so the fact that he's a prolific stage actor makes the TV work like an alias but he's in a band too and how ya doin'?

Marshall J. Flinkman's famous tangents are the comic relief segments on *Alias*, thanks to actor Kevin Weisman. "Marshall is my ode to all those kids out there who aren't in with the popular crowd. He was one of those kids who wasn't necessarily good at sports but excelled in the classroom."

Kevin was born on December 29, 1970, in Los Angeles, California. His love of acting came out at an early age: one of his first performances was in an adaptation of the television show *Gilligan's Island* in grade school. Another love was fostered in his early years: a love of music. His parents gave him his first drum set when he was 12, and he's been playing ever since. In high school Kevin was part of the band Radical Faction, and then he joined a rock band called Dagaz. His busy musical life didn't prevent him from continuing with acting, however: "I got into drama because all the cute girls were in drama. I always had a flair for it, a penchant for performing. I was always the ham of the group."

Kevin went on to study drama at UCLA's School of Theater, where he first met co-star Merrin Dungey and formed a crush on her roommate. "She wasn't down with me then," Kevin jokes, "but I bet now she's down with me." Also at school with Kevin was comedic actor Jack Black. "We used to play *Star Patrol* and a lot of games on the old PlayStation . . . ," recalls Weisman. While Merrin and Kevin would perform onstage together before *Alias*, Jack Black would occasionally jam with Kevin's band Trainwreck.

In 1991, while he was still a student, Kevin became one of the founding members of the Buffalo Nights Theatre Company. According to the troupe's Web site, "Buffalo Nights sprang from an idea where we as actors could continue to keep working on our craft and at the same time create theatre that was imaginative, provocative, and entertaining; to return to a time when going to the theatre was considered a special, cultural event and not merely as a way for members of the

Kevin Weisman is a fan favorite as Marshall, and in university he hung out with fellow comedic actor Jack Black.

entertainment industry to find new talent." To become members, actors must perform in a certain number of shows; only then are they told where the name "Buffalo Nights" comes from.

Weisman pursued music as well, performing with the band Christopher Robin for the four years he attended college in California. Once he graduated, Kevin left the band and the west coast in order to study in New York at the Circle in the Square Theatre. Kevin put great stock in the importance of training as an actor. Why? "I did a show once with a young actress who could not walk and talk at the same time. Literally. If she had a line, she had to stop moving." In November 1995, Weisman received his first television job: two lines on the show *Frasier*. Roles on *ER*, *The Drew Carey Show*, JAG, *The Pretender*, *Just Shoot Me*, and *Maggie Winters* followed: "I hoped they'd see me in hour-long stuff. Then I got a JAG and an *ER* and . . . *Pretender*. They are finally seeing that though I am an off-center guy, I can do drama shows and play real people instead of two-dimensional sitcom types. I am not a comedian. I happen to do well in that arena, but I prefer to play real people. I don't mind weirder characters because there is actually more work for me. There's only one leading man."

Kevin also had a couple of small film roles, but his main work was on television along with continuing to build the Buffalo Nights Theatre Company. He performed in the plays *Apollo of Bellac*, *Incident at Vichy*, *Salome*, *'Tis Pity She's a Whore*, *Anatol*, *The Greeks*, *J.B.*, *The Firebugs*, and *Sophistry*, to name a few. "I've always been about creating opportunities," Kevin says. "Keep working, get into a play, make a short film, use your resources. Work begets work." The company won nine Drama-Logue Awards, a Garland Award, the Revival Production of the Year Award from *LA Weekly* (for *Modgliani*, 1997) along with two other *LA Weekly* Awards, and received three Robby Award nominations. Many of its shows have been selected as the critics' choice from various publications in Los Angeles. Having garnered a strong reputation for choosing unconventional material, presenting experimental interpretations, staging unusual revivals, and delivering high-caliber performances, Buffalo Nights continues to grow as a company. "If it is a revival that we can put our own slant on, we want to do it," says

Weisman. Kevin line-produces for Buffalo Nights and joins the company productions as frequently as his schedule allows. Most recently he performed in *Crazy Drunk* by Robert Fieldsteel, taking on the role of Griffith J. Griffith in the true story of the wealthy L.A. man who shot his wife in the early 1900s and used the "alcohol insanity" defense. The theater company has also begun working with youth groups and teaching workshops.

In 1998 Weisman garnered a guest role on an episode of J.J. Abrams's *Felicity*. Kevin continued appearing on television, taking a memorable turn as the alien-obsessed character Larry on *Roswell*. In 2000 he landed a guest role on his favorite show, *The X-Files*; best of all was that the episode focused on his character, Anson Stokes. That same year Kevin also played the recurring role of Glory's minion Dreg in *Buffy the Vampire Slayer*. "It was fun but a little hellish, with four hours of makeup to put on that troll face," he remembers. "It's definitely a long time to be in that makeup, but you suck it up." He had a second opportunity to work with Sarah Michelle Gellar in the comedic television movie *Beverly Hills Family Robinson*. He also landed a role on the short-lived series *Pauly* starring Pauly Shore. Kevin had a few roles on unaired pilots as well, but nothing took off. He can also be seen in the films *Man of the Century* (written by fellow Buffalo Nights member Gibson Frazier) and *Gone in 60 Seconds*.

One thing was for certain: Kevin had left an impression on J.J. Abrams. So when Abrams began casting for *Alias*, Weisman got a call. The only problem was that the character of Marshall was supposed to be an ex-hippie in his 40s. Initially, the characterization worried Weisman: "When I read the description of this character, I called my agent and I said, 'This doesn't seem anything like me!' He said, 'No, but J.J. really likes your work and would love for you to come in and just talk to you about it.'" That's exactly what Weisman did. After some collaborative brainstorming, the two of them adjusted the character to suit Kevin. "[M]y theory behind it was, yes, [Marshall] should be very smart and technically proficient, obviously. But it would be interesting if he was kind of lacking in the social skills department. Just one of those types of people that in situations dealing with other people, that he had a hard time, completely opposite of how skilled he is when it comes to the technical and the gadgets — learned information," says Kevin.

The other character trait that emerged was the infamous Marshall "tangents." "Originally, as it was written in the pilot, Marshall was very much about the facts, so we had to create that tangent and funny stuff," claims Weisman. "They gracefully and graciously let me run my mouth, to do my own thing, and if it worked, it ended up on Sunday night. But I didn't have to do as much improvisation as the season went on because the writers locked into my Marshall mannerisms and speech patterns and they wrote some really funny stuff and solid tangents."

Marshall provided the comic levity that was very necessary in the high-drama series. And yet, Kevin was presented with another challenge: the technical know-how that came with the character. "I have to start learning the technical jargon days before. I try and get the script as soon as I can. I'll be in the car and I'll run through them or I'll have my girlfriend work on it with me. I want to get to the point where it's second nature, where I'm not thinking about it because Marshall wouldn't," Kevin explains. Weisman admits to keeping a dictionary close by in case of emergency, even though he claims that he doesn't have a problem with the technical side of things, normally: "I've got a lot of equipment at my house — my surround sound, computers — you know, all the stuff that a man has!"

While Marshall hasn't always been as active as some of the other characters on the show, there are some definite perks in the role, one of which was the opportunity for Kevin to be a character in the *Alias* video game. "For me, it was a dream come true," he says. "I'm not limited by my looks." Weisman's role has evolved over the seasons, allowing the character a little romance and adventure — and the chance to be a new parent! He was even given a drum set for Marshall's office, allowing Kevin to show off his talents. One thing hasn't changed, however, and that is Marshall's appeal: "I know what my strengths are for this character and I know viewers really respond to the comic relief element because this show is so serious. I try and give the people what they want. What I've attempted is not to be silly or funny for funny's sake, but to try and make the comedy come from this character and his difficulty in relating to people." Kevin also appreciates the fact that Marshall is a sweet man. "I get a lot of people that are in the technical world who say, 'Oh my god, that character, that's me. I relate to it.' You know, that's really cool. I've played a lot of villains, but if I'm gonna be around for four or five years, you kinda want people to like you."

When Kevin isn't busy with *Alias* he continues to perform with Buffalo Nights as well as tour with the Southern rockabilly band Trainwreck under the name Kenny Bob Thornton. Recently he has taken on producing the independent film *The Illusion* starring Kirk Douglas and directed by fellow Buffalo Nights actor Michael Goorjian (of *Party of Five* fame). The film was submitted to the 2004 Sundance Film Festival. Weisman has also had the opportunity to work with Steven Spielberg on the upcoming film *The Terminal* with Tom Hanks. "Spielberg's a big fan of [*Alias*]. I didn't even have to audition! I'm only in one scene, but it's a great scene with Tom Hanks and it's just been great for me. I owe J.J. Abrams definitely a dinner. Maybe dessert too, we'll see," he quips.

Weisman just bought a house, and as a huge fan of the L.A. Lakers, set up his own basketball hoop in the back. He's also a major gamer: he owns three consoles and is an expert at the NFL game *Madden 2004*. He continues to keep himself busy in all levels of life. "Young people often ask me, 'What should I do to become an actor?' and I say, 'Work, study hard, do everything you can to prepare yourself for that break, because it may not come more than once.'"

Greg Grunberg (*Alias: Eric Weiss*)

Agent Eric Weiss is one of the nice guys on *Alias*, or so says actor Greg Grunberg: "I'm the show's Dr. Phil. It's a nice position to be in. You know, everyone comes to me. Marshall came to me. Certainly, Vaughn and I are best friends on the show and it's nice. It's nice to be that guy that everybody wants to talk to." The amicable actor was born on July 11, 1966, in Los Angeles, California. Sandy Grunberg was mother to not one, but two performers: Greg and his brother, Brad (an actor also known as Johnny Cocktails). Raised in a Jewish family, Greg enjoyed cooking traditions while growing up: "My grandmother taught [her brisket recipe] to my mom and she taught it to me. Family recipes are the best. Nanny cooked everything with so much love; that's what makes her brisket so delicious."

While Greg befriended *Alias* creator J.J. Abrams in kindergarten, his first step into the acting world happened at Roscomare Road Elementary School. "My first part ever was that of Huck Finn in *Tom Sawyer*," Grunberg recalls. "Then in junior high at Emerson Junior High I played Colonel Purdy in *Tea House of the August Moon*. . . . I've been hooked on acting ever since." Greg graduated from University High School in West L.A. and made his way to San Diego State University, where he majored in business with a minor in creative writing. He continued to take acting classes, however, and to perform outside of university.

In his early 20s, Grunberg came to the realization that it was time to take a chance in the acting world and began auditioning for commercials. He had to make ends meet, though, and kept himself busy with a variety of jobs in order to pay his bills. He was a personal driver for director Joel Silver; worked for producer Dino de Laurentis; and started up a frozen-yogurt delivery service (Yogurt Runners), selling the product door-to-door at various businesses around town. Meanwhile, he was trying to find a commercial agent and act in student films. "I got my start . . . with a commercial for Computer Learning Center. It was so bad. I showed up two hours late and looked like hell," he says. Greg's most prominent commercial was for Rolaids; in it he played a shirtless football fan: "I actually made it onto the *Tonight Show with Jay Leno* because of it." His last commercial was a spot for Nicorette, done in 1999. "We shot it in New York, and I was pretty happy with that one," he says. "But I've never taken a puff. Relatives have called me up and said, 'I never knew you had a problem.' Pretty funny." Working in the commercial world paid off for Greg; it kept him motivated to keep striving in the acting world: "[I knew] the first time that I walked out to my mailbox expecting nothing but bills, and to my surprise there were residual checks from commercials I'd done a couple years before. I knew if the magic mailbox was going to keep delivering, I was going to have to keep acting. I knew it was something I wanted to do. I've known

CHRISTINA RADISH

Greg Grunberg is close friends with J.J. Abrams, and has starred on *Felicity* and *Alias*. Here he poses with his then-pregnant wife Elizabeth, who would soon give birth to their son, Sam.

that forever. As far as knowing I could make a living at it, that was the time that I knew the harder I worked, the more it would pay off."

His first moment on a television series was on an episode of *Melrose Place* in 1992. Grunberg remembers what came next: "My first significant acting role other than commercials was on a show called *Flying Blind* [in 1992]. I played Corey Parker's brother." In 1994 Greg had a small role on *Baywatch*, and, two years later, on *Murphy Brown*, *Ned and Stacey*, and *Relativity*. He was credited with a "special thanks" for work on the film *Buffalo '66*: "I was asked to do a voice-over for the film that turned into a very, VERY small voice-over job. Vincent [Gallo] wanted me to originally do the play-by-play for the football sequences in the film, then was later able to get the real sportscasters — so I was reduced to just a few lines." He continued garnering smaller roles on shows such as *Silk Stalkings* and performed in the television movies *Stolen: One Husband* and *Frankenstein: The College Years*. Greg was also the co-writer of a computer-animated pilot series, for which he provided his voice for the main character.

Through the 1990s, Grunberg landed small roles in films such as *Witchcraft V*, *The Pallbearer*, *The Trigger Effect*, and BASEketball. He had an uncredited role in *Picture Perfect* and a more significant role in the HBO film *Dinner and Driving*. He enjoyed working on the latter: "I'd have to say the best role I have done in film has to be in *Dinner and Driving*, where I got to play a happily married man who gives bad advice to a soon-to-be-engaged friend [Joey Slotnick]. It was also one of the first film roles I did and the writing was incredible." On television, Greg could be seen in NYPD *Blue*, *Pacific Blue*, *Profiler*, *Mike Hammer*, *Private Eye*, and Dean Koontz's television film *Mr. Murder*. Meanwhile, Grunberg's best friend, J.J. Abrams, had been working hard at creating a show about a young student starting up her life at NYU. Greg's career was about to take off.

In 1998, *Felicity* hit the airwaves. Grunberg was cast in the role of Sean Blumberg, a comedic character who had a penchant for inventing very odd things in the hope of making himself into a millionaire. The role was created especially for Greg; some of Grunberg's own characteristics were even given to Sean. "Out of necessity as an out-of-work actor, I actually invented some things. The camera vending machines that sold disposable cameras are actually mine. I leased them to the show," Grumberg reveals. Greg was one of the older actors on the show, which he enjoyed. In the middle of season 1, Greg's status went from "recurring" to "regular": "I was hoping that at some point I'd be a regular on some show. The time that that happened, I auditioned during pilot season, when new shows get the green light and production begins. I had been selected on two other shows, so that forced them to make a decision whether to sign me on as a regular. They jumped at the chance."

His character shifted as well, balancing more drama with his comedic side. Sean had to deal with the challenge of cancer as well as a budding romance with Amanda Foreman's character, Megan. "We knew each other before the show, actually," said Foreman. "We didn't have to create anything; the chemistry was there. But I should point out we never dated or anything — I'm good friends with his wife!" His family was happy about the shift to regular status. His older son adored *Felicity* even though the show was past his bedtime. His other son was too young to watch the show (at only eight months old) but was glad to have his father home for a few days during the week. In between serious storylines, however, the cast continued to joke around and have videogame sessions.

While working on *Felicity*, Grunberg was cast in Paul Verhoven's action-thriller *Hollow Man* starring Kevin Bacon. "I actually thought the audition went terrible. He [Verhoven] had a pillow in his office and I was just making fun of it. I guess the language difference, not his native tongue — he didn't pick up on it. Now we're great friends," says Greg. Grunberg played Carter Abbey, one of the six scientists working on the secret invisibility project deep underground. It was his second time working with Kevin Bacon, whom he had met on the set of *Picture Perfect*, where they played many games of backgammon to pass the time. Even though Greg claims to have been the better backgammon player, Kevin got his revenge. "[T]hey gave me a Sony Mini Disc player and headphones, which is appropriate for my character [in *Hollow Man*]. What was funny was that they made me listen to the soundtrack of *Footloose*. I enjoyed it the first five times, but after eight months I wanted to strangle Kevin. I guess I could be thankful it wasn't the Bacon Brothers," joked Grunberg. Greg also had the opportunity to be in Wendall Morris's comedic autobiographical cancer story *The Medicine Show* starring Jonathan Silverman.

In 2001 a new J.J. Abrams series burst onto the scene, starring *Felicity* alumnus Jennifer Garner. Grunberg claims that Abrams calls him up with story ideas frequently, and once he read the script for *Alias* he begged Abrams to write a part for him. Of course, Grunberg kids that he has to keep giving Abrams boxes of Krispy Kreme donuts for pulling strings. Initially Greg read for the role of Agent Dixon: "I wasn't right for it and obviously it's a major role on the show. After that [Abrams] said, 'OK, I'm going to make this happen somehow.'" In the end, Greg's big role in the pilot consisted of handing over a pen. Greg was still working on *Felicity,* but was given the opportunity to take on the recurring role of CIA Agent Eric Weiss on *Alias*. Because the shows were on different networks, Grunberg had to make a concession: he was not allowed any on-screen credit for *Alias*. The news didn't spoil his sense of humor: "What would be really funny, when [*Felicity*] ends, is that this is the way Sean has been making money — is at the CIA undercover. The crazy invention thing is just a front." His *Felicity* co-stars were supportive of his new role, and interestingly enough, Amanda Foreman would soon follow in his footsteps when *Felicity* finally ended.

Agent Weiss didn't have a first name initially. Greg had a suggestion for one, however: "[W]hen they told me that my name was Weiss, I told J.J., 'You've got to make me *Eric* Weiss, because that was Houdini's real name.'" Sure enough, Greg got his wish, and in season 3 Agent Eric Weiss became a series regular. Since gaining regular status Weiss has been allowed to show off his field skills. "I always feel like it looks like comedy when I'm doing it," he confesses. "[Director] Ken Olin always tells me to be more tough. But I think I bring a humanity that other characters don't."

When he hasn't been at work on *Alias*, Greg has been busy with other projects, including small roles in *Austin Powers: Goldmember* and *Connie and Carla*, as well as performing in the comedy *Malibu's Most Wanted* and the Coen brothers' remake of the 1955 film *The Ladykillers*.

He has also been active in the creation of a new show with J.J. Abrams, based on one of his own ideas. The one-hour series focuses on two bounty hunters and is tentatively entitled *The Catch*. "Basically, I play a bounty hunter who is trying to balance work and the pressures of a screwed up personal life. It's an action/comedy and I have a partner who keeps me in line. It will hopefully be a great ensemble show if we get a chance to actually do it," Greg says. Until then, Grunberg will remain on *Alias*.

When he's not performing, Greg is busy at home with his wife, Elizabeth, and his sons Jake, Ben, and baby Sam. He loves cooking ("My kids call themselves my 'sous-chefs'"); has just started getting into golf; played basketball in the celebrity NBA league while on *Felicity*; and, like his fellow castmate Kevin Weisman, plays drums (in the band Every Other Tuesday). He's an avid backgammon player, collecting various boards from the 1970s, and continues to invent things as well. And yes, he still finds fart jokes funny. For Grunberg, it all comes back to comedy: "I'm very comfortable with being a character actor that can hopefully step into sort of a leading character but not a leading man — that pressure of leading man. I just love what I'm doing. I'd love to be on a sitcom, because it's the easiest hours and it's what I feel really comfortable doing: comedy, just straight comedy; just out there to make people laugh. That I'd love to do, but I would not mind being an eighty-four-year-old Weiss. I would be happy doing that too. No problem. J.J., if you're listening . . ."

THE BEST FRIENDS

Merrin Dungey (Alias: Francie Calfo/Allison Doren)

Good girl? Bad girl? Merrin Dungey has been both on *Alias*. Born on August 6, 1971, in Sacramento, California, Merrin is the younger of two girls. Her sister, Channing, three years older, also found her way into the entertainment business as a production executive while her father, Don, on the other hand, works in the energy and conservation industry as a manager for the General Services Department of the Sacramento

Municipal Utility District. Channing and Merrin were classic sisters, with Merrin constantly attempting to raid her sibling's closet. Even though they are both in the same industry, the two are quite different. "If I were a shoe, I'd be a pair of red patent-leather platforms," says Dungey. "My sister? She's more like an elegant sandal."

Dungey began ballet lessons at age four, and like her co-star Jennifer Garner, continued with them into her teen years. She also played piano and competed as an ice skater for a time. Acting, however, wasn't part of the picture in her early teens with the exception of the occasional musical. Then, at age 18, Merrin ended up hosting a local teen talk show, which led to some commercial gigs. Those spots marked the beginning of her foray into the professional acting world.

After graduating from Rio Americano High School in 1989, Dungey made her way to UCLA acting school and ended up sharing a dorm with none other than *Alias*'s Marshall — Kevin Weisman. While Kevin's crush on Merrin's roommate didn't go very far, he was destined to cross paths with Merrin again. In May 2001, they both performed in the Buffalo Nights Theatre Company's version of *Anatol* by Arthur Schnitzler just before they were cast in J.J. Abrams's new show.

In her sophomore year, Dungey's talents wowed the entire school when she became the youngest person ever to win the coveted UCLA School of Theater's Annual Acting Award. "It was a big deal," says her father. "At UCLA they have four years of undergrad school and they have three years of grad school in theater, so she beat out all of the juniors, seniors, and even the grad students as the best actress. [When] she won the best actress award and we realized how truly competitive that was, then we began to understand how really talented she is." Even better, the award was presented to her by Oscar-winning actor Denzel Washington.

When she graduated from UCLA in 1993, her acting career took off as she garnered small roles on shows such as *Martin*, *Living Single*, and *Babylon 5*. In 1996 Merrin signed up for her first pilot series: *Party Girl* starring Christine Taylor. The show revolved around the character of Mary, a woman who is the queen of the New York party scene by night, but a librarian by day. Dungey was cast in the role of Wanda, a co-worker who cannot believe that Mary could possibly work where she

CHRISTINA RADISH

The beautiful Merrin Dungey didn't become interested in acting until she was 18.

does considering her nighttime lifestyle. Next came roles on *ER*, *Caroline in the City*, *Murphy Brown*, and *Seinfeld*. Sure, the roles were minor, but Merrin saw their importance: "Those nameless roles were certainly not thankless because they came at the beginning of my career, when I was grateful for any part."

Dungey also began to explore the world of stand-up comedy and signed up with the William Morris Agency after her first show. She wrote and performed in her own one-woman show *Black Like Who?* for the HBO Comedy Workspace, which received great acclaim. That success led to an opportunity to perform in the Montreal Comedy Festival *Just for Laughs* in 1998, which in turn garnered Dungey an act on Comedy Central's *Premium Blend*. She put her comedy talents to work on television as well, landing a recurring role on *The King of Queens*. "I got that job in the nick of time," she says. "I was working three day jobs: I was delivering Zone food to people like Hank Azaria, I was a personal assistant to an executive at Warner Brothers, and I was working at a bar. After the first season I was able to quit them all." Merrin also explored roles on the big screen, landing parts in *Deep Impact* and *EdTV*, and returned to the small screen for guest stints on *Friends* and *The West Wing*.

After a role in the pilot of *Malcolm in the Middle* as Frankie Muniz's teacher, Merrin was later offered the chance to return in another role: the overprotective mother of Malcolm's wheelchair-bound friend Stevie. Unfortunately, Dungey had to give up the role when another part came along — the part of Francie Calfo in *Alias*. "It was pilot season and *Alias* was one of the best scripts I'd read," Merrin claims. "I had an initial meeting with J.J. and we hit it off — it was really clicking, which doesn't always happen." As Sydney's best friend, the character of Francie helps to shape the double agent's "normal" life. "Isn't that the point, that CIA agents and people who really are sent out on missions have private lives, take their families to Disneyland?" Dungey asks. "It puts a face on the agents that are out there serving our country. The James Bond films were always exciting, but you'd care a bit more if you felt that was a real human being — you care so much more about Sydney because you see her personal life."

One of the bonuses of working with J.J. Abrams is that Merrin has been able to help shape her character's direction. One of the earlier roadblocks included Francie's relationship with Charlie, her fiancé. Realizing that the marriage would inevitably hurt Francie and Sydney's relationship, she brought the matter to J.J., who was receptive to her concerns. "I did get a couple of complicated twists in the Charlie storyline — I got to argue and get upset," she says. In the end Charlie was written out of the script, leaving Francie to open her restaurant and be Sydney's support system. Merrin also got involved with the ABC Television Network's public service initiative called "A Better Community," organized in conjunction with the Ad Council's Racial Cooperation campaign. ABC aired spots promoting racial tolerance with the help of different actors including Dungey and Jennifer Garner.

Full of energy, Merrin is the type to be the first on the dance floor. Francie, however, remained out of the spy action loop. The fact was that Francie was in need of a change. Dungey explains: "I was getting frustrated because I'd come in once a week and say, 'Hey guys, do you want to try my soup, or bouillabaisse or brownies?' I walked in my trailer and I was like, 'If I see one more apron. . . . Am I Florida on *Good Times*?'" After much collaboration with J.J. Abrams and keeping a secret as large as Sydney Bristow's, Allison Doren came along. "[In] October [2002], J.J. finally filled me in on what was going to happen with the whole doubling thing and I was like, 'What?' I was at the post office and I was on the phone in the car in the rain for thirty minutes just listening to J.J. I didn't say a word. Who doesn't want to be a bad girl? It's so much fun to be naughty. I don't have to apologize for anything I'm doing. It's very freeing to be so bold in everything that I do." As a consequence of the change, a new nickname emerged: "[N]ow we call her 'The Francinator,' which is actually Merrin's name for her," said co-star Bradley Cooper.

With the coming of Allison Doren also came a new workout regime for Merrin. Suddenly she was training with a world champion kickboxer. From cooking to killing, Merrin has gone from one extreme to another. Even with the character twist, it seemed as though Francie/Allison was fated to leave the show. Season 3 arrived and Merrin was no longer a permanent fixture on *Alias*. She did manage to reappear for a couple of episodes, however. "Oh, [Merrin's] just the greatest," says J.J.

Abrams. "Not just because she was great, but because she was back to play this character that she is marvelous at creating. We loved Merrin as an actress. Allison Doren was a chance to give her something that was meaty, that she could have fun with, and she was extraordinary, I thought. To have her come back and do this character, which gives her so much to do and has such importance to the show, was wonderful."

As to whether or not Merrin will return to *Alias* remains unclear. The fans still have hopes of a return, however: some have started up a site called "Operation: Save Allison."

Dungey has since filmed the thriller *Scream at the Sound of the Beep*. A Los Angeles resident, she keeps herself busy doing yoga or catching local bands at the Viper Room. She is also a sushi fan, as well as a dessert lover. At present she's also doing some more work on *The King of Queens* and is a regular on the WB series *Summerland*. Does Merrin Dungey find it tough to switch from comedy to action and back? Not at all: "I get to tape in front of a live audience every week on *The King of Queens* and I get to be bad and kick butt and jump down elevator shafts on *Alias*. I guess you could say I'm well-rounded."

Bradley Cooper *(Alias: Will Tippin)*

Bradley Cooper, the man behind the notepad of reporter Will Tippin, was born in Philadelphia, Pennsylvania, on January 5, 1975. Growing up with an Italian grandmother helped him gain a great love of home-cooked food, including cheesecake, seafood dishes, and homemade pasta and ravioli. It makes sense that he should have an older sister nicknamed "Noodle" by his father. It was his grandmother's culinary skills that inspired him to learn to cook: "Now I make gourmet meals just for myself — I even do the whole parsley garnish thing — and eat in front of the TV. Pretty lame, I know."

As a child Bradley wanted to be like his father and, in one case, went as far as dressing up like him. "It was in second grade — a cream-colored three-piece spring suit. The tie was a clip-on. Unfortunately, I just couldn't find a proper one that small," he confesses. Cooper gives great thanks for having had an older sister around to prevent him from being bullied for that ensemble. Feathered hair, soccer shoes, and even suspenders made it into Bradley's wardrobe in high school for a short period of time. His preference in clothing has grown more casual over the years, but he keeps various tidbits from the past, including a ragged "Naples Lobster" T-shirt from a family trip taken to Maine when Bradley was only 12. A sentimental man, it seems.

Bradley had two things going for him as a child: he lived next door to a movie theater, and his dad was a huge movie buff, so he was always in front of the big screen.

At 12 years of age, Bradley found acting inspiration from the David Lynch classic *The Elephant Man*. Released in 1980, the film was based on the true story of John Merrick (played by John Hurt), a man afflicted with a disfiguring disease. The key moment for Cooper was specific: a scene between Anthony Hopkins and John Hurt. "When Anthony Hopkins comes in and sees Merrick for the very first time, I was addicted to the way it made me feel — like, the music and everything. And movies moved me in a way that nothing else had in my life at that point," Bradley says. Little did he know that he would later take on Hurt's challenging role. Rather than pursue acting straight away, however, Bradley actually avoided acting while in high school: "Looking back, I know it had a lot to do with fear. It was just my way of avoiding doing something that put so much at stake."

Even right after high school, Bradley still didn't pursue his acting dream. "I think I wasn't really prepared to do it. But, at the same time, I'm so glad I didn't do it because, you know, there's just other things to do which, ultimately, informs your acting." So when he graduated from high school, Bradley pursued English Literature at Georgetown University instead. He left Georgetown in 1997 with an honors degree in English. He was also a medallist, having rowed for the Men's Heavyweight Crew team. And yet the acting bug remained for Bradley, even though he'd spent four years in a different program.

After graduating, Bradley made his way to New York City with the desire to enroll in the Master of Fine Arts program at the Actor's Studio at New York University. The dean of the school at the time was none other than James Lipton, best known for his television interviews with

Will's inspiration for being a journalist was the film *His Girl Friday*, but Bradley Cooper's inspiration for acting was the 1980 film, *The Elephant Man*.

celebrities on *Inside the Actors Studio*. While there, Bradley studied voice and movement along with acting. He also spent his weekends involved with a non-profit organization called LEAP (Learning through the Expanded Arts Program), teaching movement and acting techniques to inner-city children. Sure enough, Cooper was cast in the role of John Merrick in Bernard Pomerance's *The Elephant Man*, which was performed at the Circle in the Square Theatre.

While Bradley was working away at school, he had also begun to pursue a professional career. One of his first breaks was an opportunity to guest star on *Sex and the City* opposite Sarah Jessica Parker in 1998. As Jake "The Downtown Smoker," a love interest for Carrie, Parker's character, Cooper was suddenly faced with his first on-camera love scene. "The day of [the shoot], I think I brushed my teeth eighteen times," Bradley remembers. "'Whatever you do, do *not* put your tongue in her mouth,' the director warned. Great. I was a mess, sweating in my leather pants. But once the director said 'Action,' Sarah Jessica kissed *me* — and she was wonderful. I've done more sex scenes since then. They're still never erotic to me, but I don't sweat profusely anymore."

Soon after, Bradley was off on a new adventure, hosting the *Lonely Planet* show "Treks in a Wild World," broadcast on the Discovery Channel. His commercial agent sent him to an open-call audition where he was informed that the producers were looking for a person who had some experience going on extreme treks. More importantly, they were looking for someone with the sensibilities to perform these activities. The problem? Bradley had no experience whatsoever. "So I had to make up this trek that I went on and I made up this whole thing that I went to Indonesia in hunt of the, like, Komodo Dragon or something, and I made up all this bullshit. Then I got called back, and they were like, 'OK, we want to film you and you have to make up a trek in Central Park.'" After borrowing his friend's equipment, he showed up and camped in Central Park, and the producers were impressed. Suddenly they were sending Bradley off on international adventures, including sea kayaking in British Columbia and ice climbing in the Andes. After signing a $500,000 life insurance policy, the gig was his. The show was broadcast in 2000.

Bradley had a brief foray into film after his extreme adventures, landing his first feature: a role in the comedy *Wet Hot American Summer* starring Janeane Garofalo and David Hyde Pierce. While the film itself was not terribly successful, Cooper enjoyed the experience of making it. He then went on to film *Carnival Knowledge*, and soon after he landed the role of Clay Hammond in the short-lived Darren Star series *The $treet*. The television series about Wall Street stockbrokers was expected to be a hit. It only aired for five episodes, however, allowing Cooper to pursue more projects. Next, Bradley landed the role of law student Gordon Pinella in the Ben Affleck film *Changing Lanes*. Luck wasn't with him on the latter, as all of his scenes were cut. In his next project, Cooper starred in the unaired WB pilot *Wall to Wall Records*.

And then *Alias* came along. "I auditioned in New York," says Cooper. J.J. happened to be out in New York, so I met him. And we just hit it off, like, boom! And he flew me out and then I tested the next week and then I got it. No one was, like, a name or anything. J.J. really picked people that he thought, you know, that he just thought would work. Which is really great that the network allowed him to do that." It was a year after graduation, and in moving to L.A. from New York, Bradley's life was on a whole new path. He attributes getting the role to his corduroy pants: "Will is sort of a retro character. I think [Abrams] just dug the corduroy. It had nothing to do with me." He almost did not accept the role, however, as he was also scheduled to film the independent thriller *My Little Eye* in Nova Scotia, on Canada's east coast. In the end, he was able to do both — the appeal of the reporter character of Will Tippin was too strong: "As for the character, I loved the neophyte. The person who enters into this mythical world with iconic characters and is there for the audience. He's the everyman. I just wanted to say 'neophyte.' J.J. always uses that word."

Will was written as a close friend of Sydney Bristow's who was both a confidant and a possible love interest. The original name for the character was Clay, but Cooper didn't feel it was right. He mentioned the name Will, and the producers used it. To study for the role, Bradley decided to do some investigative reporting of his own and followed around a *Los Angeles Times* reporter during a mayoral campaign: "It was amazing to watch this reporter constantly eating bagels, leaving around half-empty cups of coffee, half-eaten sandwiches. . . . [T]hat insight was a wonderful thing I integrated that informs the psychology of my character." Being a part of the *Alias* team has brought about a new fascination for the production side of things. "I'm just obsessed with the process of making the show," Cooper claims. "They make fun of me for watching dailies the very second they come in."

Cooper was surprised to find his character embroiled in controversy off-screen. The Internet fans did not seem to have much time for Will Tippin. Many took issue with Will's pursuing Danny's murder. When Bradley's sister sent him some of the comments she had read on ABC's message boards, Bradley was, in his own words, ". . . a mess. It wasn't so much I felt personally [attacked], but I thought, *Oh wow, I'm totally going to get fired because they hate the character.*" Cooper did not get fired, however, and Will continued to evolve in unexpected ways. J.J. Abrams commented that "He has an important role in the show that wasn't being well-told, which is Will seems to be the person that was bridging Sydney's normal life with her spy life. The way it was being done, the audience was ahead of him the whole time, so we could never be with him. We got some letters from people who were like, 'Please kill him.' Bradley's a really good actor — he's a great guy, and I think his character's in a really good place."

Bradley is known for doing impressions of his castmates' characters, including Sloane, Sark, and CIA Director Kendall, and he isn't the only one who partakes in the fun. Cooper's on-set antics aside, when season 2 ended, we were all left wondering whether or not we would be seeing Will again. The rumors abounded until it was finally announced that Bradley would be coming back, but only as a guest star. "I miss the family a lot," he says. "But we all hang out. That hasn't changed. . . . But honestly, it's been revitalizing. It was tough playing that character. He was a victim. He was a passive character, except for the finale, when he takes charge of his life and becomes proactive. And if I do come back, it will only be under those circumstances. But I would love to come back, and I would do anything for J.J. Abrams." In the meantime, Bradley has guest-starred on the NBC show *Miss Match* opposite Alicia Silverstone.

A California resident, he also just moved to Venice from Laurel Canyon with his girlfriend from Georgetown. Having filmed *The Last Cowboy* with Jennie Garth and *I Want to Marry Ryan Banks* with Jason Priestly, both for television, it looks as though Bradley is continuing to keep himself busy.

Bradley is missed, no question. Greg Grunberg (Agent Eric Weiss) has his own comments on the issue: "I miss working with him. Bradley, if you're out there in witness relocation land, if you can hear me, it's Weiss — your instant buddy. Remember the magic tricks I showed you? I miss you. Come back, buddy!"

THE BAD GUYS

Ron Rifkin (Alias: Arvin Sloane)

As the variable villain Arvin Sloane, Ron Rifkin has become the man we love to hate. Born in Brooklyn, New York, on Halloween in 1939, Rifkin was the elder son of two and grew up in Williamsburg in what he calls a "shtetl-like community of orthodox or conservative Jews." Having 13 aunts and uncles on his mother's side, Ron was constantly surrounded by relatives. His father was an exceptional businessman working as a furrier, but that world never tempted Rifkin. Even though he had little exposure to theater as a child, it didn't stop him from discovering a love of performing at a very early age: "I had a cousin who had a one-room apartment where the bedroom area was separated from the living area by a curtain. And I would tell my cousin, 'Now I'll get behind the curtain, you announce my name first, and I'll come out singing and dancing.'" Ron credits his early love of theater to his experiences at the synagogue. With the formal separation of the women and men (men downstairs and women on the balcony) and a large stage with curtains, the theatrical production of presenting Torahs wrapped in rich velvet inspired Rifkin.

Ron explored theater in high school and studied at the Actor's Studio at New York University, but the latter did not present him with very good roles. It was the opportunity to apprentice in summer stock that gave Ron the chance to show off his skills. His first lead role was in *The Boyfriend*, which was also Barbra Streisand's first professional gig — only she had a small role! In 1960, Ron made his debut on the Broadway stage in Neil Simon's original production of *Come Blow Your Horn*. The production was a smash hit, leading to more opportunities on the stage for Rifkin. Breaking into television and film, however, was more of a challenge. His first opportunity on the small screen came in 1966, when he landed a guest-starring role on the series *Gidget* playing Sally Field's friend Mel, but the one-episode stint did not lead to anything permanent. In fact, he would not return to the small screen until he had a guest stint on *The Bob Newhart Show* in 1974. Thankfully, his off-Broadway career remained constant until the 1970s, when Rifkin hopped from one failed series to the next, including a role as an assistant D.A. in *Adam's Rib* and as Prince John in the short-lived Robin Hood series *When Things Were Rotten*. While he could be seen guest-starring on such series as *McMillan and Wife*, *Soap*, *Alice*, and *Knots Landing*, it wasn't until the hit series *One Day at a Time* that he landed a more prominent role, playing a single father to an awkward teenage son. On the big screen, Rifkin had small roles in the films *Silent Running*, *The Sunshine Boys*, and *The Big Fix*, but even then he remained relatively unknown.

During the making of the 1983 film *The Sting II*, Ron met his wife Iva, a former dancer. From there he continued to work onstage in between filming various made-for-TV movies. However, Rifkin felt his career was frozen in place: "I'd wake up in the morning, I'd be depressed, and sometimes I'd be crying. I was playing the same part over and over again — the friend of the friend of the friend. . . . I was sad about myself. I lost a sense of belief in myself. I just didn't want to be in that world." Rifkin took a step away from acting in order to explore the business world. He began his own retail clothing business, marketing a line of high-end coats that were designed by the Carole Little label.

Having established a successful business career, Ron had no intention of returning to acting until he was persuaded to join in a summer production of Arthur Miller's *The American Clock* in Williamstown,

CHRISTINA RADISH

The versatile and talented Ron Rifkin was best known for good-guy roles before he took on the part of the sinister Arvin Sloane.

Massachusetts, in 1994. It was at this point that fate took a hand in his career. Playwright Jon Robin Baitz was in the audience and was affected by Ron's performance: "[H]e told me afterwards that when I came out onstage, something happened to him. He didn't quite understand what it was but . . . he felt he was watching a man at the height of his power and he came up to me afterwards and said that he'd like to write a play for me someday. I laughed and said, 'Uh-huh, sure. Of course . . . whatever.'" Sure enough, the two men became friends and Baitz wrote *The Substance of Fire* with Rifkin in mind for the role of Isaac Geldhardt. *The Substance of Fire* is the story of Geldhardt, a troubled holocaust survivor whose life falls into decline after the death of his wife, causing his son to attempt to take over his publishing firm. Rifkin took on the lead role without question. His performance received great acclaim, garnering him an Obie Award, a Drama Desk Award, and the Lucille Lortel and Drama-Logue Awards for Best Actor. Following that, he continued performing in Baitz's plays, including *Three Hotels* and *A Fair Country*, with the former gaining him the Lucille Lortel Award and a Drama Desk Award nomination.

Rifkin hit his stride in the 1990s when he was cast as a psychiatrist in the Woody Allen film *Husbands and Wives* and then opposite both Diane Keaton and Allen in *Manhattan Murder Mystery*. He became an unofficial member of Woody Allen's stock company at that point. Then the opportunity to play Isaac Geldhardt came once more when *The Substance of Fire* was adapted for the big screen. "I don't think I could have done the film had I not done the play," says Rifkin. "I don't think I'm skilled enough to have played that character that way with such . . . well, I don't want to be self-congratulatory, but I don't think I could have given that performance had I not rehearsed it every night for two years. Don't forget, I never played that kind of part in a film before — I'd never been given that kind of role before. I'm an actor who really hasn't had those kinds of opportunities. In theater I have, and it's been great. But in film, never. In fact, the film wanted to get done without me. There were studios who . . . wanted [Baitz] to use big movie stars. Clearly I wasn't a movie star and it was a struggle and a challenge for [Baitz] and myself to work through that." Baitz insisted on Rifkin, however, and Miramax produced the film with Rifkin as Isaac Geldhardt, starring opposite Timothy Hutton, Tony Goldwyn, and Sarah Jessica Parker. He would later work with Timothy Hutton on his series *Nero Wolfe* and with Sarah Jessica Parker while guest-starring on *Sex and the City*.

His performance in *The Substance of Fire* led to a role in *L.A. Confidential* and a steady film career. Rifkin continued to balance film with theater, winning a Tony for his performance of Herr Schultz in the 1998 revival of *Cabaret*. Before *Alias* arrived on the scene, Ron acted in such films as *The Negotiator, Flowers for Algernon, Keeping the Faith*, and *The Majestic*. He continued to guest-star on television, appearing on shows such as *E.R.* and *Law & Order*. His guest-starring role on the sci-fi show *The Outer Limits* garnered him a Cable ACE nomination. And then, after years of failed television series, Rifkin hit gold with *Alias*.

J.J. Abrams was a fan of Ron's and almost had the opportunity to work with him in the movie *Six Degrees of Separation*, only Rifkin ended up backing out of the film. The opportunity to work together came again when Rifkin read the pilot script for *Alias*: "I thought the pilot was the best script I'd ever read for television. I said to J.J., 'You know, I really love Sloane, but maybe I should read for the father also.'" Victor Garber landed the role of Jack Bristow, however, and the two veteran stage actors have been kibitzing about it ever since. "Yeah, he's so jealous of me, it's sad," Garber jokes. Jennifer Garner was thrilled at the notion of working with Ron Rifkin, seeing as Ron was part of the cast of her first New York theatrical production (she was an understudy): "When Ron was cast as my boss, I just died."

Like the other members of the cast, Rifkin was attracted to the quality of writing in the script. Sloane's three-dimensional qualities also appealed: "[Sloane's] evilness is more ambiguous. There is still a lot of 'maybe' in my character." Still wearing a beard from his role in *The Substance of Fire*, Ron recommended that he keep it for the character of Sloane. "When we were doing the pilot I said to J.J. that I really wanted to go against the grain. You think of FBI or CIA people as being clean shaven and I'd like to have a bit of a beard. I also have a lot of input in terms of the way I dress on the show. Sloane's jacket is never open, his ties are always just so, the collars are very neat. Then when we see Sloane at home, I decided to wear glasses," Rifkin reveals. Considering Ron's fashion background, it makes sense that he'd be in touch with the wardrobe of his character. Don't expect any similarities between Rifkin and his character, however: "He's totally not like me. I'm a fall-apart person, very open. Everything Sloane says is carefully thought out."

One of the important things for Ron is making sure that Sloane did not turn into a two-dimensional character. As a consequence, he is constantly sharing his views with the writers. In one instance he noticed that the writers seemed to be leaning toward the idea of Sloane and Irina having an affair. He asked them to reconsider, as it was a direction that would certainly vilify Sloane further considering the medical condition of his wife. And as for his viewpoint on Sloane's obsession with the infamous Rambaldi, "Some people have trouble with the Rambaldi stuff," says Rifkin. "I have to say, [it's] because they can't quite follow it. *I* can't quite follow it and I'm playing it! Rambaldi is my primary reason for being, my raison d'être. It'd better make some sense sooner or later, don't you think?"

Ron lives in Los Angeles while filming the show but, like his co-star Victor Garber, makes his home in a Manhattan loft. Also like Garber, Rifkin's first home is on the stage. "I am a creature of the theater," Rifkin admits. "I am most comfortable onstage. More comfortable onstage than any place in the world, and that includes my own living room." On the film front, his most recent ventures have included *Dragonfly* with Kevin Costner and *Sum of all Fears* with Ben Affleck. Like many of his castmates, Rifkin also has quite the sense of humor, and is known for his wild socks as well — everything from fluffy black ones to ones with bumblebee stripes: "The real Ron Rifkin is more akin to these. I'm a nice guy, married for thirty-six years who has never killed anyone."

Lena Olin (*Alias: Irina Derevko*)

Tall, dark, mysterious, and sexy, the appearance of Irina Derevko on *Alias* was certainly a shocker for both the audience and the other characters. This is one woman you wouldn't want to cross. "I tend to get dangerous, dark roles," says actress Lena Olin, "but comedy is really much more me as a person. I'm a light, upbeat character." The sensual actress, known as the "thinking man's siren," was born on March 22, 1956, in Stockholm, Sweden. Lena Maria Jonna Olin is one of three children, and her parents, Stig and Britta, were both actors. Lena is no stranger to the public life; her parents hosted parties with such guests as actresses Liv Ullmann and Bibi Andersson, as well as famous director Ingmar Bergman. "I was used to having the stars of Sweden at our house," Olin says. "But I was more drawn to the traditional mothers who had coffee with each other. I was always pleading, 'Oh, Mommy — have coffee with the other mothers!'"

Olin claims she was an extremely shy child but had a violent temper, which came out while playing hockey. "I wasn't very big when I grew up, but I always took pride that no matter what, I can be tougher than anyone else. And I am fearless — I do not care — and so I can score the goal. . . . I was so ferocious that I was always a useful player to have on the team. It's a very useful tool for an actor to have that kind of anger, but I can control myself when I have to," she says. Lena was a stubborn tomboy who wore her hair short and stayed away from "girls'" clothing. Her mother encouraged her rebellion. Lena also hated the fact that she was the daughter of celebrities, and since she was afraid of the press, she initially decided to enroll in medical school. She caught the acting bug, however, and when she was 16, Ingmar Bergman encouraged her to go to school to get proper training.

Terrified at her audition, Olin failed at her first attempt to be accepted into the prestigious Royal Dramatic Theatre School in Stockholm, but succeeded the second time around. In 1976, Bergman gave her a small role in his film *Ansikte mot Ansikte* [*Face to Face*] and became her mentor. She began working with him extensively both onstage and on-screen. In between frequent theatrical productions, Olin had roles in the films *Picassos äventyr* [*The Adventures of Picasso*], *Kärleken* [*Love*], and *Gräsänklingar* [*One-Week Bachelors*]. Her next Bergman film was 1982's *Fanny and Alexander*. The role of Anna in Bergman's television movie *Efter repetitionen* [*After the Rehearsal*] was written especially for Lena, and was her international debut. It was the last Bergman film she would act in. "I think I was blessed. Bergman gave me such confidence in a business where confidence is ripped apart," she says.

It was Olin's performance as Cordelia in a Bergman production of *King Lear* at Stockholm's Royal Dramatic Theatre that caught the attention of Bertil Ohlsson, the executive producer for Philip Kaufman's film adaptation of *The Unbearable Lightness of Being*. "We were looking all around the world for someone who could play Sabina, but I knew I'd found her when I saw Lena Olin walking across a hotel lobby," Ohlsson remembers. "There was beauty and confidence in her walk; talking to her, you realized how smart she is, and how funny." Meanwhile, her 1986 pregnancy with her son, August, prevented her from continuing her work with Bergman on the August Strindberg stage production of *A Dream Play*, causing some friction in their relationship.

In 1988 Lena Olin burst onto the screen in *The Unbearable Lightness of Being* as the sexual Sabina, a free-spirited Czech bohemian famous for sporting a black bowler hat. It was this performance that landed her a role in *Enemies: A Love Story*, only Olin wasn't so thrilled. She had not expected *The Unbearable Lightness of Being* to be successful, nor was she ready to leave Stockholm for New York, as she had a fear of traveling and felt very shy and uncomfortable about the situation. And yet it was her role as the neurotic Holocaust survivor Masha that would garner her both the New York Film Critics Circle Award for Best Actress as well as an Academy Award nomination in 1989. Olin was still dealing with culture shock, however: "Acting is so much more serious in Sweden — remember, Bergman ditched Barbra Streisand [for a role in one of his films] because she was late for a meeting — so when I got here it was horrifying to see people even yawn on a movie set. Ron Silver yawned once, and I was shocked. It's seen as unprofessional and simply not done. If that would have happened with Bergman, that person would have been so kicked out."

Having seen her work, director Sydney Pollack went to work on rewrites for his film *Havana* that were tailored especially for Olin and made allusions to *Casablanca*, starring Swedish legend Ingrid Bergman. The 1990 film was not a success, however, and Lena's career shifted. She lost out to Melanie Griffith for *The Bonfire of the Vanities* and to

CHRISTINA RADISH

Swedish-born Lena Olin was encouraged to become an actress by none other than legendary director Ingmar Bergman.

Michelle Pfeiffer for *Batman Returns*. At that point, Olin made her New York theatrical debut in a Swedish-language production of *Miss Julie*, directed by none other than Ingmar Bergman.

Olin returned to the screen in 1993 in two films: *Mr. Jones* starring Richard Gere and *Romeo Is Bleeding* starring Gary Oldman. In the former, Olin played a therapist who falls in love with her patient. But you'll never catch Olin herself on the couch: "I don't believe in therapy. I think [the therapy trend] is a sign of our times: people want to be too polite, too nice. It's a sign of how much we've — what do you do to medical instruments? — sterilized our lives in order to be appropriate." In *Romeo Is Bleeding*, Olin took on what critics have called her most outrageous character, the Russian terrorist-assassin Mona. "I love that kind of character, because I have access to so much fury," says Olin. She continued to return to Europe to film overseas as well.

Divorced from her first husband, Olin connected with Oscar-nominated director Lasse Hallström. Olin was still in drama school in Sweden when Hallström was making a reputation for himself as a director. Over the years he watched Lena in productions at the Royal Dramatic Theatre as well as on film. Lasse would check in with Olin's manager on occasion, until finally he called up Olin personally. "It was so unlike Lasse to call up a girl and ask her to dinner," Olin claims. "He seems far too shy. And it was so unlike me to go. At that time, I was utterly possessed by work — and by my baby. I feel in a way I was saved by Lasse." The two were married in 1994, and their daughter, Tora, was born in 1995. The decision to move to the U.S. came when Olin's eight-year-old son, August, declared he was tired of being tutored in hotel rooms. They decided to stay away from Los Angeles and instead moved to Westchester, New York, into a historical home. Lena has mixed feelings about the move: "You realize, *My grandchildren probably won't even speak Swedish*. And it makes me sad but also excited, because I feel I've done something historical, in a way. I've moved a family. I've emigrated."

For the first couple of years after the move, Lena and Lasse took time off and spent it together. "Our friends would moan, 'You two are never apart!' And we'd say, 'Yeah, that's why we got married! To be with each other!'" Lena remembers. Olin returned to the screen in such films as

Night Falls on Manhattan, Polish Wedding, Hamilton, The Ninth Gate, and *Chocolat* directed by Hallström. Initially, Lena wasn't meant to be in the film. "We had a project that we really wanted to do that fell apart five days before we started shooting," she says. "So I was still very upset about that. And then we had to move on, and Lasse was going to do *Chocolat* and Miramax called and said, 'We think Lena should play Josephine.' And I read the script and I just loved the character, but I didn't see it as one of the characters I would naturally be cast for."

Olin followed up *Chocolat* by taking a role in *Ignition* and playing the vampire Maharet in *Queen of the Damned*. Then Olin was approached by J.J. Abrams about taking on the role of Irina Derevko: "I remember the first time I met with J.J., I was like, 'TV? I don't know.' And the way he started describing all the elements of Irina's character, he was very passionate." Finding Abrams's description very appealing, she began watching the show. Lena agreed to take on the role, temporarily leaving New York for Los Angeles. The immediacy of television — the short time between filming and air date — appealed to Olin. That and the character relationships underneath the action. It was a major coup for the *Alias* team. "[In] *Romeo Is Bleeding* she really demonstrated a strength, a brutality, a darkness, a mystery that felt so much like [Irina]. We needed someone who could be compassionate and loving despite an inherent malicious sense — someone who had the soft side but who was intimidating as hell," said Abrams.

Olin fit right in with the cast, and the audience loved her. "The cast and crew have a collective crush on Lena. It makes us all sit up straighter," said Jennifer Garner. Lena even resembled Garner right down to the fact that both women have large hands. The physical nature of the part appealed to her as well: "In fact, I love that part of acting. If I'm running on the show, I'm, like, 'OK, let's go,' and I want to be the first one out there. [Victor] Garber is always ten miles behind me." Olin's work on *Alias* garnered her an Emmy nomination along with Victor Garber and Jennifer Garner. Suddenly, Lena Olin was becoming a household name: "I've been acting for years in movies, and I'm getting attention from studio executives who never heard of me before the show. It's strange to me. Everybody watches TV."

When season 2 ended, rumors suggesting Olin would not be returning to the show started to circulate. There were other projects the actress wanted to pursue, and her family's home base in New York was a problem as well. Furthermore, Olin had to consider the consequences of TV exposure. "I don't want to become a commodity. I'm sure that's something Bergman would not approve of," she said. Whether or not Lena will rejoin the cast of *Alias* is still unknown. The fans have put together a campaign called Bring Back Lena (www.bringbacklena.com) and raised funds to create an ad for the *Hollywood Reporter*, with the excess money being donated to the charity of Lena's choice.

While out in Los Angeles, Lena filmed the Harrison Ford feature *Hollywood Homicide* and *The United States of Leland*. The production of her latest film, *The Swedish Job*, was cancelled. She enjoys music ("I consume music the way other people consume movies") and is a dedicated mother, choosing to stay away from roles on the stage or screen that take her away from her family. She still keeps in touch with Ingmar Bergman and keeps her Swedish roots alive by speaking her native tongue at home with her family. She calls herself an "unsocial" person, choosing to stay away from the whole concept of "stardom": "In my universe, the kids are the most important thing in my life, but I also think that it's healthy for them to see me working. Actually, it's more of a problem for my manager and my agents. They'll be, like, 'Well, you're meeting so-and-so in London next week,' and I'll tell them I can't because it's my daughter's ballet recital. I can hear them practically twisting their heads off, but that's just the way it is."

David Anders *(Alias: Julian Sark)*

David Anders Holt, known to us as Mr. Sark, is the youngest member of the *Alias* cast. Born on March 11, 1981, in Grants Pass, Oregon, to Dr. Tony and Jeri Holt, David is the youngest of four children. He has two brothers, Jason and Arik, and a sister named Maili. Like his co-stars, Anders was a performer from the get-go. "I think he's been a ham since he started walking," says his father, Tony. Still, David didn't find his way to the stage until he was a junior in high school.

A fan of music, David played both piano and drums, the latter being the instrument he played in his middle-school band. At age 17, a junior in high school, David was cast in the small role of Philip the Apostle in a regional production of *Jesus Christ Superstar* staged by Rogue Music Theatre. At Grants Pass High School, David was quite active in athletics, specifically basketball, tennis, and football. He did not pursue theater at high school until his senior year, when he was cast as George in a production of Thornton Wilder's *Our Town*. He also signed up for an experimental productions class. While his initial thought was to pursue small-college football, his priorities changed: "I was more happy onstage at that point than I was practicing three times a day. That was a choice that I made, and I was very strong about it. My mom supported me, and my dad was, 'Uh. . . .' It was a leap of faith." David was cast in another Rogue Music Theatre production, this time in the role of Freddy Eynsford-Hill in *My Fair Lady*. His performance was well received and prompted his next step — to pursue acting as a career.

When he graduated from high school, David had some choices to make. It was 1999, and the 19-year-old had the option of either attending the American Academy of Dramatic Arts in Pasadena, California, or simply jumping into the pond straightaway and seeing if he could land any roles. "I did a couple of monologues for a friend of the family and he said, 'Don't waste your time with that! Just come down here and get an agent.' I got offers from a couple of agencies so I figured, 'Why not?'" David took the plunge and made his way to Hollywood. Nervous as they were, his parents supported his decision, wanting their son to follow his dreams.

When David arrived in Los Angeles, he realized that he wasn't in Oregon anymore — it took some time to deal with the culture shock. Two weeks after he arrived, after performing in a talent showcase, three different agencies were interested in the young actor. Two were respected ones at that. David ended up choosing the largest of the three agencies, but alas, things did not go as well as he would have liked. "A lot of people think I'm so much older," he explains. "That was the bane of my existence when I moved to L.A. I always read old. I came here and I couldn't even get high school parts." He ended up switching agencies soon after.

CHRISTINA RADISH

David Anders was only 20 years old when he first appeared on *Alias* as the evil Mr. Sark.

He changed his last name from "Holt" to "Anders" when he discovered another actor was using the name "David Holt." For a year, David relied on his parents for support and worked in retail and teaching tennis to make ends meet. He was also a stunt performer/double in a few films. He took the time to get some private coaching, study with The Second City improv group, and take voice lessons as well. Still lacking a Screen Actors Guild card, David kept himself busy with auditions until he finally landed a small role in the independent film *The Source* and joined the theater group the West Coast Ensemble. With the latter, David performed in *The Diary of Anne Frank*, which received an award for Best Ensemble Performance at the Backstage West Garland Awards. More recently, he played the title role in the premiere performance of *Rockne: The Musical*. The show debuted in South Bend, Indiana, where Knute Rockne made a name for himself coaching the University of Notre Dame football team.

David's first television role was guest-starring as a high school student on the Mary Kate and Ashley Olsen series *So Little Time* on the Fox Family channel. He still wasn't getting many opportunities, however, so he found himself switching agencies once more. He moved to Silver, Masetti and Szatmary, and within two months of the move landed a great opportunity: *Alias*. "I became the quickest client to get a job," Anders reveals.

The role of Mr. Sark was initially a guest-starring role for one or two episodes. Not only that, but the character was meant to be both older and German. "We were trying to cast the role," J.J. Abrams remembers. "This kid, David Anders, came in who was twenty years old. He did an impeccable German accent. He was fantastic, but we decided he shouldn't be German, because there was another German storyline going on. We thought, 'We'll make him English,' and this twenty-year-old kid from Oregon did an impeccable English accent. He was so young, but we thought, 'Screw it. Let's say he's actually working for this big boss and have the characters comment on how young he is.' As we started to shoot it, this guy who was supposed to be in one episode was so compelling we thought, 'Let's bring Sark back again.' So we brought Sark back a few more times and then we were like, 'This guy is brilliant. Let's make him a regular.' We just fell in love with him."

Anders, however, did not believe he had made a good impression on the producers: "I thought I totally bombed the audition and then I found out I got the part from one of the wardrobe girls. She called me and said, 'Uh, David, I need your sizes for tomorrow.'" The question of Mr. Sark's ethnicity was still up in the air as well. The character was written to be from Eastern Europe, so Anders came in with a Russian accent, only the producers wanted something from Continental Europe. "I came in with a pseudo-German-British hybrid that got me the part. Then on my first day of work the script says, 'He speaks with a British accent.' Why didn't you tell me that from the get-go?" Mr. Sark debuted on February 24, 2002, as a mysterious young British villain with no first name. Anders's expectation to eventually get killed off was never met, and in 2003, David became a series regular two and a half years after graduating from high school.

Once Anders landed the role, his parents got on the promotional bandwagon within their area. His brother, Jason, set up David's official Web site in order for local fans to keep up with David's endeavors. His fan base is international, however, stretching from England to Australia thanks, in part, to his excellent accent — and he's never even been to England. "The dialect has been really challenging for me. It's not something that I started from scratch, but it is something that I want to do appropriately," he says. He had never fired anything other than a BB gun either, and yet he manages to look convincing while handling weapons for the camera.

Still teased for being the "baby" of the show, Anders also had to deal with the fact that his character had no first name. Victor Garber christened him "Steve Sark." When Anders asked J.J. Abrams about it, however, he was denied until he was recently given the name "Julian" (for which he gave his seal of approval). But who needs a first name when they've gone from being a guest star to a series regular? David's also become more recognizable on the street. One night, out with his parents for dinner, he was approached by the waiter, who asked if he was on a television show: "My mom's like, 'Oh, jeez' and clapping. I'm like, 'Yeah.' He's like, 'You're one of the best bad guys on TV.' That was great for my parents to see that, for the first time."

The character of Sark is slowly growing more unpredictable, not unlike the infamous Arvin Sloane. "I was just noticing today in the script, that the evil now, at least my evil, is beginning to have a background somewhat. What my character does is bad and awful on a lot of occasions, but to him, it may be something different. To him, it's a means to something bigger. It's obvious that he's not a mindless killer. There's something underlying it," Anders says. There is, of course, still much speculation as to what Mr. Sark's relationship is with Sydney Bristow. Early on, David's father suggested that Sark and Sydney were half-brother and -sister, which is a common hypothesis. "It would be very Luke and Leia, wouldn't it?" asks David.

In between episodes, David enjoys driving around in his Jeep Cherokee as well as checking out the local clubs to hear rock and roll bands. He'd love to be a rock star. Following in his co-star Garber's footsteps, Anders also auditioned for a now-canceled production of *Fiddler on the Roof*. He's interested in working on Broadway as well. In the summer, during his spare time, he teaches tennis to children in L.A. He is also an avid golfer, and participates frequently in celebrity Pro-Am charity events across the U.S. He continues to audition, but it's been a challenge: "It's funny — people always wait for the accent. A lot of casting directors think I'm British and twenty-eight, so that kind of hurts when I'm looking for movies." David hasn't given up the idea of attending college, but if he does, it would be to get a degree in something other than theater, thus broadening his horizons. His ultimate goal, however, is to keep acting: "I just want to keep working. Whether it be on TV, film, or stage, I just want to constantly be working. I would just love to be in film, ultimately, but I really have no control over that. I would be happy just being a working actor, someone who is not even recognized or anything. Someone who you know their face, but may not know their name, you know what I mean? I am fine being anonymous really, but that too is out of my hands."

THE NEW ELEMENT

Melissa George *(Alias: Lauren Reed)*

As the "other woman" on *Alias*, Melissa's presence has created quite a stir. And her personal background is as colorful as her character. An example: Her great-great-great-grandfather was sent to the penal colony of Australia for stealing underwear from nurses' washing lines. Born on August 6, 1976, in Perth, Australia, Melissa Suzanne George is the second eldest of Pam and Glenn George's four children. She has two sisters, Marnie (the oldest) and Kate, and a younger brother, Brett. Melissa was a straight-A student living in the suburban neighborhood of Hammersley with a loving family, Holly Hobby wallpaper, and the ambition to be a veterinarian.

At the age of seven, Melissa delved into the world of roller skating, competing at both the national and international levels, representing Australia on more than one occasion: "I won the Junior World Championships when I was fourteen or fifteen. I was very, very good. It's a really disciplined sport. You get one two-minute routine as an opportunity to do everything you've ever trained for." She also studied modern dance, tap, jazz, and classical ballet. At the same time, George ventured into the world of modeling, which interrupted much of her life at Warwick High School. About her "look" Melissa says, "[I]n my family we're all very blond but our brows are quite dark. My aunties are the same, and it's actually quite unusual, and you know, it's my trademark!" Melissa ended up winning Western Australia's Teenage Model of the Year in the early 1990s. It was then that fate took a hand in Melissa's career.

It was 1993, and the popular Australian prime-time soap opera *Home and Away* was on a nationwide search for a young actress to take on the role of street kid Angel Brooks. Melissa was scheduled to go to New Zealand for a couple of weeks with her dance troupe when a script arrived at her house for *Home and Away*. "I'd watched it every night religiously since it started," says Melissa. "I studied hard for the audition and rocked up thinking there were only four other girls going for it. Yeah, right! There were queues all the way down Hay Street in the center of Perth. Two weeks later they phoned me at home and I was invited to a second audition in Sydney. On Christmas Eve, back in Perth, they called me again and I'd got it." George was ecstatic.

It was the opportunity of a lifetime, especially considering young Melissa had no acting experience. The only problem was that the show filmed in Sydney — over 2,000 miles away. It meant that George not only had to move away from her family, but had to give up school and her skating as well. Casting agent Liz Mullinar came to her home to reassure George's parents that their daughter would be in good hands. Together with Mullinar, Melissa moved to Sydney on January 18, 1993, to a whole new life. "I was the youngest one to be brought from another state to join the show and Liz had said, 'Listen, come and stay with me for three weeks and we'll find you a place.' I ended up living there for three and a half years," recalls George. Mullinar became a surrogate parent, making sure to look out for George when the teenager was being worked too hard. "I hardly knew anything when I first arrived," Melissa says. "I had to learn how to act as I went along. After about a year I got a grip on what acting was all about and it started coming straight from my heart; I wasn't just saying the words any longer."

George was a hit as the street kid with a heart of gold, and Angel became one of the most popular characters on the soap. Melissa was an instant celebrity, and in 1994 she was awarded with the Silver Logie (Australian Emmy) for Most Popular New Talent and won the People's Choice Award for Best Actress. While Melissa's life was going well, her character continued on a roller coaster. Angel was taken in off the streets by the local headmaster and began dating his son, Shane, only to have it revealed that she had had a baby at age 15. The two became an infamous couple on *Home and Away*, but things between Melissa and her co-star Dieter Brummer (as character Shane Parrish) were rocky off-screen. "We were never friends, really, which is a real shame because we started out as really good friends, and then one started to do better than the other," she says. "There was a lot of pressure on the producers to make the relationship work between Shane and Angel, and I was the one who was always told to keep it together." Aside from the fractured relationship with her co-star, Melissa had a phenomenal time working on the show. In 1995 she won the Silver Logie for Most

CHRISTINA RADISH

Melissa George has had the most daunting task of any actor on *Alias* — being the one to step between Sydney and Vaughn.

Popular Actress and was voted Best Actress of the Year at the ITV British Television Awards.

After three years of emotionally charged work on *Home and Away*, George made the decision to leave the soap and pursue other projects. Her character's final appearance was on the show's 2,000th episode. Following her exit, Melissa delved into a few projects, including making a lifestyle video called *Mind, Body and Soul* and starting up a nightwear label called "An Angel at My Bedside." "I've diversified my talents, because I'm not going to depend on one thing," she said. "I want several options to work on, so that if something doesn't work out, I can turn my attentions to another project." Melissa was also offered the chance to follow in Kylie Minogue's footsteps and become a pop singer, but she declined, preferring to act instead. She also began exploring her passion for all things Art Deco, an interest that was sparked thanks to her grandmother.

Her next acting gig was again for television, for the *Twilight Zone*–style TV movie *Fable*, playing the title character's daughter. Following that came a small role in the Gothic feature film *Dark City* starring Kiefer Sutherland and Rufus Sewell. "To get these gigs is a dream come true," George said of the experience. She continued with a stint as a gun-slinging gal in *Tales of the South Seas* and performed on the mystery show *Murder Call*. While the opportunity to guest-star in *Roar*, the action-adventure series set in 400 AD, with fellow Aussie Heath Ledger was helpful for her career, even more helpful was meeting producer Shaun Cassidy. The producer offered the actress a role in the U.S. television pilot *Hollyweird* directed by Wes Craven: "[Shaun Cassidy] said, 'Would you like to read my latest script? I think you'd be perfect for it.' The next day I put a scene from it on tape and sent it over. They rang back and said Wes Craven and everyone had loved it and they wanted me to fly over to audition more. I just said, 'This can't be happening!'" George was on her way to Los Angeles to embark on a new phase of her career.

After the pilot was filmed, however, there were problems. The studios wanted reshoots, and there was a wait to see if the series would get picked up. So George took off for a holiday in Bali. While there with her friend Rebecca Hamilton, George met the love of her life: Chilean businessman and Bali resident Claudio Dabed. While the furniture importer/exporter was ten years older and had a three-year-old daughter, Martina, it didn't put a damper on their obvious connection. "It was such a powerful experience," says George. "We spent every day together and it was so lovely. We're madly in love."

George made the decision to move to Los Angeles, though leaving her home and family was a bittersweet experience. And then came the news that *Hollyweird* had been shelved. She decided to stick it out in L.A., however, and landed a role in the Steven Soderbergh film *The Limey* as Terence Stamp's daughter. "[Soderbergh] saw me doing my screen test. I couldn't get a visa because I wasn't a permanent resident at that time. He paid for my visa, made sure I got in the movie, and then proceeded to take us all out for dinner," she remembers. In between auditions, George continued to travel from L.A. to Bali, where she and Claudio began building their own house.

At 22, Melissa had auditioned for 20 different pilots. She finally landed a plum role in another pilot series, *L.A. Confidential.* Based on the successful film, Melissa would be taking over Kim Basinger's role. Unfortunately, the series was deemed too expensive to make by HBO, and was dropped. In 2000, George had a few pleasant experiences, the first of which was landing the role of Cleo in the cheerleader cops-and-robbers film *Sugar and Spice.* While her character was obsessed with Conan O'Brien, George didn't know who he was for some time, and was afraid to even ask! She also had a role in the John Hughes–produced dark drama *New Port South.* And in October of that year she wed Claudio in a ceremony in Bali, with her uncle, Ron, performing the service.

Also in 2000, Melissa was thrilled to land a role in the new David Lynch series *Mulholland Drive* as a 1950s-style Peggy Lee singer. Lynch cast her right after seeing her photograph. When the series was soon dropped by the networks, Lynch turned it into a film. He asked George to be a part of the project: "I was on my honeymoon in Bali and he e-mailed me that they'd make the series into a movie. 'Dear Melissa, This is your friend David. I'm wondering if you can come back to Los Angeles. I need you to shoot one scene to make this into a movie and tie your character in.' I fly back to David Lynch; I come on set — he didn't even think I'd show up, his eyes almost filled up with tears. . . . All I had to do was kiss [Laura Harring], and I flew, like twenty-three hours from Bali. You never turn down David Lynch."

Melissa's bad luck with pilots soon shifted when she took on the role of professional thief Rita in *Thieves*, co-starring John Stamos. "Melissa came in, and she was kind of the only girl who put me in my place. She gave me a run for my money," said Stamos. The show came out the same year as *Alias*, and while it was well received, it was canceled after 10 episodes. George kept plugging away. She was briefly cast in the series *Coupling* but recast because she looked too young. She garnered a role in the feature film *Down With Love* and guest stints as the lesbian babysitter on *Friends*, a scheming actress on *Monk*, and the Queen of the Valkyries on *Charmed*. All the while she was wishing that she could be on *Alias*.

Then she had the chance to audition: "I left the room thinking, *If I don't get this job, I'm going back home [to Australia]*. It felt so right. I'd turned up with the whole of Hollywood. [The producers] heard I had Wednesday off the following week, so suddenly the second test date was moved to Wednesday. I thought, *That's odd . . .* I thought, *Maybe this was a good sign*. I was the first one in to read. It just went so great that apparently when I left the room, J.J. said I had the job straightaway. He didn't call me for two days!" It was while she was filming the two-hour episode of *Charmed* that she was offered the role on *Alias*. "I was in my warrior outfit talking to J.J., saying, 'Really? I got the job? You have no idea what I look like right now.'" Melissa landed the coveted role of Lauren Reed, a National Security Agency agent who happens to be Mrs. Michael Vaughn. She was rushed out the next day to the cast photo shoots, and the rest is history. "Melissa George has a cool intelligence and a sexy confidence," says Abrams. "Though she's this beautiful and whip-smart woman, she's also able to project real vulnerability. She's complex, something this role requires." J.J. has even joked about having a mission on roller skates just to take advantage of George's skill!

George has managed to fit in with the rest of the cast without issue — she's even up to speed with the physical aspects of the work, thanks to her martial arts lessons for *Thieves* — though some audience members have difficulty with her role in Vaughn's life. Her thoughts on the issue? "Watch my character with an open mind. Don't come to any judgments too soon. I love that people are thinking that Sydney and Vaughn have to get back together, but don't make your decision about whether you hate or love Lauren too soon!"

George continues to spend her time moving from her five-level Los Angeles home in Playa del Ray on the beach to her homes in Bali and Chile. Recently Melissa's husband has begun producing a movie in which she will be making a cameo as well as helping out with the production elements. She loves cooking, watching movies with her husband, and spending time with her step-daughter. They have a dog, Cindy, and will be extending their family in the future. In the meantime, she'll keep us guessing on *Alias* while she keeps learning: "Working with those actors is the biggest reason I'm still in shock that I'm on the show, because you're looking at them, going, 'Wow. The way he just delivered that line is so fantastic.' [To work with such skilled] actors is the greatest teaching of all; you know you're only going to get better."

Internet Echelon
(*Alias* Web Sites)

Web sites are constantly changing, which makes this section a challenging one, but as it stands right now at this very moment (03.23.04, 20:15:47 EST), these are the sites that have impressed us, amused us, enlightened us, or provided us with very important intel. So, without further ado, here we go. Prepare for information download.

Top 5 General *Alias* Sites

While there are many sites out there worth noting (check out the honorable mentions section), these are the ones that stood out (in no particular order). There are also some excellent international sites worth checking out.

Alias: The TV Show
www.alias-tv.com

Classic, clean, and red, this site is comprehensive and chock-full of *Alias* info. It gives a complete and comprehensible breakdown of Rambaldi, goes through all of Marshall's gadgets from seasons 1 and 2. . . . We could go on, but we'll let you check it out for yourself.

Alias Media
alias-media.com

Also full of information, this site even has its own calendar, which lists important dates for new episodes, cast birthdays, and *Alias*-related media events — all of which you can click on for more details.

Dear Sally — Alias
www.dearsally.org/alias

Originally dedicated to *Felicity* (thus the "Dear Sally" reference), this site has now expanded to include *Alias* as well. Elegant and informative, it's a must for fans of either show.

Project Alias
www.projectalias.com

While the look of the site changes from time to time, the coolness does not. The graphics are unique to each page thanks to the *Alias* Challenge, which encourages fans to explore their artistic abilities and create banners for the site.

Alias Revolution
alias.metal-idol.net/index.php

This site is just full of fun. Be sure to check out the "How *Alias* Is Like *Star Wars*" and "Alias Arcade" sections. And don't miss the Project Christmas test.

Honorable Mentions
Mission Possible
jenah.net/mp/

We love the "Theories" section on this site, which is generally very full of information. While it's not the easiest to read, and a bit obscure to enter, it's still worth visiting.

The Secret Life of Alias
www.secretlifeofalias.com

A very stylish site. It offers "game walkthroughs" if you're having a challenging time with the video game.

Alias.Fannesite
www.neloo.com/alias/

The "Games" and "Lessons Learned" sections make this a great site.

A Free Agent
swooh.com/peon/alias/

If you have sound, be prepared: when you enter this site, you're in for a brief surprise.

The Two Evil Monks Guide — Alias
www.twoevilmonks.org/alias/aliasintro.htm

This site has a sophisticated feel to it, with lots of pics from the show. Our only complaint is that the information is pretty basic.

The Alias Addiction
www.torn-world.org/alias/

A general *Alias* site that also lists television appearances made by the cast.

Decipher
www.vegasbrite.org/decipher/decipher.htm

This site is very useful for revisiting *Alias* lingo. Want to know who the FTL are? Forget what role the DSR played? Click the "Deciphering" option and all the answers will be revealed.

Alias: Sydney
www.angelfire.com/freak/aliassydney/index.html

The pop-ups are a bit frequent, but the layout is good and it has a nice selection of wallpapers and fan fiction.

SD-6.com: Alias Info
www.sd-6.com

This general info site allows users to log into a discussion forum. It also has a link to the supercool SD-5.com: *Alias* Dossier.

Warrior Destiny Alias
www.fan-sites.org/warrior-destiny/alias/

There's no glitz or glamour with this site, but it does the job.

Alias Insider
www.aliasinsider.com/index.asp

A good general site.

Two Guys, a Girl, & Alias
alias.crankymonsters.com

Watch Marshall's proposal song over and over and over . . .

Search Engines
Alias: Sometimes the Truth Hurts
www.have-dog.com/alias/sources.html

An excellent search site that links to so many *Alias* options.

www.topsitelists.com/start/alias/topsites.html

This is another spot to check out if you're looking for *Alias* sites.

Marshall's Miscellaneous Mix
Alias: The Lost Episode
www.newbornpix.com/alias.htm

OK, fans of the show who have Quicktime capabilities *must* see this video. A spoof on the show, it's even been praised by Mr. Alias himself, J.J. Abrams.

Alias School
www.sd-12.com/

Yes, this site is exactly what you think. Perhaps even cooler.

SD-5.com: Alias Dossier
www.sd-5.com

The *Alias* Dossier (which allows you to plug in a term to find the appropriate definition) is a must if you're finding yourself swamped by the terminology used on the show.

We Want Will
www.wewantwill.com

Do you miss Will Tippin? These are the people trying to get him back on the show.

Central Intelligence Agency (Official Site)
www.cia.gov/index.html

A very cool site to check out, even if you aren't interested in joining the CIA.

Cast Sites
While there are many sites out there dedicated to the cast of *Alias*, these ones stand out.

Jennifer Garner
Jennifer Garner Fan
jennifergarner.fancube.com

This is our favorite of the sites dedicated to Jen.

Jen-Garner.net
jen-garner.net

Another excellent site.

Syd-Jen.net
www.syd-jen.net

The print is a bit small, but this is still a great site. And hey, it's red.

JenniferFan.com
www.jenniferfan.com

A general Jen site.

Perfect
www.efanguide.com/~jgarner/

Not bad. The site has a nice gallery but not a lot of info.

Michael Vartan
The Safe House
www.vartanho.com

While this is undoubtedly the best Michael Vartan site out there, it is also an excellent general *Alias* site, with probably the best news archive we've seen.

Boy Scout
web-glitter.com/boyscout/

This is the official Fanlisting site for Michael Vartan.

Michael Vartan
1000-miles.org/vartan/

Includes video clips of the actor.

Bradley Cooper
Bradley-Cooper[dot]com
bradley-cooper.com/main.html

An all-round site dedicated solely to Bradley.

Greg Grunberg
Weiss Italian Source
win.mirtilla.com/weiss/eng/

A little tough to read due to color choice, but definitely a site to see.

Greg Grunberg: A Fan Site

www.cybamall.com/greggrunberg/

Another cool site, and it has a forum dedicated to chatting about Greg.

David Anders

Official Web Site of David Anders

www.davidanders.com

David's official site is the place to go for info on the sexy villain.

The David Anders Fanlisting

fan.metal-idol.net/david/

A Fanlisting site for David Anders. A fanlisting is a place where several fans of one subject can come together and build the most complete listing possible of the people around the world who are also fans of that subject.

S A R K G A S M

www.sarkgasm.com

A fan site that includes everything you ever wanted to know about Sark, including theories, fan fiction, and more.

Kevin Weisman

Kevin Weisman — The Official Web Site

www.kevinweisman.com

Definitely cool.

Trainwreck

www.twreck.tk

The official site of Kevin's band, this site offers samples of their rockabilly music.

Lena Olin
Lena Online
www.lena-olin.com

Classy and informative.

Lena Olin
lenaolin.net

Yes, there is such a thing as a Lena-o-Meter.

Melissa George
Melissa George — The Authorized Web Site
www.melissageorge.com

A hugely informative site with articles dating back to Melissa's *Home and Away* years and exclusive interviews with the actress.

Merrin Dungey
Merrin Dungey Online
merrindungey.bravepages.com/main.htm

Very informative and very . . . pink.

Merrin Dungey Online
www.fanscape.net/merrin/

A Fanlisting site.

Victor Garber
Victor Garber Archive
vg.bozx.com

Fabulous for info on Garber as well as for pics.

Just Another Victor Garber Site
my.execpc.com/~jdungan/garber/index.html

Another good site dedicated to the actor.

J.J. Abrams Fanlisting
www.allalias.com/jj/main.php

Michael Giacchino
www.michaelgiacchino.com

Want to find out more about the man behind the *Alias* music or hear some clips? Enter here . . .

Forums
Alias Boards
www.aliasboards.com

This forum site even includes exclusive interviews with the cast. Truly worth joining.

Alias TV Show
allalias.com

Addicted to Alias
www.fanbb.com/addictedtoalias/index.php

Alias Graphics
www.s3.invisionfree.com/alias_graphics

So, You Want to Join the CIA (CIA Trivia)

Our Vision: To be the keystone of a U.S. Intelligence Community that is pre-eminent in the world, known for both the high quality of our work and the excellence of our people.

You've decided that serving your country is the way to go, and what better way to do that than to join the famed Central Intelligence Agency? Only it's not as easy as you'd think. There are so many options to explore, and so many requirements to fulfill. Below is a quiz to see just how well you know the CIA, and whether or not you would make good CIA material. No cheating; remember, you are being watched. Write down your responses for each section before checking the back of the book for the answers. Let's start off with some easy questions. Score a point for each that you answer correctly. No tooth extraction is required.

CIA History: True or False (10 points)
1. The CIA was originally just one man, a New York attorney.
2. The CIA was created in June 1942.
3. The origin of the CIA is the Office of Strategic Services.
4. President Truman went against the advice of the FBI, the State Department, and the military in order to create the Central Intelligence Group (CIG).
5. The difference between the CIG and the OSS was the fact that the CIG had access to all-source intelligence.
6. The first director of central intelligence was named Sidney.

7. The National Security Council was born at the same time as the CIA.
8. The CIA was forbidden to engage in law enforcement activities.
9. There is such a thing as the 1949 Central Intelligence Agency Act, which exempted the CIA from many of the financial limitations imposed on the dispensation of federal funds.
10. There has never been a U.S. President who has acted as the director of the CIA.

CIA Statues and Memorials (8 points)

1. The Route 123 Memorial
   a) was created to commemorate two CIA agents shot by a terrorist in 1993 while waiting to enter the agency's gate.
   b) is located by the main CIA entrance and was designed by two CIA employees.
   c) is dedicated to Lansing Bennett and Frank Darling and consists of two benches, a bluestone walkway, and a granite wall.
   d) All of the above.
   e) Only a and c.

2. The CIA Memorial Wall has
   a) 90 stars, all for the anonymous members who have died in action.
   b) 80 stars, all for the anonymous members who have died in action.
   c) 90 stars; not all are for anonymous deaths.
   d) 80 stars; not all are for anonymous deaths.

3. The Book of Honor
   a) lists only the 46 members whose names could be revealed in death.
   b) lists all the members who have died, placing gold stars where names could not be revealed.
   c) is in a book bound in Canadian leather.

d) has the CIA seal on the front in solid gold.

4. The OSS Memorial
    a) is directly opposite the CIA Memorial Wall.
    b) has only one star on its wall and includes a statue of Maj. Gen. William J. Donovan, who is considered the "Father of Modern American Intelligence Gathering."
    c) also has a book listing 116 individuals who died in World War II.
    d) All of the above.

5. The Berlin Wall Monument
    a) consists of three graffiti-ridden pieces of the original Berlin wall.
    b) is located near the Agency's northwest entrance.
    c) points from east to west to indicate West Germany and East Germany.
    d) is void of any plaque in order to reinforce the stark image.

6. The official CIA seal
    a) is made of marble.
    b) measures 18 feet in diameter.
    c) consists of an eagle, the shield, and a 16-point compass star.
    d) became the symbol of the CIA in 1949.

7. The Nathan Hale Statue
    a) commemorates the first agent to die in the line of duty.
    b) commemorates the first American to be executed for spying on behalf of the U.S.
    c) commemorates the designer of the original CIA headquarters.
    d) None of the above.

8. The "Kryptos" Sculpture
    a) is dedicated to the technological teams who have worked for the CIA.
    b) consists of steel, marble, and glass.

c) was created with the help of a CIA cryptographer and a fiction writer.

d) has an "s"-shaped screen designed to look like paper with over 5,000 letters cut into it.

CIA Employment: True or False (15 points)

1. You do not have to be a U.S. citizen to work for the CIA.
2. All potential employees must undergo a medical exam; a polygraph (lie detector) test; a psychological exam; and a thorough background check that evaluates behavior and character, reliability, and judgment skills.
3. You must be able to speak a second language to be eligible for consideration by the CIA.
4. Undergraduate students who are interested in interning with the CIA's Undergrad Scholarship Program must have a minimum 3.5 GPA.
5. If a student is taken into the internship program, they must agree to join the Agency for one and a half times the length of their sponsorship time in college.
6. The main areas of employment in the CIA consist of science, engineering, and technical; clandestine service; analytical careers; language-oriented careers; and professional services.
7. One of the most common reasons for being denied security clearance is psychological weaknesses.
8. If you are attending university and wish to attend the CIA training program, there is a required course list that includes psychology, chemistry, and political science.
9. If you are a U.S. citizen living overseas and wish to apply to the CIA, your résumé will not be accepted and your phone calls will be ignored along with your e-mails.
10. Having an undergraduate degree is mandatory for joining the CIA.
11. Most students who intern with the CIA are recruited independently.
12. If you are part of the military, you cannot transfer to the CIA in order to complete your term.

13. CIA employees can receive monetary awards for learning a foreign language and maintaining it.
14. FAB stands for "Frequent Agency Benefits."
15. The present director of the CIA was part of Bill Clinton's national security transition team.

Spies in the Movies (11 points)

1. What three female leads on *The Avengers* also appeared in James Bond films?
2. In the short-lived television series *A Man Called Sloane*, Sloane was assisted by a man named Torque. What was Torque's unique ability?
3. In *Austin Powers in Goldmember*, Nigel Powers says there are two types of people he can't stand, one of which is those who cannot tolerate other people's cultures. What is the other type?
4. Name the three actors who have played the villains in the *Spy Kids* films.
5. What is the name of villain Blofeld's cat in the James Bond films?
6. In the 1985 film *Spies Like Us*, Dan Aykroyd and Chevy Chase play two men who cheat on the CIA admissions test and are caught. The CIA recruits them anyway. Why?
7. What 1965 thriller starred Michael Caine as a spy investigating a bunch of scientists who have been brainwashed?
8. On the British spy drama *MI-5* (known as *Spooks* in the U.K.), what is Tom Quinn's undercover name at the beginning of the series?
9. In the film *True Lies*, Jamie Lee Curtis's character learns that her husband, played by Arnold Schwarzenegger, is actually a secret agent. What actress plays their daughter?
10. In the film *Harriet the Spy*, what do Harriet's friends find that could uncover her secret life? (Score a bonus point if you can name the *Buffy the Vampire Slayer* actress who played Harriet.)

Alias Episode Guide

The following guide contains spoilers for each episode (that is, the entries give away some important plot details), so if you prefer to be surprised, avoid the entries for those episodes you have not yet seen. The episode guide aims to give the reader a richer understanding of each episode and offers background material on the show's guest stars, how the various government agencies tie in to the show, and what pop culture allusions are being made either visually or through dialogue. *Alias* is one of the most complicated shows on television, so with any luck this guide will help clarify the missions and explore the development of each character and story arc. The opinions expressed in the following pages are the authors' only, so feel free to disagree. These commentaries are intended to add to the reader's enjoyment of the show, but in no way are they intended to be a substitute for watching the show. We strongly recommend renting/buying the DVDs or watching the series as it airs; if you just read the episode guide without actually watching the show, you probably won't be able to follow the plot very well. When we list bloopers and nitpicks, we offer them only in fun and not as criticisms of the show.

At the end of each entry, you will find items of special interest. **Highlight** includes something that stood out in the show as particularly funny or sad but didn't fit in the summary (and yes, we realize how often Marshall features in this one). **Interesting Fact** lists a behind-the-scenes tidbit that you might not have known about an actor or something mentioned on the show. **Name That Guest Star** gives a brief background on the major stars that appear on the show. **Did You Notice?** details something in the episode that is in the background, perhaps foreshadowing an upcoming episode or relating to a previous one. **Nitpicks** are inconsistencies that bothered us while we were watching the episode, but ones that others might be able to explain to their satisfaction. **Oops** details the bloopers and continuity errors we spotted. **What Did He Say?** is a clarification of the rather complex mission briefings that happen in each episode. Occasionally, it describes an outside mission that is not detailed by Sloane or whoever is in charge, and just explains what people are doing in the episode. **Locations** keeps track of all the places Sydney or others go in each episode. **Marshall's Gadgets** lists all the neat gizmos that the resident tech expert comes up with to send Sydney on her missions. Finally, **Music/Bands** lists all the music heard in the episode, when it is heard, and what album it is on in case the reader wants to find it. Not every feature is listed for each episode.

For each season we have listed the characters that will recur. If they continue to appear in following seasons, we don't list them again.

Starring: Jennifer Garner as Sydney Bristow

Ron Rifkin as Arvin Sloane

Michael Vartan as Michael Vaughn

Victor Garber as Jack Bristow

Bradley Cooper as Will Tippin

Merrin Dungey as Francie Calfo

Carl Lumbly as Marcus Dixon

Kevin Weisman as Marshall J. Flinkman

Greg Grunberg as Eric Weiss

Lena Olin as Irina Derevko (Season Two)

David Anders as Mr. Sark (Season Two)

Terry O'Quinn as Agent Kendall (Season Two)

Melissa George as Lauren Reed (Season Three)

Season One:
September 2001–May 2002

1.1   Truth Be Told

Original air date: September 30, 2001
Written and directed by: J.J. Abrams
Guest cast: Edward Atterton (Daniel Hecht), Jay Gerber (Professor Mizzy), Angus Scrimm (Agent McCullough), William Wellman Jr. (Priest), Ric Young (Suit & Glasses), Lorenzo Callender (Messenger), Greg Collins (Kenny), Vicki Davis (Intern), Ming Lo (Agent), Raymond Ma (Taiwanese Businessman), Miguel Najera (Agent Gonzales), Greta Sesheta (CIA Receptionist), Philip Tan (Taiwanese Security Officer), Emily Wachtel (Beth at the airline counter), Nancy Wetzel (Amy Tippin)

When Sydney Bristow's fiancé is killed by the organization she works for, she discovers that her life has been a lie.

"Truth Be Told" is an excellent pilot that not only introduces the key elements of the show — SD-6 versus the CIA, the core characters, Syd's deification of her mother and demonization of her father, Syd's parallel lives, and, of course, Marshall and his gadgets — but does so in a stylish way that emphasizes the series' thematic elements. Just as Abrams cuts between Sydney's torture in Taipei and flashbacks to her life at university and with her friends, so too does Sydney's life straddle these two very different extremes. Syd's friends have no idea what she does for a living, and similarly, the viewers are forced to put the pieces of the puzzle together to figure out what the heck is going on.

Most important, the series introduced the incredible talents of Jennifer Garner. Here was a beautiful woman who not only slipped into various disguises with the ease of a mannequin but boasted a wide-ranging acting talent that seemed refreshing and new. "Truth Be Told" was our introduction to Sydney, but by the end of the pilot we felt like we had known her for years. From her stress over her university courses to her breathless acceptance of Danny's proposal to her bewilderment when her father suddenly shows up in the parking garage ("Daddy?") to her stoned act in Taipei ("Whoa!") to her desolate fury in Sloane's office, Garner carries the episode with a grace and beauty that few actresses would be able to achieve. But nothing prepares viewers for her reaction to finding Danny's bloody corpse in the bathtub. As the situation washes over her, she moves from confusion to shock without making a sound, her mouth open and her face showing the devastation we can only imagine.

As she finally catches a breath and screams aloud, it's hard for us to continue watching this series without being on Syd's side no matter what she does. It's an astounding performance.

Victor Garber, despite playing the absentee father role, also wins us over in his very first scene as he expresses a completely unexpected reaction to Danny's request for Syd's hand in marriage. Before playing the part of Jack Bristow, Garber was a seasoned theater actor, and he steps into this role as if it were written for him. Bradley Cooper (Will) and Merrin Dungey (Francie) are good as Syd's closest, clueless friends, with Will clearly having the hots for Sydney. Michael Vartan (Vaughn) and Greg Grunberg (Weiss) only appear at the end of the episode, but the sparks from Vaughn are already flying. Kevin Weisman as Marshall J. Flinkman, the modern-day Q (without the finesse), has us at "Uh . . . h-hello," and Ron Rifkin, who has a history of playing good guys, is deliciously and subtly evil as Arvin Sloane.

The series premiere is a must-see for anyone who is a devoted fan of the show, and is a little jarring watching in retrospect because of how much the series has changed since its debut. The premiere is also amazing for the way it foreshadows the season finale, and the two episodes act as bookends of this first season (see "Almost Thirty Years").

Alias had an immediate effect on people who were still trying to come to terms with the atrocities of 9/11. With its focus on terrorist networks, American organizations trying to take them down, and the feeling of not being able to trust anyone, the show struck a chord in viewers. The real world had suddenly become a terrifying place, but through *Alias*, viewers could imagine that maybe somewhere out there was a Sydney Bristow who was working hard to preserve American values.

Though she probably doesn't look as amazing as Jennifer Garner does in a tight outfit . . .

Highlight: Jack's terse conversation with Danny. "Welcome to the family."

Interesting Fact: When Danny is serenading Sydney at her college, the clock-tower bells begin ringing and he yells for them to shut up. The bells actually went off by accident, and Edward Atterton improvised Danny's reaction. Also, fans of *Felicity* would have recognized not only Garner but Greg Grunberg (who played Ben's roommate Sean Blumberg) and Kevin Weisman (who played Earl a couple of times).

Name That Guest Star: Angus Scrimm plays Agent McCullough in several episodes in season 1. As the man called in to interrogate and sniff out suspicious SD-6 agents, McCullough is meant to elicit fear in the characters and in the audience. Casting Angus Scrimm in the part was perfect, since he's best known as "The Tall Man" in the *Phantasm* series of films. "I called Angus because I was a fan of his from

Phantasm," says J.J. Abrams. "And he was kind enough to come in and do this part. He's wonderful in the show, and he's returning in a number of episodes."

Did You Notice?: Marshall says that he wants to get the camera up to 47 snaps because it's a prime number. While this probably came off to viewers as a humorous geeky statement, it's the first use of the very important number 47 in the series (see page 302). Also, Syd's red hairdo is an homage to the excellent film *Run, Lola, Run*, about a girl who has a limited amount of time to find money for her boyfriend or he'll be killed. It's an appropriate allusion because just as Lola keeps returning to the beginning to try different means of obtaining the cash (à la *Groundhog Day*) Sydney will constantly make two steps forward and one step back throughout the series.

Nitpicks: Why didn't Syd tell Danny not to call her when he said he would? She clearly assumes her place has been bugged. Also, Syd asks Dixon how long he has been with his wife. If she's worked with Dixon closely for almost seven years, wouldn't she already know the answer to that question? And why doesn't she worry about being followed when she leaves Sloane's office and goes directly to the CIA? Considering the lengths she goes to in season 2 to mask her entrance to the CIA each week, you'd think she would have been a little more careful.

Oops: Syd leaves her cell phone on the ground in the parking garage as a decoy, but when she fights the agent it disappears from the ground. Immediately following the fight she picks it up again and jumps into the car.

What Did He Say?: Oskar Mueller has been killed. A modern-day alchemist, he had made up several plans for gadgets before his death, but his notebooks are nowhere to be found. A plan for one of his inventions has surfaced in Taipei, and Sloane sends Sydney and Dixon there to scope out the area but not to retrieve the plan. Later, when Sloane discovers the gadget has actually been built, he needs them to go back and recover it.

Locations: Taipei, Taiwan. As you watch the episodes, notice how often the same stock image of a foreign city will be reused, each time as a different place.

Marshall's Gadgets: A lighter that scrambles all video signals in a 420-yard radius, and a lipstick that is actually a camera/grid analyzer/laser that takes pictures from three axes.

Music/Bands: When Sydney and Danny meet outside the college we hear Vertical Horizon's "You're a God" (*Everything You Want*); "Goin' Our Way" by Gus (*Goin' Our Way*) plays when Sydney tells Francie that Danny has proposed; The Cranberries' "Never Grow Old" (*Wake Up & Smell the Coffee*) plays when Sydney tells Danny the truth; we hear "Under the Gun" by Supreme Beings of Leisure, from their self-titled album, when we see Sydney enter Credit Dauphine for the first time; "Trouble" by Cat Stevens (*Mona Bone Jakon*) plays as Sydney remembers when she was first recruited;

Peter Gabriel's "Here Comes the Flood" (*Revisited*) plays at Danny's funeral; we hear "Sofisticated" by the Stereo MCs (*Deep Down & Dirty*) when Sydney calls Francie from the parking garage and asks her to call back; Sinéad O'Connor's "No Man's Woman" (*Faith & Courage*) plays when Sydney walks into Sloane's office with the prototype; and we hear Vertical Horizon's "Give You Back" (*Everything You Want*) as Sydney and Jack stand near Danny's grave.

1.2   So It Begins

Original air date: October 7, 2001
Written by: J.J. Abrams
Directed by: Ken Olin
Guest cast: Evan Dexter Parke (Charlie Bernard), Aharon Ipalé (Ineni Hassan), Alex Kuz (Kazimir Shcherbakov), Ravil Isyanov (Luri Karpachev), Sarah Shahi (Jenny), Ammar Daraisen (Supplier), Azdine Melliti (Bodyguard #1), John Storey (CIA Officer), Xavier J. Nathan (French Officer), Gregory Phelan (Student), Seema Rahmani (Sara)

As Sydney tries to adjust to her new life as a double agent, she learns just how big the Alliance is and how difficult it will be to accomplish her CIA work while remaining at SD-6; Will starts to become suspicious about Danny's death.

This episode is full of Syd's growing pains as she tries to get used to her new life, and it is fun to watch for Sydney's cockiness when she tells Vaughn that operations are going to run her way or no way. For seven years she believed in something that has turned out to be a lie, but now she's convinced that she has the upper hand and is a valuable commodity to the CIA because she is on the inside of the terrorist network and can tell the agency everything (she doesn't seem to realize just how high-ranking Jack is at SD-6 and that he probably disclosed all to the CIA years ago). However, for all of Sydney's overconfidence in what she's doing, it's interesting to note that when faced with a potentially deadly situation, she turns to the people she's known longer over the people she actually trusts.

In "So It Begins," all trust begins to break down. Syd is appalled that her father knew that Danny was going to be killed. Will is distraught that Syd won't tell him what she was doing with his sister's passport in Taipei. Syd worries that Will might discover something that could be dangerous to him. Sloane begins to show suspicion that Jack might be up to something. Vaughn is worried about Syd's reluctance to keep him in the loop. And while it seems that no one trusts anyone else, the tension in all these relationships is simply the tip of the iceberg for what is to follow. By the end of the season, the rocky relationships will become the strongest and the ones that seemed so strong will fall apart. Trust is the key theme of this series, and right from the beginning it's clear that no one can trust anyone else.

The actors are far more at ease with their characters in this second episode than they were in the pilot, which was clearly filmed long before the rest of the episodes (just look at how much Jennifer Garner's hair has grown). We begin to see Will's determination to find out who killed Danny and Vaughn's growing attachment to Sydney. The bond between Sydney and Jack continues its roller-coaster ride. But the best aspect of this second episode is Sydney coming to terms with how drastically her life has changed in the last three months and how clumsily she deals with those changes. But just when we start to wonder if she's making the right decisions, the director features a beautiful montage of Sydney, alone, thinking about Danny over Kate Bush's "This Woman's Work." Suddenly we realize that her heart might not be in the game yet because it was so recently broken.

Highlight: Syd's reaction when Vaughn shows her the map.

Interesting Fact: The actor who plays Kazimir Shcherbakov is credited as Alex Kuz, which is a shortened version of his full name, Alexander Kuznetsov.

Did You Notice?: This is the first episode where we get Syd's voiceover at the beginning, but it's different than the one we hear in later episodes. In this version, she was probably told to sound upset and emotionally deadened, but instead she sounds really bored, as if she's telling her life story while filing her nails.

Nitpicks: The blood donor clinic van is a great cover — once. But Vaughn uses it every time he visits Syd on campus. If SD-6 were really watching her every move, wouldn't they pick up on the fact that she's giving an *awful* lot of blood and seems to be the only one who ever goes in? Also, when Sydney digs up the grave by herself, it looks like a perfect rectangle, as if she were a professional gravedigger or something. It's a little too precise for something she was doing quickly.

Oops: In the pilot, when Syd enters SD-6 through the white room, the door's hinges are on the right, but in this episode (and in subsequent ones) it's hinged on the left. Also, listen to the first time Syd tells Vaughn about Ineni Hassan: she calls him "Inie." Finally, when she's dressed up as the maid, she's wearing flat shoes, but when she pulls off the maid's outfit she's suddenly in heels. Where did those come from?

What Did He Say?: Dixon and Sydney's mission is to travel to Russia, where Dixon will pose as a man who is going to get some stolen foreign intelligence documents from two members of the Russian Mafia. Their job is to intercept the transaction, and Syd poses as a maid of the hotel who must break into the room, get the money that would have been used to pay for the transaction, and get it to Dixon so he can make the deal smoothly without arousing any suspicion on the part of the Russians. Later, Syd's mission is to find a nuclear warhead that has been missing for years in Virginia, and she must travel to the "address" of Ivanov Milovich.

Locations: Paris, France; Moscow, Russia; Virginia, U.S.

Marshall's Gadgets: A substance in the form of a tiny pill that, when touched, makes the person fall asleep instantly. However, it can only be used twice.

Music/Bands: Roland Gift's "Looking for a Friend," from his self-titled CD, plays when Sydney moves into her new place; we hear Kate Bush's "This Woman's Work" (*Sensual World*) as Sydney cries in the bathtub.

1.3   Parity

Original air date: October 14, 2001
Written by: Alex Kurtzman and Roberto Orci
Directed by: Mikael Salomon
Guest cast: Evan Dexter Parke (Charlie Bernard), Gina Torres (Anna Espinosa), Aharon Ipalé (Ineni Hassan), Keone Young (Professor Choy), Elaine Kagan (June Litvack), Mark Rolston (Agent Seth Lambert), Carole Gutierrez (Laura Stenson), Duane Journey (Sniper Team Leader), Luis Medina (Eduardo Benegas), Randy Mulkey (Navy Seal), Russell Alexander Orozco (M.C.), Alfonso Paz (Lead Security Officer), Tony Sears (SD-6 Agent), Anthony Vatsula (Doorman)

After Sydney retrieves a box containing a code, SD-6 realizes the only way to open it is to join forces with K-Directorate.

The word *parity* means "equality" or "equivalence," often with regard to pay or status within a business (the term *on par* is more commonly used). In math, it refers to the property of a number being odd or even as a way to detect errors in binary code. In physics, parity describes the phenomenon where a subatomic particle is symmetrical to its mirror image. A completely different use of the term refers to the act of having borne children. Someone on the writing staff knew their Webster's dictionary well, because all these definitions could describe this excellent and thrilling episode.

"Parity" is important for the introduction of the Rambaldi plot and K-Directorate. Played by the always-excellent Gina Torres, Anna Espinosa is a superb nemesis for Syd, and it's too bad she's not used longer than she is. In the past she has believed that Syd was her inferior, but throughout this episode she comes to realize Syd's a lot tougher — and smarter — than she might seem. When Syd ultimately bests

The Players

It seems in every CIA briefing we hear of another crime organization or department of the government that is somehow involved with what Sydney and Company are doing. The following is a list of the bad guys (and "good guys") who have been mentioned in episodes:

The Alliance — an organization made up of 12 SD cells and headed up by a board that meets in London, England

SD-6 — one of the SD cells of the Alliance (SD stands for *Section Disparu*, or "The Section that Does Not Exist")

FTL — an enemy of SD-6 and the U.S., its main headquarters were in Hong Kong until Mr. Sark assassinated the head of operations; it's now extinct

K-Directorate — an enemy of SD-6 and the U.S., it is a Russian underground crime organization

The Triad — a coalition of organized crime groups

The DSR — the Department of Special Research, a branch of the National Security Agency; it is determined to investigate Syd's connection to page 47

FAPSI — the federal information and communications agency in Russia (Federal'naya Agenstvo Pravitel'stvennoy Svayazi i Informatsii)

FSB — Soviet intelligence (Russia's Federal Security Service)

SVR — foreign intelligence in Russia

The Covenant — a terrorist organization of international cells composed of Rambaldi followers

Yakuza — the Japanese Mob

Shining Sword — a crime organization in the Philippines

The Trust — a highly secret government organization that is associated with Rambaldi; its financial front is Project Centigrade

her in Madrid, you can actually see a look of respect pass over Espinosa's face. Finally, she and Syd are "on par" with each other.

It appears the writers hadn't yet worked out the Rambaldi subplot when they filmed the pilot episode, because the modern-day alchemist, Oskar Mueller, turns out to have been working from someone else's plans. Sloane explains that Rambaldi was far ahead of his time and, as Pope Alexander VI's chief architect, sentenced to death for suggesting that science would some day allow people to know God. Pope Alexander VI did indeed exist, although Rambaldi is more a fictional amalgamation of Nostradamus and Leonardo da Vinci. He wrote early binary code (another reference to parity) and had drawn up plans for a cellphone and transistor radio in the 15th century.

As Syd tries to wrap her head around this new plot twist, she continues to ask Jack questions about her mother, but he's cold and pushes her away. Garber is excellent in these scenes as a father who seems to want a relationship with his daughter but doesn't know where to start. He's also clearly hiding something about her mother despite assuring Syd that he's telling the truth. The suspense created in these scenes — What does Jack know that he's not telling Sydney? Is he a good guy or bad guy? — will be the addictive part of the show that will keep viewers coming back week after week. In "Parity," Syd begins to see the pieces of her life coming together a little more manageably, and she deals with troubles as they come, whether it's a late paper for class, Francie's relationship troubles, her father not talking to her, or Vaughn being taken off her case. She'll continue to hit unexpected bumps in the road — like unintentionally kissing Will — but that's what makes her human.

This episode marks a shift in Syd's character to someone who's confident without being overconfident but also has the ability to be hurt.

Highlight: Syd in a red dress swooping down Tarzan-like from the rafters on a chain, and the ensuing fight.

Name That Guest Star: Gina Torres — who, like her character, Anna Espinosa, is of Cuban descent — is a genre queen. She appeared on *Xena: Warrior Princess* as Cleopatra and on *Hercules: The Legendary Journeys* as Nebula. She starred in *Cleopatra 2525* as Hel and in Joss Whedon's short-lived *Firefly* as Zoë, had a guest stint on *Angel* as Jasmine, and appeared on *24* in the second half of the 2003–2004 season. She married Laurence Fishburne in September 2002 and had cameos in the second and third installments of the *Matrix* trilogy.

Nitpicks: Sloane explains to the agents in the briefing who Rambaldi was and that the Oskar Mueller design from two episodes ago was actually a Rambaldi construct. Considering we later find out he's been chasing Rambaldi and his artifacts for 30 years, wouldn't he have known it was a Rambaldi design? And wouldn't he have briefed SD-6 on Rambaldi long before now? The Alliance has Rambaldi at the top of its priority list and Sloane will later brag that SD-6 has found more artifacts than any other SD cell, yet he's only mentioning it now? It seems improbable.

Oops: Near the beginning of the episode, Sydney confronts her father just outside of a parking lot to ask him questions. He refuses to listen to her, telling her she's been exposed. When he gets out of the car and is walking toward the building, he has nothing in his hands. He argues with Syd, and when he turns to walk away, a briefcase magically appears in his left hand.

What Did He Say?: Sloane explains who Milo Rambaldi was, and tells the agents that SD-6 needs two pages of machine code. They have one, but another man, Eduardo Benegas, has the other, and Syd and Dixon must go to Madrid to retrieve it. Unfortunately, when they bring back the briefcase containing the code, they can't open it and must meet Anna in Berlin to open it mutually.

Locations: Madrid, Spain; Berlin, Germany

Marshall's Gadgets: A fiberglass necklace with a mic'd pendant; a Spanish peseta that is actually a sonic-wave emitter; a pen that, when triggered, sets off the sonic wave in the peseta that shatters glass; and a remote modem to hook into the security camera system and put it into perpetual loop. Marshall's been busy!

Music/Bands: When Francie and Syd are on the couch talking about

CHRISTINA RADISH

Anna Espinosa (played by Gina Torres, pictured here with her husband Laurence Fishburne) was the perfect nemesis for Sydney, but her tenure on *Alias* was short-lived.

Jack, we hear Bill Bonk's "Rings a Bell" (*Evening Shade*); Miranda Lee Richards's "The Beginner" (*Herethereafter*) plays when Will and Syd are talking about his upcoming story on gene sequencing in virus-resistant cabbage; "Go Get It" by Spookie Daly Pride (*Marshmallow Pie*) is heard while Syd, Francie, Charlie, and Will play poker; and Ryan Adams's "La Cienega Just Smiled" (*Gold*) plays when Will and Syd accidentally kiss in the kitchen.

1.4 A Broken Heart

Original air date: October 21, 2001
Written by: Vanessa Taylor
Directed by: Harry Winer
Guest cast: Miguel Sandoval (Agent Anthony Russek), Gina Torres (Anna Espinosa), Evan Dexter Parke (Charlie Bernard), Faran Tahir (Mochtar), Maurice Chasse (Luc Jacqnoud), Bernard White (Malik Suari), Angus Scrimm (Agent McCullough), Sarah Shahi (Jenny), Arabella Holzbog (Sydney's Mom), Hector Aristizabal (Waiter), Sayed Badreya (Vendor), Jeff Chase (Bodyguard), Haley Gilbert (Rachel), Soren Hellerup (Doctor), Subash Kundanmal (Dhiren Patel), Tony Sears (German SD-6 Agent), Alex Veadow (K-Directorate Officer)

After Sydney recovers the Sol D'Oro piece of the Rambaldi puzzle, she travels to Morocco to spy on a man who might be planning a revolt at an upcoming United Commerce Organization (UCO) conference.

If one thing can be said about the writers of this show, it's that they choose perfect titles. "A Broken Heart" describes what happens to so many people in this episode. Sydney makes the first major step in her father-daughter relationship, but Jack backs away, scared that Sydney might discover the secret he's keeping from her. The look of bewilderment on Jack's face when she invites him to dinner speaks volumes: it is one of those classic Victor Garber moments where he says nothing and his eyes say everything. Francie spies on Charlie and sees him with another woman, which breaks her heart; she was insecure about him, but never thought she'd actually catch him cheating. And the titular trope is used quite literally when Sydney discovers the horrible way Luc Jacqnoud and his cronies are going to use an Edgar Peace Prize winner to crash the UCO party.

"A Broken Heart" is also the episode where things started to become very complicated for viewers. Sloane opens the show with an explanation of Rambaldi and another artifact that Syd needs to retrieve and then suddenly switches gears, sending her on a mission to stop a resistance group from raising hell at an upcoming conference. It was at this point that some fans realized they would probably have to tape these episodes and watch the scenes several times if they wanted to follow what was happening with the missions, while others decided they would just sit back and enjoy the character aspect of the show and let the missions fall into place eventually. Either way, it's the complexity that makes this show one of the most exciting on television.

Will's acting like a journalist on the scent of a good story is another great plot device that blossoms throughout the season. His blind determination to find Danny's murderers and the pain Syd feels about lying to him is a perfect illustration of Syd's major dilemma. If she tells Will what is happening, he will be killed. But by keeping secrets from him, she is allowing him to dig himself into a dangerous hole — which could also get him killed. As he follows the trail of the mysterious "Kate Jones," viewers can't help but wonder what would happen if only he knew what Syd was *really* doing on those trips. His astute comment to her — "You take an insane amount of trips" — is hilarious for its dramatic irony.

The best part of this episode is Syd's discussion with Vaughn on the bridge. After trying to bring her many lives together and watching them clash, after making a step toward building bridges with Jack only to be spurned, and after seeing the murder of an SD-operative who believed he was working for the CIA, Syd's confident exterior breaks down, and she turns to the only person

Sydney's best friends Francie and Will have no idea that she's leading a double life.

she believes she can trust. Garner is superb in this scene, not just crying but sobbing uncontrollably, on the verge of hyperventilating. She lends such humanness to her character that by this fourth episode, it's impossible to imagine anyone else as Sydney Bristow. Vaughn's reassurance to her was like a drug for the fans of the Sydney-Vaughn relationship (the "Syd-Vaughn-shippers"), and it was only the beginning of the sexual tension between them that would thrill fans in the weeks to come.

Highlight: Marshall explaining his wind filter, and the bemused looks on the faces of everyone around him.

Interesting Fact: The United Commerce Organization (UCO) seems very similar to the World Trade Organization (WTO) for good reason; in the original script it was the WTO, until the events of September 11 forced the writers to change the name.

Name That Guest Star: Miguel Sandoval (Agent Russek), is a seasoned actor who has appeared on television shows such as NYPD *Blue*, *Seinfeld*, *The West Wing*, *Law & Order*, and *The X-Files*, and movies such as *Do the Right Thing*, *Jurassic Park*, *Clear and Present Danger*, *Get Shorty*, *Crash*, *Blow*, and most of director Alex Cox's films.

Did You Notice?: Vaughn tells Sydney not to let her rage darken her. It's an interesting choice of words considering the revelation they'll later discover in "The Prophecy."

Nitpicks: When Sydney and Anna are fighting in the church, there's no way they could have knocked each other in the head with those massive posts and candlesticks without incurring some major head trauma. Also, when Sloane is briefing everyone on the next Rambaldi artifact they will look for, he calls it "Sol D'Oro," and Sydney looks confused before he says, "Golden Sun." Considering she's fluent in Spanish, why the confusion?

Oops: Syd makes a big deal to Vaughn that she could have given SD-6 the wrong number, but in fact she *did* give them the wrong number! The code ends in 0010; that's the number Syd gives to the CIA and the one Anna gives to K-Directorate, but when she repeats it back to SD-6 she ends the sequence with 1101.

What Did He Say?: Sloane explains that Rambaldi was a 15th-century Nostradamus who could see the way of the technological future. Sloane is fascinated with him because Rambaldi spent the last decade of his life working on one project, and Sloane believes it'll be the wave of the future, unlike anything anyone has ever seen. Syd's first mission in the episode is to go to a church in Spain (the coordinates were hidden in the binary code revealed in the briefcase) and recover the Sol D'Oro. Next she has to go to Morocco to monitor who Jacqnoud — a rebel leader — is meeting, because SD-6 is convinced he is planning a huge disruption. Finally, she has to head to Sao Paulo because SD-6 believes the man that Jacqnoud met — Malik Suari — is going to somehow use Dhiren Patel, an Edgar Peace Prize winner.

Locations: Málaga, Spain; Morocco; Sao Paulo, Brazil

Marshall's Gadgets: A purse with a built-in microphone and wind filter that will eliminate all wind noise up to 150 hertz.

Music/Bands: Nina Storey's "If I Were an Angel" (*Shades*) plays when Syd and Francie decide to spy on Charlie; we hear Bill Bonk's "Halfway Home" (*Evening Shade*) when Syd asks Will to check up on Francie; and Sarah McLachlan's "Angel" (*Surfacing*), a song used as the background music in many heartrending moments on television shows, plays when Sydney breaks down with Vaughn.

1.5   Doppelgänger

Original air date: October 28, 2001
Written by: Daniel Arkin
Directed by: Ken Olin

Guest cast: Tom Everett (Agent Paul Kelvin), Norbert Weisser (Jeroen Schiller), Lori Heuring (Kate Jones), Maurice Chasse (Luc Jacqnoud), Kevin E. West (CIA Officer Logan), Yvonne Farrow (Diane Dixon), Robert Bailey, Jr. (Dixon's Son), Subash Kundanmal (Patel), Pablo Santos (Roy), Kenneth Ivan (UCO Host), Jeff Chase (Bodyguard), Clint Lilley (Patel's Bodyguard), Tristin Mays (Dixon's Daughter), Kevin Mitnick (Hacker)

When Sydney pulls a switch on an operation and the phony contact fails to give Sloane a vital piece of information, Sloane begins to suspect Sydney of betraying him.

Doppelgänger is, appropriately for this episode, a German word meaning "double" or "alter ego." It has often been used in literature and literary criticism to represent good and evil within humankind, and philosopher Immanuel Kant believed there was a constant battle within oneself between an evil heart and a rational head. Books such as Robert Louis Stevenson's *Dr. Jekyll and Mr. Hyde* or Dostoevsky's *Crime and Punishment* are explorations of doppelgängers. It's an appropriate term for *Alias* to explore, considering many of the main characters might seem like good people on the outside but have their dark secrets within (or, in the case of Sloane, the opposite is true).

Syd's been living a double existence for some time now as an agent for both SD-6 and the CIA, but it's when she makes the switch with another double that she runs the risk of being compromised. This episode is full of suspense and gives us a deeper look at just how dangerous her life really is. Not only is she her own doppelgänger, but she sees in Agent Kelvin what might happen to her if Sloane were to catch on.

This episode also begins to uncover the mystery of Jack Bristow. When Vaughn unexpectedly hands Syd Jack's file, she is pleasantly surprised, but this boon will soon be her burden. Similarly, "Doppelgänger" marks the first time she expresses a desire to tell Dixon the truth, but we also find out from Vaughn why that might not be the gift she thinks it is. As Syd reads more into her father's past, imagining what it must have been like when *he* first became a double agent, the viewers also see how Jack deals with it now, accepting that when he's at SD-6 he must act like an agent of SD-6, no matter how cold, cruel, and heartless that might make him. Garber's ability to maintain a stony face while betraying a multitude of expressions through his eyes just gets better and better every week. As Jack beats a man he knows is innocent, it's almost like he's beating himself, since this man is a double too. When he calls Sydney to apologize for not making it to dinner and tells her he doesn't have time to get together, it's because he's scared to get too close to his daughter. He knows she needs her father, but he's scared his shadowy secrets will cause more pain than she can handle.

Meanwhile, Will continues to chase the story behind Danny's murder, and when he confesses to Francie what he's been doing, it puts a tiny chasm between Syd and her two best friends. Just as Syd is keeping secrets about her life from her best friends, now they, too, are keeping secrets from her, despite Francie telling Will to stop pursuing the story. But in this otherwise simple scene, viewers become aware that Syd's apartment is indeed bugged when Will receives an unexpected phone call.

But the real shocker is the ending of this episode. Sydney is just starting to get the hang of having a countermission for every mission, and she pulls it off perfectly. Until Dixon surprises her with his unexpected backup plan. The look on her face at the end of this episode shows that Sydney will have to endure many more heartbreaking realizations before she'll ever get used to her new life.

Highlight: The amazing ambulance chase at the beginning; as if emergency open-heart surgery wasn't suspenseful enough, they added a speeding ambulance!

Did You Notice?: Syd is dressed as Alice in Wonderland at the Halloween party — an appropriate outfit considering she fell down the rabbit hole when Danny died and has been watching her world turn upside down ever since. And Will comes dressed as Nixon, a subtle nod to *All the President's Men*, in which two journalists chase the Watergate scandal in the same way Will is chasing his story.

Nitpicks: Why didn't Sydney turn on the ambulance siren during the chase?

Oops: During the ambulance chase, one of the back bottom doors flips open as the vehicle turns a corner, but in the next scene when the turn is complete, it's closed.

What Did He Say?: Sloane explains that Jeroen Schiller is a man who works for a corporation in Germany that has perfected a vaccine against biological weapons. He'll give SD-6 the info for the vaccine if the organization can guarantee him safe passage to the U.S. Sydney must go in to the company, retrieve the information from the computer, and get Schiller. Later, they have to go to the plant where the company is holding the prototypes of the vaccine inhalers, get the inhalers, and blow up the plant.

Locations: Sao Paulo, Brazil; Berlin, Germany; Badenweiler, Germany

Marshall's Gadgets: A business card that, when placed on top of a computer, overrides the central processing unit and makes the computer think you are the system administrator, allowing you access to the company's files.

Music/Bands: John Wesley Harding's "I'm Wrong About Everything" (*Confessions of St. Ace*) plays as Francie and Will put up decorations for the Halloween party; and during the party we hear "Get Down Massive" by Freestylers (*Pressure Point*) and Leroy's "Trans Am" from his self-titled CD.

1.6 Reckoning

Original air date: November 18, 2001
Written by: Jesse Alexander
Directed by: Daniel Attias
Guest cast: John Hannah (Martin Shepard), Nancy Dussault (Mrs. Calder), Evan Dexter Parke (Charlie Bernard), Lori Heuring (Kate Jones/Eloise Kurtz), Eugene Lazarev (Dr. Kreshnik), Sarah Shahi (Jenny), Maurice Godin (Agent Fisher), Daniel Betances (Pearson), Neil Dickson (John Smythe), Haley Gilbert (Rachel), Arabella Holzbog (Laura Bristow), Paul Lieber (Bentley Calder), Cole Petersen (Boy), Tom Waite (Guard #1), Nancy Wetzel (Amy Tippin)

Sydney discovers that an FBI agent had been conducting an investigation into Jack Bristow and believes her father was responsible for her mother's death; Vaughn tells Sydney about a tragedy that happened to him when he was a child; Will discovers Kate Jones is a fake name for Eloise Kurtz.

And the mystery of Jack Bristow deepens. As Syd recovers from the horror of the events in Badenweiler, she makes a new discovery about her mother's death and tells Vaughn. Ever since their conversation on the bridge, Sydney and Vaughn have become closer, and Syd opens up to him about everything, whether it is her concerns about SD-6 or her father (soon she'll be telling him about her friends). But because of her heightened sense of what is right and what is wrong, she and Vaughn will be butting heads for some time over protocol versus the morally right thing to do. As they meet at a driving range, Syd once again puts her foot in her mouth by assuming that Vaughn is an agent who follows orders without any real understanding of the emotions involved. His confession to her about what happened when he was eight years old fills Sydney with regret, and this is the last time she speaks to him in such a presumptuous manner.

Similarly, Jack tells Sydney that she should know better than to jump to rash conclusions with just a few tidbits of information, but it'll take more than a stern talk on a street corner for her to listen. Syd is trying to find out about her past, and Jack is undecided about what he should tell her and what he should keep to himself. Their inexperience in dealing with the situation is what will make this journey a dangerous and painful one for both of them, but throughout season 1 Syd will learn some important lessons about whom to trust and when to question things, and by season 2 she'll be a very different person emotionally. Jack believes that by not telling Syd the truth he can protect her, just as Charlie keeps the truth from Francie to protect himself. However, in both cases the men's silence forces the women to think the worst.

An intriguing aspect of this episode is the use of John Donne's "Devotion #XVII."

Sloane tells Sydney that an organization has turned Martin Shepard into a cold-blooded killer by using a trigger, the famous "No man is an island, entire of itself; every man is a piece of the continent, a part of the main." Donne wrote the poem when he was deathly ill, and the piece is a meditation on how everyone is interconnected, and when one person dies, we all lose something: ". . . never send to know for whom the bell tolls; it tolls for thee." The poem is appropriate for this episode because Sydney watches four agents die at the beginning; their deaths are a personal loss for her and a reminder of her own mortality. Like them, she could die on active duty because someone either doesn't understand or finds out what she is doing. Likewise, she sees Shepard as a personal cause: he too was used by an evil organization to do things against his will. Perhaps she believes that by freeing him, she'll free a part of herself.

Highlight: Syd's feats of strength (and pain tolerance) on the steam ducts.

Name That Guest Star: John Hannah (Martin Shepard) is a terrific actor hailing from Scotland, who starred in the short-lived television series *MDs*. Before that, he appeared in films such as *Four Weddings and a Funeral*, *Sliding Doors*, *The Mummy*, and *The Hurricane*.

Did You Notice?: At the driving range Garner swings left-handed, but we've seen in other episodes that she's actually right-handed. The director probably asked her to change her swing so that she and Vartan would be facing each other for the scene. Also, whether or not the writers intended it, the picture of Bentley Calder looks a lot like Sloane might have 20 years ago.

Nitpicks: If Charlie had a legitimate reason for being seen with another woman, why didn't he make every effort to let Francie know about it rather than let her continue to think he's having an affair? Also, when the location names flash on the screen, sometimes it's a city and other times it's a country, which is inconsistent.

What Did He Say?: FTL, an enemy of SD-6, has vacated its base and SD agents find two birthday cards left behind. Embedded within the little birthday songs, SD-6 detects a secret code in the higher registers. There are decoders in existence, and Syd needs to retrieve one from an art gallery owner in London in order to find out FTL's new location. When Syd brings back the decoder, they discover that the code was the DNA of an FTL agent, Gareth Parkishoff, who had been assassinated by Matthew Shepard, an unsuspecting pawn who had been programmed to kill and then forget what he'd done. Syd must go to the mental hospital where Shepard is and try to get him out.

Locations: London, England; Bucharest, Romania

Marshall's Gadgets: Although Marshall's not shown explaining the items, Syd has a pair of glasses that allows her to find the safe behind the wall and a watch that helps her decode the lock on the safe.

Music/Bands: "Going, Going, Gone" by the Stars (*Nightsongs*) plays as Syd looks at a picture of her mother; at the art gallery, we hear Garbage's "Tornado" (*When I Grow Up*); as Francie waits for Charlie to take the stage in the club, we hear Huffamoose's "Zero Hour" (*I Wanna Be Your Pants*); Charlie sings John Hiatt's "Have a Little Faith in Me" (*Bring the Family*); and when Vaughn attends the funeral of the agents who died in Badenweiler we hear Lisbeth Scott's "Be Still My Soul" (from Paul Schwartz's *State of Grace*).

1.7   Color-Blind

Original air date: November 25, 2001
Written by: Roberto Orci and Alex Kurtzman
Directed by: Jack Bender
Guest cast: John Hannah (Martin Shepard), Evan Dexter Parke (Charlie Bernard), Elaine Kagan (June Litvack), Eugene Lazarev (Dr. Kreshnik), Sarah Shahi (Jenny), Mark Galasso (Ed Davis)

Sydney poses as a patient in a mental institution and must get information from another patient. What he tells her is completely unexpected.

"Color-Blind" is another exciting episode full of torture sequences, touching moments, and Jennifer Garner still doing the best sobs on television. John Hannah is excellent as the mentally unstable Martin Shepard, who has been turned into a killing machine (complete with an on/off switch) for some unknown organization. As his memories begin to collide, he must decide between staying in the mental hospital and possibly going insane or working through the difficult memories and healing himself.

Viewers get a glimpse of Syd's excellent detective skills in this episode. She discovers who the director of the institution is because of his accent and figures out exactly how Shepard's faculties are breaking down by realizing he's using the wrong crayon color. While it might seem strange that she can keep her mind so alert (especially after such an excruciating torture session), this ability foreshadows what we ultimately discover about Syd's training. She also sees a bit of herself in Shepard: he has gone color-blind as a sort of detachment mechanism. If he could remember all the horrible things he's done in color, those events would be even more horrific and real, so he's forced himself psychologically not to see or remember color. Similarly, Sydney has learned so many painful things in her life that we can't help but wonder if she has some innate detachment mechanism that allows her to continue to smile, laugh, and fulfill her missions despite knowing things that would debilitate a normal person.

The relationship between Jack and Sydney begins to heal (at least for this week) when he realizes the depth of her concern and what she believes she knows about him. His rather unpleasant first encounter with Vaughn is a sign of how their affiliation (and mutual hostility) will continue, but it also allows him to see Sydney through another person's eyes. This episode marks the first time Jack and Syd actually share a smile that's not forced or artificial.

Finally, Syd makes a step toward moving on from Danny's death. After Shepard's horrifying confession in Romania, she returns home to see history repeat itself at her Thanksgiving dinner (and she shows an enormous amount of strength in this situation) and her casual but caring chitchat with Vaughn shows that perhaps the attraction is mutual. It's interesting that Sloane sent Sydney on a mission to activate Martin's memory, knowing that doing so might reveal to her what really happened the night of Danny's death. Did he not think it all the way through, or is he more of a sadistic bastard than we thought?

Highlight: Marshall introducing Sloane to his blow-up chair and offering to inflate the couch for him.

Interesting Fact: Most people who are color-blind have trouble distinguishing reds or greens. This type of color blindness is genetically passed from the mother to the child. Total color blindness, or monochromacy, is an extremely rare condition whereby persons can only see black and white. They usually have other eye problems as well, and the disease is also a genetic one. Very rarely, color blindness can be brought on by a trauma to the brain or to the eye, but generally it's an inherited trait that is completely untreatable.

Did You Notice?: Although he is uncredited, the maître d' at the Chinese restaurant is prolific actor James Hong. His cameo is probably an in-joke — while he has appeared in dozens of movies and television shows, he is probably best known to North American audiences as the maître d' at the Chinese restaurant in the classic *Seinfeld* episode where the gang can't get a table. "Cartwright?" Also, despite Sydney's youth and relative immaturity, she immediately forgives Shepard for what he did because she realizes he was innocent; notice how Sloane won't show the same forgiveness later in "Endgame."

Nitpicks: Despite Syd's obvious display of resilience in past episodes, her getting shock treatment while lying in a vat of water only to be zapped with a cattle prod afterward seems like something that would knock even the strongest person unconscious. Also, Syd figuring out that Shepard is color-blind because he colors the sky yellow is a little too convenient — maybe the guy has an eccentric view of the world, or perhaps he's a surrealist.

...plains to Sydney at the end of the episode that the

...e possibility of a Rambaldi artifact in Tunisia. When

...discovered FTL had already left — with the artifact

...rd University for testing, and Sydney must travel to

...ia

...hepard escape from the institution, we hear The

...r self-titled album; Jude's "Everything's All Right (I

...y) plays during the Thanksgiving dinner; and as Syd

...Natalie Merchant's "Not in This Life" (*Motherland*).

1.8   Time Will Tell

Original air date: December 2, 2001
Written by: Jeff Pinkner
Directed by: Perry Lang
Guest cast: Tobin Bell (Agent Dreyer), Gina Torres (Anna Espinosa), Robert Clendenin (Kostia Bergman), Peter Dennis (Professor Bloom), Keone Young (Professor Choy), Elaine Kagan (June Litvack), Jack Axelrod (Giovanni Donato), Michael Halsey (Professor Hunt), Sam Ayers (Man on Phone)

Sydney travels to Italy to find a clockmaker who will fix a Rambaldi clock; when she returns home, she makes a disturbing discovery in her mother's books.

Time is a constant theme on *Alias*. Sydney is usually racing against time to complete a mission; the passage of time has made her miss her mother while it highlights the neglect Jack has shown as a father; time has begun to soften the blow of Danny's death; and through it all, Sydney wonders if, in the future, there will ever be a time when she can be completely honest with the friends who are closest to her. In this episode, the theme of time is brought to the fore when Sydney retrieves the most important of the Rambaldi puzzle pieces — a clock. Unfortunately, because it's half a millennium old, it doesn't work, and she must seek out a direct descendant of Giovanni Donato, the man who built the clock for Milo Rambaldi. The ensuing scene is dramatic, mysterious, and makes Rambaldi an even more intriguing character than before.

The other main theme of this episode is Syd's emotionalism. While on the surface she might appear to be keeping things more or less together — no small task considering she's lying to her friends, discovering disturbing things about her father every day, trying to maintain her status as a double agent with only one side knowing the truth, and hoping to graduate with a university degree — on the inside she can feel the panic rising. And with the worst timing imaginable, along comes Dreyer, one of Sloane's lackeys, who will be administering an emotionally based lie detector test. The scene where Vaughn tells Sydney to split her focus and she counters that it's been split too much already worries the viewer — can Sydney make it through this lie detector test successfully? If she doesn't, Sloane will have her eliminated, or at the very least tortured for information. Throughout the series, it will be repeated again and again that Sydney's emotional sensitivity is her one flaw, and while it's her humanity that always puts her in the most dangerous situations, it's what makes viewers so sympathetic to her week after week.

Near the end of the episode, Syd makes a shocking discovery within her mother's books, and despite Jack's warning in the previous episode about jumping to conclusions, it would seem there is only one conclusion to draw. Her actions in subsequent episodes will either drive a final wedge between her and Jack or bring them closer together.

Highlight: Marshall realizing the magnitude of Rambaldi's designs: "That sound, you know, that boom? That's my mind blowing!"

Interesting Fact: This is the last time we'll see Anna Espinosa, who seems to drop into oblivion. The Espinosa character provides an opportunity for Sydney to have a nemesis who is her equal while being her opposite, and Anna's departure is an opportunity lost. Gina Torres felt the same way when asked about it two years later: "I would absolutely love to reprise my role as Anna; I think so much was left unsaid. She just kind of disappeared, and I think Sydney's due for another ass-whuppin' from Anna. I fought her three times; every fight I ever engaged in with Sydney I won. Which was shocking! I mean, I couldn't believe it. I'd read it episode after episode; I'd go, 'I kick her butt *again*? She's the lead of the show! I'm the guest villain!' Maybe that's one of the reasons why I never came back!"

Did You Notice?: Anna sports the Rambaldi tattoo on her hand, even though we only see it briefly. The symbol — <0> — looks like a mathematical formula stating that something is simultaneously less than and greater than zero, a conundrum that is no doubt something Rambaldi was exploring at some point.

Nitpicks: Syd tells Will that she's going to be getting a lie detector test at work. Since she knows the apartment has been bugged by SD-6, why would she tip off Sloane that she knows about the upcoming test? Also, Marshall explains that the Donato clock has to be set to 12:22 to see the star chart, yet Sloane concludes that the star chart refers to a place at 2:22 a.m., which seems like a slip of the tongue. And if it was so easy to get out of the engineering lab by leaping out of a window, why did Syd take such great pains to get in? Finally, each of the Rambaldi artifacts points to the place where the next one is hidden, yet the artifacts weren't scattered around the world until *after* Rambaldi's death and *after* he had created these maps. Perhaps the writers are attributing that discrepancy to the fact that Rambaldi was a prophet and *knew* where the pieces would be scattered.

What Did He Say?: The clock Sydney retrieves had been made by Giovanni Donato, who died in 1503, which is intriguing, since the star chart is for a night in 1523. It had been commissioned by Rambaldi and it's significant because he hid codes in his artwork. The clock has a date on the back, a date in history where absolutely nothing happened. Syd must go to the direct descendant of Donato to get the clock fixed. When Syd visits Donato he describes the "magnific order of Rambaldi," a group of people bearing the Rambaldi symbol who pledged to protect his creations. Unfortunately, most modern-day members have gone rogue and only want the creations for themselves. Later, when Syd returns from her mission, Marshall explains that when the clock is set at a certain time it reveals a star chart for a very specific time and place on earth — August 16, 1523, at 2:22 a.m., on Mount Aconcagua on the Chile-Argentina border. Sydney and Dixon must go to that place in order to find the next, and most important, piece of the puzzle — Rambaldi's journal.

Locations: Oxford, England; Positano, Italy; Mount Aconcagua, Argentina

Music/Bands: As Will and Syd chat we hear Ivy's "Edge of the Ocean" (*Long Distance*).

1.9   Mea Culpa

Original air date: December 9, 2001
Written by: Debra J. Fisher and Erica Messer
Directed by: Ken Olin
Guest cast: Miguel Sandoval (Agent Anthony Russek), Tobin Bell (Agent Dreyer), Timothy Landfield (Kretchmer), Christopher Thornton (Nevil), David St. James (Mr. Franco), Jon Curry (Phillips), Yvonne Farrow (Diane Dixon), Timothy Halligan (Dr. Mallaska), Richard F. Whiten (Officer Pollard), Kaline Carr (Franco's Assistant), David Franco (Guard), Maurice Irvin (Man in the Couple), Cosimo Fusco (Logan Gerace)

As Sydney worries about Dixon's health now that he's in a coma, Sloane takes a drastic measure and Will makes contact with someone who knows what happened to Eloise Kurtz.

A very exciting episode and one of the best of the season so far, "Mea Culpa" will have you on the edge of your seat from beginning to end. Sydney seems far more at

CHRISTINA RADISH

What makes Arvin Sloane such an amazing character to watch is that he's not completely evil — despite his self-serving endgame, he truly loves the people who are closest to him.

ease playing the double agent now and moves between her two lives more seamlessly, but when she's faced with a snag — Dixon getting seriously hurt on the job — she's forced to expose herself and put both of them in danger.

For all of Sloane's evil ways, we see a small spark of humanity in him in this episode as he's put on his own emotional roller-coaster ride over his conviction that Sydney is not duplicitous. He opens up to Sydney in a more personal way than he ever has before, and by the end of her mission in Tuscany, the look of relief on his face is as palpable as it is on Vaughn's and Jack's. But, as fans of *Alias* know too well by now, relief and calm are fleeting feelings on this show.

Meanwhile, Will makes strides with his story when he looks into the mystery of the brooch. Will was a difficult character for many fans to deal with at the beginning of the show. Syd-Vaughn-shippers didn't like the idea that Will and Sydney might become an item, and wanted him gone (we will admit that during the first season we occasionally wished for a stray bullet to fly in Will's direction). Other fans were annoyed that he wasn't heeding Syd's urgings to leave the story alone and worried that he might get her in trouble. But detractors were forgetting that Will is unaware of Sydney's real job — he has no idea that Sydney is working in a dangerous profession. He doesn't know of the existence of Michael Vaughn. All he knows is that his best friend's fiancé has been murdered, the police never found the killer, and there are several suspicious things that have happened since then. He doesn't want something to happen to Sydney, and he's always been working in her best interest. The scenes that depict him finding out more about the brooch are gripping — as he asks whoever is listening to call him, as he responds to anonymous messages, and as he makes a discovery in his car that convinces him he is being followed. With this episode Will moves from an occasionally annoying character to an intriguing one on the trail of his own mystery, just like Sloane and Sydney.

As if threats against Will or scenes with Syd and Sloane aren't suspenseful enough, the scene where Syd fulfills her mission in Tuscany takes the tension one notch higher. In "Color-Blind," Vaughn and Jack meet for the first time and they immediately begin trying to one-up each other. That initial rivalry explodes in this episode as each man argues that he knows what's best for Sydney and that the other's actions will kill her. This competition will continue beyond season 1, with each man trying to prove that he loves Sydney more than the other.

"Mea Culpa" — the phrase is a Latin term meaning "I'm guilty" — is an episode that's actually more about the men surrounding Sydney and how they're all doing things that could hurt her. Sloane, Jack, Vaughn, Will, Dixon, and even Marshall all impact Sydney in a potentially negative way and make her already difficult life that much more complex. Each man will learn that Syd is a big girl who can make her own decisions. For some this will be a positive discovery; for others, not so much.

As viewers, we can only hope that someday Sydney might learn to stay out of parking garages.

Highlight: Will's unexpected phone call when he's with Francie and the creepy voice on the other end. Definitely one of the highlights of the season.

Interesting Fact: Yvonne Farrow (Diane Dixon) has chemistry with Carl Lumbly for good reason: she played opposite him in the television series *M.A.N.T.I.S.*, as did Gina Torres.

Nitpicks: I don't care how strong Sydney is, there is no way she could have taken a fall like that and stopped herself by hooking her leg over the rung of the ladder without dislocating her leg *and* breaking the rung of the ladder. Also, why didn't SD-6 have a unit nearby to extract her and Dixon? Six months earlier she would have been forced to call SD-6 — why change protocol now? And why does Jack always show up late to every mission briefing? Finally, when Francie asked Syd to go shopping with her on Saturday, Syd would have already known how long she was going to be away, so why did she say yes?

Oops: When Jack talks to Marshall, Marshall pulls off his headphones and has them around his neck. But when the camera angle is on Jack, filmed over Marshall's shoulder, Marshall doesn't have the headphones on. Also, when Will and Francie are watching a movie at her apartment, he goes to the fridge to get two beers, but when he pulls them out of the refrigerator, their caps have already been removed. Those must be some pretty flat beers.

What Did He Say?: A U.S. bank was robbed by men who were working for Ineni Hassan. Two of the men rerouted funds to Hassan's bank account, and SD-6 is worried he will use the money to partner with a hostile country and provide it with arms.

Syd's mission is to go to a party held at Hassan's accountant's house in Tuscany, get Hassan's account number from the accountant's computer, and dead-drop it at Danatti Park. Vaughn explains that SD-6 is actually looking for revenge because Hassan recently double-crossed them. The CIA wants SD-6 to have the money so it can see how SD-6 spends it. Later, Syd must travel to Geneva to get Hassan's account number from a safe deposit box after discovering the computer file only has the name of the bank.

Locations: Mt. Aconcagua, Argentina; Tuscany, Italy; Geneva, Switzerland

Marshall's Gadgets: A device that "sucks" the information from a computer's hard drive and transfers it into the internal flash ram; a cellphone with a biometric sensor that takes a picture of a fingerprint and then makes a latex copy of it

Music/Bands: Smashmouth's "Diggin' Your Scene" (*Astro Lounge*) plays when Syd enters Gerace's party; when Jack talks to Marshall, the techie is listening to Munkafust's "Sacred Way" (*Welcome to Playtime*); we hear Duncan Sheik's "Out of Order," from his self-titled CD, when Sydney reassures Francie she's happy that Francie is engaged.

1.10   Spirit

Original air date: December 16, 2001
Written by: J.J. Abrams and Vanessa Taylor
Directed by: Jack Bender
Guest cast: Miguel Sandoval (Agent Anthony Russek), Scott Paulin (Robert Stoller), Aharon Ipalé (Ineni Hassan), Christopher Thornton (Nevil), Scotch Ellis Loring (Agent Gordon), Sarah Shahi (Jenny), James Warwick (Severn Driscoll), Conrad Gamble II (Bodyguard), Erica Inez (Hotel Manager), Kevin McCorkle (Agent), Don Took (Agent Grey), Scott Vance (Security Section Agent #1), Nancy Wetzel (Amy Tippin)

Sydney is suspicious of her father when a last-minute transmission saves her from being tagged as a mole; Will gets one step closer to SD-6.

"Spirit" contains one of those great moments that fans wish could go even further (they'll get their wish by the end of the season). After months of muttering to ourselves, "If only you guys knew what Syd was really doing, it'd blow your mind . . . ," Sydney finally speaks without thinking and tells Will to stop bothering her about her job, that he should be thanking her instead. It's interesting, however, that he's lecturing her on how dangerous her job has become while he is chasing down an organization he believes murders people. In this episode Will hears the name SD-6 for the first time and is able to hear Eloise Kurtz get murdered on tape. He no longer seems to have any worries about what Sydney might think of his following the story because it now seems so much bigger than Danny's murder.

Just as Will is keeping secrets from Sydney, Syd is wondering how many secrets her father is keeping from her. She has learned how to tell when someone is lying to her based on how they blink their eyes, and this week she discovers it's one of her dad's "tells" as well. His answer to one of her blunt questions causes her to remember a similar answer he gave to a question she posed when she was a child, and once again the past comes back to inform the present. But just as Jack's blinking eyes are what give him away in this episode, they're what she'll need to save her life in the next one. Vaughn's latest disastrous meeting with Jack gives Jack the upper hand in the "who loves Sydney best?" competition, but it's interesting how Vaughn will repeat back to Sydney what Jack said; it's as if Vaughn's listened to Syd's father, thought about it, and realized Jack is right. If you think of these early episodes with the hindsight of later ones, it's easy to imagine just how annoyed Jack could be with Vaughn. Like Will, however, Vaughn's just doing his job based on the suspicions he has and isn't trying to hurt anyone.

Finally, Sloane almost becomes human in this episode. Along with glimpses into his past, we discover, after many hints, that his wife is dying of lymphoma. Sloane's a man who works for the wrong side but isn't completely bereft of morals. He doesn't coldly issue hits on agents; rather, he realizes those orders are for the good of the operation. His treatment of Emily later in the season will open up more of his humanity, and it was perfect timing on the part of the writers to show this side of Sloane at this moment. Enough time has passed since Danny's death to allow viewers to get over that shock, but enough details are left sufficiently vague to allow us to continue happily hating Sloane.

Highlight: Vaughn giving Syd a surprise Christmas gift.

Interesting Fact: Although Sydney travels to Semba Island off the coast of Kenya, it's a fictional place made up for the episode.

Name That Guest Star: The character David McNeil, who appears in "Spirit," "The Coup," and "Page 47," was uncredited each time he was on the show. He was actually played by Ken Olin, who has directed more episodes of *Alias* than anybody else.

Did You Notice?: The suits, cars, and camera-lens tint in the scenes set in Cuba all evoke *Our Man in Havana*, the film based on Graham Greene's 1940s novel. The book is the story of Jim Wormold, a vacuum cleaner salesman in Havana whose daughter is prone to extravagant shopping sprees. He can't afford to keep up with her, so he accepts a job as an intelligence officer for the British Secret Service. When he can't find any news to pass on, he begins making up stories. Only when things begin going wrong and the stories become reality does he realize he's in trouble.

Nitpicks: What's with Hassan's new identity? Did he go to Driscoll and say, "Make me look like Saddam Hussein"?

What Did He Say?: By using the account numbers Syd got in "Mea Culpa," SD-6 has noticed Hassan communicating with someone on the remote Semba Island. Severn Driscoll is a master forger who lives on the island, and SD-6 thinks he's made a new identity for Hassan. Syd must travel there and find out what Hassan's new identity is.

Locations: Semba Island, Kenya; Havana, Cuba

Marshall's Gadgets: A pair of "super-swank" glasses that take photos and have telephoto lenses; a cellphone fitted with a card that will descramble any door keycode system so Syd can get into Driscoll's hotel room.

Music/Bands: As Francie, Will, Sydney, and Amy play Boggle, we hear "Santa's Dilemma" by Klyph Black (no album); Thunderball's "Domino" (*Scorpio Rising*) plays when Sydney first arrives on Semba Island; Freedy Johnston's "Love Grows (Where My Rosemary Goes)" (*Right Between the Promises*) plays when Syd and Will discuss her gift from Vaughn.

1.11   The Confession

Original air date: January 6, 2002
Written by: J.J. Abrams and Daniel Arkin
Directed by: Harry Winer
Guest cast: Aharon Ipalé (Ineni Hassan), James Handy (Arthur Devlin), Francesco Quinn (Minos Sakulos), Vincent Lappas (Techle), J. Anthony McCarthy (Bouncer), Matthew James Williamson (Bodyguard)

When the CIA decrypts the Cyrillic codes in Sydney's books and discovers orders to kill, Syd can no longer deny her suspicions about her father.

"The Confession" features Victor Garber at his cold, emotionless best, while at the same time depicting Jack's struggle to be a father to Sydney in some meaningful way. Usually Jack walks through every scene with a hard, stony look on his face, but as mentioned earlier, every once in a while there's a look of real pain and suffering that flashes in his eyes. What other actor on television can convey so many emotions without ever uttering a word? Garber does it brilliantly every time.

In this first time that Syd and Jack work together on a field op, Jack puts himself in major danger to protect Sydney, and he mentions how much he hates that she

That Strange Little Pen

Several times on *Alias* when Jack has needed to speak to Sydney at SD-6 without anyone listening in, he pulled out a pen to jam the radio frequencies so they could speak in private. The pen is capable of jamming the frequencies for one minute before it needs to be recharged — or so Jack says the first time he pulls it out — but the pen has been extremely inconsistent.

"Truth Be Told" — This is the first time that Jack uses the pen that jams the frequencies in the office so that he and Sydney can have a private conversation. If you time the scene, almost 60 seconds pass before the pen stops, which is very nicely done on the part of the writers and directors.

"The Confession" — Jack uses the pen frequency jammer, but it beeps after 70 seconds rather than 60.

"The Solution" — Jack pulls the top off his pen and says, "We've got two minutes." But the two previous times he's used it, they've only had one minute.

"Salvation" — When Jack pulls out the pen that distorts the recording devices so he can talk to Sydney, he uses it for *exactly* one minute, which is quite a feat on the part of the director.

"The Two" — Sydney uses her own variation on the pen when she activates an anti-eavesdrop watch that allows her to talk to Jack for two minutes.

works in this business. Later he pulls her aside at SD-6 and makes another awkward attempt to be a sort of father to her, and she's so touched by it that when Vaughn tells her immediately afterward what the CIA has discovered, she's overwhelmed with mixed feelings. Once again a character's hope and happiness is short lived, and Syd sees the gains she and Jack have made in their relationship slipping away as quickly as they had occurred. Just as Jack has taken risks for Sydney's protection — sacrificing

Russek, fighting with Vaughn over the Tuscany dead-drop — she now makes excuses for him, but in the end she knows there's only one thing she can do.

Meanwhile, Vaughn is also on a mission for personal reasons. He deals Syd the crushing blow that he knows will change her mind — he tells her that Jack Bristow caused his father's death. Syd knows that while she might be thrilled with the possibility of developing a friendship with her father for the first time in her life, Vaughn has been denied that chance and she can't go on lying to herself about it. Michael Vartan makes a major impact in this episode. Up to now he's been an interesting character who's provided some scrumptious eye candy for those viewers who are so inclined, but his character's personality has been rather dull and Vartan has had to play him without the on-screen charisma of someone like Victor Garber or even Ron Rifkin. Admittedly, it's difficult to act in an episode with someone of Garber's caliber and not come off as dry in comparison, but Vartan hasn't really been given much of a chance to shine. In this episode, as Vaughn struggles with his frustration with Sydney, tries to double-cross her, and then admits what he's done, we feel a real sympathy for him and hope that he can find some inner peace.

Despite all the ups and downs of each character's development, the bombshell that is dropped at the end of this episode is worth the entire hour. Even if you figured it out ahead of time, the looks on everyone's faces are priceless.

Highlight: Sydney going to Will's house and just crying, and his acceptance of it.

Nitpicks: SD-6 has satellite hookups everywhere; why doesn't anyone ever see Sydney doing things she shouldn't (putting Hassan on a chopper in this episode; putting Dixon on a CIA chopper in "Mea Culpa")? Also, Sydney would have had an alias in Athens, but Dixon runs in and calls out her real name. Finally, when Sydney is trapped in the weapons bunker she's covered in gas, yet when the explosion goes off and she's really close by, she doesn't catch on fire. With that much gas on her, the tiniest ember from the explosion would have set her alight.

Oops: Sydney needs to get a retinal scan on Sakulos, but her hair is completely obscuring her right eye, and it wouldn't have been possible to scan both his eyes if one lens in the glasses was covered. Also, when Sydney first walks into the room, Sakulos is sitting with three women. When the camera cuts back, there are four.

What Did He Say?: As soon as Hassan's death was announced, Minos Sakulos, a man who was practically Hassan's second-in-command, began trying to contact Hassan's old clients, saying he had a package and was accepting bids. Syd must go to Club Panthera, which is Sakulos's cover, and get specs of the package because SD-6 fears it might be nuclear.

Locations: Athens, Greece; Crete, Greece

Marshall's Gadgets: A pair of sunglasses that scans a person's retinas, then transfers the code to a remote computer that creates a pair of contact lenses with the retinal information encoded.

Music/Bands: When Sydney walks into the club in Athens to see Sakulos, the song playing is DJ Teebee's "Rave Alarm" (*Through the Eyes of a Scorpion*); Sting's "Someone to Watch Over Me" (*At the Movies*) is heard when a distraught Syd appears on Will's doorstep.

1.12 The Box, Part 1

Original air date: January 20, 2002
Written by: Jesse Alexander and John Eisendrath
Directed by: Jack Bender
Guest cast: Quentin Tarantino (McKenas Cole), Joey Slotnick (Agent Steven Haladki), Agnes Bruckner (Kelly McNeil), Sarah Shahi (Jenny), Patricia Wettig (Dr. Judy Barnett), Jennifer Tung (Toni), Ben Bray (Tchen), Kristof Konrad (Endo), Igor Jijikine (Chopper), Dave Lea (Ice), Jeff Wolfe (Gonov), Randy Hall (Security Agent #1), Lawrence Lowe (Security Agent #2)

A group led by a spurned former SD-6 agent, McKenas Cole (Quentin Tarantino), breaks into SD-6 in order to steal something from the vault for "The Man."

This fantastic two-part episode was a delight for Quentin Tarantino fans. The man who wrote and directed *Pulp Fiction* and *Reservoir Dogs* has never been more than a campy actor, but his overdramatized lines and his urban street talk — "we want a little sumpin-sumpin from the vault" — are always amusing for fans of his work. In this episode he plays the crazy white guy who talks the talk brilliantly, but his character is also a tragic one.

Like most people at SD-6, Cole believed he was working for the CIA when he went to Chechnya undercover in 1996. When he and the other agents were captured, he told his captors that he was working for the CIA, but the CIA denied any knowledge of him. He believes that denial was made by SD-6, and he has now returned to confront his Judas Iscariot. Sloane seems amused by Cole's pain and anger and sees him as nothing more than a harmless idiot. But he doesn't realize what Cole is capable of. After all, Cole's got . . . The Box.

Meanwhile, Sydney and Jack — two agents working to bring down SD-6 — might be the organization's saving grace. The two of them working together in the agency's

Quentin Tarantino may be one of the most celebrated directors in Hollywood, but McKenas Cole is the one with The Box.

underbelly to save the other SD-6 agents is thrilling, as we hope this will be the credibility Syd believes she still needs from Sloane. Ironically, she's trying to thwart Cole, who feels the same pain of betrayal as she does. She must be thinking about how she could have been the one charging into SD-6 fully armed and demanding information if she had handled things a little differently. The difference is, Cole doesn't realize the whole truth about SD-6, which is strange considering who he's working for; wouldn't The Man have told him the truth?

Over at the CIA, Vaughn is under investigation for his attachment to Sydney beyond the call of duty. Just as Sydney's emotional attachments to people constantly put her in danger, so too are Vaughn's feelings putting him at risk, which results in his being asked to withdraw from Sydney. However, her sudden decision to leave SD-6 has put Vaughn in a precarious position, and both he and Jack will be trying to change her mind.

Will takes another step toward discovering SD-6 now that he actually has the name of the group, although his assistant researches the name and says it's a chemical name for an artificial sweetener. It seems like the perfect name, actually, since SD-6 tricks its agents to work for them under artificial pretenses and makes it seem like they're making the world a "sweeter" place. Cole, on the other hand, knows otherwise.

Highlight: Tarantino's goofy and campy acting skills; his repetition of the words "The Box" throughout the episode is so over the top it's hilarious. Sloane: "I can't be the first person to have difficulty taking you seriously, can I?" Cole: "While that was a moderately clever retort, I'm the man holding The Box."

Interesting Fact: In an attempt to distract his captors, Marshall says to them, "As luck would have it, I'm feeling kind of a Stockholm Syndrome thing happening right now." *Stockholm Syndrome* is a term used to describe the strange phenomenon of a hostage feeling sympathy toward his or her captors and eventually siding with them. It got its name from a 1973 bank robbery in Stockholm, Sweden. Four hostages were taken and held captive in the bank vaults, and six days later they tried to avoid being rescued. They refused to testify against their captors and even raised money for their defense. Similar cases have emerged since, the most famous being the case of Patty Hearst. After she was kidnapped and reputedly tortured by the Symbionese Liberation Army, she sided with them and helped them rob a bank.

Name That Guest Star: Quentin Tarantino is best known for his one-two punch of *Reservoir Dogs* (1992) and *Pulp Fiction* (1994). Hailed as a wunderkind at the time, Tarantino suddenly became very overexposed, appearing in bad movies and participating in parodies of his movies and himself. He seemed to disappear from the scene until he released his comparatively lackluster *Jackie Brown* in 1997. He re-emerged in 2003 with the brilliant *Kill Bill* films. J.J. Abrams was a fan of Quentin Tarantino's work and decided to see if he would appear on the show: "I knew Quentin a little bit from years ago. I just heard he was a huge fan of the show and he was interested in being a part of it and I called him and we made it happen. We were writing a part that I thought would be really funny and perfect for him."

This is also Patricia Wettig's first episode on the show. She is married to Ken Olin, executive producer and director on *Alias*, and the two had worked together on the show *thirtysomething*, of which J.J. Abrams was a big fan. She played Nancy Krigger Weston and Olin played Michael Steadman.

Did You Notice?: This episode proved that Jack Bristow was not the one calling Will with the disguised voice (as some viewers initially thought); when Will gets one of the phone calls, Jack is trapped in an elevator with no cell signal. Also, this two-parter obviously pays homage to *Die Hard*, a movie about terrorists who take over an L.A. office building and demand the code to a safe. The writers acknowledge that when Cole's people pull into the parking garage in a van that says "McTiernan Air Conditioning." It's a nod to John McTiernan, who directed *Die Hard*.

Nitpicks: The driver of the A/C van that Cole's men use to break into SD-6 spots Sydney and Jack heading toward the elevator to go into SD-6. Why doesn't he radio the others to let them know two agents have just entered the building behind them? Also, why didn't Sydney just stay in the wall vent at the end? Why go up into the ducts when she knows how much noise that will make? Finally, it seems a little convenient that Sydney was able to spot the compact on Marshall's desk (which is absolutely covered in other gadgets) when Jack does a quick camera sweep of the office.

Marshall's Gadgets: Although he made it for another op, Marshall still has a gadget that comes into play in this episode. He has hidden a code scrambler in a compact, and Sydney tries to get it to scramble the code on the vault.

Music/Bands: As Sydney and Vaughn commiserate about losing their parents, we hear Enya's "How Can I Keep from Singing" (*Shepherd Moons*); Rob Zombie's "Dragula (Si Non Oscillas, Noli Tintinnare Mix)" (*American-Made Music to Strip By*) plays as Cole and his crew run through the hall to beat the laser beams.

1.13   The Box, Part 2

Original air date: February 10, 2002
Written by: Jesse Alexander and John Eisendrath
Directed by: Jack Bender
Guest cast: Quentin Tarantino (McKenas Cole), Joey Slotnick (Agent Steven Haladki), Agnes Bruckner (Kelly McNeil), James Handy (Agent Arthur Devlin), Jennifer Tung (Toni), Ben Bray (Tchen), Kristof Konrad (Endo), Igor Jijikine (Chopper), Dave Lea (Ice), Jeff Wolfe (Gonov), Geta Sesheta (CIA Secretary)

When Vaughn finds out something is happening at SD-6, he rushes over to try to save Sydney; meanwhile, the CIA discovers what Cole was looking for.

In this second part of "The Box," everything becomes even more exciting. Sydney discovers another double agent involved in the operation, Weiss threatens the very slimy Agent Haladki, Cole begins to lose it, and Sloane makes a major sacrifice to save SD-6.

Many of the events in the previous episode find a resolution in this conclusion. Vaughn was questioned by a psychiatrist — Judy Barnett — in the previous episode about being too attached to Sydney, and his actions in this installment prove that she was right. The question is, if it's in the CIA's best interest to protect Sydney, why is that a problem? His attachment keeps her alive; otherwise she'd be in Haladki's hands. Interestingly, in season 2 Vaughn will realize that it's *because* of his attachment to Sydney that they've been able to make so much headway in taking down the Alliance.

Sydney and Jack had a brief discussion at the beginning of the previous episode about Jack's bombshell at the end of "The Confession," but through the events of this two-parter, Sydney and Jack realize what a great team they make, and the ending of this episode is a touching one. The music on this show is always superbly chosen and appropriate to the scene, character, and episode, and the use of Fleetwood Mac's "Songbird" to close out "The Box" is perfect. With all the excitement in Sydney's life, Will's comment that her life is so normal compared with his is hilarious in its irony.

Poor Vaughn loses face in front of Devlin because of his inexperience in the face of danger. Jack has talked down to him repeatedly, Hassan double-crossed him, he's been taken off Sydney's case twice, and now he's being forced to see a psychiatrist. But in the end he comes through, proves himself a worthy field agent (we finally get to see Vaughn in a fight, although he doesn't seem too shaken when he kills a man), and gives Sydney a pep talk to convince her of her importance to the CIA and the United States. Vaughn will eventually prove himself in front of everyone, but this episode sees his first big breakthrough in the eyes of Sydney, the CIA, and Jack. "The Box" is a fantastic two-parter that broke convention (no foreign locations, no mission assignments) and kept fans riveted for two weeks.

Highlight: A toss-up between Cole's announcement over the P.A. system — "Dear person beating up my men . . . I am now standing in Sloane's tastefully minimalistic office . . ." — and his recollection to Sydney about their meeting five years earlier.

Interesting Fact: The Box that Cole fondles throughout the episode was actually found in Disney's Prop and Drape department, and *Alias* prop master Christopher Call speculates that it was originally used to hold mechanical pencils and drafting tools.

Did You Notice?: Dixon does the same thing Cole had done in 1996 — contact Langley to help him out. Both have the same feeling of being let down, although Dixon has no idea that the CIA does in fact answer his call. Also, the ship that Will visits to get the envelope is the *Alba Varden*, which is the name of the South African ship in *Lethal Weapon II*.

Nitpicks: Sydney tells Vaughn that she has no idea who has infiltrated SD-6, yet she heard Cole disclose his identity to Sloane *and*, just moments later, she explains who Cole is in front of Toni. It seems Syd's been hit in the head one too many times in this episode. Also, Sydney creates a makeshift wrench when she runs out of carbon dioxide, yet we can see another fire extinguisher right around the corner. And it's a little strange that Dixon would know the server number to contact Langley — how would SD-6 agents know that information and not be in danger of finding out the truth? Finally, when Dixon tells Jack that he's going to contact the CIA, he's sitting right next to him, yet when he *does* contact them, he's suddenly across the room from Jack.

Oops: When Endo radios Cole and Sydney begins beating him up, Cole can hear her hitting Endo, but no one is actually holding down the button on the walkie-talkie, so how could Cole be hearing anything? Also, when Cole is sitting over Toni, the camera cuts to Sloane, who no longer has the needle in his neck. When it cuts back a moment later, the needle is back in.

Marshall's Gadgets: Again, the gadget that comes into play in this episode was made for an earlier op in Lisbon, but it's an earring that explodes when thrown. The explosion causes a diversion, buying the SD-6 agents time.

Music/Bands: When Will tells Francie about the story he's pursuing, we hear "Rockaway" by Jesse Harris & The Ferdinandos (*Crooked Lines*); the show closes to the sounds of Fleetwood Mac's "Songbird" (*Rumors*).

1.14   The Coup

Original air date: February 24, 2002
Written by: Alex Kurtzman and Roberto Orci
Directed by: Tom Wright
Guest cast: Evan Dexter Parke (Charlie Bernard), David Anders (Sark), Allison Dean (Stella Campbell), Keone Young (Professor Choy), Ray Laska (Floor Manager), Stephen Liska (Ilyich Ivankov), Jorgo Ognevovski (Lavro Kessar), Patrick Pankhurst (Brandon Dahlgren), Christopher Grey (Security Guard), Douglas Robert Jackson (Dealer), James Lew (Quan Li), Joe Toppe (Security Officer), Frank Patton (Roulette Dealer), Bobby Rodgers (Reverend), John Fletcher (1st Card Player), Hamilton Mitchell (2nd Card Player)

While Syd is trying to decide whether to drop her school studies or not, she discovers that Charlie had an affair while dating Francie. Meanwhile, there's a new player in town associated with The Man.

It has been firmly established on this show that Syd's private life is inextricably linked to her crime-fighting one. Because of her sensitivity for the feelings of others, especially her friends, Syd always tries to support Francie and Will when things happen to them, even if she's trying to break into a casino in a disguise. In "The Coup," when Syd finds out that Charlie cheated on Francie, she's heartbroken for her best friend and ultimately must be the bearer of the bad news. Francie's response to Sydney shows some underlying hostility that Francie has been harboring for some time. She calls Sydney "elitist" and says she's changed since starting her new job (which was seven years ago, so how long has she held this grudge against Syd?), and as anyone would in an uncomfortable situation such as this one, Francie says a lot of things that she probably doesn't mean. Telling Francie about Charlie was one of the only moments of honesty in Sydney's life, and it's thrown right back in her face. She can probably only imagine what would happen if she told Dixon the truth about what she was doing.

Meanwhile, after breaking the news to Syd about her mother a few episodes ago, Jack begins to feel paternalistic toward his only daughter, and in his ham-fisted way he stumbles through a casual question — how is school going? — only to discover that being a father isn't that simple. Sydney tries to open up to him, but he isn't prepared for her response and takes another step backward in their relationship. However, his subsequent call to her, which is the first time he initiates a discussion and a meeting, is a wonderful moment on the show: they stand together and he tells her some things about her childhood. Jack just might be a good father after all — one who keeps secrets from her, is about as warm to her friends as an ice rink, and tortures people on the side, but a good father nonetheless.

Finally, Sydney's offer to Vaughn in "The Box" to get together and go to a hockey game is dealt with as he explains to her what he wishes their relationship could be like. It seems that Sydney brings out the best in the men who are closest to her. These guys, who once could barely string a sentence together in her presence without feeling awkward, are now opening up to her in ways they've never been able to before. The gradual development of Sydney's relationships with Vaughn and Jack is brilliantly handled by the writers on the show. They continue to keep an excellent balance between character development, the overall arc of Sydney's double agent duties, and her weekly missions. By the season's mid-point, there has still not been a misstep.

Highlight: Syd teasing Will about his hickey.

Interesting Fact: When David Anders first appeared on *Alias* as Sark, he was only 20 years old. And the British accent is fake; he's American. Also, it's interesting that Lumbly's alias is a Jamaican man; he's Jamaican by birth.

Nitpicks: McNeil gives Will the passcode to the computer room at a major corporation; McNeil hasn't been there in over eight years and the passcode has never changed? Also, Sydney's paper in her English class is entitled "F. Scott Fitzgerald: The Tragic Hero." That's subject matter for first-year undergrad essays, not an upper-year graduate paper. And Marshall gives Sydney a talk about the excruciatingly tight security at casinos, yet after she and Dixon get fingered as imposters they make it out of the casino without a problem? Finally, why is Sydney always unarmed in dangerous situations? She always seems to be up against the world's *worst* shots, and while the ending of this episode has one of the series' excellent trademark cliffhangers, the enemy shooters must have been myopic to have missed her.

Oops: When Will interviews McNeil, he has the tape recorder phone hookup attached to the bottom part of the receiver. In that spot, it would only pick up his part of the conversation, and he wouldn't have recorded any of McNeil's words; he's supposed to attach it to the earpiece end of the phone.

What Did He Say?: An unknown man entered the FTL headquarters in Hong Kong and assassinated the head of the corporation at the same time McKenas Cole entered SD-6. Nobody knows who the man is, but he stole a Rambaldi artifact and works for

The Man. This new group on the scene contacted K-Directorate to discuss sharing Rambaldi information, and SD-6 has found out that Brandon Dahlgren, a go-between for K-Directorate who lives in Las Vegas, will be receiving a phone call with details of the meeting. Syd and Dixon must find a way to intercept that phone call and, if they are successful in doing so, go to the meeting.

Locations: Hong Kong; Las Vegas, Nevada; Moscow, Russia

Marshall's Gadgets: Marshall makes an exact replica of Dahlgren's ring that contains a bug. There's also a razor prism that cuts into the fiber-optic cable at the casino while giving Sydney access to the data stream.

Music/Bands: As Syd puts makeup on Will's neck to cover his embarrassing hickey, we hear "Shoot the Moon" by Norah Jones (*Come Away with Me*); Chantal Kreviazuk's "Green Apples" (*Under These Rocks and Stones*) plays as Syd comforts Francie when Francie realizes Sydney was right.

1.15　　Page 47

Original air date: March 3, 2002
Written by: J.J. Abrams and Jeff Pinkner
Directed by: Ken Olin
Guest cast: Sarah Shahi (Jenny), Amy Irving (Emily Sloane), Michelle Arthur (Abigail), Jorgo Ognevovski (Lovro Kessar), Bryan Rasmussen (Officer Cohen), Don Took (Agent Grey)

Vaughn asks Sydney to use Sloane's wife to place a bug in his house, and Sydney discovers a horrible prophecy hidden in the Rambaldi manuscript.

An excellent episode full of suspense, "Page 47" brings two storylines together that had thus far been kept separate. Will has gotten too close to SD-6 through his Deep Throat contact, and Sloane insists that he must be stopped. The ensuing scene of Will's capture is an exciting one, and any viewer would think that Will must be trying to convince himself that the situation is a joke of some kind. After all, Will is a film buff, and only in the movies does someone get bugged, kidnapped, and beaten in an abandoned warehouse. However, when he wakes up with a splitting headache, he realizes that what he's been through is real.

Will's storyline inadvertently comes together with Syd's when Sydney goes to Sloane's house and brings Will. Jack and Vaughn both show slight disconcertment when she tells them she's going to bring Mr. Tippin to the mad tea party, and it's one of the first times the two men agree on anything. The look on Sloane's face when Will walks through the door is worth the entire episode, and the subsequent discussion over the dinner table with the whole gang — about the evil boss who would kill you if you spoke out against him — is one of the best scenes of the season. Amy Irving is excellent as Emily Sloane, and through her we see a teensy bit of humanity in Sloane while being shocked that someone as endearing and big-hearted as Emily could be married to someone who just might be the epitome of evil.

Meanwhile, Sydney talks to Vaughn about the Rambaldi manuscript with the missing page. He tells her that the whole Rambaldi cult seems like the sort of stuff people wearing pyramids on their heads might believe in, but despite being skeptical of the whole "prophecy" issue, he is being forced to pursue it. Later, Sydney will have a similar discussion with Sloane, in which she tells him that she doesn't really believe in the Rambaldi prophecy and he admits that he's obsessed by it. But what she discovers at the end of this episode might make a believer out of anyone.

Highlight: Vaughn and Sydney's discussion after she mentions how impressed she is by a bug Vaughn gives her. Vaughn: "You should see the guys who make it. It's like they've never seen sunlight." Sydney: "You should meet Marshall."

Interesting Fact: Will suggests that he and Sydney should see *North by Northwest*, an interesting choice for both of them, since it's a film about an ad executive who is mistaken for a government agent and pursued by spies across the country.

Name That Guest Star: Amy Irving, who plays Emily Sloane, had her first memorable movie role in *Carrie*, when she played Carrie's best friend, Sue. She has since appeared in movies like *The Fury*, *Micki + Maude*, *Who Framed Roger Rabbit*, *Traffic*, and *Tuck Everlasting* (alongside Victor Garber). She was married to Steven Spielberg from 1985 to 1989, and they have one son. J.J. Abrams was excited about her debut in "Page 47": "We got to introduce Amy Irving as Mrs. Sloane, and she is wonderful. The whole sequence where they're having dinner at Sloane's house is the first time we got to see Sloane in that world."

Did You Notice?: Sloane lies to Sydney about where the journal is being sent for analysis.

Oops: The timing is all off in this episode. Sloane shows Jack some videotape of Will visiting McNeil in prison "a few hours ago" and says that it was his third visit and something must be done, so Jack arranges to have Will bugged for his next visit to the prison. But when Will goes to see McNeil, he tells him about the computer files he retrieved after their second visit, making the current visit their third. Earlier in the episode, Will wakes up in the morning and tells Jenny that he's going to interview McNeil. He calls Sydney, who is still in Moscow, to tell her some news. Then Sydney chats with Francie in the living room on what appears to be the same morning that

Will called her — she is back from Moscow already? Perhaps Marshall has constructed a transporter beam for Sydney and a time machine for Sloane?

What Did He Say?: Ilyich Ivankov, who was the head of K-Directorate, was the man killed in the previous episode and his body has been returned to his agency. Sloane believes that Sark has kidnapped Kessar, K-Directorate's second-in-command, and he may be killed also. By analyzing the videotape that Sydney has captured, Marshall believes that Sark is Irish, and SD-6 has located a plane in Tunisia that is ready to fly to Galway, Ireland, leading them to believe the meeting point between K-Directorate and Sark will be in Tunisia. Sydney must intercept Rambaldi's journal — the item changing hands — and bring it home.

Locations: Sekhira, Tunisia

Marshall's Gadgets: Although we don't see Marshall briefing Sydney, she sprays people in the face with something that renders them unconscious.

Music/Bands: John Mayer's "No Such Thing" (*Room for Squares*) plays as Will and Jenny discuss the award Will has been nominated for; we hear "Landslide" from Smashing Pumpkins (*Pisces Iscariot*) when Francie and Syd take their engagement rings off together; Abra Moore's "Home" (*No Fear*) plays when Emily asks Sydney to dinner; and "Feelin' the Same Way" by Norah Jones (*Come Away with Me*) plays when Syd is preparing for dinner and chatting with Francie.

1.16   The Prophecy

Original air date: March 10, 2002
Written by: John Eisendrath
Directed by: Davis Guggenheim
Guest cast: Roger Moore (Edward Poole), Lindsay Crouse (Dr. Carson Evans), James Handy (Director Arthur Devlin), Derrick O'Connor (Alexander Khasinau), Joey Slotnick (Agent Steven Haladki), Castulo Guerra (Jean Briault), Wolf Muser (Ramon Veloso), Amy Irving (Emily Sloane), Joe D'Angerio (Dr. Watterson), Robert Arce (Hobbes), Allen Williams (Senator Mark Townsend), Lilyan Chauvin (Signora Ventutti), Anya Matanovic (Opera Student), Joseph Vassallo (Vatican Station Chief)

Sydney undergoes various tests administered by members of the government's Department of Special Research (DSR) as they try to determine if she plays a role in Rambaldi's prophecy.

"The Prophecy" moves away from Syd's personal life (there isn't much development between her and Vaughn or her and Jack) and focuses almost entirely on

Rambaldi's prophecy. Up to now we've seen the maniacal search for Rambaldi artifacts carried out by people on power trips, but now we see that there's actually a government-sanctioned group of people who follow the word of Rambaldi and are testing it for its veracity. Despite being a nonbeliever, Syd is caught in the middle. What if Rambaldi is a complete fraud? What if all the DSR's tests are just a load of bunk, and Sydney's actually right — there is no proof of the prophecy? Sydney's back is against the wall, because at this point it doesn't matter if she is innocent of every-thing; the DSR people have been given the legal right to treat Syd however they want, and all of her personal rights seem to have been waived. It's an interesting concept, similar to the one presented in the movie *Minority Report*, that someone could be arrested for a crime they will commit in the future.

The scene between Emily and Sydney is a touching one as well; Sydney shows an ease around Emily that she doesn't have with a lot of people. Later she will say that Emily is like a mother to her, and that would explain why, when Emily makes a rather shocking statement, Sydney chooses to turn a blind eye rather than mention it to anyone.

The second plot in "The Prophecy" involves Sloane's interaction with the Alliance. Having Roger Moore play Edward Poole, the British head of SD-9, was a stroke of genius on the part of casting. It's as if James Bond himself has shown up to pass the torch to Sydney Bristow as this generation's secret agent of choice. While he's not on screen for long, his presence is large and effective, and Sloane's actions and reactions in this episode show a vulnerability that we've only seen when he's around Emily. Sloane is as capable of being manipulated as he is of manipulating others, and what he does in this episode will come up again in season 2 (although there it'll be to his advantage). Sloane is slowly becoming the most fascinating character in the series as we receive small hints about his past and his strange, conflicting beliefs. Does he share a connection to Rambaldi? And, in turn, to Sydney?

Highlight: The scene of Vaughn and Sydney breaking into the Vatican set to The Hives' "Hate to Say I Told You So."

Interesting Fact: J.J. Abrams was thrilled to be able to cast Roger Moore, one of his childhood heroes. At the time of filming this episode, he told reporters, "When I found out it was a possibility that he could work on *Alias* I just went insane. When I went to see my first James Bond movie, for me, that was just who James Bond was." To which Roger Moore countered, "Well, you see, [he's just saying that] because he couldn't get Sean Connery."

Name That Guest Star: It's not really necessary to explain who Roger Moore is. Best known as "Bond, James Bond" (1973–1985) Moore is the perfect actor to guest star on *Alias*. When Moore was working on *Alias* he said, "I would hate, as Bond, ever to have come across somebody like Jennifer Garner. She's far too pretty, she's far too young, and she's far too talented and athletic."

Did You Notice?: Lindsay Crouse is probably most recognizable to *Alias* viewers who have also watched *Buffy the Vampire Slayer* as Professor Walsh. Interestingly, she played a similar character on that show — a government researcher who was intent on taking down Buffy.

Nitpicks: The DSR is clearly an *X-Files*-inspired organization, but did the interrogator have to look *exactly* like Cigarette-Smoking Man?

Oops: During the interrogation, when Sydney is given the tests, her eyes are staring forward on a monitor, yet in the background you can see her looking up and down constantly.

What Did He Say?: The surveillance photos Sydney took in Brazil identified Alexander Khasinau as "The Man." He used to be a highly decorated member of the KGB, but he now has ties to the Russian Mafia and heads up a far more dangerous organization. He is the one Sark contacted when the Rambaldi manuscript was stolen. He's now gone missing and SD-6 must be careful making its next move. Sloane talks to Jack privately, telling him that Khasinau must be killed but the Alliance won't allow it — five of the Alliance's voting members are former Soviet bloc and will elect to save Khasinau.

Locations: Rio de Janeiro, Brazil (the location is never stated, but the instantly recognizable statue of Christ the Redeemer tips us off); Rome, Italy; Montreal, Canada; London, England

Music/Bands: Bill Bonk's "World Gone Mad" (*Spaghetti Western*) plays when Will and Francie talk about basketball; Hathaway's "Feels Like Home" (no album) is heard when Francie asks Sydney if her "prophecy" has come true yet; Sydney and Vaughn break into the Vatican to the sounds of The Hives' "Hate to Say I Told You So" (*Veni Vidi Vicious*); and Mint Royale's "From Rusholme with Love" (*On the Ropes*) is playing when Syd joins Will and Francie at the Zebu Lounge.

1.17   Q & A

Original air date: March 17, 2002
Written by: J.J. Abrams
Directed by: Ken Olin
Guest cast: Terry O'Quinn (Agent Kendall), Joey Slotnick (Agent Steven Haladki), Jon Simmons (FBI Officer), Andrew A. Rolfes (Guard), Lisa Dinkins (FBI Agent Baker), Frank Hoyt Taylor (FBI Agent Dunn)

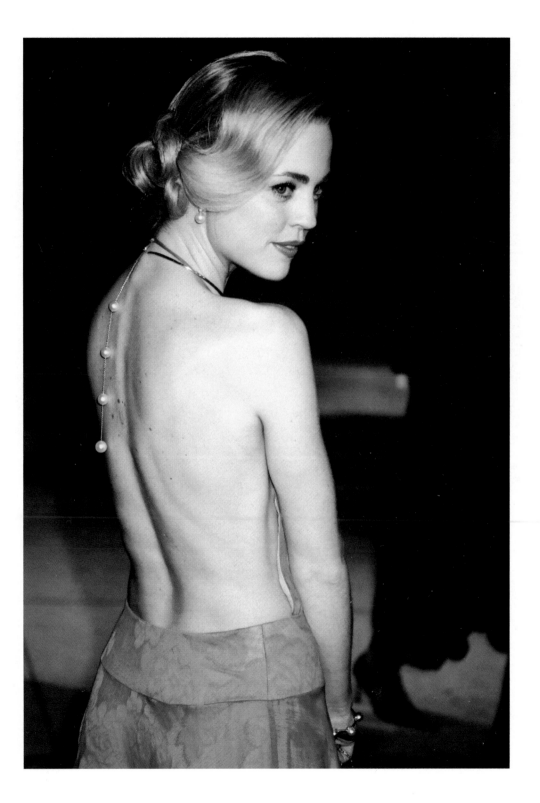

When Sydney is taken in for questioning by a special division of the FBI, she must recount her life story and explain how she ended up at SD-6.

The flashback episode. Most television shows do it at some point, and for a series as complicated as this one, it was inevitable. "Q & A" offered the show an opportunity to bring in a new audience while being a primer for recently converted viewers or longtime watchers who needed a quick review. But unlike most series, where the writers get tired at some point during the season and slot in a tedious segment in which the characters hang out on the couch saying, "Do you remember that time when . . . ?" this episode actually introduced new material, maintained a fast-paced storyline, and even presented more information in the flashback sequences than we'd gotten originally.

As Sydney describes how she first entered the world of SD-6, we see footage of her working her way up through the ranks, whereas earlier, when she'd told Danny who she was, we got a very quick retelling of events. She finally defines oft-used words like *black ops*, which have always been used but never fully explained to viewers. Certain new scenes, like when Sloane welcomes Sydney to SD-6 as if he's never met her before, have a resonance with longtime viewers who know that Sloane has known Sydney since the day she was born. We get a quick glimpse at Sydney's many outfits, a recap of who Rambaldi was and why so many people are looking for his artifacts, and an overview of the most important moments thus far for anyone who might be too bogged down in the details each week to be able to step back and see the broad picture.

Meanwhile, Jack and Vaughn work together harmoniously for the first time as they try to find a way to rescue Sydney. Haladki becomes even slimier than before, and Weiss proves that his loyalty lies with friends over protocol. Vaughn tells Sydney what he thinks of her, and Jack refers to her using an affectionate term for the first time. But as the episode comes to its thrilling climax, Sydney has a revelation that changes the course of her life — and the direction of the series.

Highlight: Jack threatening Haladki: "If you report this conversation, you'll never wear a hat again."

Interesting Fact: Sydney rattles off three international disasters: India, 1992; Japan, 1996; Germany, 2001. These incidents are fiction, which makes sense considering how inappropriate it would have been to have taken real-life tragedies and made up a reason for why they happened.

Did You Notice?: In the final scene, Sydney's wearing Marshall's "super-swank" sunglasses, or at least an exact replica of them. Also, this is the first time an episode of *Alias* begins where it ends, a plot device that will be used a lot more in the future. Finally, the scene of Will and Francie on the couch eating popcorn was a nice touch given that Sydney's life seems to be the stuff of movies, and they watch the chase scene as if it's fiction and not something that's actually happening.

Nitpicks: Why, for an operation this covert, did Jack and Vaughn use agency-issued vehicles? Couldn't they have gone to a Budget car rental dealer to get Sydney some wheels? Also, considering that short wig was something Sydney pulled on quickly in the trunk of a car, how could it have stayed on underwater like it was glued to her head? Finally, why didn't any police scuba divers jump into the water to see what had happened?

Oops: When Sydney's car goes underwater, the windows are already down (which is how it fills up so quickly), yet when she tries to escape she rolls the window down.

Music/Bands: Smashmouth's "Diggin' Your Scene" (*Astro Lounge*) plays during the montage of Sydney's various missions and disguises.

1.18   Masquerade

Original air date: April 7, 2002
Written by: Roberto Orci and Alex Kurtzman
Directed by: Craig Zisk
Guest cast: Peter Berg (Noah Hicks), Angus Scrimm (Agent McCullough), Patricia Wettig (Dr. Judy Barnett)

Sydney runs into an old flame while on a mission in Vienna, but Dixon doesn't believe he is to be trusted.

A "masque," or a dance of masked figures, was a common form of entertainment in the medieval periods in England, France, and Italy, where it first gained prominence. The masque in England was most popular during the reigns of Elizabeth I, James I, and Charles I, when it was an elaborate combination of dance, performance, poetry, and song. The more intricate courtly form of the masque evolved from the folk tradition of "mumming," in which masked revelers would roam from house to house, enter, perform a small play, and then pass a hat around for coins. By the reign of James I the masque was so spectacular that guests would first walk through the streets in their costumes before arriving at the palace, where they would put on a stage play complete with sophisticated set designs and storylines. Shakespeare's *Love's Labour's Lost* and *The Tempest* feature versions of the masque, and poets such as Sir Philip Sidney and Ben Jonson actively wrote masques for their sovereigns. Today the masque is remembered in the form of masquerade balls and is still seen in opera or in films such as *Eyes Wide Shut*. It's a fitting theme for *Alias* because so many of the characters are wearing masks of their own, performing their own little dances around friends and family, and keeping secrets about who they are.

In this episode, there are several masquerades. Sydney and Jack now know that Laura Bristow is alive and are surprised to discover that someone close to them knew it and has been keeping it a secret from them. Sydney learns that her father suffered a lot of grief when she was a child, and he had been hiding his true guilt and sadness by gradually pulling away from her over the years. The scenes of Jack almost begging Sydney not to pursue a search for her mother are heartrending.

Later, Jack puts on a front for the counselor, but she sees through the charade. His reaction to her accusation is one of the highlights of this episode. In a subtle way he challenges this person who is supposed to understand human nature when he asks her how she expects someone in his position to act; after all, his life and Sydney's are 24-hour masquerades. Meanwhile, Will and Francie inadvertently find out that Sydney has been keeping things from them, and they vow to pull off her mask and reveal who she really is and what is really going on.

At the masquerade ball, Sydney discovers her dance partner is someone from her past, and the arrival on the scene of Noah Hicks is an intriguing development, albeit one that didn't exactly sit well with the Syd-Vaughn-shippers. Sydney and Noah's relationship is one that was never reconciled to either's satisfaction (a misunderstanding five years prior left both of them hurt and confused). But Noah immediately appeals to Sydney in that he offers her a chance to be in a relationship where she's not lying to anyone and her partner is heroic and clearly hates Sloane. Is Noah someone she can trust, or does Sydney have to face the prospect of yet another loved one deceiving her in some way?

Highlight: Francie and Will speculating on what Sydney was doing in Italy.

Name That Guest Star: Actor/writer/director Peter Berg starred on *Chicago Hope* from 1995 to 1999 as Dr. Billy Kronk. While on the show he tried his hand at directing and has since directed films such as *Very Bad Things* and *The Rundown.* His most recent acting credit, aside from *Alias,* is in *Collateral* with Tom Cruise.

Did You Notice?: This is the fourth time that Roberto Orci and Alex Kurtzman have co-written an episode, and each time they switch whose name is listed first.

Nitpicks: Sydney sits through the briefing meeting with Sloane (where Marshall is covered in hives), argues with him afterward, leaves the office, and then goes out into the parking garage where Jack meets her. Presumably at some point after leaving Sloane's office and before entering the parking garage she receives the earrings from Marshall, yet when we see him explaining the earrings to her in flashback, he is no longer covered in hives — something he had all over his face just moments earlier. Did she go back to

SD-6 later even though she was supposed to leave for Vienna immediately?

What Did He Say?: Kyle Wexler, one of two undercover agents at the Russian embassy in Vienna, has sent a communiqué saying that Alexander Khasinau has converted $250 million in assets into cash. He's got all of Khasinau's transactions on a microchip that he will pass off to Sydney at a masquerade ball in Vienna. Later, Sloane explains that Khasinau has bought two Westbury 23 supercomputers (interesting that when you add 23 and 23, you get 46 — just one number short of the magic 47). These computers are capable of accounting for the Rambaldi artifacts Khasinau already has and figuring out the pieces he's missing. Syd and Noah must steal the data core.

Locations: Mt. Sabasio, Italy; Vienna, Austria; Arkhangelsk, Russia

Marshall's Gadgets: Diamond earrings that emit an infrared pulse. The agent passing off the microchip to Sydney will be wearing contact lenses that allow him to see the pulse and determine where she is. Later, although we don't see Marshall brief her on the gadget, Syd and Noah use a camera that emits a bright light that renders the enemy unconscious.

Music/Bands: "Plus Bele Que Flor . . ." by Anonymous 4 (*Love's Illusion*) plays when Sydney reaches the peak of Mt. Sabasio; when Will makes chocolate chip pancakes we hear "Lay Your Weary Body Down" by Gigolo Aunts (*Pacific Ocean Blues*); The Doves' "Break Me Gently" (*Lost Souls*) is heard when Sydney and Noah try to decrypt the microchip; and as Syd and Noah get a little closer in the cabin we hear Depeche Mode's "Dream On" (*Exciter*).

1.19   Snowman

Original air date: April 14, 2002
Written by: Jesse Alexander and Jeff Pinkner
Directed by: Barnet Kellman
Guest cast: Peter Berg (Noah Hicks), Natasha Pavlovich (Irina Derevko), Stephen Spinella (Mr. Kishell), Boris Lee Krutonog (Igor Sergei Valenko), Angus Scrimm (Agent McCullough), Paul Lieber (Bentley Calder), Patricia Wettig (Dr. Judy Barnett), Richard F. Whiten (Officer Pollard), Don Took (Agent Grey), Scott Vance (Agent Douglas)

As the CIA is on the trail of a K-Directorate assassin called "The Snowman," Sydney finds video footage of her mother.

"Snowman" is an excellent episode that gives viewers a glimpse of what Jack Bristow really went through 20 years earlier when he discovered his wife was a traitor. The ongoing theme throughout the series is deceit, whether for honest reasons or devious ones. Laura Bristow lied to Jack and Sydney for her own gain, while Sydney lies to Will and Francie for their protection. In "Q & A," Kendall questioned Sydney's loyalty and common sense when he asked how an intelligent girl like her could have believed SD-6 was actually a good organization. Similarly, it's hard for the characters on this show not to wonder how Jack could have had the wool pulled over his eyes by Irina Derevko for an entire decade. For someone trained to catch a person in a lie, how could he not have seen through her deceit?

When old flame Noah Hicks (played by Peter Berg) shows up in Sydney's life, she's torn about her feelings for him.

In "Snowman," viewers — and Sydney — see firsthand just how Jack could have been duped. Sydney finds the video footage retrieved from Khasinau's data core in the previous episode and watches her mother call her father a fool and explain how she deceived her husband. Later, when we watch Jack view the same footage, the look on his face is an extension of the grief we learned about in "Masquerade." Once again Jack goes to bat for Sydney against his better judgment when he begs Sloane to leave Noah alone and not imprison him based on SD-6's suspicions. But the viewer can't help but wonder about Jack's motive. He's actually sided with Sloane on this issue and doesn't trust Noah any more than Dixon does. Does he believe that Noah might actually turn out to be a traitor? If so, will it show Sydney firsthand what he'd gone through with Irina? At this point viewers are pretty certain of Jack's love for his daughter, that he would never do anything to hurt her intentionally, but maybe through this bit of tough love he might show her that *not* trusting someone can hurt less than trusting them and being caught off guard.

Meanwhile, Sydney is cornered by her two best friends when they confront her about her plane ticket. It's a close call, but it reminds her once again just how dangerously close she keeps coming to hurting Will and Francie. The distraught look on her face afterward is a window to her thoughts: if they ever find out what she really does for a living — that her life has been a bizarre lie to them for the past seven years — will they react the same way Jack did when he found out the truth about Irina? Is she living the same lie that her mother once did?

Highlight: The footage of Irina Derevko explaining her mission to the KGB.

Did You Notice?: In the video footage that Syd watches, Irina Derevko is played by Natasha Pavlovich. Though Lena Olin hadn't yet been cast in the role, this actress speaks with a heavy Russian accent, something Olin won't use later. Also, she refers to "Project Christmas" for the first time, something that will play a much bigger role in season 2. Finally, the scene in which Sydney is left dangling is reminiscent of *Mission Impossible*, where Tom Cruise's character is left hanging by Jean Reno.

Nitpicks: The getaway at the beginning of this episode is even more outlandish than any James Bond opening sequence. If Sydney and Noah had been extracted by a helicopter it would have been believable, but a large airplane? The speed at which the craft was traveling would have been enough to snap both their backs as soon as the wire had been connected. It was a spectacular scene to watch, but too far-fetched.

Oops: When Marshall is demonstrating the armband to Sydney and Noah, you can hear him clicking it off before the music comes in. We should have heard both simultaneously or, more likely, not heard the beep of the armband at all.

What Did He Say?: Marshall reconstructed some data from the server files and located Calder's home in Australia; Sydney has to go there, get him, and bring him back.

Locations: Bogotà, Colombia; Cape Town, South Africa; Mackay, Australia

Marshall's Gadgets: An armband that emits a sound that cancels out all noise when triggered; a wireless modem that can pull information off a server when held three inches away from it.

Music/Bands: Matt Beckler's "From the Summer," from his self-titled CD, plays when Francie and Will talk about how they're going to bring up the plane ticket with Sydney; when Jack and Sydney discuss Noah we hear Jeff Buckley's "Lover, You Should Have Come Over" (*Grace*); "Ready Steady Go" by Paul Oakenfold (featuring Asher D, *Bunkka*) plays while Sydney and Noah are on their mission; Hathaway's "There's Something Better" (no album) is heard when Sydney sits in the bathroom and regrets lying to Francie and Will; and "My Favorite Regret" by Gigolo Aunts (*Pacific Ocean Blues*) plays when Syd tells Noah she can't join him on the island.

1.20   The Solution

Original air date: April 21, 2002
Written by: John Eisendrath
Directed by: Daniel Attias
Guest cast: James Handy (Director Arthur Devlin), David Anders (Mr. Sark), Tony Amendola (Agent Tambor Barceló), Kirk B.R. Woller (Exterminator), Amy Irving (Emily Sloane), Michelle Arthur (Abigail), Alec Maray (Sial), Al Faris (Salim Wahid), Zuhair Haddad (Sayyad), Nameer El-Kadi (Algosaibi)

Sydney proposes a mission that will use a fake Rambaldi artifact as bait to bring Khasinau to the CIA.

"The Solution" is an episode that brings many former storylines back into play and alludes to earlier episodes. While "Q & A" might have refreshed some memories and introduced the main elements of the storyline to new viewers, it overlooked Will's tracking down leads to SD-6 (which was last mentioned in episode 15). That plotline comes back to the fore when Will's source reveals who kidnapped him in "Page 47." His subsequent confrontation with his kidnapper sparks the events that will follow in the next two episodes.

Sloane is also reminded of former events when the assassination of Jean Briault (from "The Prophecy") is used against him to threaten Emily. When Sloane is confronted with proof that Emily knows more about SD-6 than she should, it's not surprising that he pleads for her to receive the mercy he refused to show Danny under the same circumstances. It's also interesting that when telling Sydney that knowledge of SD-6 is like a virus that needs to be contained, Jack uses the same words Sloane did in "Truth Be Told," as if the line is part of an upper-management SD-6 handbook. Will Sloane take the Alliance up on its offer?

As Sydney loses faith in her mission again, Vaughn is there, as always, to prop her up. He explains how important she is to the agency, and he pulls out the same map he'd shown her in "So It Begins." But where he'd used that map earlier to prove to her that she was naïve and cocky, he is now using it to show her how fruitful her efforts have been. His assurances also give her the confidence to propose her own CIA mission for the first time.

All these strands are woven together in this episode to show just how tight the writing has been all season and to prove to viewers how important it's been to tune in every week. Missing just one small piece of information at this point would really confuse a novice viewer, and it's this efficiency that makes *Alias* so exciting week after week. Where other series might have stand-alone episodes or throwaway episodes that

Languages

Sydney has shown a remarkable dexterity with languages, and she is fluent in several. So far we've seen her speak 15 languages on the series (mostly Russian, which is appropriate considering her mother is Russian):

Chinese — Truth Be Told, Prelude
Arabic — So It Begins
Russian — So It Begins, Parity, Page 47, Dead Drop, Endgame, Reunion, Full Disclosure, The Frame, Blood Ties
Spanish — Parity, Doppelgänger, Countdown, A Missing Link, Legacy
German — Doppelgänger, Double Agent, Second Double, Succession
Romanian — Reckoning
Italian — Time Will Tell, The Prophecy, Trust Me, The Two
Malaysian — The Solution, Rendezvous
Hungarian — The Indicator
Japanese — The Counteragent
Hindi — The Passage, Part Two
Vietnamese — A Higher Echelon
French — The Two
Bulgarian — The Nemesis
Korean — Crossings

can be missed without losing sight of the big picture, *Alias* always has so much on the go that the writers can't afford to lose a week. As Sydney comes closer than she knows to Dixon finding out the truth about her duality or Will discovering what her real job is, other elements of the story come flying together to send viewers toward the season's thrilling conclusion. Will Jack discover who Will's source is? Will the persistent Will uncover the truth about Sydney? Will Sloane be forced to lose Emily or will he exercise a double standard? Will Dixon discover that Sydney's been betraying him?

And will Marshall be able to sell one of his pop-up books to a children's publisher?

Highlight: Sark challenging Sydney to a latajang duel.

Interesting Fact: This is the first time we hear Vaughn speaking French; Michael Vartan lived in France for many years and is fluent in the language.

Nitpicks: Vaughn shows how incompetent he is with undercover fieldwork in the final scene. As Sydney is challenged by Sark to a duel, he keeps yelling in her ear, "Is he asking you to fight him? What is he doing now?" as if she could somehow answer him. He seems to yell the entire time in fact, and Sydney's just lucky that Sark can't hear him through the earpiece.

What Did He Say?: For the first time, the mission statement comes from Sydney. She explains that a year ago some SD-6 agents broke into a museum in Algiers to steal artifacts (Sloane believed there would be Rambaldi artifacts among them). The agents were caught and SD-6 killed them before they could talk. Sydney proposes breaking into the museum and stealing some objects, then leaking word to the black market that among the items was a second Rambaldi ampule of liquid. She suggests they bait Khasinau with this fake news. Later, Vaughn leaks information that the ampule is owned by a splinter group of the Raslak Jihad and that Khasinau is willing to pay for the vial in diamonds. Khasinau will be sending Sark as his representative.

Locations: Algiers, Algeria; Denpasar, Indonesia

Music/Bands: Syd, Francie, and Will discuss their rodent issues to Ray's "Do You Care?" (no album); Trickside's "Coming Down," from their self-titled CD, plays when Will tells Abigail to publish his story if he disappears; and when Sydney tells Francie about Noah, we hear "I'm Gone" by Alison Krauss and Union Station (*New Favorite*).

1.21   Rendezvous

Original air date: May 5, 2002
Written by: Erica Messer and Debra J. Fisher
Directed by: Ken Olin
Guest cast: David Anders (Mr. Sark), Derrick O'Connor (Alexander Khasinau), Joseph Ruskin (Alain Christophe), Wolf Muser (Ramon Valoso), Kamala Lopez Dawson (Dr. Lemon), Amy Irving (Emily Sloane), Philippe Bergeron (Lucques Trepanier), Christopher Dukes (Alpha Team Leader), Yvans Jourdain (Second Door Guard), Angela Nogard (Makeup Artist), Tom Waite (Interrogator)

As Sydney travels to Paris to obtain a Rambaldi document, Will meets up with his source — in the same city.

"Rendezvous" is easily one of the top-five episodes of the season. Erica Messer and Debra J. Fisher also penned the equally fantastic "Mea Culpa" earlier in the season, and their style includes bringing many storylines together — all of which impact Sydney in some way — while keeping viewers tense with excitement. *Alias* has developed its signature of ending each episode with a cliffhanger, but this episode ends with several, sending every storyline into hyperdrive just in time for the season finale.

Sloane renders himself a sympathetic character throughout this episode. Given a reprieve on the fatwa the Alliance was about to put on his wife's head, Sloane looks inward and finally expresses guilt and remorse for what happened to Danny. While even his current situation couldn't make anyone forgive him for what he's done in the past, we can't help but wonder if he might think twice the next time an agent slips up. The writers cleverly use Sloane's situation with SD-6 to make the doctor's "happy" declaration at the end of the episode a positively devastating one.

Over at the CIA, Weiss gives Vaughn a wake-up call when he confronts him about what happened in Denpasar. Before, Vaughn's concern for Sydney's well-being might have been questioned by others, but it always ended up being a positive thing for the agency. This time, however, Vaughn committed a pretty big mistake that has cost the CIA dearly, and Weiss tells him things must change. It's one thing for the CIA's psychiatrist to tell Vaughn that perhaps his relationship with Sydney is an inappropriate one, but with Weiss taking the fall for him, it really hits home for Vaughn.

The best part of this episode involves Will. Throughout the season he's been acting in what he thinks are Sydney's best interests even when he should have been backing off, and he believes that his actions could prevent further murders by the mysterious "SD-6." In this episode he gets a small taste of what Sydney's life is like when he goes undercover with Jack's help, but their operation has a shocking ending. The look on his face when the red-haired lounge singer leaps into the room where he's being held captive, the wish fulfillment we all get when he finally sees Sydney performing her kick-ass moves in the club, and Will's comment on the whole fiasco when Syd and Jack argue in the car — "Who *are* you people?!" — make for the highlight of the season.

When Sydney gets a chance to speak with Will calmly afterward, his reaction to the situation is one few people would have predicted. Will has proven himself a loyal friend, and even when he doesn't know the whole story behind a situation, he's smart enough to know when it's time to shut up and stop asking questions. That Dixon has gotten so close to Sydney's secret (when he remembers her words from "Mea Culpa") is less worrisome when we see the positive way that Will interprets Syd's actions thus far. However, the shocking ending to this episode — the most upsetting one so far — shows us what happens to people who find out Sydney's secrets.

Highlight: Will's scream when Sydney shows up to rescue him.

Interesting Fact: Jennifer Garner is actually doing the singing in the lounge scene. Just when you thought the lady couldn't have any more hidden talents . . .

Did You Notice?: Just before the story cuts to a meeting of the Alliance, we see a stock shot of the Houses of Parliament in London, England, which makes it look like the Alliance meets there.

Nitpicks: In "The Solution," Jack tells Will not to ask his contact for a meeting because it would be a dead giveaway; in this episode he tells him to insist upon a meeting.

What Did He Say?: Sark and Khasinau will be meeting in a Parisian club so that Sark can hand over the Rambaldi ampule to Khasinau. Khasinau needs the liquid to make the invisible ink readable on a Rambaldi document that he has. SD-6 will give Sark a fake ampule, and Sydney will retrieve the real document from Khasinau's safe and replace it with a counterfeit.

Locations: Denpasar, Indonesia; London, England; Paris, France

Marshall's Gadgets: A ring that is a cardiac event recorder. Khasinau's safe opens when it detects Khasinau's heart rhythms, so when Sydney holds the ring over a part of Khasinau's body, it will record his pulse and send the ECG data to Dixon's cell phone. Dixon will then be able to trick Khasinau's safe by using the heart rhythms.

Music/Bands: Jacintha's "Autumn Leaves" (*Autumn Leaves — Songs of Johnny Mercer*) plays when Sark and Khasinau first enter the club; Jennifer Garner sings the Buddy Johnson classic "Since I Fell for You"; and Maren Ord's "Just Like You" (*Waiting*) plays when Will and Sydney talk at the CIA safehouse.

1.22   Almost Thirty Years

Original air date: May 12, 2002
Written and directed by: J.J. Abrams
Guest cast: David Anders (Mr. Sark), Derrick O'Connor (Alexander Khasinau), James Handy (Director Arthur Devlin), Joey Slotnick (Agent Steven Haladki), Elaine Kagan (June Litvack), Wolf Muser (Ramon Veloso), Ric Young (Suit & Glasses), Amy Irving (Emily Sloane), Michelle Arthur (Abigail), Emily Wachtel (Worker)

Will is kidnapped and tortured by Suit & Glasses, and Jack, Vaughn, and Sydney work together to try to get him back while discovering what The Circumference really is.

"Almost Thirty Years" is a brilliant episode that brings the entire season full circle. "Truth Be Told," the series premiere (also written and directed by J.J. Abrams), opened with Sydney sitting in a chair in a torture room in Taipei. The season finale ends with her sitting in exactly the same chair, in exactly the same room. Episodes like this one reward the loyal viewership and prove to the audience that there are some executives who assume viewers have higher IQs than fruitflies (which the executives on most other series do not).

The tables have turned in many ways in this episode, and where a year ago Sydney was being tortured by the creepy Suit & Glasses man, Will is now in that unfortunate position. At the time, Sydney was just discovering the truth about SD-6 and her place within it; now, Will is just finding out about Sydney's real identity. Will shows how strong he is both physically and mentally, and Bradley Cooper does a superb job in the torture scenes. Will has always been a bit of a comic character, but the way he stands in the alleyway near the end of the episode, bruised and beaten, is an extraordinary moment.

The episode also brings back a device we saw very briefly in "Truth Be Told": the hovering red ball that Sydney disabled in Taipei. When we see it again, it suddenly takes on far more significance, as we know the importance of the object, who its creator was, and the danger of someone like Khasinau owning it.

Meanwhile, both Jack and Vaughn are coming under fire for the opposite reasons. Vaughn's interrogation by the CIA reveals that his affection for Sydney has perhaps come at a cost to the agency, but his ultimate decision will show that he's learned something from the death of his father and he's not about to make the same mistakes. In contrast, Sydney asks Jack to help her, and he responds by saying she must learn to be more like him — more strategic than emotional. The irony is, Jack *does* let his emotions dictate his actions occasionally, and when he finally figures out who Will's source is, the ensuing scene is grotesquely satisfying for viewers.

Just like the previous episode, this one ends with multiple cliffhangers. Dixon confronts Sydney after he untangles her myriad lies, but her response is unsatisfactory for him. Will he trust her when the new season begins? Sloane comes clean with Emily, but what he does next leaves viewers speechless. And finally, Sydney comes face-to-face with "The Man," and the result is one that will definitely shape the year to come.

In a season that began with Sydney not trusting (or even knowing) her father; happily working for the U.S. government (or so she thought); and enjoying the company of Will and Francie, trusting friends who had no reason to doubt her, it's amazing to sit back and realize just how far she's come. She has graduated from innocence to experience, gotten to know her father and finally begin a relationship with him, met a man who allows her to open up with her innermost thoughts, and discovered that her mother is alive. Will has lost his best friend and worked on a story that he believed was rather simple in the beginning only to end up caught in a web of espionage, bugged brooches, kidnapping, and tooth extraction. Sloane's confidence has been shaken by the realization that what he's done in the past is now coming back to haunt him, and that his position within the Alliance may not be as secure as he once thought.

But the many revelations experienced by the characters in season 1 are nothing compared with what awaits them in season 2.

Highlight: Jack interrogating the mole.

Interesting Fact: Since Lena Olin had not yet been cast, the woman who appears at the end of the episode is April Webster, the show's casting director.

Did You Notice?: The song playing while Emily drinks her wine is "Canzone del Salice" from Verdi's *Otello*, which is the aria sung by Desdemona shortly before her husband, Othello, kills her.

Nitpicks: The plane that Vaughn, Jack, and Sydney take to Taipei looks really phony dangling in the air — you can't help but look for strings attached to it. And near the end, why does Vaughn *just stand there* when Sydney is running at him, waving her arms and yelling for him to run? A trained agent should know better.

Oops: Despite the size of The Circumference, the square footage of the warehouse holding it would have prevented it from getting that high. It would have flooded that room, but there's no way it would have caused the tidal wave in the corridor outside in those proportions. Also, when Sydney is talking to Jack, she says that the CIA has the page Khasinau wants and SD-6 has the ampule, but it's actually the other way around.

Locations: Taipei, Taiwan

Music/Bands: Natalie Merchant's "My Skin" (*Ophelia*) plays when Sloane tells Emily the truth about SD-6; as Sydney and Vaughn walk through the nightclub we hear "Music: Response" by the Chemical Brothers (*Surrender*); "Overseer" by Supermoves (*Snatch* soundtrack) plays when Sydney finds the door to room 47; and "Canzone Del Salice" by Miriam Gauci (from Giuseppe Verdi's *Otello*) is heard as Emily and Sloane drink their wine.

Season Two:
September 2002–May 2003

Recurring characters in season 2: David Anders (Mr. Sark), Terry O'Quinn (Assistant Director Kendall), Patricia Wettig (Dr. Judy Barnett)

2.1   The Enemy Walks In

Original air date: September 29, 2002
Written by: J.J. Abrams
Directed by: Ken Olin
Guest cast: Derrick O'Connor (Alexander Khasinau), Stuart Yee (The Tester), Jamie McShane (CIA Agent), Dayna Adams (Receptionist), Chris Harrison (Reporter #2),

Todd Karli (Newscaster), Roger Lim (Gasping Body), Tricia Nickell (Reporter #3), Danny Romero (Reporter #1)

Upon escaping from Taipei, Sydney talks to a psychiatrist about a new troubling problem in her life — her mother. Meanwhile, Will is forced to make a terrible public "confession" in order to stay alive.

There were some naysayers who believed there was no way the writers could keep up their unfaltering momentum of season 1 past the season finale. "The Enemy Walks In" proves them wrong. Season 1 was about Sydney discovering life-altering truths about SD-6 and her father, working for the CIA as a double agent, and trying to keep her friends from finding out what she does for a living. By the beginning of season 2 she has come face-to-face with her mother, made amends with her father, and dealt with Will's discovery of the truth. Not to mention that she's making progress in taking down SD-6. And the twists and turns just keep on coming.

This is an excellent episode (not surprising given the writer) and while Sydney is going through some new turmoil, it's similar to what she's endured in the past. Before she could barely stand the sight of her father; now it's her mother. Facing her mother (and the shock of what Derevko does to Sydney when she sees her) is almost more difficult for Sydney to handle than the troubled feelings she'd had about Jack a year ago. Sydney grew up knowing her father was cold and distant, but she believed her mother was a saint who died when she herself was a child. Now she's faced with the monstrous reality of who her mother really is, and it's far worse than anything she ever imagined about Jack.

Seeing Vaughn for the first time in the episode was a huge relief to fans who had waited all summer for the certain confirmation of his death. The thrilling scene that follows when Sydney discovers him sparks the new direction of their relationship for this season. No longer will those fleeting glances between them be noticed only by the fans.

Will once again talks to Syd in a way that makes us proud of who he's become. Gone is the earnest reporter who didn't know when to quit no matter how loudly we shouted at our television sets for him to back off the story and listen to Syd. When Jack steps in and tells Will what must be done to save his life, though, our pride in him turns to sympathy for him. The lie he tells the press (and worst of all, Francie) discredits everything Will has worked his entire life to accomplish. Every story he's ever written becomes a fiction. Francie looks at him like she doesn't know him anymore. Everyone who knows Will believes he's been keeping secrets and is a completely different person than they thought he was, and Will — while knowing that it's in fact Syd who is living the lie — keeps his mouth shut and goes along with everything. And the lies are more far-reaching than we might initially think. Will wrote human interest stories on topics such as the Mexican migrant worker who learned to read (the piece that Emily Sloane loved so much) — imagine how his subjects are being treated now that he's "admitted" to making stories up.

Emily Sloane, however, is not around to be offended by Will's confession. Sydney's eulogy for Emily is touching — and timely considering what has been happening in Syd's life. Her own confession, that Emily has always been like a mother to her, stands in stark contrast to Syd's experiences with her own parents. Now, just as she loses an affectionate, sympathetic mother, she's gained a new, dangerous one. Derevko is not an enemy that Sydney can turn her back on. She could be the catalyst that will bring down SD-6. She carries secrets that would be invaluable to any counterterrorist (or terrorist) organization. And later in the episode, when Sydney encounters Derevko a second time in Barcelona, Sydney's hatred turns to confusion when Derevko acts out of character and mutters an ominous phrase that could actually be the subtitle to this series: "Truth takes time." It's not hard to see that Emily Sloane really was the true, honest mother that Syd should have had. Or was she?

Highlight: Marshall demonstrating the use of the cellphone and getting involved in an imaginary argument with his mother.

Interesting Fact: Michael Vartan was pleased with the explanation for his character's dilemma last season. "I was kind of worried when I first read [the premiere episode]," he said. "I thought, *What kind of crazy f---ing thing are they going to come up with? I hope it's not, like, 'Well, he had an oxygen capsule in his heel.'* I was very happy to see that it was something a lot simpler than I could have dreamt up."

Did You Notice?: The moment when Sydney plunges the adrenalin into Vaughn's chest is right out of Quentin Tarantino's *Pulp Fiction*.

Nitpicks: Dixon reports that Sydney used a different call sign in "Mea Culpa" and tells Sloane that he found her stealing something from an underground vault in "Almost Thirty Years." Jack anticipates this discussion and tells Sloane that he himself issued the call sign in "Mea Culpa," but he never explains what Sydney took from the vault in "Almost Thirty Years" and Sloane never asks. Does Sloane suspect Sydney or was this an oversight by the writers? Finally, are we to assume that Sydney went into radio silence while rescuing Vaughn? Otherwise, Dixon would have heard the whole thing.

Oops: When Derevko is speaking to Sydney in the opening scene, Syd's blue hair is alternately straight and then curled under as the camera keeps cutting back to her, presumably revealing which scenes are from the season 1 finale and which ones were filmed for the new episode.

What Did He Say?: When Sydney gets back to SD-6, Sloane tells her about Jean-Marc Ravais. He's a man who helped finance Khasinau and his operations with Derevko, and Sydney must break into his office and plant a bug so they can listen to his conversations with Khasinau. The bug works: they hear Khasinau mention a bible, and Jack tells Sydney and Vaughn that the CIA must get this item. They must intercept the handoff from Ravais to Khasinau that will be happening in Barcelona.

Locations: Cap Ferrat, France; Port of Barcelona, Spain

Marshall's Gadgets: A wiretap that's actually in the wire so that Sydney can plant it inside a phone and have it be undetectable.

Music/Bands: When Sydney rescues Vaughn, the song playing is Daniel Lenz's "Spy" (no album); Rosie Thomas's "Farewell" (*When We Were Small*) plays when Will is going through withdrawal in Syd and Francie's apartment; and when Will and Syd talk, we hear "I Wanna Stay" (*Night on My Side*) by Gemma Hayes.

2.2   Trust Me

Original air date: October 6, 2002
Written by: John Eisendrath
Directed by: Craig Zisk
Guest cast: Tony Amendola (SD-6 Agent Tambor Barceló), Wolf Muser (Ramon Veloso), Joseph Ruskin (Alain Christophe), J.D. Hall (Judge Freid), Wendle Josepher (CIA Agent Vicki Crane), Soren Hellerup (Petr Fordson), James Kohli (Concierge), P.J. Marino (Felon), Scott Alan Smith (Chris Schmidt), Benson Choy (Soldier), Joel Guggenheim (Agent on Call), Alex Morris (Homeless Man), Sam Alyia Sakio (Burly Security Guard), Krikor Satamian (Mohammed Naj), Kevin Sutherland (Monitoring Agent), Michael Yavnieli (Driver)

Irina Derevko turns herself in to the CIA, a development that leaves Sydney, Jack, and Vaughn shaken and suspicious of her motives.

Just when it seems things couldn't get any weirder for Sydney, Mommie Dearest suddenly shows up, turns herself in, and claims she'll cooperate with the good guys to take down the bad. Of course, the very notion is laughable to Sydney and Jack, who know exactly what this woman is capable of. One of the highlights of this season will be watching how Sydney, Jack, and Vaughn interact with Derevko and slowly change their minds about her. Is she for real this time, or will she repeat her betrayal from so many years ago?

That question becomes central to this episode when Syd is sent on a mission, for the first time with advice from Derevko. Vaughn urges her to take it. Jack pleads with her not to. The scene echoes the one from "Mea Culpa" in which Jack and Vaughn argued about different avenues Sydney could take and which one might kill her. This time, however, it's Vaughn who wants to take the chance and Jack who prefers to play it safe.

"Trust Me" introduces the new CIA headquarters where Sydney will work (the old office building set has been scrapped for the rotunda set) and has an excellent scene that shows how Sydney will enter the building incognito each time she arrives. Previously, Sydney simply met Vaughn; she never actually ventured into the CIA building except for that first time, red-haired and determined. Now, with Derevko locked up in the building and cleverly refusing to see anyone but Sydney, she is forced to meet there and to deal with her new boss, her former nemesis Kendall. The tension between the two characters is beautifully played throughout the season by Jennifer Garner and Terry O'Quinn.

That said, the interplay between Kendall and Sydney is nothing compared with that between Syd and Derevko. Lena Olin is perfectly cast as the mysterious mother/wife/traitor: her stare is piercing, her voice is haunting, and she looks so much like Jennifer Garner it's scary. Derevko's sudden appearance conjures up many things: Sydney's inner turmoil about her mother and the lies that have been told to her; Vaughn's anger about what happened to his father; and Jack's seething fury about how Derevko weaseled into his life, made him believe she loved him, and destroyed him. Sydney, despite her own tumultuous feelings, finds herself caught between the two men, with Vaughn asking her to put her feelings aside and speak to Derevko to help the CIA and with Jack angrily urging her *not* to go to Derevko, explaining that Derevko knows how to stir up whatever feelings Syd thinks she might be able to suppress. Sydney wants to deny that this monster is her mother, but looking at Derevko she can't help but see herself — from the obvious physical resemblance to the way Derevko tucks her hair behind her ear exactly as she does.

The scenes of Vaughn and Sydney going to see Derevko are haunting. As the camera slowly moves down the hall with the characters, the iron bars lift before them rather than keep them out, and the glass wall separating the monster from her prey becomes visible. There is a definite evocation of Hannibal Lecter in these scenes, as Derevko quietly moves toward the glass each time and always seems to answer a question with a more personal question. The ambient wind-like noise, always present in the background, adds to the frightening quality of these scenes. As viewers, we haven't gone through what these characters have presumably endured and can only imagine what must be racing through their minds as they approach the cell. But the atmosphere that has been created produces a chill in us that helps us to understand.

Highlight: Jack stiffly giving Francie interior decorating advice.

Name That Guest Star: Wendle Josepher, who plays Vicki Crane, appeared in two episodes of *Roswell*, and her boyfriend, Larry, was played by none other than Kevin Weisman.

Nitpicks: When Syd is in Helsinki she's wearing a disguise. Yet when she walks into Kendall's office she's wearing the same disguise. She kept the disguise on for a 12-hour plane ride? Also, last season Kendall was FBI (for an investigation that was being covered by NSA) and now he's CIA? The FBI, NSA, and CIA are three separate organizations; when is he going to choose one and stick with it? How is he able to glide from one organization to another so easily?

Oops: When Sydney is in Rabat, the huge bandage she'd had on her shoulder is gone and there's no sign that she was even shot.

What Did He Say?: SD-6 discovers that for years Irina Derevko would find dirt on everyone and store it on a disk, then blackmail them into working with her. The blackmail disk is now in Rabat, being held by Mohammed Naj, a Derevko operative, and Sydney must get to it. Once Sloane gets his hands on it, he immediately blackmails someone on the list named Petr Fordson. Meanwhile, Derevko tells Sydney to go to Fordson and steal a camera, one that Sloane is on his way to retrieve at the same time.

Locations: London, England; Rabat, Morocco; Helsinki, Finland

Marshall's Gadgets: A regular metal detector that will find the safe, and a stethoscope attached to a cellphone. When Sydney types 793793 into the cellphone, the stethoscope will decode the safe's combination.

Music/Bands: Catie Curtis's "Fusco's Song" (*A Crash Course in Roses*) plays when Will talks to Francie in her restaurant about doing business with mobsters; "Touch Me" by the Supreme Beings of Leisure (*Divine Operating System*) is playing in the club in Helsinki; and we hear Bob Dylan's "Shelter from the Storm" (*Blood on the Tracks*) during Syd's final confrontation with Derevko.

2.3　　Cipher

Original air date: October 13, 2002
Written by: Alex Kurtzman-Counter and Roberto Orci
Directed by: Daniel Attias
Guest cast: Janet MacLachlan (Jane Banks), Mark Colson (Ops Director), Endre Hules (Mr. Vashko), Strahil Goodman (ASA Techie #2), Tom Kiesche (Cooper), Keith Lewis (Novak), Ilya Morelle (ASA Techie #1), Weston Blakesley (Barfly), Joel

Birthdays

Michael Vaughn, born November 27, 1968; Michael Vartan, born November 27, 1968

Will Tippin, born August 3, 1973; Bradley Cooper, born January 5, 1975

Arvin Sloane, born October 31, 1950; Ron Rifkin, born October 31, 1939

Sydney Bristow, born April 17, 1975; Jennifer Garner, born April 17, 1972

Francie Calfo, born January 3, 1975; Merrin Dungey, born August 6, 1971

Marcus Dixon, born August 14, 1955; Carl Lumbly, born August 14, 1952

Marshall J. Flinkman, born December 29, 1964; Kevin Weisman, born December 29, 1970

Jack Bristow, born March 16, 1950; Victor Garber, born March 16, 1949

Guggenheim (Agent on Call), Paul Mendoza (Bartender), Alex Morris (Homeless Vet), Kavita Patil (Desk Attendant)

Sydney must find out why Sark has patched in to a satellite; Jack worries about the influence Derevko will have on Sydney; Will undergoes hypnosis to help the CIA.

Everything on this show is a cipher that begs to be decoded. Whether it's a note in a Rambaldi document, a missive from the enemy, or Jack Bristow himself, everything and everyone has something to hide. And that something will eventually be discovered.

The best parts of this episode are the scenes with Jack. When he goes to the CIA psychiatrist in the beginning to ask her to help him keep Sydney away from Derevko, her response is a little surprising and rather harsh. She knows Jack's background and she knows what Derevko is capable of, yet her answer shows a complete lack of human compassion. She treats him like a jealous father rather than a concerned one. Later, when Jack confronts Derevko himself, the showdown is one viewers had been waiting for since we found out Derevko was still alive. We know it has taken every ounce of strength Jack has to get himself there, but Derevko seems unshaken by his presence. And then she asks him a question that is like a bomb, reopening the case on Jack as a duplicitous father. Could he have done something to hurt Sydney in the past?

Will and Vaughn meet for the first time, which is an amusing moment. Will clearly catches on immediately that Vaughn could be a guy Sydney might have eyes for, and if he hadn't already begun to back off on his pursuit of her, this meeting certainly clinches it for him. Will's cooperation with the CIA to get a lead on Sark forces him to undergo a painful hypnosis that brings him back to the most frightening moment in his life, showing just how brave and heroic Will has become. Vaughn clearly likes him and appreciates what Will has done, as will be seen in upcoming episodes.

Meanwhile, another mystery gets underway as Sloane begins to suspect that someone is taunting him about Emily. Sydney has her suspicions about Sloane's complicity in Emily's death, but in this episode we see Sloane begin to come a little unhinged as he first tells Jack to keep an eye on him and then gets a mysterious phone call. Is someone on to Sloane? One thing is for sure — the writers on *Alias* certainly know how to keep viewers glued to their sets week after week, whether it's with a focus on the personal storylines like the ones in this episode or the action sequences and cliffhangers that give the series its uniqueness.

Highlight: Sydney luging to and from the launch site.

Nitpicks: Whenever characters go to incredibly cold regions, they never have any face coverings. In Siberia, Syd has icicles forming on her face, which is beet red, but she doesn't think to put on a scarf? And though the luge scenes are really amazing, there's no way Sydney would have made it out of those ducts without being burnt to a crisp.

Oops: Marshall tells Sydney that the luge will go 150 mph, which means she'll be able to do the 2-mile duct in 12 seconds. His math is way off — at 150 mph, she can cover 2.5 miles in 1 minute, and about 0.04 miles per second. So in 12 seconds she would get as far as about half a mile. She would have to go four times as fast to cover 2 miles in 12 seconds, but if the luge were really going 600 mph, it would have shot out from under her, leaving her on the launch pad.

What Did He Say?: Sydney tells Kendall what she learned from Sloane: The camera she had retrieved in the previous episode is a prototype of one located in a satellite that will be launched into space on the orders of one Mr. Sark. The camera is capable of penetrating solid matter up to 100 meters deep, and they find out what Sark is looking at: the outline of the Rambaldi symbol in the snow in Siberia. By hypnotizing

Will they are able to get the code to a music box Rambaldi had hidden in that location in Siberia, and Sydney travels there in order to retrieve the song.

Locations: Sri Lanka; Siberia, Russia

Marshall's Gadgets: One of the coolest gadgets yet, Sydney's toy this time around is a briefcase that turns into a luge.

Music/Bands: When Sydney tells Will that he's going to be getting his Standard Operating Procedure from Vaughn, we hear Saint Low's "Spanish Moss," from their self-titled album.

2.4   Dead Drop

Original air date: October 20, 2002
Written by: Jesse Alexander
Directed by: Guy Norman Bee
Guest cast: Marisol Nichols ("Rebecca Martinez"), Daniel Faraldo (Manolo), Carol Androsky (N.A. Moderator), Jim Hanna (Claus Richter), Dato Bakhtadze (Russian Security Guard), Scott Donovan (American Tourist), Ira Heiden (Techie), Kevin Sutherland (CIA Operative)

When no one listens to his warnings about Derevko affecting Sydney, Jack takes desperate measures to prove to Sydney that he's right.

It's a wonder that Sydney Bristow has managed to retain her sanity thus far. Children from homes far less broken than hers have been destroyed by what has happened within the family fold, and yet the Bristows are easily the most messed-up family on television and she has learned to deal with it. Is she suppressing her feelings as she has been trained to do for so many years? Or could it be that she lives in a constant state of hope that things will get better? She thought her father was a deadbeat until he proved himself otherwise. She thought her mother was dead, but she's alive. Now that she sees her mother is a murdering traitor, maybe Sydney believes that she will change and they might have a mother-daughter relationship after all.

And nothing scares Jack Bristow more than that possibility.

In this episode he continues his desperate pursuit to get Sydney away from Derevko. Barnett has refused to listen to him, Kendall believes the information they get from Derevko is more important than any harm it's doing to Sydney, Sydney believes she's in control, and Vaughn is willing to concede to whatever decision Sydney makes. You might damn Jack for what he ends up doing at the end of this episode, but he's acting out of fear and love for his daughter. Only he knows exactly what Derevko is capable of, and he doesn't believe that a leopard can change its spots. The questionable aspect of what Jack does, however, has to do with the potential danger in which his actions could put Sydney.

Just as Jack feared, Sydney is almost elated at the prospect that Derevko might have positive motives for helping out the CIA. So far all of the information she has given Sydney has saved Sydney's life and put Syd one step closer to taking down SD-6. As she tells Vaughn about how Derevko has been assisting the CIA, there's a palpable look of happiness and hope on Sydney's face. When Vaughn diplomatically explains that while her father is going through a rough time he himself trusts her instincts, she realizes that she might have a true ally she can trust — something she hasn't had in a long time. She also reveals to Jack that as soon as she takes down SD-6 she is leaving the CIA, and if Derevko can help her reach that goal more quickly, then she will use her.

One thing about Derevko is undeniable: she is brilliant. No matter what Sydney brings to her, Derevko is able to decode it in a matter of minutes. Are these "secret codes" preplanned? Did Derevko plant them herself so that she could show how quickly she could decode them? Or is she really so intelligent that she can work out a complex terrorist message with a pencil and a pad of paper? Either way, her brilliance shines in every episode, making her an important ally for the CIA but at the same time an incredibly dangerous enemy.

Highlight: Vaughn's answer to Derevko when she goads him. Derevko: "How do you say thank you to the woman who killed your father?" Vaughn: "You don't."

Interesting Fact: Jack tells Sydney to retrieve the copy of *War and Peace* at FAPSI headquarters in Moscow. FAPSI stands for *Federal'naya Agenstvo Pravitel'stvennoy Svayazi i Informatsii*, or Federal Agency for Government Communications and Information, the equivalent of the Agency of National Security in the U.S.

Did You Notice?: This episode has the third reference to author Leo Tolstoy in the series. In the series premiere, when Sydney writes up her report for the CIA, Vaughn tells her it's "Tolstoy-long"; in "Cipher," one of the code words Will discovers under hypnosis is *Tolstoy*; and in this episode, the map they are looking for is hidden in a copy of *War and Peace*, written by Tolstoy.

Nitpicks: A skeleton key is one whose bits have been filed down so that it can open several locks. Marshall mistakenly calls the keys on the medals "skeleton keys"; if they were, Syd would need only one to open the various locks. And how did Sydney manage to avoid hypothermia, having been in water as cold as that in Siberia?

Oops: Dixon warns Sydney that the water will freeze over within four seconds if she falls through the ice, and that's exactly what happens. Yet when she gets pulled out of the ice at the beginning of the episode, we see the water rippling on the surface for the rest of the scene, and it never freezes over again.

What Did He Say?: Jack tells Sydney that Sark got away from Siberia and went to the Falkland Islands, where he met with Claus Richter, the man who had been in Barcelona three weeks earlier when the CIA was there trying to retrieve the bible, which they now know is Derevko's operations manual. Sloane thinks Derevko gave Richter the bible, and now SD-6 has Richter in custody. He is bleeding from his fingernails and they believe Sark used some sort of chemical weapon on him. Derevko tells Sydney about a map that is hidden in a book, and it gives the location of the bible. Sydney must try to retrieve it.

Locations: Moscow, Russia; Madagascar

Marshall's Gadgets: Since Syd is going in disguised as an army major, Marshall hides three skeleton keys in her medals.

Music/Bands: As Syd and Will talk in her apartment about him helping the CIA we hear "Oh Do Not Fly Away" by the Innocence Mission (*Small Planets*); in Madagascar, the song playing is Michelle Featherstone's "Stay," from her self-titled album.

2.5   The Indicator

Original air date: November 3, 2002
Written by: Jeff Pinkner
Directed by: Ken Olin
Guest cast: Amy Aquino (Agent Virginia Kerr), James Lesure (CIA Agent Craig Blair), Stephen Markle (Senator Douglas), Kevin West (SD-6 Agent Kelsey), Newell Alexander (Congressman), Dan Istrate (Public Employee), Vladimir Skomarovsky (Valery Kolakov), Kevin Sutherland (CIA Agent), Loren Haynes (CIA Strike Team Leader), Sarah K. Peterson (Sydney at Six Years Old)

When Sydney goes to Budapest to find out what the "next generation" secret weapon is, it leads her to a terrible truth about an incident from her childhood; Sloane admits to Jack that Emily's death wasn't caused by lymphoma; Derevko is moved away from the CIA and may receive the death penalty for her lies.

Everyone keeps secrets on *Alias*, but no one can keep them for long. Earlier this season Derevko asked Jack if Sydney knew what he had done to her; in the previous episode, Jack staged a scene to make Sydney believe him over Derevko. And in "The Indicator," it all blows up in his face.

Last season, in "Spirit," Vaughn caught on to something Jack did for Sydney's safety and fought with him about whether or not what he did was right. Jack impatiently yelled back that he always keeps Sydney's best interests in mind, and sacrificing another person for Sydney's life is within the realm of good fathering as far as he is concerned. While Vaughn never agreed outright, the look on his face showed that he believed Jack was probably right. In this episode, however, Vaughn once again catches on to what Jack did in the previous episode and calls him on it. Again Jack begins yelling about Sydney's safety, but he's not so sure of himself this time. What he did in "Dead Drop" could have killed Sydney, and he knows it.

And then we discover that Jack's "protection" of Sydney goes back further than last season. In season 1's "Snowman," Sydney watched her mother on tape referring to "Project Christmas." Earlier this season, Sydney mentioned to Jack that she has gaps in her childhood memories from the time her mother disappeared. In this episode she goes to Budapest to find a secret weapon that is being developed and is shocked by what she finds. When she catches the man responsible for the development of the weapon, she finds a curious puzzle in his house and puts it together in a matter of seconds. Confused, and deep down knowing what is going on, she becomes determined to find out what happened to her as a child and makes a horrible discovery. What she learns changes everything — her relationship with her father, her work at the CIA, her entire life. She confronts Jack in one of the series' most painful scenes in recent memory, and even if we've agreed with his questionable actions thus far, we can't help but wonder how a father could do what Jack did to his little girl. While clearly born of the pain he felt after Derevko's betrayal, what he does removes any notion of free will from Sydney's life.

Jack has lied about so many things on the show, and Sydney always finds out, always gets upset, and always forgives him eventually. Has it ever occurred to him that maybe she can deal with the truth?

Highlight: Will's Narcotics Anonymous group showing up at Francie's restaurant opening and Francie complaining that none of them will drink.

Interesting Fact: Amy Aquino appeared on *Felicity* as Felicity's counselor. Also, on an interesting note, Merrin Dungey claims that Francie's restaurant has a secret name printed on the wall by the window, which is an inside joke between herself and the set designer. Rumor has it that it's "JJ's Mistake and Grill — Open 15 Seconds per Episode."

Did You Notice?: Sydney's code name for the CIA has been changed from Freelancer to Mountaineer.

Nitpicks: Agent Kerr tells Sydney that hypnotic regression therapy is very dangerous, yet no one seems to warn Will of this when the CIA asks him to do it.

What Did He Say?: Niels Hater, a man who had been selling intel to SD-6, has been killed in Vienna. Sloane believes Hater was killed by The Triad, a coalition of organized crime groups. The Triad used to deal in drugs and prostitution, but now it deals in weapons. Hater's last communiqué to Sloane mentioned a "next generation" of weaponry, located in Budapest. Sydney must go there and find out what kind of weaponry he was referring to. Once she discovers the weaponry she must capture Kolakov, a former member of the KGB now with The Triad and the man in charge of the "weapons development," so to speak.

Locations: Vienna, Austria; Budapest, Hungary; Buenos Aires, Argentina

Marshall's Gadgets: Hidden inside a lip gloss is a miniature camera with a compressed air injector. Sydney aims the lip gloss tube at a ceiling and the cameras will shoot out and into the ceiling, allowing her to monitor certain areas of the building.

Music/Bands: Zero 7's "This World" (*Simple Things*) plays as Syd visits her mother's empty cell; at the grand opening of Francie's party we hear "Brimful of Asha" by Cornershop (*When I Was Born for the 7th Time*) and "When I Get You Alone" by Thicke (*Cherry Blue Skies*); Beck's "The Golden Age" (*Sea Change*) plays when Syd tells Will about her mother; and we hear Joni Mitchell's "River" (*Blue*) when Sydney confronts Jack at the end of the episode.

2.6 Salvation

Original air date: November 10, 2002
Written by: Roberto Orci and Alex Kurtzman-Counter
Directed by: Perry Lang
Guest cast: James Handy (CIA Director Arthur Devlin), Stephen Markle (Senator Douglas), Austin Tichenor (Doctor Nicholas), Amy Irving (Emily Sloane), Daniel Faltus (Jan Spinnaker), Kevin Sutherland (Agent), Hope Allen (Waitress), Glenda Morgan Brown (Flight Attendant), John Patrick Clerkin (Priest), Timothy de Haas (Doctor #2), Ira Heiden (Rick, CIA Techie), Mette Holt (Nurse), John Koyama (Patient Zero), Alex Morris (CIA Homeless Man), Cliff Olin (Cliff), Robert Martin Robinson (Doctor)

Sydney's anger with Jack and refusal to listen to him causes him to turn himself in the same way Derevko did; Sloane decides to find out once and for all if Emily is dead; Vaughn hires Will to do research for him on a freelance basis.

Husbands, wives, children, mothers, fathers, siblings — family members can cause us more anguish and trauma than anyone else, and we love them more than anyone

Even when he's deceiving her, everything Jack does is out of love for his daughter Sydney. Or is it?

else. We reserve our most bitter arguments for them, and our deepest affection. No matter what someone in our family does, it's the familial bond that makes us come back and try to work out our feelings about the situation.

Jack tries to talk to Sydney and tell her there's a reason for his doing what he did to her. But she won't listen to him, and her response to him — that when he looks at her she believes he sees his greatest mistake — is like a knife through his heart. Sydney has found out that her mother will be receiving the death penalty, and it's too much for one daughter to have to endure all at once. Jack questions the logic of saving someone as evil as Derevko (and when Sydney discovers in this episode that Derevko tested the effects of viruses on her own operatives it makes her that much worse), but Sydney can't escape the reality that no matter what, Derevko is her mother. One of the things that makes Jack such a sad character is that his good intentions get caught up in his bad communication skills. We know that Jack loves Sydney more than anything, but the psychiatrist questions his motives, Derevko taunts him about what he did to Syd, Vaughn believes he would put Sydney in danger to cover his own tracks, and now even Sydney refuses to believe his intentions were honorable in any way. Her reaction to finding out what he did in Madagascar — she now views Jack and Derevko as equals on the scale of evil — seems extreme considering the résumé that Derevko has amassed is far more sinister than Jack's. But Sydney has always been emotional — it's what makes her such a sympathetic character — and her reaction is believable given the circumstances.

Jack's next step forces Sydney to listen to what he has to say and proves that while Sydney and Jack aren't the best communicators, they do care a great deal for one another and their love for each other can forgive any transgression. Sydney then shows she's learned a thing or two from her parents when she spins a wild tale in a last-ditch effort to save both of them. Even if it doesn't work, there's no doubt Mom would be proud.

Meanwhile, Sloane continues to be haunted by his wife. In the previous episode he admitted to Jack that he had accelerated her death but had done so out of love. Now he has discovered in a wine glass traces of a substance that can fake a person's death. He believes he spots Emily downtown near a church, and Jack suggests a way to find out if she's actually dead. Sloane's discovery steps up the mystery, and Sloane shifts from being an evil dictator character to a tortured husband who believes his wife has come back for vengeance. He loved her more than anyone, and he killed her. But wouldn't any of us do the same thing . . . for family?

Highlight: Vaughn telling Sydney a joke.

Interesting Fact: Victor Garber is completely computer illiterate and hates scenes where he has to use computers or computer terms. "I'm totally not in this century," he says. "Computers confuse me."

Did You Notice?: This episode is the only one in which James Handy makes an appearance as Director Devlin this season. Also, Jack's code name at SD-6 is Blackbird, and Syd's is usually Bluebird.

Nitpicks: In this episode Syd asks the doctor what the first sign of the viral infection is, and he tells her it's bleeding from the fingernails. Yet Jack had already told her that in "Dead Drop." Considering Sydney has a photographic memory for everything, why wouldn't she have remembered this detail? Clearly the line is there to remind viewers, but instead of having her ask the doctor, the writers should have run a voiceover of Jack telling Sydney about the symptom and her remembering him telling her. And what is with the cricket noises we always hear in the place where Vaughn and Sydney conduct their covert meetings? Also, it seems rather convenient that while the contact with the Circumference liquid happened months ago, Vaughn is only showing symptoms of exposure now, *exactly* when they've become aware of the virus. Finally, Jack turning himself in for conspiring against the CIA is a potentially dangerous situation for Sydney — if he's in prison and Sloane finds out why, wouldn't it expose Sydney as a double agent?

What Did He Say?: Sloane tells Sydney that Mr. Sark might be developing a biological weapon from a new virus, and the Alliance believes he tested it on Claus Richter. Twenty-three patients have been found in Geneva with the same virus (23 being just less than half of 47). Sydney and Jack must travel there to get a sample of the virus and bring it back.

Locations: Geneva, Switzerland; Washington, D.C.

Marshall's Gadgets: A briefcase that injects an anesthetic into the room, and anti-anesthetic medication for Jack and Sydney to take ahead of time so it doesn't affect them.

Music/Bands: When Syd and Will talk at Francie's restaurant we hear Violent Femmes' "Blister in the Sun" from their self-titled album; Andy Hunter's "Go" (*Exodus*) plays when Jack and Sydney are on the plane to Geneva; "Violent Rain" by Gus Black (*Uncivilized Love*) plays when Vaughn and Will meet; "A Place Called Home" by Kim Richey (*Rise*) plays when Vaughn tells Syd she talks in her sleep.

2.7   The Counteragent

Original air date: November 17, 2002
Written by: John Eisendrath
Directed by: Daniel Attias
Guest cast: Austin Tichenor (Doctor Nicholas), Petra Wright (Alice), Chris Ellis (CIA Agent Chapma), Victor McCay (CIA Agent Rudman), Stephen Davies (Sark

Associate), Stephen Mendillo (Henry Fields), Jim Hanna (Claus Richter), Michelle Arthur (Abigail), Reamy Hall (Nurse #2), Don Took (Agent Grey), Ivan Borodin (Lab Technician), Peggy Goss (Attending Nurse), Joel Guggenheim (Agent on Call), Mak Takano (Ryokan Guard)

When Vaughn becomes deathly ill, Sydney strikes a deal with Sark in order to retrieve the antidote; Will discovers some Project Christmas questions on a 1982 IQ test.

Ah, the moment that Syd-Vaughn-shippers had been waiting for. He's in a bed, she's next to him holding his hand, she realizes how much she loves him, and then his girlfriend walks in? No, no, no — that's not how it's supposed to be! Sorry, Alice, but this is Sydney Bristow you're up against: a woman who can travel halfway around the world to retrieve an antidote that will save the life of the man she loves. You'll just have to move over . . .

"The Counteragent" was definitely a good episode for fans who wanted Vaughn and Sydney to get together. It moves away from the Derevko-Jack situation slightly, although Derevko does play a role in helping Sydney help Vaughn (and when she talks to Vaughn about his feelings for Sydney, you can't help but like the gal for a few brief moments). The desperate measure that Sydney takes when in Estonia proves just how much she cares about Vaughn and forces us to acknowledge what a powerful alliance she and Sark would make if they were on the same side. Although Jack helps her out because he knows how much Vaughn means to her (even if he can't stand the guy half the time), he does say something to her that's rather nasty considering the things he himself has done in the name of love. It's an odd thing for Jack to say, even if it is related to Derevko.

Meanwhile, Will does the research that Vaughn pays him to do, and while he comes up empty at first, it's Francie who notices that something is amiss in the IQ test he has brought home. Yes, folks, believe it or not, Francie is still on the show. One of the very few disappointments of season 2 is that Francie has been reduced to this tiny character on the side, puttering about in her restaurant and getting a line or two (if that) per episode. Although her character will come into play a lot more in the second half of the season, the writers could have done something more with the fact that now both Will and Sydney know something they can't tell Francie.

Finally, Sydney fulfills her mission in Tokyo, in a fantastic scene that sees her dressed up like a geisha. Jennifer Garner plays the scene to the hilt, with the small walking movements, the way she holds herself, and the mixed fear and determination she shows when faced with Sloane. She has worked so hard to bring him down; is this, in fact, the end of him? By the end of the episode, Sydney and the viewers will realize that it takes a lot more than Sydney acting on her own to destroy Sloane.

Highlight: Vaughn chasing Sydney at the end of the episode, sending viewers to the edges of their seats as they wait for the big kiss . . .

Interesting Fact: The geisha costume was one of the most elaborate created for the show, especially since eight copies had to be made. Multilayered and very specific in its design, the outfit forced costume designer Laura Goldsmith to rely on outside technical advice. She was also unable to use proper kimono fabric, as no two rolls of the fabric are the same and so many copies had to be made. The concept of the costume originated with makeup artist Angela Nogara, and the wig was also very complex. Hair designer Michael Reitz used the traditional method — which includes beeswax — for seven wigs, with each wig taking 20 hours to create. In 2003, Nogara won the Emmy for Outstanding Makeup for a Series (non-prosthetic) for this episode.

Did You Notice?: This episode has Ron Rifkin's second naked scene, and he often jokes that Victor Garber will be next to bare all. In an interview on *Canada AM* Rifkin reiterated his theory, to which Garber responded, "It is *not* gonna happen, and he's lying and he's just brought it up because I'm so insecure about it." Garber added that he's not sure why they keep giving Rifkin the naked scenes when the writers have Michael Vartan and Bradley Cooper in the cast.

Nitpicks: Although Will is more "in the know" than he was a season ago, isn't it a little risky for Sydney to be telling him everything about Project Christmas? If Vaughn hired Will to do some work and didn't give him any details, maybe she should have taken that as a sign that the information is classified and it isn't for her to tell Will about it. And why is the patient in Geneva (in the previous episode) sealed in an incubator, while Vaughn is simply lying on the bed despite being infected with the same virus?

Locations: Paldiski, Estonia; Tokyo, Japan

Music/Bands: As Sydney explains Project Christmas to Will, we hear Debbie Weisberg's "Home" (*Acoustic*); "Slumber My Darling" by Yo-Yo Ma, featuring Alison Krauss (*Appalachian Journey*), plays while Syd sits at Vaughn's bedside; Peter Gabriel's "I Grieve" (*Up*) plays when Vaughn awakes; and we hear Sheryl Crow's "I Shall Believe" (*Tuesday Night Music Club*) when Syd and Vaughn hug back at the CIA.

2.8 Passage, Part 1

Original air date: December 1, 2002
Written by: Debra J. Fisher and Erica Messer
Directed by: Ken Olin
Guest cast: Pasha D. Lychnikoff (Zoran Sokoloff), Shishir Kurup (Saeed Akhtar), Kiran Rao (Lead Soldier), Chayton Arvin (Soldier), Rahul Gupta (Passport Officer),

Keith Lal (Porter), K.T. Thangavelu (Woman), Richard F. Whiten (Security Section Agent)

Derevko insists on accompanying Jack and Sydney on a mission; Sloane receives proof that Emily's still alive; Vaughn gives Will names of students who got perfect scores on the IQ tests.

Not surprisingly, Sark wasn't being completely honest with Sydney in the previous episode (is anyone ever completely honest on this show?) When he shows up with a very-much-alive Sloane in the SD-6 boardroom at the end of "The Counteragent," it's everything Sydney can do to keep the shocked look off her face. Having a sworn enemy in their midst mirrors what has been happening over at the CIA. Just as Vaughn, Jack, and Sydney vehemently protested the presence of Irina Derevko despite the CIA's belief that she could be of value, now Sydney and Dixon argue that Sark has no place at SD-6 and will betray them the first chance he gets. Sloane, on the other hand, says that because Sark "turned himself in" (just as Derevko did) he can be trusted. Of course, Sloane does not tell them the real reason he has allowed Sark into SD-6. Sydney and Jack can't help but wonder, however, if Sark knows about Derevko. Or worse, does Sloane?

This episode is all about trust. Sloane trusts that Sark is telling the truth; Sydney and Dixon don't trust Sark at all. Derevko asks to be let out of her cell to accompany Sydney on a mission, but she refuses to give any information and expects the CIA to trust her. Sydney no longer trusts the CIA, and doesn't know if she can trust Derevko. Jack absolutely distrusts Derevko, but trusts Sydney's instincts. Devlin doesn't trust that Will can work for the CIA because of his reporter's past. In the end, it doesn't matter who believes whom; at some point *someone* has to trust someone else or there will be a stalemate all around.

The two "love" scenes in the episode contrast and parallel each other brilliantly. In a lovely soliloquy, Vaughn tells Sydney about his father's watch and why it stopped the moment he met her. It's a touching moment, and very unlike Vaughn, who usually can't think of the right thing to say around Sydney. Jack and Irina, on the other hand, also have a "moment" over an accessory — a necklace. Their faces come close to one another as she lifts her hair to let him place the object on her neck, and the tension is electric. One would expect a sudden kiss to pass between them — if the necklace weren't full of C-4 and Jack hadn't just threatened to blow her head off if she steps out of line. (It kind of kills the mood.)

Sloane, meanwhile, receives a phone call from someone claiming to have Emily, and he demands proof. As a shocking package arrives in the mail and he stares at the proof that his beloved wife is alive, Derevko, Jack, and Sydney arrive in New Delhi

CHRISTINA RADISH

Sloane and Sark in happier times.

and the ensuing scenes of Derevko and Jack bickering are brilliant. Lena Olin and Victor Garber play off each other so well, viewers are totally convinced this is a dysfunctional couple that has gone through hell and Sydney is the only child stuck in the middle. The moments where they argue on the plane and on the train are perfect "divorced parents" gems with which many viewers can probably identify. Let's hope those viewers can identify with the Bristows standing together, finally working as a family unit, holding machine guns, and blowing away the enemy. One can only imagine what a lovely event the Bristow family Christmas would be . . .

Highlight: Jack and Derevko arguing about Sydney's love life.

Did You Notice?: From this point on, there will be no voiceover at the beginning of each episode explaining what the show is about.

Nitpicks: Jack is worried that Derevko might have told Sark that he and Sydney were double agents. But wouldn't Sark have put that together by now? If he has a conversation with Sloane about the Rambaldi artifacts that Sydney has recovered for the CIA, that would tip off Sloane pretty quickly that Sydney's been on some missions that weren't sanctioned by SD-6. Also, again Sydney tells Will some top secret information about Sark; while Will is now "in the know," doesn't she worry that if he knows too much he could end up like Danny?

What Did He Say?: Zoran Sokoloff is a black-market dealer who works with Sark. He has offered Sark a set of communication codes used by Uzbekistan's ground forces. If SD-6 doesn't retrieve the codes a neighboring terrorist organization will get them, allowing them to track the Uzbeks' movements and destabilize their forces in Asia. Once they obtain the codes, Jack and Sydney discover they are actually codes for six nuclear warheads that Sark has hidden somewhere. Derevko explains that the warheads are in Kashmir, in the stronghold for the People's Revolutionary Front, and clearly Sloane and Sark have some deal with that group.

Locations: Uzbekistan; New Delhi, India

Music/Bands: As Sydney chases Sark's car up the mountainside, we hear Creedence Clearwater Revival's "Bad Moon Rising," originally off their *Green River* LP. As Will and Sydney talk in her bedroom, the song playing is "Almost Ran" by Josh Canova (*Common Divide*); and in the final scene, where the Bristows are ambushed and forced to fight back, we hear U2's "Walk On" (*All That You Can't Leave Behind*).

2.9   Passage, Part 2

Original air date: December 8, 2002
Written by: Crystal Nix Hines
Directed by: Ken Olin
Guest cast: Derek de Lint (Gerard Cuvee), James Lesure (CIA Agent Craig Blair), Marshall Manesh (Hari Singh), Wolf Muser (Ramon Veloso), Iqbal Theba (General Arshad), Joseph Ruskin (Alain Christophe), Ira Heiden (Rick, CIA Techie), Andy Gatjen (Aide), P.D. Mani (PRF Guard)

Derevko makes a surprising move in Kashmir; Sloane tells the Alliance that he's being blackmailed; another Rambaldi artifact is discovered.

And the Bristow family laughs just keep on coming. As the bickering continues (along with the occasional soothing reminiscence about a toaster), Derevko guides Jack and Sydney through a minefield (a metaphor for the journey the three have taken this season). The threesome makes it to the nuclear facility, where once again trust, or lack of it, threatens to hinder the operation. Despite everything Derevko has done for the CIA, and despite Sydney beginning to think of her as a mother, Jack has always stood his ground, having been betrayed by Derevko to a degree no one else has. But he finally lets his guard down — and it's the wrong moment to do so. The resulting scene — Derevko appearing in the doorway with Gerard Cuvee — is devastating for Sydney, for Jack, and is a shock for the viewers, who were beginning to trust Derevko as well. The fact that the man she is with was not only her KGB supervisor but the very person who chose Jack Bristow as the target for Derevko's ingratiation makes the scene all the more upsetting for Jack and Sydney.

But should we trust everything we see? The twists and turns that follow are what make this show so much fun to watch each week, and Derevko's revelation to Sydney about what really happened in Taipei seems to be exactly what Sydney has wanted to hear all along. Just as the flower they find in Kashmir seems to be able to live forever, so does love — or a daughter's longing for her mother's affection.

Back in L.A., Sloane is being blackmailed, and he travels to London to come clean finally with the Alliance about what has been happening to him. While the Alliance chooses to support him in his efforts to find the person who is blackmailing him, the group has some bad news for him as well. Will he ever see Emily again? Is she actually alive or is he being tricked? Interestingly, in Kashmir, Sydney asks if all this trouble was over a flower. Little does she know how much that question actually applies to Sloane's life.

Highlight: Marshall's little victory dance when his liquid tracer works.

Did You Notice?: Sydney says she's writing her dissertation, which is a quick explanation for why we never see her in school anymore. Also, the head of the Indian Army tells Vaughn he looks just like his father, something Derevko said to him a few episodes back.

Nitpicks: Vaughn goes to the Indian Army official and begs him to call off the air strikes. The man refuses to listen to him and goes ahead with the attacks. Yet when Jack gets into the helicopter, he tells Vaughn to call off the strikes, which Vaughn does — and they immediately stop. Why would the official listen to Vaughn now when he refused to before? Also, Sloane had a chip put in his neck that allows the Alliance to listen in on every conversation he has. Wouldn't Alliance members have heard the telephone conversations he's been having with his blackmailer? Wouldn't they already be aware that something is going on with Emily? Finally, if Derevko were "The Man," the one that Khasinau admitted and Sark agreed was the boss of the operation, why would she be answering to someone else? It doesn't make a lot of sense.

Oops: Flying to New Delhi would take Vaughn approximately two days with the time difference, and New Delhi is 13.5 hours ahead of L.A. In this episode, Vaughn appears to leave L.A. and arrive in New Delhi in a couple of hours, which is physically impossible.

What Did He Say?: Vaughn finds out that the nukes have been set to be activated at 1700 hours, but he doesn't know what that will mean for Sydney. She has the control codes and believes she can deactivate the nukes, but she must get to them before 1700 hours. Kendall finds out that the Indian government has discovered there are nuclear weapons in Pakistan and will launch an air strike within 24 hours, and Vaughn decides to go to India to try to get the government to stop the strikes.

Locations: Srinagar, India

Marshall's Gadgets: Marshall puts a liquid tracer on Sloane's bearer bonds so they can follow where the bonds go.

Music/Bands: As Sydney plays mini-golf with Will and Francie, the song we hear is "Emotional Rescue" by The Rolling Stones (*Emotional Rescue*).

2.10 The Abduction

Original air date: December 15, 2002
Written by: Alex Kurtzman-Counter and Roberto Orci
Directed by: Nelson McCormick
Guest cast: Petra Wright (Alice), Ric Young (Suit & Glasses), Faye Dunaway (Ariana Kane), John Balma (Thatcher Powell), Don Took (Agent Grey), Charles Constant (Desk Attendant), Kenny Gould (Guard)

Marshall accompanies Sydney on a mission to London; the head of Alliance counterintelligence arrives at SD-6 to ascertain what has happened to Emily; Francie begins to suspect that Will and Sydney are keeping a secret from her.

Finally — an episode revolving around Marshall! Kevin Weisman has consistently played Marshall as one of the funniest, clumsiest, sweetest characters on television, and the writers clearly knew he was a fan favorite. With "The Abduction" he gets the chance to prove that he can act throughout an entire episode, not just in briefing scenes where he introduces his technogadgets. Every scene with Marshall in this episode is a highlight, from his admitting that he Photoshops pictures to send to his mother, to hyperventilating on his first plane ride, to overacting his role on his mission in London, to shouting at a guard in Ewok. His frightened yet sincere comment to Sydney — "It's my job to keep you safe" — has a hilarious irony that only Marshall could muster. It's his innocence that makes Sydney's decision about whether or not to let the CIA extract him from SD-6 all the more difficult. Like Dixon, Marshall is proud to be "one of the good guys," and she knows it'll break his heart to discover the truth. But if she leaves him where he is, he could not only put himself in danger, but also undermine the CIA's mission.

Jack squares off against Ariana Kane, played with an evil finesse by the legendary Faye Dunaway. The scenes of the two of them mentally sparring are wonderful, and Sloane shows a lot of pride for Jack's being able to hold his own against this daunting woman. Jack has a lot to handle in this episode as he moves from Ariana Kane to Irina Derevko, confronting her and telling her that he believes she's in cahoots with Sark. He clearly fears the developing relationship between Sydney and Derevko, and their embrace at the beginning of the episode — the first physical contact Sydney has with Derevko — definitely proves that he has every right to be scared.

Will has been playing a smaller part in recent episodes, but in this one he plays an important role — he becomes what Sydney must have been like so many years ago. After Francie asks Will and Sydney why they stop talking every time she enters a room, Will's guilt is overwhelming. He recognizes the way he used to feel when he knew

CHRISTINA RADISH

Marshall finally goes out on a field mission, and to everyone's surprise (including his own) becomes a hero. We always knew he would.

Sydney was keeping something from him though he couldn't put his finger on it, and now he's an accomplice to that deceit. Just as Sydney used to question lying to her friends, her family, and her co-workers, now Will wonders if he's doing the right thing. Sydney shows how much she has learned when she explains the difference between a "loving lie" and a deceitful one. If lying to Francie will save Francie's life, then Sydney is willing to do it. After all, she knows better than anyone what would happen if Francie were told the truth.

Highlight: When Sloane tells Sydney that she'll be going on the mission with Marshall and Marshall responds, "Marshall who?"

Name That Guest Star: Faye Dunaway is a Hollywood legend. She has been nominated for three Academy Awards in the Best Actress category for her work in *Bonnie and Clyde*, *Chinatown*, and *Network*; she won for the latter. In addition to those films she has starred in *The Thomas Crown Affair*, *Three Days of the Condor*, *The Handmaid's Tale*, *Don Juan DeMarco*, and *The Rules of Attraction*, and she always has several projects on the go. She has been nominated for 11 Golden Globe Awards and has won three, and she won an Emmy in 1994 for her work in *Columbo: It's All in the Game*. Talking about Jennifer Garner, she said, "She reminds me a little bit of Audrey Hepburn — she really does." Interestingly, Dunaway was one of the original actresses considered for the part of Derevko.

Did You Notice?: Faye Dunaway played the evil mother in *Mommie Dearest*, a movie about Christina Crawford's harrowing childhood with her mother, Joan Crawford. On *Alias*, she is guest-starring on a show that features a daughter coming to terms with her evil mother.

Nitpicks: As Sloane is torturing Sark, he puts a glass ball in one cheek and pulls the belt tight, saying the glass could break. Yet a moment later when Sark spits it out,

Sloane hasn't loosened the belt at all, meaning Sark could have spit the ball out at any time.

Oops: When Marshall yells at the guard in a language Sydney doesn't understand, he explains that it's Ewok, "the official language of the indigenous creatures on the planet Endor." While there *is* a planet Endor in the movie *Return of the Jedi*, the Ewoks lived on one of Endor's moons (also named Endor), a tidbit of geekiness that Marshall should definitely have known.

What Did He Say?: The Echelon satellite system is used by the NSA to monitor communications such as faxes, calls, and e-mails for certain keywords, allowing the organization to detect threats to the country. Sark believes Gerard Cuvee might have access to the system through a terminal he keeps in Paris. Sydney and Sark must go there and bring the terminal back. Vaughn tells Sydney to install a deletion program that will wipe the terminal clean before Sloane can read what's on it. When Sloane gets the terminal and finds that the information is gone, he sends Sydney and Marshall to London to get Cuvee's copy of the files; Marshall must go because Sydney will need someone who can "crack polymorphic algorithms" on-site.

Locations: Paris, France; London, England

Marshall's Gadgets: A magnetically charged hub that breaks through steel and emits a tear gas to disable the guards once it gets through.

Music/Bands: As Syd and Will talk about Francie's suspicions, we hear Chumbawamba's "Don't Try This at Home" (*Readymades*); when Sydney and Marshall are at the symphony in London, they are listening to Johann Sebastian Bach's "Sleepers, Awake"; "Beauty of the Rain" by Dar Williams (*The Beauty of the Rain*) plays as Marshall says goodbye to Sydney at the airport; and Boomkat's "The Wreckoning" (*Boomkatalog*) plays at Francie's surprise party.

2.11   A Higher Echelon

Original air date: January 5, 2003
Written by: John Eisendrath
Directed by: Guy Norman Bee
Guest cast: James Lesure (CIA Agent Craig Blair), Ric Young (Suit & Glasses), Faye Dunaway (Ariana Kane), Ira Heiden (CIA Agent Rick McCarthy), Elizabeth Penn Payne (CIA Print Technician), John Christopher Storey (CIA Video Technician), Mark Humphrey (SD-6 Technician), Nelson Mashita (SD-6 Op Tech Agent), George Tovar (Waiter), Shawn Michael Patrick (SD-6 Forensic Expert)

Marshall is threatened with torture by Suit & Glasses and agrees to re-create the Echelon program; Ariana Kane suspects Jack and takes measures to prove he's a threat; Derevko offers her help at a steep price to the CIA.

"A Higher Echelon" is one of the few episodes of *Alias* that doesn't seem to have much of Jennifer Garner in it and instead acts as a sort of bridge episode, with very little Rambaldi or sad Sydney moments.

Marshall continues to be a focal point as he undergoes torture and receives threats against his mother. He eventually caves under the pressure and agrees to help Cuvee. Throughout the episode he is under immense pressure, and not being a properly field-trained officer, the viewer worries that he will succumb to pressure and threats against his mother, the person he cares about more than anyone. But despite everything that Marshall is threatened with — not to mention that Sloane doesn't seem to care one iota for his safety — what he eventually does shows a brazenness that viewers might not have thought this mama's boy had in him. He proves that he's a true hero, loyal to his country and to his boss, who shows no loyalty in return.

Back in L.A., Ariana's suspicions cause her to make a move that infuriates Jack. He must turn to the CIA to help him, which it does, but in a great scene where he squares off against Ariana in a restaurant, he makes a major error, and the scene is so intense you'll be on the edge of your seat. Now he's on the lam from SD-6, although he still turns to Sloane — which might have been a bad idea.

Finally, Kendall makes a surprising call when he allows Derevko on to the Echelon server after the CIA is shut down by a virus. Despite all the correct information Derevko has supplied to the CIA and the fact that she made a reference earlier to the virus being like "quicksand," Kendall finally giving in and letting Derevko see some of the United States' most top-secret, confidential, and privileged information seems completely out of character and, frankly, pretty stupid. The CIA has techies that rival Marshall in smarts, and it just seems absurd that the director of operations would allow a well-known terrorist, murderer, and enemy of the United States (who was due to be executed just a few days before) to see this information. Was it a good call, or will it be the CIA's downfall?

Highlight: Marshall revealing the "code" he's worked out for the tooth puller.

Interesting Fact: In one of the best moments of the episode, Marshall grabs Sydney and says, "My name is Marshall J. Flinkman. I'm here to rescue you." The line is from *Star Wars*, when Luke Skywalker says the same thing to Princess Leia (with his own name, of course).

Nitpicks: See the last paragraph of the summary, above.

What Did He Say?: Marshall was abducted by an associate of Gerard Cuvee. When he and Sydney were in London, Marshall e-mailed the Echelon data to SD-6 and it came through in pieces; an error holds up one of the pieces in Ho Chi Minh City and Sydney must go and retrieve it. The CIA must find the same breach on Echelon that Cuvee found, and if they can close it, there's no way even Marshall could get in.

Locations: Ho Chi Minh City, Vietnam; Mexico City, Mexico

Music/Bands: When Sydney tells Francie about Vaughn we hear Jude's "All I Want to Do" (unreleased); "Just Go On Home" by the Mojo Monkeys (*Hang*) plays when Will talks to Francie at the restaurant; Marshall downloads an MP3 of Sammy Hagar's "Serious JUJU" (*Serious JUJU*); Kinky's "Noche De Toxinas" (*Kinky*) plays when Syd finds Marshall; and we hear Matthew Good's "Weapon" (*Avalanche*) as Marshall returns to SD-6.

2.12   The Getaway

Original air date: January 12, 2003
Written by: Jeff Pinkner
Directed by: Lawrence Trilling
Guest cast: Courtney Gains (Holden), Faye Dunaway (Ariana Kane), Amy Irving (Emily Sloane), Ira Heiden (CIA Agent Rick McCarthy), Kevin Sutherland (Agent Blake), Doug Kruse (Patton Birch), Roger Ranny (Black Sweater), Sonny Suroweic (Leather Jacket), Phillipe Simon (Claude Rousseau), Laurent Alexandre (Airport Security Guard), Don Took (Agent Grey)

Jack is a wanted man after Ariana Kane discovers he was lying; tension erupts when Sydney finds out that Vaughn has known about the Alliance's investigation of her father; we find out who was orchestrating the Emily conspiracy.

While this is an episode about people making narrow escapes — Jack (twice), Sydney and Vaughn, Sloane — it's more about relationships between people, and what impact those relationships can have. If you are so close to a person you work with that you become blind to all reason, it's usually a safe bet that your job performance will suffer. But in many cases on this show, it's the characters' love and loyalty that help them do what they do better.

In the first case, Jack turns to Derevko for help when he realizes he and Sloane are being set up. This request is a *huge* step for Jack to take considering not long ago he would seethe every time Sydney mentioned Derevko's name. Even upon returning from Kashmir with Derevko he had informed her that he didn't trust her and believed she would turn on him with Sark. Derevko's managing to close the access points to Echelon in the previous episode would not have been enough to make him trust her, but it seems he has pondered everything that has happened between them. Is he making a huge mistake, or is Derevko finally atoning for her sins? Jack is only human, after all, and Derevko used to be a person he loved above everyone else.

In contrast, Sydney and Vaughn's relationship takes a turn for the worse when she believes she *can't* trust him. When she loses her cool and yells at Vaughn that she is sick and tired of his making decisions for her own good, we can't help but agree with her. While Vaughn is supposed to follow protocol, and while he did believe he was keeping her safe in not telling her, he must begin to understand that Sydney is a big girl and can take her share of problems, and she almost always makes the right decision. Vaughn clearly realizes that she might have a point, and his ensuing conversation with Weiss (who is back after having been shot in the neck in "Trust Me") is a real eye-opener for him. As Weiss points out, Vaughn keeps repeating that his closeness to Sydney is a detriment, when in fact it could be the thing that has helped them hurt SD-6 as much as they have (it's an interesting moment, considering last season it was Weiss who said that Vaughn's closeness to Sydney was a problem). Sydney and Vaughn's "first date" is a thrilling moment for fans, even if it doesn't exactly end the way we might have hoped.

And finally, there's the relationship between Sloane and Emily. As he told Jack, Sloane put the drug in Emily's drink to prevent her from suffering later, and from the private moments between the two, we know that claim to be true. For all of Sloane's evil, conspiring ways, there is no doubt that he loves Emily above all else. Later we will discover that much of what he has been doing thus far is *for* Emily, but the revelation at the end of this episode is mind-boggling. We must think back to "Almost Thirty Years" and the scene where Sloane tells Emily on the beach what SD-6 really is and what he's done. The look of disappointment and shock on her face is too much for Sloane to bear — and almost too much for us to bear as well. If the person you loved most was disappointed with something in your life, what would you do to get rid of the thing they hate? The irony is, what Sloane does at the end of this episode is something he would kill anyone else for even contemplating.

Highlight: Weiss asking Vaughn to tell him about Sydney and saying that he revealed his deepest emotions to Vaughn when his dog peed on the carpet.

Interesting Fact: The movie rolling at the beginning of the episode in the theater is *D.O.A.*, a film noir released in 1950 and remade in 1988 starring Dennis Quaid. The film is about a man who enters a detective's office to report a murder — his own — and recounts the tale of how he was mysteriously poisoned and then found his killer after being given a week to live. Since Jack seems to have been set up in the matter of Emily's kidnapping and is a dead man if SD-6 finds him, the film is an appropriate one.

Did You Notice?: At the beginning of the episode, as Jack is running from the theater, Sydney pulls up in a car. He stops and says, "Sydney?" and she tells him to get in. This is a great throwback to the pilot, but the tables have been turned: in the pilot, Jack pulled up to Sydney in a car and yelled for *her* to get in.

Nitpicks: Make sure you watch the episode before reading on. . . . At the end of the episode, we discover that Sloane himself has orchestrated the entire ruse about Emily's death. There was no blackmailer (Sloane hired him); Ariana Kane was set up to get her out of the way; Sloane apparently cut off Emily's finger; and he put the VTX in her drink to stage her death and then bury an empty coffin. But if you go back and look at all the scenes, he seems to have gone to some very unnecessary trouble, and some parts of the ruse don't add up. First of all, the glass of wine in the bathroom: Why would Sloane have put it there, looked completely stunned, rushed to the televisions in a total panic, and called downstairs? He's not being watched (we know this because the Alliance doesn't know it's happening), so why the big act? Secondly, he would have had to have met with Emily to cut off her finger — or at least have gotten someone else to do it — and then hired a "blackmailer" to call his office and threaten him. If the Alliance had chipped his neck, how was he able to do all this without them hearing what he was up to? Sure, there's a possibility he made some arrangements through a secure server — like the way he e-mailed Jack in this episode — but there's no way he could have pulled off the whole plan that way. How did he get away with no body in the coffin? There are many questions that remain unanswered, and while all of it made for exciting, suspenseful television, Sloane's methods and the way he acted when he was alone don't seem very logical after we discover the answer to the mystery.

Oops: When Jack reads Sloane's e-mail you can hear Sloane's voice dictating it, and he starts off, "Jack, I'm sending this through a secure server. I'm sorry." But when you look at Jack's screen, it simply says, "Jack, I'm sorry."

What Did He Say?: The Triad (see "The Indicator") has developed a "quantum gyroscope missile guidance system" that can make something as banal as a 1970s-era scud missile into a high-tech cruise missile. A man named Carl Shatz is taking a prototype from Nice to Berlin and Sydney must intercept it.

Locations: Nice, France; the Philippines

Marshall's Gadgets: A ring that can cut through anything; in this case, it's used to cut fabric.

Music/Bands: Sydney toys with the airport security to the sounds of No Doubt's "Hella Good" (*Rock Steady*); Beck's "Guess I'm Doing Fine" (*Sea Change*) plays while Sydney shares cocktails with Francie; and we hear Charles-François Gounod's "Salut Demeure" when Sloane arrives in the Philippines.

2.13 Phase One

Original air date: January 26, 2003
Written by: J.J. Abrams
Directed by: Jack Bender
Guest cast: Jean Pierre Bergeron (Gils Nacor), Angus Scrimm (SD-6 Agent McCullough), Rutger Hauer (Anthony Geiger), Elizabeth Penn Payne (Techie #1), Ira Heiden (Techie #2), Kevin Sutherland (Techie #3), Mark Galasso (Tactical Medic), Lyle Killpatrick (Police Officer), Alex Morris (Homeless Vet)

After Sydney gets her hands on "the silver bullet," the CIA *finally decides to move in and take down the Alliance once and for all.*

That lingerie! That escape! That confession! That kiss! That *other* kiss! That phone call! That *ending!* "Phase One" was hands down the most jaw-dropping hour of television these two authors have ever seen. It was easily the biggest episode of *Alias* to date, and it took everything we've come to know about the show's main theme and turned it on its head, creating an entirely new series by the episode's end. What other series would have the nerve to build up to something for a season and a half and then *end it* — in this case, end the plotline that provides the backbone to Sydney's main conundrum as a double agent?

In the hands of another cast of writers, "Phase One" would have signaled the end of the series. It would have simultaneously been the greatest episode of all and "jumped the shark" (to use an increasingly loathsome phrase) by wrapping up so many tension-ridden storylines that it would have left nothing else for fans to wait for. Remember what happened to *The X-Files* after Mulder and Scully kissed? But never fear — we're in far more skilled hands here. A single episode containing the demise of SD-6, the end of Dixon's obliviousness to what Sydney has been doing, a long-awaited kiss between Sydney and Vaughn (and two other people who are far more surprising), and the death of a major character is the stuff of series finales, not midseason episodes. And yet, by the end of "Phase One," viewers were on the edges of their seats, their attention riveted on the new possibilities the writers had left open for these characters. The writers ended one show and began a new one, all at once. How could they have re-created the show (midseason, no less!) without completely ruining everything viewers had come to love? Easy. By not changing the most important part — Sydney.

"Phase One" was clearly written to attract new viewers, since its lead-in promised major ratings. Kendall briefs everyone on information the longtime viewers already know, but his summary allowed the new viewers to catch up to what was going on. Then, by putting all their eggs in one basket, so to speak, the writers showed the

Red Moments

After sporting the now-famous red wig in the pilot episode, Syd has found herself in some other pretty snazzy red outfits. Bright red is often used in the show; here are some of the more noticeable red moments, or ones that held some significance:

"Truth Be Told" — the legendary *Run, Lola, Run* hair and the T-shirt and skirt to match; the red dress Syd wears at the embassy

"Parity" — the dress Syd wears in Madrid, just before she fights Anna Espinosa

"A Broken Heart" — the sunglasses and Marshall purse Syd carries in the Moroccan market; the car wash

"Reckoning" — Amy Tippin's hair; the head doctor's desk in the asylum

"Color-Blind" — the lighting when Martin Shepard recalls the photo of Syd; Syd's dress at Thanksgiving dinner

"Mea Culpa" — the jacket the potential "hitman" is wearing

"Spirit" — the bright red flowers Syd looks at while talking with Vaughn; the "super swank" red sunglasses she wears while under the alias of Victoria King

"The Confession" — Syd's sunglasses and spicy flapper dress

"The Box, Part One" — the bag Syd carries through the air ducts

"The Coup" — the chair in the Moscow warehouse where Sark holds his meeting

"Page 47" — the blanket on Will's bed; Syd's red bikini top, with shoes and purse to match

"The Prophecy" — Syd's parachute in Rio; the robe she wears while undergoing tests

"Q & A" — the swank red sunglasses — they return

"The Solution" — the tank top Syd is wearing while she pounds the punching bag

"Rendezvous" — Syd's wig on the mission

"Almost Thirty Years" — The Circumference

"Trust Me" — Jack's suggestion that Francie paint her restaurant red; Will's community-service outfit

"Cipher" — the full-body luge suit, with matching glasses

"The Indicator" — Francie's restaurant (she certainly took Jack's advice)

"Passage, Part Two" — Syd's mini-golf ball at the end of the episode, which looks very similar to a larger version we saw in season 1

"A Higher Echelon" — Syd's little hat and outfit in Mexico City

"The Getaway" — the funky glasses that go with Syd's punk look, which also includes red fishnets and a vinyl red-and-black bra

"Phase One" — the lingerie and the airplane's interior décor

"Double Agent" — Emma and James's hotel room in Berlin

"A Free Agent" — the jacket Aaron is wearing at the aquarium

"Endgame" — the red soccer ball Aaron kicks around

"Countdown" — the interior of the monastery and the monk's outfit

"Second Double" — the fetish wear

"The Telling" — the flashing red light that bathes Syd as she wakes up, dazed, in the alleyway

"The Two" — Syd's Ferrari, dress, and wig

"Reunion" — the top the Mexican girl is wearing; the dress Syd dons when she goes to the party with Vaughn; the walls in Vaughn's hotel room

"A Missing Link" — Syd's fingernails when she's Julia Thorne

"Repercussions" — the pay phone Syd uses; the hotel's carpets and doors; the maroon-colored top Syd is wearing when she chases Sloane's kidnappers; the casino's tables and walls

"The Nemesis" — Weiss's and Vaughn's hockey jerseys; the wallpaper in the place where Vaughn and Syd follow Doren

"Prelude" — the blood on Sydney's hospital gown

"Conscious" — Brezzel's front door; Kaya's hair; the red light that shines in several scenes of Syd's dream

"Remnants" — the red-and-black-checkered shirt Syd wears when she goes to see Will

"Full Disclosure" — the light on Sydney's hair when she first sees Lauren and Vaughn together

"Crossings" — the flare

"After Six" — the red dress Lauren chooses over the black one; the sweater Syd wears on the plane

"Blowback" — Lauren's wig

"Façade" — Syd's wig and jacket

"The Frame" — Syd's wig; Senator Reed's tie and couch; the shawl Olivia is wearing when Jack speaks to her; the glass map

"Hourglass" — the red font Jack always types in when messaging Irina; the glow in Conrad's monastery; Syd's red turban; Lauren's bedroom walls and the walls of Olivia's study

"Blood Ties" — Sloane's tie; the glow in the CIA safehouse

"Legacy" — one of the cords attached to Nadia for reading her brain patterns; the liquid Vaughn pours on Dr. Lee; the red glow in the cargo plane

newbies just what was so appealing about *Alias* — Sydney's sexy disguises; exciting action scenes; quick banter; fast-paced drama; and a cliffhanger ending. Sydney's amazing feat on the plane near the beginning of the episode is one of the most exciting undercover ops we've seen her tackle, and Weiss and Vaughn cheering her on from afar is great.

Anthony Geiger has stepped in as Sloane's temporary replacement at SD-6, but Sloane has left a few surprises in his wake for Geiger to find, including a huge one that exposes Jack. When a compromised Jack telephones Sydney to give her a cryptic warning, her response is immediate shock. This is the moment she had been dreading for two years, and now it has arrived. "Phase One" is an episode that will be remembered for all the huge moments listed above, but it's the little moments like this phone call that rewarded the longtime viewers. Or the look on Dixon's face as he speaks to his wife, realizing his life is forever changed. Or the juxtaposition of Dixon watching the CIA enter the building, knowing

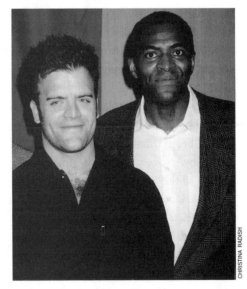

CHRISTINA RADISH

As SD-6 crumbles around them, Marshall and Dixon have no idea what they are about to face, and that their lives have been based on a lie.

what's happening, and Marshall munching away on his cocktail wienies, completely oblivious, not realizing the danger he's in. Both Dixon and Marshall are characters viewers hold deep in their hearts, and we feel for them in a way we were unable to feel for Sydney back in the pilot episode when we really didn't know her very well.

With the excitement of Sydney finally fulfilling her mission and Vaughn and Sydney finally expressing their love for one another, the writers *still* managed to one-up themselves with the very shocking ending. On the one hand, what happens to this character is sad given she's barely spoken an important word all season. But the potential destructiveness that arises from this final scene is infinite, and we realize that while "phase one" of this series is now over, we cannot wait for phase two to begin.

Highlight: Apart from what has been mentioned above, Geiger torturing Jack is particularly harrowing and excellent.

Interesting Fact: This episode originally aired immediately after Super Bowl XXXVII, which would explain the sexed-up bikini shots in the opening sequence.

Name That Guest Star: Rutger Hauer, who plays Anthony Geiger, is best known as the replicant Roy Batty in *Blade Runner*, the 1982 Ridley Scott film starring Harrison Ford. Hauer is outstanding in the movie and showed real promise, but after starring in the 1985 film *Ladyhawke*, he seemed resigned to taking B-movie roles. He has since appeared in several fantasy, science-fiction, and horror films, and has played many vampires (including Lothos in the 1992 film *Buffy the Vampire Slayer*). His last major role was in the 2002 George Clooney film *Confessions of a Dangerous Mind*.

Did You Notice?: Vaughn tells Sydney he can't sleep when she's in the field, something Derevko told her she had intuited in "The Passage, Part 1." Also, the recurring background characters get no respect on this show. Take Ira Heiden, for instance. All season he's been referred to as "Techie" during the end credits. Then he was "Rick, CIA Techie" before finally graduating to the more prestigious name of "CIA Agent Rick McCarthy." Now, suddenly, in this episode, he's back to being "Techie #2." This happens to all the "techies" on the show who only appear in the end credits and get very few lines, if any. Can't the characters at least keep their full names?

Nitpicks: While the scene where Sydney finally tells Dixon the truth shows what phenomenal actors both Garner and Lumbly are, the repetition of that tired phrase "You have been working for the enemy you thought you were fighting" is *so* overdone it actually detracts from her heartbreaking admission. And when Sydney wraps the wire around Nacor's neck, why doesn't it pierce the skin? It's very thin and she's pulling it pretty tightly around his neck, choking him.

Oops: When Syd makes her first entrance in the black outfit, she's not wearing the red bracelets that she will later use to overpower Gils Nacor. It's a good thing he made her change. Also, Francie tells Sydney and Will that the restaurant has made a profit in only six months, and it opened in "The Indicator," episode 5 of season 2. Yet in the previous episode, Weiss says he's been in the hospital for three months, and he was shot in "The Enemy Walks In," the season premiere. So how much time has really passed?

What Did He Say?: The CIA has discovered there is a server 47, a secret server of the Alliance. It is on a 747, being watched over by Gils Nacor. The plane only lands for refueling and for Nacor to pick up a new escort to keep him company. Sydney has to be the escort in order to access the server.

Locations: "Over the Atlantic"

Music/Bands: During Sydney's lingerie modeling at the beginning of the episode we hear AC/DC's "Back in Black" (*Back in Black*); Lenny Kravitz's "American Woman" (*Greatest Hits*) plays as Syd goes through the motions to enter the CIA; Groove Armada's "Hands of Time" (*Love Box*) plays when Will and Francie are in the kitchen; and we hear "Use Me" by Bill Withers (*Still Bill*) when Sydney is having dinner with Francie and Will.

2.14   Double Agent

Original air date: February 2, 2003
Written by: Roberto Orci and Alex Kurtzman-Counter
Directed by: Ken Olin
Guest cast: Olivia d'Abo (Emma Wallace), Constance Brenneman (Christine Phillips), Ethan Hawke (James Lennox), Ira Heiden (Techie #4), Michael Mastro (Arden Jezen), Michael Yavnieli (Techie #2), Joel Guggenheim (Techie #3), Steve Heinze (Ranking Agent), Bru Muller (Negotiator), Terry Urdang (Techie #5)

When an agent is killed in public in Berlin, the CIA sends Sydney to recover her partner. In the meantime, the CIA discovers Project Helix, a new technology capable of reshaping a person's face and body to look exactly like someone else's.

After the shocking revelations of "Phase One," any episode would be a disappointment, but "Double Agent" is surprisingly good and shows that the writers have no plans to slow down and take it easy for a while. The opening sequence, showing two people in bed then hunting each other in the hotel room before the female half of the couple is standing half naked on a Berlin street covered in explosives, is intense and terrifying. As she stands shaking on the corner, completely helpless and being forced to sing "Pop Goes the Weasel," we wince in horrible anticipation every time she says the word "pop." Olivia D'Abo only appears briefly in this episode, but she leaves a powerful impression.

CHRISTINA RADISH

James Lennox (Ethan Hawke) must convince Sydney that he is telling the truth, but she doesn't know if she can believe him.

Because this is the first episode after the dissolution of SD-6, Sydney's mind is still reeling with the possibilities — could she really be free? Is it true that she could meet Vaughn for lunch, or enter the CIA building through the front door? As she stands in the rubble of what was once SD-6, she has a feeling of freedom that she doesn't quite know what to do with. However, with Dixon and Marshall still in debriefing, she knows the worst is not yet over.

The big-name guest stars continue to appear, with Ethan Hawke starring as James Lennox, the partner (and, it turns out, fiancé) of the woman from the beginning of the episode. Sydney can't help but see herself in him. He doesn't have an SD-6 to deal with, but the woman he loves died because she was compromised by being with him. Could the same thing happen with Sydney and Vaughn? Is it possible someone could take advantage of one of them while posing as the other? What easier way to weasel into someone's heart and gain their trust?

The double Lennox situation Sydney finds herself in at the end of the episode is an intriguing — if unoriginal — plot device, with origins back in biblical times. In *1 Kings*, King Solomon is faced with two women claiming to be the mother of a child. Solomon finally figures out who the real mother is when he threatens to cut the child in two and give half to each woman: the real mother is the one who pleads with him not to kill the baby. Sydney uses a similar tactic at the end of the episode to determine which Lennox is the real deal, although the back and forth up to that point keeps viewers guessing.

Finally, the scene all the Syd-Vaughn-shippers have been waiting for happens, but the two have an unexpected "audience" without Sydney's knowledge (the "ew" factor is definitely heightened in this scene). Not for the first time, Sydney's professional life (and the technology she has learned about in this episode) follows her home, but when she finally puts the pieces together to discover what is going on, will it be too late?

Highlight: The shocking beginning with Emma Wallace on the street.

Interesting Fact: The big finale of "Phase One" involving Francie was supposed to have been the ending of this episode, but the writers decided to put all of the shocks into the previous hour. Considering what we learn about Project Helix, putting that ending here would have been more effective. Also, Olivia d'Abo, who plays Emma Wallace, is the second cousin of Miriam d'Abo, who was the Bond girl in the 1987 film *The Living Daylights*.

Name That Guest Star: Ethan Hawke is one in a crop of young Hollywood actors that appeared in the late 1980s. His breakout role was in *Dead Poet's Society*, and he went on to star in other timely films such as *Alive, Reality Bites, Before Sunrise, Snow Falling on Cedars*, and *Training Day*, for which he was nominated for an Academy Award as Best Supporting Actor. He met his wife, Uma Thurman, on the set of *Gattaca* (which also starred Jude Law), but they broke up in late 2003. He's an ambitious actor who tends to take roles that establish him as a "thinking person's actor," and his movie choices just get better and better. If you liked his work in "Double Agent," check him out in the movie *Tape*, a little-seen Linklater film that he appears in with Robert Sean Leonard and Uma Thurman.

Did You Notice?: If Sloane already knew Jack and Sydney were double agents, that might explain the mysterious letter Sark gave him in the back of the ambulance in "The Counteragent." Also, Vaughn jabs a needle in Jezek's neck and tells him he has a short time to live before he'll have a heart attack. It's a very "Xena" moment — she would always perform a neck pinch on her victims that would slowly cut off the blood supply to their brains and kill them if they didn't tell her everything in time. Finally, this is the first time a real name (Osama bin Laden) is used on the show when the characters talk about terrorists.

Nitpicks: While Jennifer Garner has a body that is nice on anyone's eyes, the constant wet bikini/lingerie/rubber suit moments are becoming a little repetitive and gratuitous. We can't help but wonder what an episode would look like under a female director. Also, when Lennox gets back to the CIA, he tells everyone about his undercover op. Since they're CIA, and so is he, wouldn't they already know the details of his operation?

Oops: When Lennox #2 calls in to the CIA as he's racing toward the railway yard, he says he was captured in Concho Caya, when in fact the place is called Cayo Concha (the writers could have included this slip intentionally to suggest that the character isn't telling the truth, but that conclusion is never made by the CIA).

What Did He Say?: Emma Wallace, the agent who was killed in Berlin at the beginning of the episode, was working for two months undercover to gain the trust of Dr. Renzo Markovic, a former research and development scientist who is developing a classified technology under the heading "Helix." He has received bids for his technology from terrorist organizations. Emma was sent on the mission with her partner, James Lennox, who is missing. When last heard from, he was heading to Cayo Concha, off the coast of the Dominican Republic, and the CIA is hoping to find Lennox there. Sydney must go in undercover to try to retrieve him. Arden Jezek is Markovic's chief of security, and he would have access to Helix and know where Markovic is keeping it. Later, Jack explains to Sydney that Project Helix is a next-generation molecular gene therapy, meaning a patient's face and body can be reshaped to look exactly like someone else's. The only way to tell the original from the copy is with an ocular scan. The schematics for Helix are in Poland, and Sydney must find them and destroy them.

Locations: Cayo Concha, Dominican Republic; Poland

Music/Bands: "Moving in Stereo" by The Cars, from their self-titled debut, plays as Sydney is by the pool in a blue bikini; Coldplay's "God Put a Smile upon Your Face" (*A Rush of Blood to the Head*) plays at the end when Sydney and Vaughn have their bedroom encounter.

2.15   A Free Agent

Original air date: February 9, 2003
Written by: Roberto Orci and Alex Kurtzman-Counter
Directed by: Alex Kurtzman-Counter
Guest cast: Christian Slater (Neil Caplan), Yvonne Farrow (Diane Dixon), Lindsey Ginter (Tom Cesaretti), Michael Enright (Antonyn Vasilly), Tracy Middendorf (Elsa Caplan), Arthur Young (Aaron Caplan), William Dennis Hunt (Claude Sheurer), Simon Gray (Peter Kunz), Paul Michael (Tobias Denney), Evan Arnold (David), Ahmed A. Best (Seth)

Kendall refuses to accept Sydney's resignation from the CIA; Dixon expresses how he feels about Sydney's having lied to him; Sloane kidnaps a mathematician and asks him to piece together the Rambaldi artifacts to build something.

Although the last episode contained the Project Helix revelation, it didn't address the biggest fallout of the events in "Phase One": what will happen to Dixon and Marshall; what will Sydney's mission be now that she's fulfilled her duty; where has Sloane disappeared to. Because it didn't address these plot points, "Double Agent" felt more like a "filler" episode, one that was stuck in to pass the time until the writers could address the larger issues. As a result, "A Free Agent" feels like the episode that *should* have followed "Phase One."

Now that Sydney has brought enough information against the Alliance to shut the entire operation down, she realizes she doesn't have much of a purpose at the CIA. Being an agent isn't what she wants to do with her life. In "Double Agent" she witnessed the worst possible outcome of being an undercover operative in the agency, and the life she has been leading for the past eight years isn't one she's eager to continue. The problem is, she's proven herself *so* worthy to the CIA and her efforts have been *so* effective that Kendall isn't about to let her go that easily. His loathsome response to Sydney might seem like blackmail, but it's actually the only option he has. Sydney has arrived at a crossroads in her life — she is graduating from university and believes it is time she graduate from the CIA as well.

Until she gets the congratulatory phone call from Sloane. It's at that moment Sydney realizes her mission was twofold: to bring an end to the Alliance and to make Sloane pay. She's only fulfilled half her mission. Sloane's mocking voice on the other end of the phone is enough to bring that reality right to her, and she begins to reconsider her plans (it's appropriate that she's wearing her graduation gown when he does make the call). However, no matter how much Sloane has done to her in the past, when he vows to kill her if she comes anywhere near him, the threat seems pretty empty.

Once Sydney has dealt with the worst person in her life, she has to turn to the one who's been most wronged by her: Dixon. This is a man who has fought by her side, saved her life (and she's saved his), and been a close friend to her. He has now been put in exactly the same position she once was in and believed what she did at the time. His headspace is where Sydney's was at the beginning of season 1, so his anger toward her is understandable. (Marshall, on the other hand — now the king of the CIA techies — seems unfazed by what has happened, but then again, he was never that close to Sydney.) As Dixon says, if Sydney was so concerned about what might happen to him if she told him the truth, why tell him only when it was for her own benefit? It does seem like a rather selfish thing that she has done. However, later in the episode, in the touching moment between Dixon and his wife, Diane turns on him for the same reason he has turned against Sydney — she feels like she doesn't know him anymore and can't believe he lied to her. Diane is the most important person in Dixon's life and the last person he would ever want to hurt. He must realize the predicament Sydney was in and her reasons for not telling him about SD-6.

One aspect of this show that sets it apart from others of its kind is the weight put on love and marriage. A loved one's disappointment can carry so much weight it can alter the way the other person thinks and acts. Dixon has worked his entire life to get to where he is, and he believed he was fighting for the good guys. Now that he *knows* he would be fighting for the good guys, he walks away from the CIA because Diane asks him to. Similarly, despite everything Sloane worked for and how far he got with the Rambaldi material, when Emily showed disappointment in him for being associated with an organization like SD-6, he walked away from it. Jack is someone who can see a lie coming a mile away, and his stony demeanor makes him the best actor among all the agents — no one can see through him when he's undercover. Despite his gift of intuition, his heart seemed to make him close his eyes when he was married to "Laura," and he refused to even consider that she might be a spy working against him. In this episode, Neil Caplan follows the more traditional character role of a husband agreeing to help out a madman to keep his wife and child safe. Later we'll discover he's more like the other men on this show than we might have originally thought.

Highlight: Jack's comment about Kendall blackmailing Sydney into staying: "Legally he's right; ethically he's an ass."

Name That Guest Star: Christian Slater is the latest A-lister to appear on the show. He comes from the same generation of actors as Ethan Hawke, although he got his start at a younger age, appearing in *The Legend of Billy Jean* when he was 14. He moved on to star opposite Sean Connery in *The Name of the Rose*, but he got his big break in the classic teen angst film *Heathers*. He's since starred in films such as *Young Guns II*, *Pump Up the Volume*, *True Romance*, *Interview with the Vampire*, *Murder in the First*, and *Windtalkers*.

Did You Notice?: At the beginning of the episode it looks like Vaughn and Sydney never went back to have the dinner that was in the oven. Also, when Sloane calls Sydney, it's a scene reminiscent of the end of *Silence of the Lambs*. Like Clarice, Sydney is having a celebratory moment, and like Hannibal Lecter, Sloane tells her not to come after him. There's also an allusion to *Raiders of the Lost Ark* in the scene where Sydney and the goon fight near the airplane propeller.

Oops: Vaughn refers to a Rambaldi device as a "sixteenth-century neutron bomb," but Rambaldi actually lived in the 15th century.

What Did He Say?: Neil Caplan is a mathematician from Cal Tech. He specializes in Knot Theory, the math of geometric objects and how they fit into one another. Sloane took all of the Rambaldi artifacts that were left at SD-6 and is looking for a way to piece them together. Jack believes that Sloane is building a weapon with the Rambaldi puzzle pieces. When the CIA discovers the techie guy's eye implant and sees Sloane make a phone call to arrange transport for the Rambaldi artifacts, Jack believes the call was made to Sloane's contact in the Mojave Desert. Later, Sydney and Vaughn track Sloane to Switzerland.

Locations: Mojave Desert, California; Switzerland

Music/Bands: When Vaughn and Sydney wake up together, we hear Jimmy Eat

World's "My Sundown," from their self-titled album; Evan Olson's "I Can't Forget" (*Red*) plays when Sloane calls Sydney to congratulate her; and as Vaughn confronts Sloane's contact in the bar, we hear The Vines' "Get Free" (*Highly Evolved*).

2.16   Firebomb

Original air date: February 23, 2003
Written by: John Eisendrath
Directed by: Craig Zisk
Guest cast: Eli Danker (Ahmad Kabir), Lina Patel (Alia Gizabi), Yvonne Farrow (Diane Dixon), David A. Kimball (Fleming), Roy Werner (Bob Squad Leader), Bonita Friedericy (Joyce), Ken Lally (Lead Agent)

Kendall becomes frustrated when Sloane eludes the CIA again; Sloane meets with a warlord in Kandahar about his new Doomsday Device; Sydney tries to find Sloane, but because Dixon has refused to help the CIA, her life could be in danger.

If this episode's theme is heat, then Kendall is the episode's hothead. In "Firebomb" he reaches a new level of loathsomeness as he chastises Sydney for not dealing with Sloane more effectively, refuses to listen to her when she complains that the CIA is doing nothing to bring in Sloane, and then has the nerve to tell her that the next time the CIA loses Sloane it'll be her fault. Shut *up*, Kendall! Sometimes this character doesn't seem very realistic — someone in his position doesn't have the time to play petty little mind games. Interestingly, Sloane is seen as the quintessential monster, yet when Sydney's life is in danger at the end of the episode, Kendall tells everyone to pull out and just leave her. He shows the same lack of concern for her that Sloane had shown for Marshall in "A Higher Echelon," which is strange considering that just one episode ago, Kendall was practically blackmailing Sydney to stay at the CIA.

Sloane continues his mysterious mission. In the previous episode he mentioned he was nearing the end of a 30-year odyssey, and considering that's how long he's been chasing the Rambaldi artifacts, we know he's planning something pretty big. In this episode he angrily tells Sydney he's doing something that's bigger than the CIA or SD-6, but he remains cryptic about his idea that will "influence an existing world order I believe to be corrupt," as he explains to Ahmad Kabir. Although we don't see Neil Caplan, his work on the device results in a weapon Sloane decides to "test out" in Mexico City. This device is so original, awesome, and horrific that we can rest assured the writers aren't falling asleep on the job. The scene that Sydney and Vaughn discover upon entering the church is one few viewers will ever forget.

Kendall (Terry O'Quinn) and Sloane work for opposite sides of the game, but both of them cause Sydney endless aggravation.

Will is back in an important capacity. When he's not kissing Francie, he's proving to be an important asset to the CIA, and there's a delicious satisfaction in seeing Will arrive at his first strategy meeting, looking scruffy and unkempt, and then show up the two Harvard graduates and their lame suggestions. His idea — forget playing around with Kabir's enemies; it's his ex-wife who will have the strongest emotional attachment to him (whether love or hate) and could be the biggest asset to the CIA — is consistent with the ongoing theme of the show: the ones you love the most can quickly become the ones you hate the most. But, as we discover with Dixon, sometimes a loved one's safety is more important than a spouse's disappointment, and he makes a heroic return to the show.

Highlight: Syd telling Vaughn the best part of the hockey game is the zamboni.

Did You Notice?: This is the first time Sydney has been disguised as an older woman rather than a sexy younger one.

Nitpicks: First of all, the product placement of the Ford Focus is downright shameful in this episode. It's one thing for someone to hold up a Coca-Cola in the scene of a television show or a movie, but the characters in this episode have turned into walking advertisements for the car (which was part of a sponsorship deal the series had with Ford). In the previous episode, the camera zoomed right in on the make and model number, and in this episode, Vaughn calls Marshall and tells him to find Sydney before rattling off the make, model, and color of the car, only for Marshall to say that he has been looking to buy one. Ugh. John Eisendrath must have been horrified when he was forced to put all of that nonsense into his script. Secondly, when Sark shows up to steal Sloane out of the back of the car, why doesn't Sydney lock the doors (the car has a child lock for the back seats that would have prevented Sloane from leaving) or slam on the brakes? And by the way, for such a great car, it fell apart pretty easily in the car chase scene. Also, if Sydney's body temperature dropped to room temperature in Kabir's house, you'd think she'd be shivering and her teeth would be chattering, but she acts like nothing is different when she's running around in the cold suit.

Oops: Kendall and several others keep referring to the Swiss bank as "Amcorp" (and they pronounce the *p*), but as Sloane and Sydney leave the building you can see the name of the bank is "Amcor." Also, when Sydney is in Kabir's house and Vaughn is instructing her where to go, he tells her to run down a flight of stairs and turn right, but she turns left at the bottom, which is the only way to go, and says the wall has been sealed. If she was supposed to go right, wouldn't the other wall have been the one that's been sealed over?

What Did He Say?: Sloane has been spotted with Ahmad Kabir's men. Kabir is a well-known warlord connected to the Taliban, but the CIA doesn't know exactly where his compound is located. A year prior, Agent Dixon was assigned to steal missiles from Kabir, but Kabir doesn't know Sloane was connected to Dixon. Later, after Sydney returns from Mexico City, Marshall explains that the device that went off in the church was a high-energy pulse weapon that caused everyone's body temperature to immediately increase by about 2,000 degrees so that they were incinerated. It only affects organic material, which is why the church itself didn't burn down. It can also affect computer circuitry (which doesn't make sense if it only attacks organic materials), so if it is aimed at the sky, it could bring down an airplane.

Locations: Kandahar, Afghanistan; Mexico City, Mexico

Marshall's Gadgets: Because the sensors in Kabir's compound can detect body heat, Marshall creates a cold suit for Sydney that will drop her body temperature to room temperature, thus keeping her from being detected by the cameras.

Music/Bands: As Francie talks to Sydney and tells her she's been acting weird, we hear Duncan Sheik's "On a High" (*Daylight*); David Gray's "Freedom" (*A New Day at Midnight*) plays as Sydney and Vaughn talk in her apartment.

2.17   A Dark Turn

Original air date: March 2, 2003
Written by: Jesse Alexander
Directed by: Ken Olin
Guest cast: Richard Lewis (Counterintelligence Analyst Mitchell Yeager), Ravil Isyanov (Karpachev), Thomas Urb (Ilya Stuka), Michael Yavnieli (Techie), Yoshio Be (Chinese Captain), Michael Komurov (Russian Bodyguard), Jon Dixon (CIA Officer), Ryan O'Quinn (Driver)

Derevko is let out again on a couple of CIA missions; a counterintelligence officer shows up at the CIA to investigate Vaughn, and Sydney must decide where her loyalties are; "Francie" is manipulating Will.

After several episodes of guest stars and side plots, we return to the complex relationships of our core characters in this exciting episode. "A Dark Turn" is an hour about intimate trust. Jack and Derevko were once intimate as husband and wife, but Jack's trust was clearly misplaced and he will be forever haunted by his having been blind to Derevko's deceit until it was too late. Sydney has had to live with the knowledge of what happened between her parents for the past year, and it has undoubtedly caused more than a little paranoia in her own life about whom to trust and whom not to. So we can't blame her for being confused when a counterintelligence officer suddenly shows up and tells her that Michael Vaughn is a suspicious person.

Mitchell Yeager has appeared on the scene, and he has reams of evidence against Vaughn. Vaughn's been meeting with people who have known terrorist affiliations. He has changed his cell phone four times in the last few months. He might have a program called Xenon on his computer that only a terrorist would have. Sydney's immediate and loyal response is to roll her eyes at the mere suggestion that Vaughn might be up to something, but then Yeager reminds her that her father had made the same mistake years before. Even Sydney has noticed that they never discuss her mother — could Vaughn be planning some sort of revenge on Derevko? The scene where Sydney opens Vaughn's laptop while he's in the shower is a suspenseful one, and we can't help but recall a similar scene in "Double Agent," where Agent Wallace opens Agent Lennox's computer — and what happens to her as a result. Syd's mother and father have lied to her repeatedly, and two years ago she discovered her whole life was a lie — why should she trust Vaughn?

Jack makes a questionable move when he tells Kendall to let Derevko out on two missions, claiming he'll know when and if she's deceiving him. Just when we're about to say, "Riiiiight," he reminds Kendall that since Derevko faked her death so many years earlier, he has become the world's leading expert on who she is and how she operates. He has probably played every moment of their marriage over in his head hundreds of times, wondering when she was slipping out of the room to spy on him, when she was reporting back to associates, and how he could have let all this slip under his radar. But in life the heart often wins out over the head, and in a shocking moment, we wonder if Jack really *is* free from Derevko's spell. We mentioned in the summary of the previous episode that sometimes the ones you love the most can become the ones you hate the most; so too can ambivalence develop, allowing you to love and hate a person at the same time.

Meanwhile, Evil Francie is playing head games with Will and using him as an entry into the inner workings of the CIA. Will completely trusts Francie, but why shouldn't he? Unlike everyone else on this show, she seems to be unaffiliated with anything he and Syd do, and there's no reason to be suspicious of her. Our sympathies are roused for him as he begins to have dreams of exposing Sydney, which is one of his worst nightmares.

But all of these deceptions pale in comparison with what happens as the episode comes to a close. As we watch Jack's face as the bitter realization of what is happening washes over him, we can't help but feel for him. Our first thought is: How could he have let this happen again? But Derevko is smart, a great actress, and seems to be soulless. Anyone capable of feeling the pain and heartbreak that Jack Bristow has endured will be no match for someone like her.

Highlight: Stuka playing the knife game with Derevko and her response. Despite being evil, she is so much fun to watch when she's in the field that it's too bad they don't let her out more often.

Name That Guest Star: Comedian Richard Lewis is playing against type in his appearance on *Alias*. Most recently he's been appearing as himself on HBO's *Curb Your Enthusiasm*, and prior to his *Alias* guest spot he played Rabbi Richard Glass for a stretch on the WB's *Seventh Heaven*. When he guested on *Alias* he joked, "Playing a CIA agent on *Alias* wasn't much of a stretch — considering I learned to live undercover during my entire adolescence."

Did You Notice?: At the hockey rink you can see the Canadian flag and the Olympic flag featured prominently, and an American flag has been added to the other wall. Later, in "The Telling," the Olympic flag has disappeared and the Canadian and American flags are the only ones there.

Nitpicks: While it might have been a good call to let Derevko out for the Bangkok operation, why did the CIA let her hold on to the Rambaldi manuscript and take notes? What Rambaldi wrote in his journals is volatile stuff, and not exactly information you want in the hands of a terrorist. And now that Sydney and Vaughn know that Syd's place was bugged, why aren't they going to his apartment just to be on the safe side, since it's clear Sydney's being targeted?

Oops: In the opening sequence when the elevator begins to drop suddenly, Karpachev and his men hit the floor hard. In fact, the force would have immediately thrown them upward, in the opposite direction the elevator was going.

What Did He Say?: Luri Karpachev is a former arms dealer with links to the Mafia, and he was a contact of Derevko's. Sloane used to have dealings with him and probably still does. Derevko explains that Karpachev keeps a keycard in his wallet that Sark stole, and it opens a safe in which Sloane believes Karpachev's keeping a Rambaldi manuscript. However, the manuscript was sold to another person, Ilya Stuka, who is in Bangkok. The manuscript is Rambaldi's study of the human heart, which is important because of Rambaldi's obsession with and belief in immortality.

Locations: Bangkok, Thailand; Hong Kong, China; Panama

Music/Bands: LaTour's "Blue" (*LaTour*) plays in the Bangkok nightclub; we hear "Righteously" by Lucinda Williams (*World Without Tears*) when Syd talks to Vaughn in the bar.

2.18   Truth Takes Time

Original air date: March 16, 2003
Written by: J.R. Orci
Directed by: Nelson McCormick
Guest cast: Amy Irving (Emily Sloane), Christopher Curry (Heinz Brucker), Kevin Sutherland (CIA Agent Blake)

When Sark and Derevko are traced to Stuttgart, Emily and Sloane are forced to go into hiding, and Emily discovers what Sloane has been up to.

There's an ironic moment in "Truth Takes Time" in which Sloane takes a flabbergasted Emily onto his plane (she had no idea he had one), introduces her to Derevko (who Emily thought was dead), and then proceeds to tell her that he's in pursuit of the truth. Well, aren't we all, Arvin, aren't we all.

"Truth Takes Time" is a great installment that shows while a husband might be willing to do anything for his wife, maybe his wife just wants to do what is right. Poor Emily, who has been through so much — finding out her husband is managing a terrorist operation and sticking by him; faking her own death and having to leave behind her loved ones; being shuttled off to a cabin in the Philippines; having her finger cut off; believing her life has returned to some semblance of normalcy before being whisked away to go into hiding again — now receives one shock after another, and it's too much for her. The worst part is that she believed if she stood by a known murderer and even mangled her own body for him, things would change and she might get back the man she once thought she knew. Imagine her horror when she realizes he hasn't stopped any of his activities, even if they are for her sake.

Meanwhile, Jack is dealing with the guilt of what happened with Derevko, but surprisingly, he's given operational control at a time when you'd think he'd be removed from the case for being so close to the subject that he compromised the previous op. Derevko, for all her evil ways, shows that she's still a mother at heart when she can't bear to leave Sydney in a building that's about to explode. Sydney surprisingly doesn't seem too shaken up by the knowledge that her mother has betrayed her father again and instead has an even fiercer resolve to find both Derevko and Sloane.

When Emily confronts Sydney, Syd looks at her with the same disappointment that Dixon had shown Sydney a few episodes ago. Here is the one person that Sydney could always trust, the one person who had never betrayed her — and she's betrayed her. This is behavior Sydney has come to expect from Derevko, but not from Emily. Emily can feel that look of censure on Syd's face, a similar look to the one she herself had given Sloane in "Almost Thirty Years," but she follows through on the reason she came and Sydney decides to trust her.

The end scene between Sloane and Emily is one of the most touching, beautiful scenes in season 2. Emily stands in their Tuscan villa, wringing her hands because she's about to betray the man she loves more than anything, only to have him confess to her that he's done the very thing she has always wanted him to do. When Sloane realizes the truth, the shattered look on his face is heartrending. He's done some terrible things, but we can't help but feel what he's feeling in this scene. He can't believe what Emily's done to him, but at the same time he sees the love in her face, and his is reflected right back at her. He forgives her instantly, and her heart forgives him. This entire scene is played with no words, only actions — Emily's look of regret; Sloane's hands coming up to her face. Amy Irving and Ron Rifkin are phenomenal in this scene, and their actions make what's about to happen all the more devastating. Truth does take time, but sometimes it comes too late.

Highlight: The uncomfortable silence after Marshall asks Jack how he managed to plant a transmitter on Derevko.

Did You Notice?: In "The Enemy Walks In," Derevko shot Sydney in the shoulder. In this episode, Sydney shoots Derevko in the same shoulder.

Nitpicks: Even Marshall's biggest fans have to admit that sometimes he takes so long to get to the point you just want to slap him, but why is Jack always *so* annoyed with him? The way he fiercely yells, "What is it, Marshall?!" in this episode is completely uncalled for, even if his nerves have been on edge lately. Also, Sark disables Derevko's transmitter by shocking her with heart defibrillators. Even if they were posing as pharmaceutical company representatives, what the heck was he doing with those in his briefcase?

Oops: In a few shots where we see Emily's hands, she appears to have 10 fingers. Considering there's no way she could have had the other one attached (and we saw she only had nine at the end of "The Getaway"), how did that happen? It looks a little too real to be a prosthesis.

What Did He Say?: Jack is now in charge of operations and Kendall has been demoted. Jack says he put a passive transmitter in Derevko that will go off in 12 hours. Later, after Derevko and Sark obtain a disk in Stuttgart, Will explains that the disk could have the DNA of millions of citizens on it. Marshall says that if you know someone's exact genetic coding, you could poison the water supply so it would kill only that person.

Locations: Tuscany, Italy; Stuttgart, Germany; Florence, Italy

Music/Bands: Josh Kelley's "Amazing" (*For the Ride Home*) plays during the dinner scene when Francie gives Vaughn the tie; Eastmountainsouth's "So Are You to Me," from their self-titled CD, plays when Syd and Vaughn are lying in bed.

2.19   Endgame

Original air date: March 30, 2003
Written by: Sean Gerace
Directed by: Perry Lang
Guest cast: Christian Slater (Neil Caplan), Tracy Lynn Middendorf (Elsa Caplan), Yvonne Farrow (Diane Dixon), Yasen Peyankov (Morgan Nickovich), Eve Kagan (Sorority Girl #1), Stacey Scowley (Sorority Girl #2), Arthur Young (Aaron Caplan), Jess King (Cell Block Guard), Justin Wade (Drug Store Employee), Sean Casey (Sedan Agent)

As Sloane mourns his wife, Sydney tries to find Neil Caplan, the mathematician who was kidnapped in "Truth Takes Time." But when Jack discovers the truth about Neil's wife, he stops wanting to help her.

Jack can't possibly last long as director of operations at the CIA. First he's asked to head up an operation to find Derevko (a case he's far too close to) and now he's faced with another case that hits too close to home. When Sydney goes to interview Elsa Caplan, Neil Caplan's wife, she discovers that Elsa is actually Russian Intelligence and married Neil under false pretenses. Elsa has put a cyanide capsule in Neil's arm that will kill him in a matter of hours. Jack, of course, takes this tidbit of information and can see Elsa as one person only: Irina Derevko.

Despite everything Jack has said to the contrary, he has not accepted what Derevko did. He has not tried to move on with his life, and he proved a few episodes ago that even though he has studied Derevko for decades, he *still* can't tell when she's lying or telling the truth. When Jack confronts Elsa and tells her who "she" is, it's clear he's come a little unhinged. After all, he's not actually describing Elsa but Irina, and his threat to take Aaron away from her hints that perhaps he raised Sydney as some kind of revenge against Derevko. When Elsa breaks down in front of him there's a small change in his facial expression that suggests maybe he's finally able to see that the woman standing in front of him is not Derevko. Elsa claims she loves Neil and that what began as a sham is now a truly loving marriage. Can Jack believe her after hearing those very words spoken to him so long ago? It's only when Neil makes a confession of his own that we're reminded Jack also kept secrets from Derevko. Irina might have married him on false pretenses, but Jack also hid things from her, and it was those secrets that brought about his downfall in the end.

It seems every family on this show keeps secrets from one another — Jack discovers the wife of Neil Caplan (played by Christian Slater) isn't who she seemed in the beginning.

Diane and Dixon have come to an understanding, as it was inevitable they would. Just as Emily realized in her last moments that despite Sloane's murderous ways, deep down he was still the man she loved, so too does Diane now know that while she didn't know the truth about what Dixon did for a living, she knew the man, and he's a good man worth fighting for. Unfortunately, Dixon made a fatal error in the previous episode, and with Evil Francie's help, a classic "eye for an eye" scenario is effected in the shocking finale of this episode. The pursuit of Rambaldi has now ended three marriages.

Highlight: Weiss's comment to Vaughn when he agrees to help Sydney behind Jack's back: "If we end up sharing a cell in a federal prison, I'm not giving you a drawer."

Interesting Fact: The Web site Francie sends Will to, www.bouillabaissecentral-.com, doesn't exist. However, a parody site is up at the intentionally misspelled www.bouillabaisecentral.com.

Did You Notice?: Jennifer Garner pulled out her West Virginian accent to play the sorority girl. She's claimed in the past that it comes out when she least expects it to — usually after a couple of glasses of wine.

Nitpicks: The cryptic message Sydney gives to Vaughn over her cell phone is a little too over the top; of all the sentences she says to him, he just happens to choose the one that contains the message *and* manages to decipher it within seconds? If Vaughn could really do that, he wouldn't be a field agent — he'd be working with Marshall.

Locations: Moscow, Russia; Spain

Music/Bands: Luce's "Good Day" (*Luce*) plays when Sydney tells Vaughn he can have a drawer at her place; we hear "Rain City" by Turin Brakes (*Ether Song*) as Diane and Dixon talk about their future together; "Cannonball" by The Breeders (*Last Splash*) plays when Sydney leaves the pharmacy with the sorority girls; Bering Strait's "Porushka-Paranya," from their self-titled CD, plays when Sydney is in Russia.

2.20   Countdown

Original air date: April 27, 2003
Teleplay by: Jeff Pinkner
Story by: R.P. Gaborno
Directed by: Lawrence Trilling
Guest cast: Danny Trejo (Emilio Vargas), Jonathan Banks (NSA Director Frederick Brandon), Amanda Foreman (Carrie Bowman), David Carradine (Conrad), Jimmie F. Skaggs (Captain), Carlos Cervantes (Panamanian Detective), Allen Evangelista (Janov), Ryan Honey (Delta Force Leader), James Carraway (Proteo di Regno)

When the CIA discovers a Rambaldi prophecy stating that a major world-changing event will be happening in 48 hours, they must try to determine what it will be and stop it; a grief-stricken Dixon wonders if he can go on after losing Diane; Sloane makes a life-altering discovery in Nepal.

"Countdown" is about making decisions with one's heart rather than with one's head. Most of the characters have been under an extreme amount of stress, and two of them are experiencing intense grief and are unable to think clearly. Jack refuses to take Dixon off field duty despite evidence that he should because of his own feelings of guilt over having lied to Dixon for so long about SD-6. It's just one more bad decision in a string of them Jack has made since becoming head of operations. Dixon is suicidal, taking drugs and acting suspiciously on the job. Sloane has given up on his quest to discover what Rambaldi was trying to do and travels to a remote part of the world for revenge. Sydney begins keeping secrets from Vaughn to help her old friend Dixon. And to add to the stress, there's a possibility that a catastrophe of untold proportions could be happening within 48 hours.

Carl Lumbly does a superb job in this episode, as Dixon wavers between sanity and a complete breakdown throughout. At times he appears to be OK, and then he loses his cool and does something that is completely out of character. It's no surprise that by the end of the episode he doesn't seem to be thinking at all any longer, just taking out his anger on the closest person he can find. The writers do a great job of setting up Dixon's ultimate act of desperation, and Lumbly plays it brilliantly.

Marshall has an immediate connection with Carrie Bowman, the new assistant from NSA who has arrived to research the Rambaldi artifacts, and it's hilarious watching how her one compliment to Marshall in front of everyone reflects on his face as love at first sight. Their conversation about Rambaldi is an illuminating one for viewers looking for a broader perspective, and they are able to express how conflicted they are about the implau-

CHRISTINA RADISH

After the tragedy of the previous episode, Dixon appears to be hanging by a thread, and Sydney must stop him before he goes too far.

sibility of this man's prophecies despite evidence that he was right without bringing the show down into Mulder and Scully territory.

The most intriguing part of the episode, however, involves Sloane. He has sacrificed 30 years of his life in pursuit of the life's work of a man who lived 500 years earlier, and recently his search has been spurred on by the hope he could give this knowledge to his wife to save her. Now he appears in Nepal a broken man who realizes he has wasted his life and become a hateful person, betraying everyone he loves along the way. As he meets with the mysterious Zen master and is given the next clue to the puzzle, Conrad's words, "Your journey has just begun," signal an exciting new direction for the show. Since the revelation has occurred at a very specific time, Sloane has now become part of Rambaldi's prophecy, and next season we'll find out how.

CHRISTINA RADISH

Emilio Vargas (played by Danny Trejo) has no idea what he's about to encounter when Dixon shows up at his house.

Highlight: Marshall telling Carrie about his agnostic parents.

Name That Guest Star: Danny Trejo, who plays Emilio Vargas, was a drug addict as a child and became a criminal as he got older. He spent 15 years in various penitentiaries and finally ended up at San Quentin prison in California. There he became the lightweight boxing champion of his cell block, and when he was released he decided to quit the drugs and alcohol once and for all. He became a counselor to his friends, helping them kick their bad habits, and one of those friends worked in Hollywood. When Trejo accompanied him to the set of the film *Runaway Train*, another person recognized him for his boxing talents in San Quentin and asked him to train actor Eric Roberts to be a boxer for the movie. As a bonus, Trejo also made an appearance in the film. It was his first foray into movies, but his weathered face proved that what he had been through made him a unique commodity to directors, who started casting him as a thug in various movies. Since then he's appeared in dozens of movies, such as *From Dusk Till Dawn*, *Con Air*, *Reindeer Games*, *Spy Kids*, *Bubble Boy*, and *xXx*. He continues to volunteer as a drug counselor.

Amanda Foreman continues the *Felicity* alumni trend on *Alias*. Best known as Megan Blumberg, *Felicity*'s creepy roommate, she won over audiences on the show as the crazy Goth girl who was the complete opposite of straitlaced Felicity.

David Carradine, part of the legendary Carradine family, got his first big break in the 1972 television series *Kung Fu* as Kwai Chang Caine, a Shaolin monk who has escaped to America after killing the Chinese Emperor's nephew. The show had its own *Star Trek*-like spinoff in 1992 with *Kung Fu: The Legend Continues*. Carradine has appeared in dozens of movies, including the recent Quentin Tarantino duo, the *Kill Bill* movies, as the titular Bill. Interestingly, both Quentin Tarantino and Vivica A. Fox, who also stars in *Kill Bill*, have appeared on *Alias*. That Carradine plays a monk in *Alias* is not a coincidence, and when J.J. Abrams sent him a few episodes to get an idea of what the show was about, Carradine was hooked immediately. He was thrilled to find out that he would play the character who basically starts the whole quest for Sloane, but it's not clear if he will return to reprise the character. He loved being on the show. "It's a very emotional show," he said afterward. "It's not just shoot 'em ups and intrigues and stuff like that. Basically, what this show's about is love and lost love and loyalties and betrayals and all of these really deep emotions that go on. It's the ties that bind and the fact that there's more going on than we can possibly realize, and I know that's true." Carradine developed a lot of respect for Abrams while on the set and compared him to his other current director. "He reminds me of a pint-sized Quentin Tarantino. There's that same boundless enthusiasm and total knowledge of film."

Nitpicks: Sydney says that, like Dixon, she was back at work immediately after Danny's death, but in fact she stayed away for over three months before being forced back. Also, the plot device of starting the show at the climax and then going backward in time to lead up to that moment has been used a few times on this show so far, and by season 3 it will become a tired and lazy device used by the writers to create intrigue at the beginning. The fact that it's overused on *The West Wing* and has been for years only makes it worse that *Alias* is latching onto it. It doesn't work very effectively in this episode, although episodes like "Phase One," which return to the opening scene a quarter of the way through the episode rather than lead up to it throughout, use the device far more successfully.

Oops: Dixon clicks the bomb remote and says the bomb will go off in 30 seconds, but if you time the scene from the moment he starts the timer to the moment it hits 0, about a minute goes by.

What Did He Say?: Frederick Brandon and Carrie Bowman have arrived from NSA as part of a task force charged with locating and studying Rambaldi's work. Carrie says that because of Marshall they have a breakthrough; he had copied and catalogued all the pages of the Rambaldi heart journal before Derevko stole it. In the corner of each page was a DNA string, and when they are put together they match the DNA profile of Proteo di Regno, a man in Panama City, and his DNA is the code key to page 94 of the Rambaldi manuscript. This page foretells the dates of major catastrophes, and the next date is in 48 hours. Later in a briefing, Jack explains that a truck is being held in a cargo-freight area in Cartagena, and all intel is suggesting that di Regno's heart is on it. Sydney must secure the truck and find out if the heart is a bomb. If the CIA doesn't retrieve the heart by midnight, the yard is rigged with C-4 explosives that will destroy everything.

Locations: Panama City, Panama; Guadalajara, Mexico; Nepal; Cartagena, Colombia

Music/Bands: Lizzie West's "Prayer" (*Holy Road*) is heard after Diane's funeral;

"Más" by Kinky, from their self-titled album, plays when Sydney and Vaughn enter the club and see the Mexican wrestlers fighting; and as Sydney and Vaughn eat ice cream and she confesses to him that she's been lying, we hear Aretha Franklin's "You're All I Need to Get By" (*30 Greatest Hits*).

2.21 Second Double

Original air date: May 4, 2003
Teleplay by: Crystal Nix Hines
Story by: Breen Frazier
Directed by: Ken Olin
Guest cast: Robert Joy (Hans Jurgen), Joel Swetow (Jens), Michael Canavan (Special Agent McCain), Kristopher Logan (Garth), J.P. Romano (French Guard)

Evil Francie hypnotizes Will so that he'll look suspicious, which leads the CIA to believe he's not Will but the other Project Helix double; Sloane visits Jack and proposes that they work together again.

"Second Double" is a harrowing episode because it's one of the only times the audience isn't playing a guessing game. Instead, we know the truth and must endure the characters' trying to figure out what's true. Will has once again become Sark's target, just as he was at the end of last season, and it's hard to watch Sydney hoping against hope that he is in fact the real Will, but starting to believe he isn't. Jennifer Garner and Bradley Cooper handle their scenes together beautifully. Will struggles to remember ordinary things and Sydney's face becomes sadder and sadder, and she's as anxious to believe him as he is to be believed. When he leans forward and says, "I swear it's me," her heart is breaking. If it's Will, then they need to figure out what's wrong with him. If it's not Will, then she's probably looking at his murderer.

When Sydney turns to Francie and finally tells her the truth, we wince in our knowledge that Sydney's misplaced loyalties are about to get her in a lot of trouble. It's also hard not to be baffled by Sydney's spilling the beans once again when it's convenient for her — has she still learned nothing from Danny's death? Is it really safe for "Francie" to know about all this? And considering there's potentially a double out there and she's trying to prove it's not Will, wouldn't she start to be suspicious of everyone? In "Truth Takes Time," when Francie gave Vaughn the tie, Sydney looked perplexed and noticed when Francie seemed to forget about people they'd gone to high school with. For someone who has the same deep-seated intuition as her father, why doesn't Sydney investigate further? Up to now she's been able to keep everything secret from Francie, yet when Will calls her in a panic, she not only takes the call but tells Will top-secret information (again) right in front of Francie. What kind of "secret" agent has Sydney become? If Will is the double, then whoever is doing this is targeting Sydney's friends. If Will is not the double, then he's clearly been framed to look like he is. Therefore, once again, whoever is doing this is targeting Sydney's friends. Yet she never suspects Francie? Merrin Dungey has played both Francies so well that we can easily tell the difference between the old and the new character, yet Sydney seems oblivious.

The most hurtful part of this episode is when Will tells Sydney he can't trust her anymore. His harsh words that follow — that meeting Sydney ruined his life — cut deep, but while they might sound cruel, he's in a headspace right now that makes the statement true for him. And seeing him tortured, drugged, and then lose his job and his reputation all because of her, it's true for us as well. Notice how Sydney doesn't actually look surprised when he says it. She's matured enough to know that what he said is the truth.

Highlight: Sloane suddenly showing up in a restaurant where Jack is eating and telling him he misses his poker face. On the one hand, it seems there's no truer description of Jack Bristow; on the other hand, he *does* let his emotions slip occasionally and his eyes speak volumes.

Interesting Fact: When this episode first aired it was immediately followed by "The Telling," as if it were a two-hour season finale.

Nitpicks: When Dixon goes to see Will in the cell, Will is being held without proof that he's the double, yet Dixon grabs Will by the throat and the guard does absolutely nothing. Why is there a guard present if he's going to be so ineffectual? Also, Jack discovers that Will's fingerprints were put on the trigger after it had already been wiped. Considering that would be a pretty easy thing to check for, why didn't SD-6 notice the CIA had done exactly the same thing back in "A Higher Echelon" when Ariana had been hot on Jack's trail? In that episode Jack had the CIA fake where he had been several times (and put his fingerprints on things).

What Did He Say?: Kendall is back on the case and says that through Tippin's intel (a nice irony), they've discovered Hans Jurgen is the man whose equipment was used to create the gene therapy that produced James Lennox's double and a second one. A CIA contact has tracked Jurgen to a sex club in Berlin. When Sydney and Vaughn go to the club and blackmail Jurgen, he tells them Markovic would have been at a server farm, where he would have done the actual body-switching.

Locations: Berlin, Germany; Marseilles, France

Music/Bands: Macy Gray's "Speechless" (*The Trouble with Being Myself*) plays during Sydney and Vaughn's tryst at the beginning; we hear The Lawyer's "I Wanna Mmm" (CD single) at the sex club in Berlin; "Corps à Corps" by Glendooz (no album) plays when Vaughn pretends to be drunk in Marseilles.

2.22   The Telling

Original air date: May 4, 2003
Written and directed by: J.J. Abrams
Guest cast: Jonathan Banks (NSA Director Frederick Brandon), Amanda Foreman (Carrie Bowman), Kevin Bowens (Alpha Team Leader), Jon Dixon (CIA Agent), Kent George (Sloane's Guard), Paul Keeley (Police Officer), Michael Yama (Chinese Agent)

Will discovers the other double is someone named A.G. Doren; Derevko confronts Sydney to tell her what she has been doing; Sloane kidnaps Jack to inform him of the Rambaldi device; Sydney makes a horrible discovery.

So much happens in "The Telling" that there was little need to put it together with "Second Double" to make an exciting season finale. This fast-paced episode wraps up most of the storylines of season 2, leaves a few mysterious ones open, and lights the sparks that will form the basis of season 3. And it contains a whopper of a cliffhanger that no fan would have been able to see coming (unless they'd read spoilers).

As if to round out Sydney's season 2 relationship with her mother, in an echo of "The Enemy Walks In," she again faces Derevko with no backup, with her guard down, and with Derevko forcing her to listen and hurting her physically. Derevko, as always, is unreadable in this scene, and we don't know if she's telling the truth about anything anymore. Maybe she does love Sydney, but she said the same to Jack years ago. She might want to help her daughter, but she said she wanted to help the CIA at the beginning of the year and look how well that turned out. This scene is bookended by the final scene between Derevko and Sydney in Mexico City on the roof of the building, and Derevko's ominous words to Sydney set up a new quest for her daughter (if Derevko is to be believed) and show that Syd's ongoing conflict with Sloane is far from over.

In one double-cross after another, the CIA is foiled no matter what they try, and Jack pays the price by being kidnapped by Sloane. Sloane seems to have a renewed passion for the work of Rambaldi, and the gleeful way he leans over Jack, telling him what he's about to accomplish, makes him seem like a borderline madman. Jack gets his own jab in, as we knew he would, but Sloane is about to piece together the ultimate Rambaldi artifact. Because we never get to see what it is, the move creates suspenseful anticipation for season 3.

Meanwhile, Will uncovers a big clue relating to the identification of the other

Sydney becomes suspicious of "Francie" and realizes she might not be who she seems.

There's an obvious romantic spark between Carrie Bowman (played by Amanda Foreman) and Marshall when she arrives at the CIA.

double, and it ties back to the Project Christmas investigation from earlier in the season. Suddenly, this person who's been doubling as Francie doesn't seem evil so much as a helpless pawn of an agency that forced her to become who she is. Now she's not only had her life mapped out for her against her own will, but she's stuck in a body that isn't hers. The scene where she and Will face off in the kitchen is a sad one, not only for him but for her as well. Her reaction when she fights Will shows that despite all the evidence thus far, she's human, and she's capable of caring for someone.

Despite the action sequences, the emotional scenes, and the revelations to this point in the episode, nothing can prepare us for what happens next. When Sydney returns home, viewers are again one step ahead of her and fear for what could happen to her. All seems to resolve itself until the episode does a strange cut and she wakes up in an alleyway. What happens next is mind-blowing and a testament to the writers of this show. Sydney discovered so much about herself in season 1 that there was some worry the writers would lose steam. They didn't. Then "Phase One" ended *Alias* as we knew it and threatened to make the show predictable and repetitive. But it didn't. Now, the writers have thrown an entirely new curve ball: Sydney is right back to

Sydney in Wonderland

Sydney's journeys for the first three seasons are as complicated as anything on television, and they leave not only her, but also the viewer, disoriented and confused. No wonder the writers have chosen Lewis Carroll's Alice books — *Alice's Adventures in Wonderland* and *Through the Looking-Glass* — to emulate throughout the series and to draw parallels between Sydney and another female who finds herself with strange people who aren't what they seem. "It obviously is deliberate that we are making plays on *Alice in Wonderland*," says J.J. Abrams. "We might not be the most well-read writing staff ever hired, but we know *Alice in Wonderland*, so that is definitely something intentional. The feeling of Sydney being displaced and trying to figure out who she is, where she belongs, and where she comes from — she is so clearly Alice in this world." We see a rabbit figurine beside Sydney's bed and a rabbit doll sitting on her pillow in scenes from her childhood, but there have been other, more specific, instances that liken Sydney's crazy journey to Alice's:

"Time Will Tell" — At the end of the episode, Sydney falls down a deep hole like Alice did when she entered Wonderland.

"A Broken Heart" — Vaughn's girlfriend's name is Alice.

"Doppelgänger" — Sydney dresses up as Alice in Wonderland for her Halloween party.

"Snowman" — Syd uses the code name "White Rabbit."

"The Telling" — Sydney smashes through a mirror before passing out after her fight with Allison Doren. When she wakes up in Hong Kong, Sydney calls the CIA and uses the term "Confirmation: Looking Glass."

"Succession" — A CIA agent is beheaded, something the Red Queen always threatened to do to Alice in *Alice's Adventures in Wonderland*.

"Reunion" — Sydney tells Weiss that her mother had bought her a first edition of *Alice in Wonderland* when she was five years old, but she lost it in the fire at the end of season 2. Weiss buys Sydney a third edition to replace it.

"Crossings" — While waiting in Sydney's apartment, Jack reads her copy of *Alice's Adventures in Wonderland*.

square one, just like she was at the beginning of season 1, wondering what has happened to her, who has betrayed her, and what has her life become. This show continues to re-create itself, and just when you think it can't get any better, it does.

Highlight: The ending.

Interesting Fact: Harry Houdini's birth name was indeed Ehrich Weiss.

Did You Notice?: Will discovers that the other name on the DNA string for Project Helix is A.G. Doren. It's interesting the writers chose a name with these initials, because A and G are two of the four DNA bases used in genetic code sequencing (A = adenine; G = guanine; T = thymine; C = cytosine).

Nitpicks: Derevko says that when she was at the CIA, the CIA had 24 artifacts and Sloane had 23, but the NSA actually had one of them — di Regno's heart. Derevko would know that because she raided the NSA to try to get it.

Oops: Sydney and Jack left the CIA at the same time to do their separate ops — Jack headed to NSA and Sydney headed to Zurich. Yet they both arrived at exactly the same time, and as Sydney was opening the Rambaldi crates in Zurich, Jack was leaving the NSA with his item in hand. How is that possible?

What Did He Say?: Derevko corners Sydney in the ice rink and tells her that Sloane's warehouse, where he keeps the Rambaldi artifacts, is in Zurich at 266 Kroner Strasse. She says that she wants to help Sydney, and while she's able to betray the CIA, she can't do the same to her daughter. She explains that she was actually behind the raids on SD-6 and the CIA in "Phase One" and describes how she was able to escape. When she had been on the Echelon system she discovered where the CIA had been holding their Rambaldi artifacts (at the NSA) and she told Sloane, who organized a raid on the offices and retrieved all of them. Later, Sloane explains to Jack that he has all 47 pieces of the Rambaldi puzzle and will construct a machine called *Il Dire*, or "the telling."

Locations: Zurich, Switzerland; Stockholm, Sweden; Mexico City, Mexico

Music/Bands: As Sydney and Vaughn discuss going on vacation while they're in Stockholm, we hear Fleetwood Mac's "Bleed to Love Her" (*Say You Will*).

Season Three:
September 2003–May 2004

Recurring cast for season 3: Kurt Fuller (Robert Lindsey), Amanda Foreman (Carrie Bowman), Mark Bramhall (Andrian Lazarey)

3.1   The Two

Original air date: September 28, 2003
Written by: J.J. Abrams
Directed by: Ken Olin
Guest cast: Oleg Taktarov (Volkov), Adam Alexi-Malle (Bernard), Michael Berry Jr. (Scott Kingsley), Emma Bering (Receptionist)

Sydney tries to adjust to having her life stolen from her after she wakes up in Hong Kong with no memory of the previous two years.

"The Two" is a whirlwind of a season premiere, and it had to be good after the stunning conclusion to season 2. The episode begins exactly where "The Telling" had left off, and by the time Sydney gets to L.A., she's asking the same questions the fans had been all summer: Where has she been for two years? Is Will dead? Is Francie? Where is Irina? Where is Jack? And how is it possible that Vaughn has gotten *married* while Sydney was gone?! The writers cleverly keep the viewers as confused as Sydney throughout as she discovers Dixon is the new director of operations at the CIA and Vaughn is a schoolteacher, overhears Weiss saying something about the "Covenant," and finds out her father was apparently far more loyal to her than Vaughn in her absence. The entire episode is shown through Sydney's eyes, and we never see what Vaughn is really thinking or what really happened to Jack until Sydney does.

The title of the episode, "The Two," not only refers to the two missing years of Sydney's life, but also underscores the constant dichotomies present in the episodes. Everyone on the show seems to have two faces, and just as Sydney gets comfortable with one, she realizes there's another. There are two women in Vaughn's life now. Sydney has two men who mourned her more than anyone else when she died. The CIA is always pitted against a terrorist organization, in this case the Covenant. Sydney wonders who *she* has been for the past two years. And surprisingly, Sloane has resurfaced as if he were his own doppelgänger, someone who runs a world health organization called Omnifam that conducts major research into finding a cure for cancer and helps hungry children worldwide. Yes, *Sloane*. His story about *Il Dire* (the

Despite our anger at Vaughn moving on in his life, we can't help but feel sorry for him now that his world has been turned upside-down.

machine he spent half his life constructing and finally put together in "The Telling") pumping out only the word "Peace" and changing his life is so unbelievable it's a wonder anyone actually fell for it. Is that really all it said? And was it telling him to devote his life to peaceful work? Where did he get that idea, from the lyrics of "One Tin Soldier"? Sloane killed a *lot* of mountain people to get to that word, and it's going to take more than a charitable organization to make Sydney trust him again — if ever.

The two standout scenes in the episode are the contrasting meetings Sydney has with her father and with Vaughn. When she meets her father, whose prison sentence has turned him into Grizzly Adams, the look on his face upon seeing her is one only Victor Garber could muster. His face is a mixture of shock, relief, overwhelming joy, sadness, and regret all at once. He's overjoyed that she's alive, but we can tell his imagination is trying to comprehend what she must have gone through over the past two years and what lies ahead of her. She pours her heart out to him, telling him Vaughn is married, which has been the biggest shock of all for her. Jack hisses that Vaughn was never good enough for her (a sentiment he's always harbored), and she takes that sentiment and confronts Vaughn with it later in the episode. What she says to Vaughn in the corridor echoes the feelings all fans had when we saw that wedding band on his finger at the end of "The Telling." Jennifer Garner is brilliant in this scene.

Did Vaughn betray her? Is Sloane really a good guy? And could the person on the video Jack reveals to his daughter at the end of the episode really be Sydney?

Highlight: "I've lost my keys. Where are they?"

Name That Guest Star: Versatile character actor Adam Alexi-Malle starred in the Steve Martin film *Bowfinger* and has appeared in movies such as *A.I.: Artificial Intelligence*, *The Man Who Wasn't There*, and *Hidalgo*.

Did You Notice?: When the CIA agents first pull into the alleyway in Paris right before their job, you can see a sign that says *Société de fabrication de Montmartre*, which means "Manufacturing Society of Montmartre." It's appropriate, considering Sydney has manufactured her entire story about remembering the facility. Also, the final scene of Sydney showing up at the CIA with the desired object after being considered an enemy parallels her barging into Sloane's office in "Truth Be Told" with the Rambaldi artifact after Sloane had assumed she'd defected.

Nitpicks: Why doesn't Weiss get chastised for blatantly ignoring Dixon's order to abort the mission, which resulted in all the agents getting killed?

Oops: Sydney's watch says 11:05 when she activates the anti-eavesdropping device, but 90 seconds later, it has the same time on it. Also, the Lazarey in the photo isn't the same actor who will later play him. And Arvin Sloane's name is misspelled as "Sloan" on the cover of the magazine.

What Did He Say?: In Dixon's first briefing as director of operations (that we see), he mentions a new organization, the Covenant, a group that remains elusive to the CIA. Scott Kingsley was a CIA asset and engineer who developed a spy aircraft that could fly undetected by radar. He had been heading to Avignon to deliver the schematics of the plane when he was killed and the chip containing the schematics was taken by the Covenant. This spy drone has the capacity to be converted into a delivery system for biological weapons, and in the Covenant's hands the specs could be very dangerous. The CIA will raid the building where they suspect the Covenant has hidden the chip and get it back. After Sydney runs away from the mission, Lindsey has her listed as an enemy of the state, and a CIA contact tells Syd that Volkov, the hitman for the Covenant, will be delivering something in Prague, most likely the chip.

Locations: Hong Kong, China; Lyon, France; Paris, France; Zurich, Switzerland; Prague, Czech Republic

Marshall's Gadgets: An anti-eavesdrop device that Sydney uses when she goes to meet Jack, similar to Jack's pen from seasons 1 and 2.

Music/Bands: Limp Bizkit's "Rollin' (Air Raid Vehicle)" (*Chocolate Starfish and the Hot Dog Flavored Water*) plays when Sydney pulls up in the red Ferrari to meet Volkov; we hear "I Feel Love" by The Blue Man Group (*The Complex*) when Sydney shows up in Prague, encounters Volkov, and later walks into the CIA; and Rickie Lee Jones's "On Saturday Afternoons in 1963," from her self-titled CD, plays when Sydney confronts Vaughn at the end of the episode.

3.2 Succession

Original air date: October 5, 2003
Written by: Roberto Orci and Alex Kurtzman-Counter
Directed by: Daniel Attias
Guest cast: Brad Greenquist (Otto), Al Sapienza (Tom), Ilia Volok (San'ko), Andrew Borba (Jim), Stephanie Venditto (Cathy), Fabio Serafini (Pieter Klein), James K. Ward (Ulrich Rotter), Bill Bolender (Oleg), Heidi Dippold (Executive Assistant), Igor Korosec (Janitor)

As the CIA learns more about the Covenant, Sydney begins to suspect the terrorist group might have been behind her disappearance; the Covenant demands Sark's release from CIA custody.

Where "The Two" was pretty one-sided, allowing viewers to align themselves with Sydney and rediscover who she was alongside her, "Succession" moves the point of view to the other characters, and now we see a second side. Weiss explains to Sydney exactly what she doesn't want to hear — that Vaughn's wife is a good person, and that Vaughn really didn't move on quickly but mourned Syd's death for a very long time. Weiss will become one of Sydney's closest friends (a replacement for Will, in a way), for the first part of the season, but sadly, he's dropped halfway through.

When Sydney goes to see Vaughn at his new job, he answers her tirade from the previous episode, and while his words might seem harsh (especially when he pointedly tells her he doesn't regret moving on), they're fair. What seems like a couple of hours to her was two long years for him — exactly the length of time he and Sydney had spent together before she went missing. We know how much he loved her, and we can only imagine what he went through. While the rest of this season will slowly piece together where Sydney has been for the past two years, we'll get only brief glimpses of Vaughn dealing with the pain of losing Sydney, or Jack desperately trying to prove that his daughter's alive. Vaughn's words here are full of pain and anger. He went through hell losing her, and now that she's back, she can't stand the sight of him.

Sydney is able to vent some of her frustrations on her foil, Director Lindsey, who rivals Kendall in the degree to which Sydney hates him. The fights she has with Lindsey are similar to those she had with Kendall, although Lindsey seems to be a more obviously evil character than Kendall, constantly sabotaging what she is trying to do. He represents everything she finds frustrating upon her return, not least of which is the support group Dixon talks her into joining. Sydney listening to these agents pouring out their biggest fears is not helpful to her at all and is, in fact, detrimental to her recovery. Sydney has shown strength of character that rivals anyone else on the show, and we've watched her bounce back from one betrayal after another, proving time and again that no matter how emotional she is, she seems to be able to weather any storm that comes her way. Compare the way she deals with trauma with Dixon's approach in "Countdown" and "Taken," or Vaughn's in "Legacy." Both men put their anger and sense of betrayal before all else, which leaves other people in danger, while Sydney momentarily buries her feelings and handles herself professionally while in the field (even if she occasionally puts her foot in her mouth, as she does at the end of this episode).

Sydney's new knowledge — that while she was missing she killed an innocent man — amplifies her distress about her missing years, and her frustration over not knowing who she was or why she can't remember anything is the worst part. Sydney Bristow is one of the most sensitive, empathetic, self-sacrificing characters on television, and the thought that she could have killed someone in cold blood will haunt her throughout the season. Her encounter with the doctor in the laboratory in this episode only compounds her questions rather than answering any of them.

Sark is back, and he will become a major character for this season. David Anders's Sark may have all the emotion of Spock, but Sark is so much fun that we don't care. He's meant to be that way — someone who has a quick wit about him, knows exactly what to say to hurt someone, but who never laughs, gets angry, or seems passionate about anything. How many characters on television can show almost no emotion and yet be so engaging to watch?

Highlight: Jack saying the message from *Il Dire* was akin to that of a fortune cookie.

Did You Notice?: When Sydney sees her name on the Agents Killed in Action plaque, Cece DeStefano and Scott Chambliss are the agents listed below her. Chambliss is the production designer on *Alias* and DeStefano is the show's art director. Also, Jack's typing "Distinguished Composer Looking for Music Lover" is a nod to Victor Garber's musical background.

Nitpicks: Despite the years of service Jack has given to the CIA, it's unlikely that he would be given his old job back immediately upon his prison release, especially considering Sydney blackmailed Director Lindsey to procure that release. Also, the computer voice on Jack's computer that reads Irina's replies to his messages is unnecessary: he's not illiterate. And when the extra cars show up in the desert, Sydney immediately says she doesn't want the Covenant to think the CIA has double-crossed the organization. Why doesn't she think *she* is being double-crossed by the Covenant?

Oops: Jack says Sydney killed Lazarey eight months ago, and in the next scene Sydney says it happened nine months ago.

What Did He Say?: Two CIA agents were kidnapped by the Covenant when the elevator they were in was airlifted out of the building; the Covenant has placed its ransom demands beneath a seat in a movie theater. When Sydney retrieves the demands and discovers the Covenant wants Sark, Lindsey explains that Sark has given them all the information they'll probably get out of him, and the Covenant will probably kill him anyway, but the CIA later discovers that Sark has an inheritance of $800 million from his father, Andrian Lazarey, and the Covenant wants his money to bankroll its operation. He retrieved the money from a vault in the basement of a club, and Sydney needs to find out how to get into the vault.

Locations: Berlin, Germany; Munich, Germany; Zurich, Switzerland; Sonora Desert, Mexico; Frankfurt, Germany

Music/Bands: REM's "Bad Day" (*In Time: The Best of REM, 1998-2003*) plays in Sydney's apartment while Weiss helps her move in; when Sydney arrives in the nightclub in disguise, we hear Starecase's "Bitter Little Pill" (*First Floor*).

3.3   Reunion

Original air date: October 12, 2003
Written by: Jeff Pinkner
Directed by: Jack Bender
Guest cast: Mark Ivanir (Boris Oransky), Scott Adsit (Pierre Lagravenese), Elizabeth Penn Payne (Carolyn), Pierrino Mascarino (Science Ministry Official), Arthur Darbinyan (Ministry Official), Deeonna Lanay (Young Girl), Patricia Rae (Young Girl's Mother)

Sydney works with Vaughn's wife for the first time, and Jack must stop Marshall from identifying Sydney as the assassin who killed Lazarey.

Syd has adjusted to her new life pretty well considering what she went through. Weiss continues to hang out at her place, to offer her a shoulder to cry on, and to help her through everything (Weiss is truly one of the unsung heroes of the show). He steps into the roles both Dixon and Vaughn played in her life in the early episodes, and when he asks her if she lost anything she really cared about in the fire, she only names one thing rather than dwelling on all that's gone. The truth is that Sydney's lost everything, but the material things don't count compared with losing the love of her life.

We finally meet Lauren, Vaughn's new wife. Melissa George will be a lot of fun to hate this season, but in the beginning, she's painted as a sympathetic character. We imagine her as a woman who met Vaughn and fell in love and has probably heard him talk about Sydney and what she meant to him. Sydney posed no threat, however, because she was dead. Now everything has changed and Lauren knows that Vaughn still cares for Sydney — it's obvious in everything he does and says, even when he's telling Lauren that he loves her and not Syd. In these early episodes, we actually feel a twinge of sympathy for this woman, who will be revealed as a very different person by season's end. The argument between Lauren and Sydney in the briefing room parallels what's going on in their lives: Sydney argues for a return to the old way of doing things; Lauren insists the new ways are better.

Because Sydney can't rely on Vaughn, Jack is now the only person she turns to when she needs to vent her frustrations or voice her deepest fears. She knows what he did for her while she was gone, and the two of them are the only ones who know the crime she committed during her two-year absence. In the previous episode, Jack confronted Sloane, snarling that he would bury him for being complicit in Sydney's disappearance (a suggestion that Jack takes as fact). In this one, as he sees Marshall and Lauren getting close to a possible ID on the Lazarey assassin, he goes to great lengths to cover it up, putting his job and credibility on the line in the process. Sydney might have lost a lot when she went missing, but the one thing she has gained is a stronger bond with her father.

Highlight: Marshall's comment as he, Sydney, Vaughn, and Lauren all stand together, silent, in a room: "Awkward."

Interesting Fact: When Sydney says that she had a first edition of *Alice's Adventures in Wonderland*, at best she had a first edition of the second version of the work. The book was originally released in 1864, but when Lewis Carroll saw the poor reproduction quality of John Tenniel's drawings, he was very distraught and had all the books recalled (about 15 copies escaped collection). A second "first edition" was released in November 1865 (although it was stamped 1866), and only about eight copies of the original 1864 edition have been located.

Nitpicks: It's never really clear why Sark is trying to procure Project Medusa, since it doesn't fit in his plans.

CHRISTINA RADISH

At the beginning of season 3, Weiss takes the place of Sydney's best friends Will and Francie, who are no longer around to listen to her. The difference is, she doesn't have any secrets to keep from Weiss.

Was he originally planning on breaking Bomani out of prison by bringing down a satellite? Or was he just attempting to acquire the technology for a purpose to be named later? And if the audio communication to Weiss is in Sydney's glasses when she's in Mexico, how does she continue to communicate with him after Oransky smashes the glasses?

Oops: When Jack comes down the hall to Dixon's office, his CIA identification tag is on his left lapel. When he's in Dixon's office, it's on the right, and then later it moves back to the left.

What Did He Say?: Project Medusa is an operation that can knock out satellite systems, which cripples networks and can make them blind to any attack. Boris Oransky supervised the development of Project Medusa, and the satellite that went down in Gorky Park was actually his own — he sent it down on purpose to watch the Russian nuclear-reaction protocol in action. He took pictures of how the Russians dealt with

297

the situation and discovered the high-level officials were evacuated to a bunker. He believes that the final schematics of Project Medusa are there and he's given the coordinates to Sark. The CIA must get to the bunker before Sark does.

Locations: Moscow, Russia; Mexico City, Mexico

Marshall's Gadgets: A pair of sunglasses with audio and one gigabyte of memory to hold the photos Sydney can take while wearing them, which she does by pressing a button on the side of the glasses.

Music/Bands: Patsy Cline's "She's Got You" (*Patsy Cline's Greatest Hits*) plays as Sydney and Weiss chat in her apartment over drinks; we hear "Pa Ti Pa Mi" by Puya (*Union*) when Sydney enters the marketplace in Mexico City; Whiskeytown's "Choked Up" (*Lost Highway: Lost and Found I*) plays as Sydney and Weiss talk about Lauren and Vaughn; and "Something Else" by Gary Jules (*Trading Snakeoil for Wolftickets*) plays when Sydney finds the copy of *Alice's Adventures in Wonderland* on her desk.

3.4   A Missing Link

Original air date: October 19, 2003
Written by: Monica Breen and Alison Schapker
Directed by: Lawrence Trilling
Guest cast: Justin Theroux (Simon Walker), Clifton Collins, Jr. (Javier Perez), Ray Proscia (Laszlo Bogden), Elizabeth Penn Payne (Carolyn), Carlos Del Olmo (Bouncer), Fernando Jimenez (Police Officer), Marco Zunino (Hotel Manager)

When a freelance terrorist-for-hire refers to Sydney as "Julia," Sydney receives a hint about where she's been for the past two years.

"A Missing Link" is the first episode written by Monica Breen and Alison Schapker, but thankfully, it's not the last. It's an hour full of twists and turns, shocking revelations, and painful decisions. The first shock comes when Sydney plans to approach a man named Simon Walker and offer him her services in order to find out more about the job he's about to undertake, only to discover that they were associates and lovers when she went by the alias "Julia." She recovers quickly, but Vaughn, listening in, becomes suspicious. We've watched people change, switch sides, and betray the ones they love — a major motif on the show — and while Vaughn would never want to believe that Sydney could be one of those turncoats, it's not an altogether preposterous idea given that she's gone missing for two years. Vaughn doesn't need to worry for long, though, because Jack's got a trick up his sleeve that will surprise everyone — most of all Sydney.

From there, the episode is filled with action-packed suspense — Sydney having to break into a hotel room to prove herself to her new co-workers; an enemy who will recognize her walking into the room where she's pretending to be someone else; a heartpounding scene of Marshall trying to upload phony records to Interpol in time to save Sydney's life; and the shocker of an ending.

The relationship between Sydney and Vaughn takes one step forward, two steps back in this installment. The wonderful scene of the two of them on the plane, joking about Marshall's choice of lipstick colors (that Vaughn holds his own throughout the scene, as if he actually knows what he's talking about, is priceless) reminds us of how easy their relationship used to be. They could talk to one another and joke about seemingly mindless things — that's what brought them together in the first place and made them so good together. But it all falls apart quickly when Vaughn suspects Sydney is keeping a secret from him and is then forced to lie to Lauren about it. Even when Sydney insists that she never meant for him to have to keep secrets from Lauren, it doesn't change the fact that he must do so nonetheless. The writers have cleverly handled the progression of emotion in each of the characters. Sydney went through anger and hostility, even denial, when she realized Vaughn had moved on. Vaughn stood there and took it when she lectured him about loyalty and how he has none, and then he gave it back to her when he tried to explain what his life has been like. Sydney has since tried to smooth things over, but the awkwardness and tension hang over them in everything they do. Lauren is caught in the middle: on the one hand she is hurt that Sydney has come back, as she realizes this could spell danger for her marriage; on the other hand she has resolved to make the transition as easy as possible.

But in the final scene, Sydney has the last word, and what she says to Vaughn will cut him as deep as the knife she plunges into him. We all know that she's playing a part in order to convince her colleagues she's onside, but at the same time, could she have meant what she said?

Highlight: The look on Carrie's face as Marshall reads off his list of unisex names (where's Sydney/Sidney on that list?).

Name That Guest Star: Justin Theroux, who plays Simon Walker, has appeared in movies such as *Romy and Michele's High School Reunion, American Psycho, Mulholland Dr., Zoolander,* and *Charlie's Angels: Full Throttle,* and on HBO's *Six Feet Under* as Joe. He's an American actor, so the British accent is fake.

Nitpicks: Sydney being able to read Lazarey's lips saying the word "Julia" seems pretty far-fetched for such a grainy video feed. And Vaughn questions how easily Sydney slipped into the role of Julia, as if she had already known about the other alias, yet we've seen time and again that Sydney adjusts to any sort of surprise without betraying it — she's a master of hiding her emotions when the circumstance calls for it. So why does he become suspicious this time? Also, there is *no* way Sydney could have survived the leap from the hotel balcony into the swimming pool unless the pool was 50 feet deep or so. That balcony was at least 10 stories up, and the average hotel swimming pool might be 12 feet deep at its deepest end. Not only should she have cracked her skull on the floor of the pool, but her wig would have come off on impact, and it remains completely intact. Did she staple it to her scalp?

Oops: Jack says he's been asking himself for over a year why Sydney would have killed someone, but she killed Lazarey eight months ago. Also, when Sydney makes the dive into the pool, she doesn't have the necklace on her anywhere.

What Did He Say?: Lauren explains that a four-man team broke into a lab in Cannes that was on the cutting edge of research into virus vaccines. They stole vials that contained a strain of the Ebola virus, but one vial was broken and infected a team member, so the CIA needs to interrogate him in the hospital to find out why the other vials were taken. Sloane later tells Lauren the viruses will be used to fashion a designer bomb that will only affect people the Covenant is targeting specifically, leaving all others unharmed. Sydney joins Simon Walker's team and will break into a storage facility owned by the disease-control ministry and steal a biological agent that will help the Covenant create the bomb.

Locations: Sevilla, Spain; Zurich, Switzerland; Pamplona, Spain

Marshall's Gadgets: A tracking device hidden in a tube of lipstick that Sydney can adhere to an item so Marshall can track its whereabouts. Later he gives Sydney a device that works like an X-ray and stethoscope in one for cracking a safe. Marshall will link to it with software that will decrypt the combination.

Music/Bands: We hear three songs by Chucho Merchan: "Fumba Rumba" plays when Sydney first walks into the club to meet Simon; "Emotion Lotion" plays when Sydney leaves the club with Simon; and "Kool as a Rool" plays when Simon hands Sydney the file with the details (the band seems to have a fondness for rhyming titles).

3.5   Repercussions

Original air date: October 26, 2003
Written by: Jesse Alexander
Directed by: Ken Olin
Guest cast: Justin Theroux (Simon Walker), Clifton Collins, Jr. (Javier Perez), Djimon Hounsou (Kazari Bomani), Garret T. Sato (Yakuza Pit Boss), Virginia Pereira (Receptionist)

After the Covenant releases Kazari Bomani from prison, the CIA must disable a computer virus that Bomani is after.

In all three seasons of *Alias*, we see people keeping secrets, telling lies to others, and doing horrible things either of their own volition or because they've been forced to do them. But we've also seen secrets get out, and when another party is hurt by them, the actions have repercussions. In this aptly titled episode, everyone faces repercussions for their actions.

Sydney helps save Vaughn's life after she almost killed him in "A Missing Link," but her desire for truthfulness doesn't go over very well with Lauren, who had been told a lie about what really happened to her husband. When she finds out what Sydney did to Vaughn, her annoyance with the Lauren-Vaughn-Sydney triangle turns to outrage, and she insists that Sydney request a transfer to another office. Vaughn, meanwhile, is lying in a hospital bed and enduring nightmares about Sydney and what she did. His subconscious clearly wonders if she meant her final words, but it also suggests that he feels guilty about what's happened. The image of her stabbing him weighs on his mind because he wonders if Sydney might have been justified in what she did. By the end of the episode, Lauren has regained her confidence in her marriage and even develops a tenuous friendship with Sydney when they are both involved in an action-packed car chase with Lauren at the wheel. The scene is amusing, as Lauren appears to be giddy over her field assignment.

Sloane helped put away a criminal — Kazari Bomani — and when Sark secures Bomani's release from prison, Sloane will have to face the repercussions. Sark has been very active this season: the Covenant got him out of CIA custody; he's bankrolling the Covenant's operation (though he's clearly annoyed by the lack of respect he's been given); he broke into a facility to steal vials of the Ebola virus, which he mutated to create a designer bomb; and now he's breaking Bomani out of prison by using that very bomb to affect everyone but Bomani. Of course, this act will have its own repercussions, which Sark will deal with later.

And finally, Jack faces the repercussions of interfering in Sydney's relationship with Simon Walker. Once again, he works behind the CIA's back in order to help her, but when he's not careful, he ends up putting Sydney in danger. The scene of Simon taunting Jack with stories of Syd's "sexual depravity" is very funny, because we watch Jack's stony face change and his eyes betray his true feelings. We know it can't end well for Simon, but if something happens to Simon, will that close off a very important avenue to Sydney regarding her lost years?

Highlight: Marshall slapping Sydney's ass in the casino, and the look on her face when he does it.

Number 47

The number 47 is a fascinating digit, and some people believe it's the most commonly chosen random number in the universe. In other words, if a room of people were asked to randomly choose any number and write it down, more people would select the number 47 than any other number. There is a 47 Society at Pomona College in Claremont, California, dedicated to documenting all major cases of the number 47 (www.47.net). Many people believe there's a magical essence to the number. On *Star Trek*, the writers used to slip in obscure references to the number just for fun. But on *Alias*, the number 47 is integral to Rambaldi's works, and it appears everywhere. At the end of the second season, Sydney crashed through a mirror — a reference to Lewis Carroll's *Through the Looking Glass*. Therefore, in season 3, the number 47 often appears in reverse, as 74, as if to suggest that many things Syd sees in season 3 are mirror versions of reality. The following is a list of all the references to 47 up to the end of season 3 (warning: list contains spoilers for some episodes):

"Truth Be Told" — Marshall shows his camera, which takes 42 snaps; he says he wants to get it up to 47, "because that's a prime number."

"Reckoning" — In the briefing, Jack mentions that FTL has moved its heavy equipment, including the T-47s.

"Spirit" — Syd asks Severin Driscoll if he's staying in room 47 at the resort.

"The Coup" — When David McNeil tells Will about the computer room, the room's pass code is 4747.

"Page 47" — Aside from the title of the episode, Vaughn explains that in Rambaldi documents, page 47 is always the most important. When page 47 is uncovered, we see why.

"Q & A" — Haladki tells Vaughn that so far, 47 of the Rambaldi prophecies found have proven correct.

"The Snowman" — When McCullough is interrogating Noah, he mentions that $47 million was transferred to a bank account and then withdrawn.

"Almost Thirty Years" — Khasinau has built The Circumference and has hidden it in an underground lab in Taipei, in room 47.

"The Enemy Walks In" — The CIA tries to intercept the "bible" at Pier 347 in the Port of Barcelona.

"The Indicator" — Sydney uses port 47 to hook her computer into the network.

"The Counteragent" — The pass code to the facility in Estonia is 2664729.

"The Abduction" — Sydney and Marshall take a 747 to London, and Marshall memorizes the flight manual.

"A Higher Echelon" — First, when Sydney goes to retrieve the missing Echelon data, it's on a hard drive in room 147. Then, she discovers that Marshall is being held on the 47th floor of a building.

"The Getaway" — When Sydney and Dixon are undercover in the airport, he poses as a priest asking for donations and makes 47 euros.

"Phase One" — Sydney must try to get access to SD-6's server 47, which is housed on a 747.

"Double Agent" — James Lennox is being held on a sublevel floor, in room 47.

"A Free Agent" — Caplan's magnometer is in a vault in Switzerland, in box number 4747.

"A Dark Turn" — When Luri Karpachev and his men enter the elevator, they press the button for floor 47. Later, when we see the CIA's satellite codes, the first set of figures is X8471.

"Countdown" — Proteo di Regno's DNA is the code key to page 94 of the Rambaldi manuscript (94 ÷ 2 = 47).

"The Telling" — Derevko tells Sydney that Sloane has 23 Rambaldi artifacts, and the CIA has 24, equaling 47. Sloane is putting the machine together on floor 47 (the floor number is never stated, but in the stairwell you see the CIA agents pass floor 46, go up one more flight, and enter through the doors).

"The Two" — When Sydney is in the hospital, her heart rate is 74, an inverted 47.

"Succession" — The number 74 appears at the beginning and end of the original code to the vault.

"Reunion" — Jack says that the satellite fell from orbit at 4:47 Moscow time. Later, as he's uploading the program that will corrupt Marshall's attempts to identify Sydney in the photo, the camera cuts away when it's 47.4227 percent completed.

"A Missing Link" — When Sydney is posing as Julia Thorne and breaks into the hotel to steal the necklace, the second number on the combination to the safe appears to be 74.

"Repercussions" — Lauren's and Sydney's pagers read **47**911 when Dixon calls them.

"Conscious" — As Sydney is running down a corridor in her dream, she passes by a door with a huge 47 on it, which is the room she's wheeled into while she's unconscious. At the end of the episode, she finally enters the room in her dream.

"Crossings" — The plane that Sydney and Vaughn are on at the beginning of the episode is number N9**74**8C.

"After Six" — The bottle of wine Sydney must retrieve is a Château Margot 1953. In a pie chart or when dealing with percentages, 53 combines with 47 to make 100.

"Façade" — The deactivation code that Daniel Ryan gives Dixon is 594-**47**7-459-1124.

"Taken" — The lab at DSR is in room 74, and while Sydney makes her way to lot 45, we see lot 47, which appears to be a box filled with glass vials.

"The Frame" — When Lauren calls up the user IDs of the people who have accessed her account, we see that Jack's is 02**47**85.

"Blood Ties" — Jack says that Sydney was born in April 1975, which means she was conceived in 19**74**, the more important date from a Rambaldi standpoint. Jack also says that Weiss lost contact with Lauren between 2:10 and 2:**47**. And Marshall says the surveillance tapes are from "the 74th." In the Chechnyan prison, Nadia is lying in bed 407.

"Resurrection" — Sydney discovers she's "S.A.B. [Sydney Anne Bristow] Project 47."

Interesting Fact: Walker's hotel room is actually located in downtown Los Angeles's Standard Hotel.

Name That Guest Star: Djimon Hounsou (pronounced Jie-mon Hahn-soo) was born in Benin, Africa, and after doing some bit roles in television and film, he got his break in *Amistad* playing Cinque, and on *ER* playing a Nigerian refugee who bore deep scars on his back and deeper ones emotionally. Since then he's appeared in *Gladiator*, *The Four Feathers*, *Lara Croft Tomb Raider: The Cradle of Life*, and was nominated for an Academy Award for Best Actor in a Supporting Role for his turn in *In America* playing Mateo, a man dying of AIDS.

Did You Notice?: After Marshall and Sydney take out the guys in the casino backroom, he grabs a handful of chips.

Nitpicks: An issue never addressed is that while Sydney might have saved Vaughn's life by putting the tracker on him, she allowed a dangerous biological agent to go missing, and that very agent was used to create the bomb that killed 800 people.

Granted, 500 were dangerous prisoners, but 300 were innocent guards. Can she sleep well at night knowing that Vaughn is alive but 800 people are dead as a result?

Oops: When Sark opens the briefcase of money, watch the two stacks in the upper right-hand corner. The top bills flutter in the wind, and you can see the "bills" underneath are just blank pieces of paper. Also, Marshall's high-school photo shows him sporting a haircut and wearing an outfit that's clearly from the mid-1980s, which is when Kevin Weisman would have been in high school. But Marshall Flinkman is six years older than Weisman and would have been 16 years old in 1980, which is too early for him to have been making that particular fashion statement.

What Did He Say?: A plane has dropped a biological weapon on a prison in Siberia, and all 300 guards and 500 prisoners are dead except one — Kazari Bomani, the largest arms dealer in Africa (which explains why in the previous episode the Covenant was after the virus that could kill anyone they wanted while leaving others unharmed). After Sloane is kidnapped and released by Bomani, he tells Sydney that his contacts in the Japanese Mafia (the Yakuza) have created a computer virus that writes itself into networks, and it cannot be destroyed. Sloane has also given Bomani this information, and he explains to Sydney that the CIA cannot destroy the virus or he will be killed (and Sloane thinks this will convince Sydney how?). Sydney tells Dixon what Sloane has told her, and they come up with a plan for Sydney and Marshall to go to Osaka to disable the files. Marshall proves he can count cards, which will ensure them an invitation to the backroom for cheating.

Locations: Paris, France; Mexico City, Mexico; Le Havre, France; Osaka, Japan

Marshall's Gadgets: A Texan string tie that, when pulled, shoots bullets.

Music/Bands: "Psycho Slam" by Beamish plays when Marshall and Sydney arrive at the casino; Wyclef Jean and Kenny Rogers's "Kenny Rogers — Pharoahe Monch Dub Plate" (*The Ecleftic*) plays as Marshall plays blackjack; we hear "Ooh Child" by Lady Laistee featuring Sweetness (*Black Mama*) when Weiss is in Vaughn's hospital room talking about an old crush; and "Ooh Child" by Beth Orton (*Other Side of Daybreak*) plays when Sydney returns to Vaughn's room and sees him with Lauren.

3.6   The Nemesis

Original air date: November 2, 2003

Written by: Crystal Nix Hines

Directed by: Lawrence Trilling

Guest cast: Peter J. Lucas (Tupikov), Merrin Dungey (Allison Doren), Colin Campbell (Heinrich Strauss), Alec Mapa (NSC Techie), Dougald Park (Robert Lange), Zoran

Radanovich (Cell Leader), Emma Bering (Receptionist), Martin Horsey (Man), Krassimir (Bulgarian Cop)

Sydney discovers that Allison Doren is alive and vows revenge against her; the NSC gets one step closer to discovering the identity of Lazarey's assassin.

While the nemesis of this episode's title is obviously Allison Doren — the woman who killed Francie and tore Sydney's and Will's lives apart last season — it could also very easily be Sloane. Sloane has dogged Sydney's life more than anyone else (and it's finally stated here that he was entirely behind Doren's physical reconstruction and actions), and in this episode, when Sydney officially becomes his handler, she finally has him under her thumb. Sloane begins his turn as a double agent within the Covenant for the CIA and tells Sydney that he misses many things from his former life, chief among them

CHRISTINA RADISH

While Carl Lumbly and Merrin Dungey are good friends in real life, Marcus Dixon and Allison Doren are mortal enemies.

Sydney's trust. But no matter how many things Sloane does to make himself look like a good person, Sydney knows what he is capable of, and she will never trust him again.

It's great to see Merrin Dungey again. We get a flashback to Francie's death in "Phase One" (which was probably filmed for that episode and used here instead), and it reminds us of one of the many things Sydney has lost in her life because of her job. Doren is as cold and calculating as Francie was warm and friendly, and while Sark shows a moment of emotion (the shock on his face when he sees her for the first time makes us wonder if there's actually someone who Sark cares about), what happens at the end of the episode doesn't seem to affect him in any way. We discover that Rambaldi's journal contains a formula for a medicine that seems to heal the most life-threatening wounds and probably has something to do with Rambaldi's interest in immortality.

Meanwhile, the writers are careful to continue the plotline of Sydney trying to discover what happened in her missing years, and this episode is the first time she tells

Jack she is willing to undergo treatment to get the secrets out of her head, no matter how dangerous the procedure may be. Now that Lauren has been removed as Sloane's handler, it means she can devote more time to her search for Lazarey's killer. She finally discovers the name Julia Thorne, but only when she keeps the intel she finds at NSC and allows the techies there to decipher it rather than taking it to Marshall. Clearly she suspects someone at the CIA has been messing up her operation and keeping her from the truth. But as Vaughn says at the beginning of the episode, what will happen if she finds out Vaughn is helping thwart her search?

Highlight: The look on Vaughn's face when Marshall tells him that he got the looks and Marshall got the brains.

Interesting Fact: The Web site www.toureurope.eu doesn't actually exist.

Nitpicks: While Marshall's little song-and-drum routine was pretty funny, it seems a little over the top (even for Marshall) that he would have lugged in an entire drum kit, which we've seen in the background in other episodes, and have had time to actually practice the song in the office. Considering the elaborate routine the agents have to go through to get into the CIA rotunda each time (see the opening moments of "Resurrection"), it would have been very hard for Marshall to go through that procedure and carry drums with him (not to mention that the security guards would have wanted to look at every inch of those drums for possible explosives). The writers have taken Marshall's quirkiness a little too far this time, and this stunt was clearly a way to show off Kevin Weisman's drumming skills. Also, when Sydney's in the club trying to find Robert Lange, she walks up to the first guy, holds her hand over the necklace, and then faces away from him while Vaughn tries to get a match on him. How did she expect to get an ID that way? Finally, Vaughn seems to have recovered pretty quickly for someone who was dealing with a stab wound and a collapsed lung in the last episode.

What Did He Say?: Sloane has some intel for Sydney and has encrypted it in a photo of the Vatican at toureurope.eu. The intel states that German hardware engineer Robert Lange designed a program that gives access to a Russian arsenal. The device interfaces with security systems and acts like a key, opening them up to whoever is trying to hack into them by bypassing all security codes. Lange has surgically altered his face now that he realizes the Covenant will do anything to get the software from him, and he'll be meeting with a man named Heinrich Strauss to get his new identity papers. The Covenant knows about the exchange and will be there to kidnap him. Later, after the incident in Milan, Marshall says there was a chip in Lange's tooth that contained an RFID — a radio frequency identification. This device acted as a transmitter, allowing Lange to open the vault wirelessly — like using the EZ Pay system at a gas station.

Locations: Strasbourg [actually spelled *Strassburg*], France; Moscow, Russia; Milan, Italy; Zurich, Switzerland; London, England; Prague, Czech Republic; Sofia, Bulgaria

Marshall's Gadgets: A miniature X-ray in a necklace that can read skeletal structures and determine who has had facial reconstruction. Marshall also gives Sydney and Vaughn a device that homes in on the frequency of Lange's RFID chip.

Music/Bands: Jet's "Last Chance" (*Get Born*) plays when Sydney is running at the very beginning of the episode; Underworld's "Rez" (*1992–2002*) is the first song that plays in the club; "A/Klimatize" by Helix plays as Sydney leaves the first guy at the bar; and "Nocturne of the Sea" by Stephen James Edwards also plays in the club.

3.7   Prelude

Original air date: November 9, 2003
Written by: J.R. Orci
Directed by: Jack Bender
Guest cast: Clifton Collins, Jr. (Javier Perez), Luis Antonio Ramos (Mexican Detective Sanchez), Adrian Sparks (Dr. Siegel), George Kee Cheung (Minister Woo), Lorenzo Caccialanza (Team Leader), Gino Montesinos (Rebel Leader), Dennis A. Pratt (Kenneth Blake), Kevin Sutherland (CIA Techie), Nando De Stefano (Passing Man), Johnny Michaels (Police Officer)

Sydney's nightmares begin to haunt her, and she finds a huge clue about her disappearance; Lauren and Vaughn hit a wall in their relationship.

"Prelude" is an excellent episode that combines the best elements of *Alias* with some of the most incredible graphic sequences we've seen on the show. The hour opens with images of an angel statue and birds filmed with psychedelic colors, followed by an incredibly disturbing dream sequence of Sydney pulling a long, bloody tube from her abdomen (the scene is very graphic, and fans with weak stomachs should be forewarned). The dreams that Sydney was warned about in "Succession" are starting to happen, but she was told that the nightmares would have some bearing on reality. We'll soon find out what both sequences mean. Her horror at what she's seen in the dream forces her to turn to the director of the support group and ask about the surgery to recover her memory, but when he shows her what resulted when another agent tried the same treatment, the image is almost as terrible as her nightmares.

Meanwhile, the three men in Sydney's life all try to help her with what she's doing, despite her having difficult feelings regarding each of them. Sloane gives Sydney an integral piece of her puzzle, handing her a key and a set of codes that don't make any sense to her at first. Jack discovers that Javier Perez, the jerk within Simon Walker's crew, is about to spill the beans on who Julia Thorne really is, and he doesn't hesitate in finding a way to deal with the problem. But Vaughn takes the biggest risk of the three.

With the help of Sark, Lauren has discovered the truth about Sydney, and we can't help but feel sorry for her as she asks her husband how he could have betrayed her in this way. Vaughn's biggest fear has come true, and we know he's probably run this scene through his head a million times, but it's still not going to work out in his favor. Unfortunately, just as Vaughn did what he was told, so did Lauren, and we immediately lose all sympathy for her when we realize Sydney's life is in jeopardy. Though his wife has just discovered his deceit, Vaughn puts Sydney's well-being first, and what he does next will put not only his job on the line but his marriage as well. The scene at the airport is filled with tension surrounding both Sydney's escape and what might happen between her and Vaughn as they say good-bye to one another. Despite Vaughn's telling Sydney in "Succession" that he has "moved on," has he really done so?

The end of the episode throws everything into chaos as Lauren makes a surprise announcement at the CIA, and Sydney's discovery in Italy creates more questions for her while snatching away her opportunity to find answers.

Highlight: Sydney "staging" her hostility toward Sloane for Minister Woo.

Interesting Fact: When fighting the two guards at the party, Sydney picks up a pair of sais, Elektra's weapon of choice in *Daredevil*.

Did You Notice?: Scenes in *Alias* that are set in Mexico are often shot with a yellow tint, which was a technique used in the film *Traffic* to differentiate between the story-line in the U.S. and the one in Mexico. Also, in the dream sequences, we hear church bells, the same sound we heard in "The Two" when Sydney was coming out of the grogginess induced by the tranquilizer dart.

Nitpicks: Sark tells Lauren he's put a weight-sensitive charge under her car so, if she leaves the car within 30 minutes, it will explode. But what's to stop her from using her cell phone and alerting the CIA that Sark is in the parking garage?

What Did He Say?: In a clever throwback to seasons 1 and 2, Sloane conducts the briefing at the CIA. He says that the Covenant is sending him on his first operation, which involves a maser (which Marshall explains is a microwave laser that pinpoints its power into a focused beam). Sloane explains that he must go to a function in China and retrieve the device because China intends to launch a maser attack from a satellite, meaning they could kill from space. The effects of a maser beam include tissue damage and brain hemorrhaging, so it appears that victims have died of natural causes. Sloane wants Sydney to accompany him on the mission.

Locations: Nogales, Mexico; Beijing, China; Rome, Italy

Marshall's Gadgets: One of the coolest gadgets ever — a tiny car that camouflages itself in its immediate surroundings (Sydney can keep it in her makeup compact), it has a camera on the front so that Marshall can guide it by remote control, and when it gets next to the security system, it can disengage it. He also gives Sydney a device to attach to the maser; it will corrupt the chip within the maser and create a new one that Sydney will give to Sloane to give to the Covenant.

3.8 Breaking Point

Original air date: November 23, 2003
Written by: Breen Frazier
Directed by: Daniel Attias
Guest cast: Erick Avari (Dr. Vasson), Pruitt Taylor Vince (Campbell), Richard Roundtree (Brill), Javier Grajeda (FEMA Supervisor), Fred Saldone (FEMA Guard), Hector Atreyu Ruiz (Guiding MP), Pancho Demmings (Security Station MP #1), Travis Aaron (Security Station MP #2), John Eric Bentley (MP #2), Robert W. Sudduth (College Kid)

When Sydney is taken to a facility to be interrogated by the NSC about her life as Julia Thorne, Jack and Vaughn conspire to get her out.

For two years we've watched Vaughn and Jack battle with one another over who loves Sydney more. Jack is annoyed by Vaughn's affections toward his daughter, and Vaughn sees Jack as an overbearing father who sometimes goes too far and often can't be trusted. But in "Breaking Point" they are forced to work together, and for the first time we see some easy banter between the two. This is an excellent episode that has action, betrayal, switched loyalties, and humor.

Several times in this series the U.S. government has been portrayed as being as dangerous as — if not more than — the very terrorist organizations it tries to bring down. In "Q & A," Sydney is interrogated by the FBI and realizes that the Department of Special Research can keep her indefinitely just because it suspects she's part of a prophecy made over 500 years earlier. In "The Two" Sydney is declared an enemy of the state. And in this episode the NSC wants to subject Sydney to rigorous bouts of physical torture to get her to talk. Despite Lauren's pleas to Vaughn that Sydney is safe in the hands of the government, Vaughn knows the truth, and he and Jack will do everything in their power to get her out of there.

The banter between Vaughn and Jack provides one of many humorous moments in the episode. They chat cavalierly about Jack's incredible "storage facility," a place that will take on greater significance later in the season. They both deadpan while Jack tries to remove a bullet from Sloane — Vaughn: "I didn't know you wore glasses." Jack: "Only during surgery." An ease seems to develop between them. Sadly, it will be lost in upcoming episodes. Because they're working together for the same goal — to save Sydney — they can momentarily forget their differences and find common ground, but soon Jack will go back to hating Vaughn, and vice versa.

Meanwhile, at Camp Williams, Sydney undergoes extreme torture but doesn't crack. But when Lindsey finally checks Sydney's file and discovers her biggest vulnerability — something that is used several times against her throughout the series — he finally figures out how to get her to talk. Just as the NSC discovers Sydney's weakness, Sloane tells Jack that his weakness is Jack and Sydney. Sloane performs a stunning act of self-sacrifice to save Jack's life and explains it's because of how much Jack and Sydney mean to him, that they're all he has left. While it always appears that Sloane's endgame is a selfish one, it's difficult to shrug off his declarations of love for Jack and Sydney, because he's had several chances to hurt and/or kill both of them, but he's never taken those chances. In return, sometimes against their better judgments, Jack and Syd have often helped Sloane. Could Sloane be telling the truth, or is this just another part of his master plot to win their trust only to turn around and stab them in the back?

Highlight: Jack putting on the blue-collar "Noo Yawk" accent and using phrases like "freakin' nightmare."

Interesting Fact: Erick Avari, who plays Dr. Vasson, is no stranger to scenes with Jennifer Garner: he played Elektra's father in *Daredevil*.

Name That Guest Star: Richard Roundtree is best known as the original badass John Shaft from the early 1970s blaxploitation films and has appeared in dozens of films and television shows, including *Man Friday*, *Se7en*, *AntiTrust*, and the 2000 updated version of *Shaft* as Shaft's Uncle John Shaft. Pruitt Taylor Vince is a character actor who has appeared in films such as *Mumford*, *The Cell*, *S1m0ne*, and *Monster*.

Did You Notice?: Campbell reveals his real name is Schapker; Alison Schapker is one of the writers on the show. Also, Sydney's attempted prison break is reminiscent of a similar scene in *Terminator 2*, right down to the guards grabbing her and dragging her back.

Nitpicks: On the mission at FEMA, Sloane patches in to the phone line so all calls are rerouted to his phone, yet when Jack is leaving, the guard phones Director Blackman and the call goes to him rather than to Sloane. Why wouldn't Sloane keep the connection going until the very last minute? Also, when Lauren comes into

Marshall's office to speak with Vaughn, Marshall slips out and leaves his work on the screen. He was working on a way to break into NSC, a place Lauren works for, and knowing that she was working against Sydney, why would Marshall just leave everything visible for Lauren to see? Finally, how neural stimulation works is never explained, but how can Sydney's memories be retrieved if she's not conscious to relay them?

What Did He Say?: Sloane tells Jack and Vaughn that Sydney is being held at Camp Williams, a place where the U.S. government interrogates terrorists. He knows a way to get them into the place and make it look like the Covenant broke in.

Music/Bands: "Funktion Dunktion" by Freddie Funk plays on a nearby radio as Jack plays chess with Brill; we hear Marva Whitney's "What Do I Have to Do to Prove My Love to You?" (*It's My Thing*) when Jack goes into the FEMA building as the computer technician.

3.9   Conscious

Original air date: November 30, 2003
Written by: Josh Appelbaum and André Nemec
Directed by: Ken Olin
Guest cast: Erica Leerhsen (Kaya), David Cronenberg (Dr. Brezzel), Gerard O'Donnell (Agent Scrimm), Daniel E. Smith (Steven Dixon), Tristin Mays (Robin Dixon), Dan Warner (FBI Agent Reims), Susan Han (EMT), Sarah K. Peterson (Young Sydney), Boris Hamilton (Customer)

Sydney undergoes a procedure whereby her lost memories may be recaptured by her entering a dream state and reenacting the previous events.

"Conscious" is an amazing episode to watch, and David Cronenberg plays a delightfully loony doctor whose techniques may be questionable, but they offer results. Cronenberg, like Alfred Hitchcock, often has cameos in his own films, but who knew he could act with such humor and quirkiness? He comes off as an older version of Crispin Glover, with a similar way of muttering and moving about in front of the camera. It's apt that he would appear in this episode, as the nonlinear dream sequences are very similar to scenes you'd see in a Cronenberg film.

Sydney's dreams offer the viewer some insight into what might have happened in the two years she was missing, and they contain many symbols that have obvious meanings and some underlying ones. In one, a young Sydney goes to a birthday party, and when adult Sydney cuts the cake, Lazarey is standing there and blood seeps out of the cake, a reference to her belief that she killed him. In another Vaughn is in the ambulance with Sydney, showing her desire that he'd stayed with her rather than going off with Lauren (we know he wasn't in the ambulance because when he arrived at the scene, she was gone and her "remains" were all that stayed behind). Dr. Brezzel warns her in advance that her new memories may be traumatic, but they won't necessarily be real, even though they'll seem to be.

Her dreams, however, offer more insight on the symbolic level. Dreams of childhood indicate a longing to return to a life that was easier and had less responsibility. Sydney is six years old in one scene and is suddenly an adult slicing the cake in the next cut, showing how quickly she believes she's grown up and that her father (who is standing behind the cake) is responsible for determining her adulthood when she was only a child. Birthday cakes symbolize that one's wishes will come true. Dreaming of fathers signifies one's need to be self-reliant and also suggests authority or protection, and when he disappears suddenly, it means that Syd no longer feels protected by him or anyone. When she was gone for two years, Jack was unable to help her.

A dream about fighting indicates inner turmoil. It can denote a struggle that went on in the past, or one that continues in the present. It's appropriate that Sydney fights with Lauren — the one person who prevents her from achieving happiness in the present and who might have been involved in her past — and then herself. In the fight with herself, one self wears black, a symbol of danger, depression, sadness, mystery, and hatred, and the other self wears white, a symbol of purity, dignity, peace, and new beginnings. A fight to the death indicates an unwillingness to accept or face a real conflict in one's life. It's a perfect scene on the metaphorical level, as Sydney has always had both sides warring within her. Now more than ever she's afraid of the things she might have done, of the person Julia Thorne might have been, and she has a desire to kill the bad part of herself. But at the same time, she knows there's still an innocence within her, as things seem to happen to her — she is not the one making them happen. Again, her childhood was snatched from her, and she's still seeking a return to that more innocent time in her life.

Dreaming of riding in a car indicates ambition and the ability to move from one stage of one's life to another. Sydney is confused when she's in the car and has no idea where she's going, showing her uncertainty about where she's been for the past 24 months. Because she doesn't know where she's been, she's unable to move forward. She's also the passenger in the car, symbolizing her lack of control over her life and the feeling that someone else is forcing her to do things and go places against her will. Dixon is driving the car, which is interesting — perhaps Sydney believes that unlike her, he's regained control over his life and is now leading her to her next stage. That she's a "passenger" will also take on more significance later in the season. In this scene and in others, the color red shines on her, a color that has serious emotional meaning and indicates passion, anger, sexuality, and warning.

"Conscious" is a brilliant combination of intrigue, acting, and storytelling that will lead Sydney to her next clues while offering subtle hints to the viewers of what the rest of the season holds.

Highlight: Jack's response when Syd questions whether or not the metal detector will work if the object is not metal: "Then we're screwed. Not an entirely unfamiliar situation."

Interesting Fact: Dr. Brezzel says that dreams are made up of *a priori* and *a posteriori* information — both terms refer to how one arrives at a conclusion. A priori knowledge is knowledge one has without any physical evidence (e.g., the existence of God), whereas a posteriori knowledge is a conclusion one arrives at *after* the evidence has been collected (e.g., a child may learn not to touch a hot stove after actually touching a hot stove and realizing it's hot).

Name That Guest Star: Canadian David Cronenberg is the director of such groundbreaking films as *Scanners*, *The Dead Zone*, *Dead Ringers*, *Naked Lunch*, *Crash* (winner of the Jury Special Prize at the Cannes Film Festival), *eXistenZ* (winner of the Silver Berlin Bear at the Berlin International Film Festival), and *Spider*. He has had several film roles (often playing doctors) in movies such as *Nightbreed*, *To Die For*, *Last Night*, and *Jason X*.

Did You Notice?: When Weiss and Marshall are playing poker in Sydney's dream, the Rambaldi clock from "Time Will Tell" is sitting in the middle of the table.

Nitpicks: Syd seems pretty functional moments after flatlining on the table.

Oops: As Dr. Brezzel talks to Vaughn, Sydney, and Jack while eating his "facon," the piece he's eating keeps getting longer and shorter.

What Did He Say?: Lauren, Vaughn, Jack, and Sloane all decide that they will say Lauren was abducted by the Covenant, which still has Sydney. Jack and Vaughn will say they were off investigating the accusations against Sydney. To add authenticity, they'll tell the CIA that the Covenant wants the Rambaldi device in return for Sydney.

Locations: New Haven, Connecticut

Music/Bands: Captain Luke and Cool John's "The Chokin' Kind" (*Outsider Lounge Music*) plays when Sydney and Dixon are driving in the St. Aidan in Sydney's dream; MC Honky's "Sonnet No. 3 (Like a Duck)" (*I Am the Messiah*) is heard when Marshall and Weiss are playing cards.

3.10   Remnants

Original air date: December 7, 2003
Written by: Jeff Pinkner
Directed by: Jack Bender
Guest cast: Bradley Cooper (Will), Merrin Dungey (Allison Doren), David Cronenberg (Dr. Brezzel), Ivo Lopez (Emilio Gamboni), Gerard O'Donnell (Agent Scrimm), Tony Guma (Ben), Paul Ganus (Desk Attendant), Joey Nader (Bellhop), Sean Casey (NSC Agent), Mark Galasso (NSC Agent #2)

Sydney finds Will in witness protection, as she believes he might have some information that would help her; the two of them find the latest piece to the Rambaldi puzzle.

When you've been watching a series for three years, you get attached not only to the show but to the characters as well. In this episode, Sydney seeks out Will not only to see if he might have any knowledge of the phrase "St. Aidan" from her dream, but also to gain some closure. Undoubtedly she's wondered how he's doing and where he is, especially since they had been best friends for years, and by her finding him, it gives us closure as well. We've followed Will's journey for the past two seasons, and it's wonderful to see him again and find out what he's been doing.

The scene where Sydney first walks up to him at the construction site is tension-ridden and full of drama. Bradley Cooper is great as the guy who has mourned the death of his best friend, discovered his lover has been long dead, and lived the nightmares of realizing he was sleeping with the enemy when he believed her to be Francie. Now he's faced with the ghost of Sydney showing up in his new life, and he's obviously going to be a little unhinged. Sydney's begging him to ask her something that would prove it's her brings back memories of "Second Double," when Will did the same thing. Just as she did throughout season 2, she spills the beans on everything to Will (and we hope that by doing so she isn't putting his life in serious jeopardy once again) and he helps her on her latest mission. His new life as a construction worker hasn't challenged him mentally in any way, and it's clear he's been itching to do something interesting again. Solving puzzles is what he used to do as a journalist, and now he's able to do so again.

Sydney and Will's relationship moves to a new level, and the moment they're back together they're able to talk with ease. But when Will finds out that Allison Doren is still alive, a cloud moves over his face and we know that she's been haunting him for two years. Not only did she kill Francie, but he suspected she killed Sydney, and if there's one person he's vowed revenge against, it's her. The scene where Will and Allison come face-to-face once again is a painful one, and Will's emotional reaction afterward is poignant.

Meanwhile, Lindsey has stooped to new lows, asking Sloane for a shocking favor. Even more shocking is that Sloane accepts the offer — or does he? As much as Sydney cringes whenever Sloane mentions a father-daughter bond between them, he has often tried to protect her and thwart anyone who tries to hurt her. The way he acts in this episode for Sydney is the opposite of the way Sark conducts himself with regard to Lazarey — the latter pair may have a blood tie, but there is no love lost between them. Now that we know Lazarey is alive, we can breathe a sigh of relief that Sydney didn't actually murder someone. But Lazarey's presence — and the concern he shows for "Julia" when talking to Will — just opens up more questions.

Will returns and puts on a great act during a field mission with Sydney. "You know what I mean? You do, you cheeky little bastard . . ."

Now Sydney has a new puzzle to solve, and as Will retreats to his other life of normalcy, they agree not to talk about certain matters that have passed between them. When a friendship is based on opening up and divulging deep secrets, sometimes it's nicer not to ruin a moment by discussing it.

Highlight: Will saying he's been waiting to sleep with Sydney for eight years.

Interesting Fact: Verlustzeit, the name of the hotel Syd and Will go to in Graz, is a German word meaning "lost time." Also, St. Aidan is an Irish saint whose birth was heralded by strange omens and who is known for his kindness to animals.

Did You Notice?: This is the first time we hear Sark's first name, which is Julian (interesting that it's very close to Julia, which was Sydney's alias while in the Covenant).

Nitpicks: In "Conscious," Jack insists that for the sake of authenticity, Sydney must beat up Lauren to make the CIA believe she was really taken by the Covenant. So why does Sydney get to return to the CIA without a scratch on her?

Locations: Wisconsin; New Haven, Connecticut; Warsaw, Poland; Buenos Aires, Argentina; Moscow, Russia; Graz, Austria

Music/Bands: Peggy Lee's "Fever" (*The Best of Miss Peggy Lee*) plays when Will and Sydney catch up at the safehouse; we hear "My Goddess" by The Exies (*Inertia*) when Syd and Will check into the hotel room; and "Take It Off" by The Donnas (*Spend the Night*) plays when Will and Syd go to the safe deposit box in the hotel.

3.11 Full Disclosure

Original air date: January 11, 2004
Written by: Jesse Alexander
Directed by: Lawrence Trilling
Guest cast: Terry O'Quinn (Agent Kendall), Bill Bolender (Oleg), George Gerdes (Analyst), Steven Shaw (Minister), Yasha Blackman (Man in the Wheelchair)

Sydney is kidnapped by Agent Kendall, who finally tells her what happened to her during the time she was missing.

Season 1 of *Alias* was about Sydney discovering that SD-6 and Sloane were not what she thought they were, finding out that her mother was alive, and realizing that she'd been lied to for years. Season 2 was about discovering that her father had programmed her from a young age and learning that her mother had betrayed her once more. Now, in season 3, Sydney has been trying to put together the pieces of her life from the previous two years, and she discovers that she was the victim of — herself.

So far Sydney has seen a video of her killing Lazarey, but she later discovered that Lazarey is still alive. Lazarey's hand was buried in a box for some reason. She knows that her alias was Julia Thorne and that she had worked with Simon Walker at one point. She spent time in Italy (and was taking some prescription medication) in an apartment that she visited in "Prelude," and either she entrusted Sloane with the key and address or he was setting her up by telling her that she had done so. There is a scar on her stomach that baffles her. The Covenant had something to do with her kidnapping, and she suspects Sloane did as well. While her dreams in "Conscious" might have contained some clues about her life and her emotional well-being, they didn't answer any questions or give her any clues other than the mysterious phrase "St. Aidan," which led her to Will, who led her to the realization that Lazarey is alive. Where before it seemed a little baffling that she would know about St. Aidan and Will when Will had never mentioned the name to her, now it seems clear that Lazarey must have told Sydney about his association with Will, and her memory stored it so that she could retrieve it in "Conscious."

Finally, with "Full Disclosure," Sydney gets the answers she's been looking for. We discover that Agent Kendall was not being straight with her in "Q & A" when he said he was with the FBI. He reveals the existence of "Project Black Hole," a government project that is looking for Rambaldi objects, and says Sydney has been invaluable to them because she has found a quarter of the objects they now possess. For some reason, when Sydney disappeared and was believed dead, she turned to Kendall — not Jack or Vaughn — and told him that she was alive and explained what had happened to her. The reason he hasn't stepped forward until now is because she asked him not to tell her.

With that statement, Kendall begins filling us in on where Sydney has been, including the devastating scene of her watching, paralyzed, as Vaughn scatters her ashes and her father looks on, shattered, both men believing she's dead. The scene is heartbreaking and morbid: Sydney attends her own funeral and watches the impact her death has on the people closest to her. We see the *Clockwork Orange*–like torture she undergoes at the hands of the Covenant as its agents use physical and emotional means to break her spirit and convince her she's someone she is not. Kendall explains how, even under the most extreme circumstances, Sydney's father's programming has trained her body how to respond to the torture and her mind to stand up to the techniques, and what she does in the name of self-preservation is surprising.

When she tries to return to her life, Kendall uses her (just as so many have used her before) as a double agent, and after she sees Lauren and Vaughn together she loses all desire to go back to being Sydney Bristow. The line, "He loves me; nine months is nothing," is a sad one for its dramatic irony, and we realize that though Sydney thought she started to deal with her overwhelming loss in "The Two," she had already endured the pain of losing Vaughn over a year earlier. The biggest shock is what the scar on Sydney's stomach means — in a gruesome experiment, the Covenant has figured out a way to bring Milo Rambaldi back into the world through Sydney, whom they believe is the Chosen One. After the Covenant steals her eggs, she and Lazarey team up to find and hide Rambaldi's DNA to prevent the Covenant's master plan from happening.

The problem with the episode is the logic of Sydney asking to have her memory removed. The Covenant has her eggs, and if they find Rambaldi's DNA they will attempt to breed a child by combining the two. After everything she has gone through to prevent that from happening, why would she have her memory removed? Her memory contains the only knowledge of the whereabouts of the DNA; of who Lazarey is and his complicity in helping her hide the DNA; of who she's been for the past two years; of what she's been through and the knowledge she's gained of the Covenant's endgame. Why would she have all that removed and put herself back to square one? She never told Kendall where she hid the DNA, and if she really wanted it destroyed, why not burn it? Or go out into the desert and pour it into the sand? Why did she keep it intact, in a safe deposit box, under the very name by which the Covenant knows her?

Now that Sydney has finally gotten answers as to her whereabouts, it might seem like she can move forward. But when Lazarey mysteriously mentions "The Passenger" to her at the end of the episode — and a new enemy is unveiled — a whole new mystery begins.

Highlight: Marshall insisting he didn't put a tracer on the cube and then breaking down and admitting he did.

Did You Notice?: The voice that asks Sydney to kill the man in the wheelchair is Quentin Tarantino's, meaning McKenas Cole is affiliated with the Covenant. Also, the dream sequence at the beginning of "Prelude," where Sydney was pulling the long bloody tube out of her abdomen, could have been symbolizing her knowledge that her eggs were being used as a link to Rambaldi and that the Covenant was going to create test-tube babies.

Nitpicks: On the video she sent to Kendall, Sydney's hair is different lengths, with short strands at the front and longer, wavy ones at the back, yet when she was found in "The Two," which was two days later, her hair is one length, and much longer. How did it grow so quickly? Also, in addition to the nitpicks listed in the episode guide above, we also discover that Dixon has known all along what happened to Sydney and claims he "couldn't say" anything about it. He sort of insinuates a "now we're even" attitude, but then he softens and says he knows what she went through at SD-6 and has forgiven her. But knowing what she, Jack, and everyone else have endured trying to find the truth, why did Dixon stay mum on the subject? Because Kendall told him that Sydney didn't want to know? (Dixon's knowing the truth might explain why he was the driver of the St. Aidan in Sydney's dream in "Conscious," suggesting he's been in control the entire time.) And why didn't the CIA have snipers at the ready for added security when Lazarey got to the hospital, or at least have the ambulance pull right up tight against the emergency room door? Finally, how exactly did the Covenant retrieve Lazarey's hand? Not only is it buried in the rubble of the caved-in mountain, but it's trapped in the cubbyhole.

Locations: Patagonia, Argentina

Music/Bands: No Doubt's version of Talk Talk's "It's My Life" (*The Singles, 1992-2003*) plays when Sydney first becomes a double agent for Kendall, is spying on the Covenant, and is walking down the street.

3.12　Crossings

Original air date: January 18, 2004
Written by: Josh Appelbaum and André Nemec
Directed by: Ken Olin
Guest cast: Griffin Dunne (Leonid Lisenker), Isabella Rossellini (Katya Derevko), Arnold Vosloo (Mr. Zisman), Byron Chung (Colonel Yu), François Chau (Mr. Cho), Leo Lee (Mr. Kwan), C.W. Pyun (Ki-Jong), Emma Bering (Sloane's Secretary), John D. Kim (Soldier), Randall Park (Korean Soldier)

When Vaughn and Sydney travel to North Korea to retrieve a Covenant defector, they are captured by the North Korean Army; Jack joins forces with a new ally to try to get Sydney back; Lauren shows her true colors.

In yet another example of beginning the episode with the climax and then going back in time to lead us up to that moment, "Crossings" opens with Vaughn and Sydney kissing one another before being led outside to stand in front of a firing squad. If there was ever a powerful opening, this is it. Sydney and Vaughn have been through so much together (and the viewers now know that there's a possibility they could get back together if Lauren gets out of the way soon), and now it appears they'll die together.

The most intriguing character in this episode is Jack. When Sydney goes missing, he immediately contacts Irina for help. She sends someone who goes by the name "The Black Sparrow" and knows how to use a shish-kebab skewer as a mean weapon. The ensuing scenes of Jack and Katya working together are great, and Isabella Rossellini brings a mystery and beauty to the role, matching Katya's sexual aggression to Jack's stony indifference. On-screen, the combination is electric. She hints that Irina is still very much in the picture and tells Jack that some day Irina's intentions will be made clear. The condition she names for agreeing to help Sydney — that Jack must kill Sloane in return — puts Jack in a difficult position, but he goes ahead with the plan in order to save his daughter. The result of Katya's scheming (it's not exactly clear why she does what she does other than to suggest that, from afar, Irina is still messing with Jack's life) destroys the trust Jack has tried to build with Sloane, and the scene of Sloane telling Jack what it was like to barely escape a K-Directorate assassination attempt years earlier is eerie.

Lauren has finally been unveiled as a Covenant operative (to the viewers only), and while she appeared to be a somewhat weak character before, she'll become far more interesting in the weeks to come. The parallel between her situation with Vaughn and Irina's with Jack years earlier might seem a little too convenient (and in a

AVIK GALBOA/WIREIMAGE.COM

Married to one, in love with the other — what a mess Vaughn's gotten himself into.

way, it is), but it'll allow the writers to explore Jack's still-simmering resentment about what happened to him and how he treats Vaughn once he finds out the truth. The writers try to create sympathy for Lauren by having her stare wistfully at a picture of her and Vaughn, but like Irina, Lauren doesn't seem to have any genuine affection for Vaughn, and the calculating way she reports to her superiors the whereabouts of Vaughn and Sydney shows that she wouldn't hesitate if she were asked to kill him in cold blood. Ah, all the more reason for us to hate her.

Highlight: Katya's last line to Jack and the look on his face.

Interesting Fact: On the plane, Vaughn is reading Italo Calvino's last book, *Mr. Palomar*, which is about a man who is so befuddled by the world around him that he develops a strange ordering system to help him understand everything. It's a philosophical look at what happens when we become so obsessed with understanding everything that we miss out on the big picture and the beauty around us. Also, J.J. Abrams knew that Isabella Rossellini would be a perfect fit for the show, and she was eager to see what he could do with her. "J.J. said, 'Are you athletic?' and I said, 'Well, I don't know; I do some yoga, some Pilates,'" she recalls. "So I might be in for a big surprise. I am getting a little bit on the side of a little old lady, but I'm sure that J.J.'s going to make me look like Uma Thurman in *Kill Bill*, so why not, no?"

Name That Guest Star: Isabella Rossellini, a former model, is the daughter of Ingrid Bergman and Roberto Rossellini. A shrewd and very talented actress, Rossellini chooses her parts wisely, and she has starred in films such as *Immortal Beloved*, *Big Night*, *Roger Dodger*, and *The Saddest Music in the World*. Actor, producer, and director Griffin Dunne directed *Addicted to Love* and *Practical Magic*, and he has appeared in films such as *An American Werewolf in London*, *Johnny Dangerously*, *Quiz Show*, and *Piñero*.

Did You Notice?: When Sark is pretending to be CIA, he puts on a fake American accent, but you can still hear tinges of his real British accent behind it. It's a clever detail considering David Anders is actually American and in this scene is playing a British man trying to put on an American accent and not succeeding very well. Also, Sark tells Lisenker that his name is Agent Hollier — Christopher Hollier is one of the writers on the *Alias* team.

Nitpicks: Now that we know Lauren is Covenant and has been the whole time, it makes many of her earlier actions (or inactions) inconsistent. In "A Missing Link," she doesn't alert the Covenant that Sydney has infiltrated Simon Walker's group. In "Nemesis," Sloane is working as a double agent within the Covenant, and Lauren doesn't tell anyone. In "Prelude," Lauren looks genuinely terrified of Sark, yet if she's really an insider, she would have known he was part of the Covenant, and considering the way she fights later in the season, she wouldn't have batted an eye if someone suddenly surprised her in her car. In the season finale, she's going to reveal that she's known a lot more about Sydney than she's been letting on, which means she would have known Sydney was in the Covenant, that Sydney's name was Julia Thorne, and that she killed Lazarey, yet when Robert Lindsey sends her on a wild goose chase for the NSC, she follows orders as if she has no idea that Sydney is actually Julia. Also, Sydney and Vaughn's finding the abandoned truck in North Korea seems a little too convenient.

Oops: Jack has said many times that he was married to Irina for 10 years, but in this episode Katya mistakenly says they were married for five.

What Did He Say?: The FCC found a phantom account, and encoded within the fake stocks was a message: a Covenant official wants to defect and will turn over everything he knows about the Covenant. Sydney and Vaughn must go to North Korea and meet with him.

Locations: Q-Gong Province, North Korea; Gai Li, North Korea; Zurich, Switzerland

Music/Bands: Damien Rice's "Delicate" (*O*) plays when Sydney and Vaughn return to the CIA with Lisenker.

3.13   After Six

Original air date: February 15, 2004
Written by: Alison Schapker and Monica Breen
Directed by: Maryann Brandon
Guest cast: Vivica A. Fox (Toni Cummings), Quentin Tarantino (McKenas Cole), Ian Buchanan (Johannes Gathird), Laetitia Danielle (Saleslady), Alex Stemkovsky (Tuxedoed Guard)

Sark and Lauren begin systematically killing all of the Covenant cell leaders in order to gain power while Sydney tries to obtain a microchip with the names and locations of those leaders.

"After Six" is an episode in which several characters become introspective and open up to others about their deepest feelings. Dr. Judy Barnett returns to counsel first Sydney, who is confused and upset by what happened with Vaughn in North Korea, and then Sloane, who has been in a depression and needs someone to talk to. Jack is involved in both situations, but where Sydney is concerned he obviously shows more protectiveness. In "Remnants," despite the inroads Jack and Vaughn made toward something resembling camaraderie in "Breaking Point," Jack told Vaughn he would not let his daughter become Vaughn's mistress, and Vaughn should try pushing Sydney away. He said that if Vaughn really cared about Sydney, he'd be cruel to be kind. Unfortunately, though Vaughn tried to follow Jack's advice in "Crossings," it broke his heart to do so, and he apologized to Sydney and explained why he was acting cold. Now Jack realizes he must appeal to Sydney, not Vaughn, and in this episode he tells Sydney to request another partner on her mission to Athens. Clearly Jack doesn't want to see Sydney hurt the way he was, and he can no longer trust Vaughn to push her away.

In Zurich, we see Sloane shooting a green liquid into his arm (an act that will take on more relevance in "Blood Ties") and telling Jack he needs to see a therapist. The ensuing scenes with Judy Barnett (who, incidentally, did her thesis on Sloane, which seems odd — by the way she talks it seems that she knew he was a leader of a terrorist cell when she was doing her paper, yet Sydney and everyone else at SD-6 was kept in the dark) are full of mystery and intrigue. Sloane keeps coming close to telling Judy something big, but then pulls back at the last minute. As viewers, we're not sure if Sloane is stringing Judy along or if he really has a secret to tell — his conniving has become so much a part of his character that it's hard to take anything he says or does as sincere.

The comedy in this episode comes with Marshall (as usual). All season long he's been trying to win over his pregnant girlfriend's heart and convince her to marry him, and only when she goes into labor in this episode does she agree. The scene of Weiss acting as minister (ordained by the online Internet Church of Mammals) and Carrie running out the door to cries of "I love you, Mrs. Flinkman!" only to hurl back at Marshall that she's keeping her last name, is hilarious. Marshall is the innocent on the show, and everyone wants to see him happy. Fatherhood will turn him into a caffeine-ridden basket case by the end of the season, but that's what makes him so much fun. Quentin Tarantino also returns for a bit of amusement, and his scene in this episode — "Did I just blow your mind?" — is as campy and over the top as those in "The Box" episodes.

The best part of "After Six," however, belongs to Sark and Lauren. While Vaughn

While Lauren had very little chemistry with Vaughn, she's amazing on screen with Sark.

325

and Lauren had very little chemistry and were quite boring compared with the fireworks that characterized the relationship between him and Sydney last season, Sark and Lauren are amazing to watch when they're together. Lauren is a different person when she's Covenant, and her milquetoast British CIA persona gets buried under a far more brutal, sexually charged one. The scenes of them working together and getting off on doing so are brilliant, and Melissa George really comes to life when paired with David Anders. The duo provides a great sadomasochistic element to the series, one that actually seems strengthened by Lauren's betrayal at the end rather than weakened by it.

Highlight: Vaughn's response when Weiss admits to having feelings for both Posh and Sporty Spice: "Who didn't?"

Interesting Fact: "After Six" marks the first time that a female has directed an episode of *Alias*. Also, despite loving the costumes on *Alias*, Vivica A. Fox revealed that she used something of her own in the club scene. "[The producers] were, like, 'We want her to be hot!'" she says. "So I said, 'Let me break out something from my closet,' and I went and got this sexy little blue dress and they were, like, 'Perfect!' I don't get a chance to play bad characters that often. I was just a bitch on wheels."

Name That Guest Star: Vivica A. Fox has starred in several movies, such as *Independence Day*, *Soul Food*, *Why Do Fools Fall in Love*, Quentin Tarantino's *Kill Bill* films, and *Beauty Shop*. Ian Buchanan is most recognizable to soap opera fans — he played Duke Lavery on *General Hospital*, James Warwick on *The Bold and the Beautiful*, and Joshua Temple on *Port Charles*.

Did You Notice?: Alongside Quentin Tarantino and David Carradine, Vivica A. Fox becomes the third person involved in Tarantino's *Kill Bill* to appear on *Alias*. Also, we know that McKenas Cole is on to Sark the moment Cole walks into the room because of the bottle of champagne he's carrying. In "The Box, Part 2," he explains that he always has a bottle of champagne when he's the victor. Also, Cole's fascination with Sark's haircut is an inside joke: when David Anders shaved his head, people joked that viewers might turn away the same way they did from *Felicity* when star Keri Russell cut off her hair.

Nitpicks: How did Sydney and Vaughn get out of the electrified vault when the pipe was fractured? It wouldn't have been able to withstand their weight. Also, how would the Covenant have gotten a photo of Vaughn and Sydney kissing in North Korea, which is presumably what Cole gives Lauren?

Oops: Judy Barnett claims to have done her post-doctoral thesis on Sloane, but there's no such thing. One can do a doctoral thesis to get a Ph.D. and then do post-doctoral work in that area, but there's no such thing as a post-doctoral thesis.

What Did He Say?: Leonid Lisenker, the Covenant defector from the previous episode, planted a microdisc with the Doliac Agenda on it (a playbook for the Covenant that contains all the leaders' names and locations) in a chalet owned by an arms dealer, and now the CIA is keeping tabs on the chalet to find a way in. The security system was created by Toni Cummings, who used to get charged for breaking security systems and now builds them. Sydney and Weiss must pose as diamond dealers who want an elaborate security system and find out how Cummings built the one in Chamonix. Meanwhile, Sark confronts Lauren with the idea of killing the six Covenant leaders and demanding more power within the organization by threatening to send the leaders' access keys to the CIA.

Locations: Chamonix, France; Zurich, Switzerland; Berlin, Germany; Athens, Greece; Salzburg, Austria; St. Petersburg, Russia

Marshall's Gadgets: A camera that Sydney and Vaughn put into the side of a mountain in Chamonix that allows Marshall to do surveillance on the chalet to see if there's a way to bypass the security system. To get Sydney and Vaughn into the building, he gives them an inflatable Kevlar ball that tricks the guns into expending their bullets, a suit that offsets the electrified vault, and a sealant that they shoot over the acid spouts.

Music/Bands: We hear Jonny Lang's "Give Me Up Again" (*Long Time Coming*) when Vaughn and Weiss play pool; "Panhandle Stomp" by Johnny Lee Schell plays as Sydney microwaves her dinner and her father shows up; and The Crystal Method's "Starting Over" (*Legion of Bloom*) plays when Syd and Weiss enter the club to talk to Toni Cummings.

3.14 Blowback

Original air date: March 7, 2004
Written by: Laurence Andries
Directed by: Lawrence Trilling
Guest cast: Patricia Wettig (Dr. Judy Barnett), Fritz Michel (Vault Manager)

As the CIA begins to suspect that there's a mole in its midst working for the Covenant, Vaughn and Sydney go on a dangerous mission during which Vaughn's feelings are revealed; Sloane discloses a dark secret from his past to Dr. Barnett.

"Blowback" experiments with a formula used in movies like *Pulp Fiction* and several television shows, where the same scene is played more than once, but from different points of view. Unfortunately, it doesn't work. The episode feels repetitive, and while the second half of the episode reveals a different point of view, the writers show

Who's Your Daddy?

In "Blowback," Sloane suggests that Sydney might be his daughter, but it's not the first time he has hinted at a father-daughter connection:

"Color-Blind" — Sloane says that he believes in Sydney as if she were his own daughter.

"Time Will Tell" — Sloane tells Jack that he worries about Sydney like she was his own daughter.

"Mea Culpa" — Sloane tells Syd that he's actually known her since she was born and adds, "I've always thought of you as my daughter."

"Page 47" — Sloane tells Jack that "there are some truths Sydney must never learn."

"Masquerade" — Jack tells Sloane that if Sydney were his daughter, he'd understand how Jack felt. Sloane looks taken aback for a moment before responding that he's used to filling in for Jack when Jack's been indisposed.

"Almost Thirty Years" — Sloane tells Sydney that watching her grow up has been as rewarding as having children of his own. Jack, listening in, mutters, "Bastard."

"Firebomb" — When Sloane has Sydney tied up in Kabir's compound, he tells her she is his proudest accomplishment.

"Truth Takes Time" — Sloane tells Derevko that he and Emily love Sydney "as if she were our own." Derevko tells him never to talk about his love for Sydney again.

"The Two" — Sloane says to Sydney, "I loved you like a daughter," but when he suggests that at times he's felt like she looked upon him as a father, she grabs him by the throat.

> "Blowback" — Sloane admits to Dr. Barnett that he had an affair with Irina Derevko, and while he never tried to prove that Sydney is his daughter, he believes her strength comes from him.
>
> "Hourglass" — Jack tells Sloane that he knows Sloane tried to take Sydney from him and that Sloane is jealous that she is his daughter.

too much of what we've already seen and don't make it different enough to merit a second viewing. For example, the episode opens with Lauren waking to Vaughn sitting next to the bed and looking at his father's watch. When the second half of the episode returns to the same scene, we witness almost the entire conversation again, where the writers could have gotten away with just showing the last few lines before Lauren takes a call from Sark. They expect us to remember tiny details from season 1 that take on huge significance two years later, yet they don't assume we'll remember a conversation that we heard 20 minutes earlier? Also, the so-called "different perspectives" play the same scenes we've already seen rather than shooting them from another character's point of view, which is laziness on the part of the writers and director. When Vaughn calls Lauren on his cell phone, we only see it from his point of view the first time, so the second time should have been entirely from her point of view. Instead, just the last couple of lines are from her perspective.

Despite the episode's repetitive nature and the tedium that plagues the second half, it still has its moments. Sark and Lauren once again light up the screen — their phone conversations are full of innuendos and tension, and Lauren shows an excitement during the car chase that turns into more of a teasing later. It appears that Sark is becoming attracted to her, but she's so cold that she has her bit of fun and then leaves him in the bed.

Sloane reveals a secret to Dr. Barnett that he's been hinting at for two and a half years now on the show, and the possibilities for storylines are endless. What if Sydney *is* his daughter and Jack has no idea? Jack's discovery that his marriage to Derevko was all a sham has devastated his life, but he loves Sydney more than he even loved his wife, and to have her taken away from him on top of everything else that has happened would utterly destroy him. And what would Sydney do if she thought for a second that Sloane was actually her father?

The scene in Lisbon brings several emotions to the surface. Sark shows that he has

Sloane, Jack, Irina, and Syd — they put the "fun" in dysfunctional family.

feelings for Lauren when he asks Vaughn to throw down his weapon if he loves Sydney. Sark believes that if Vaughn admits to loving Sydney, then maybe Lauren will be more loyal to him. But when Vaughn does what Sark says, Lauren's jealousy leaps to the surface. She's never loved Vaughn, but she hates the thought of losing to Sydney. Sark, in turn, shows *his* jealousy when he hands off the bomb to Vaughn along with a surprise. Sydney remains neutral throughout, but *we* know what she's thinking. The earlier scenes of Lauren not realizing the significance of Vaughn's father's watch while Sydney clearly does, show immediately who cares about him more. The scenes also prove that Sydney is willing to put Vaughn's thoughts and feelings above her own when it counts. Although Vaughn goes back to Lauren upon his return and Sydney goes out with Jack, it's clear that they really want to be with each other.

Highlight: Jack looking at Marshall's picture of baby Mitchell, muttering a dispirited "Cute" and attempting a smile (that fails miserably) before walking away.

Did You Notice?: Lauren in the red wig is a visual throwback to Sydney in "Truth Be Told." Also, Sydney says Vaughn kissed her in North Korea and she kissed him back, but it was actually the other way around.

Nitpicks: Once again (see "Fireball") the sponsorship deal *Alias* has with Ford makes its way into an episode as Vaughn and Sydney run through a parking garage and yell, "Get in the F150!" Ugh. Not only do they choose the fancy Ford pickup, but Lauren and Sark are driving away from them in a Ford Mustang, and as Sydney and Vaughn exit the parking garage, they're stopped by a Ford Focus. Despite the Ford product placement that promotes Ford products, not a single airbag deploys in the F150 or the Focus, which doesn't say much for the safety of either vehicle considering how hard Vaughn actually hits the car. And how did they start the F150? Were the keys just in it? They didn't hotwire it. Also, for someone who is worried about professionalism, Dr. Barnett is wearing quite the revealing dress for her dinner with Sloane. Finally, Marshall will hack through the firewall of another hacker in "Unveiled," which has to be practically impenetrable, yet he says he can't hack into the facility in Vancouver because it's state of the art. No matter how sophisticated someone's computer network is, it should be no match for Marshall.

Oops: When the chase in the parking garage is shown the second time, you can see that Lauren and Sark's back window has been shattered before Sydney actually shoots at them, and one scene later it's intact again. Also, you can see there is no one in the car that gets totaled on the street as it spins toward the camera.

What Did He Say?: Dixon briefs everyone on Shining Sword, a group in the Philippines. An operative there has a plasma charge — a tiny bomb that could take out a city block — and is shipping it to a European cell. The operative might have archived the material on a server in Vancouver, giving its schematics and whereabouts, and Sydney and Vaughn must go there to upload the information to Marshall. There is suspicion about a mole in the CIA (why that would be announced to a room of people where the mole is most likely sitting is odd), and the CIA will be interviewing agents.

Locations: Zurich, Switzerland; Vancouver, Canada; Lisbon, Portugal

Marshall's Gadgets: An electronic sniffer that can detect a bomb. The gadget is pretty standard, but Marshall adds the plasma bomb to the list of explosives the device can sniff out.

Music/Bands: Blur's "Song 2," from their 1997 self-titled album, plays during the car chase in the parking garage; and "Carnival Town" by Norah Jones (*Feels Like Home*) plays when Jack asks Sydney out to dinner.

3.15   Façade

Original air date: March 14, 2004
Written by: R.P. Gaborno and Christopher Hollier
Directed by: Jack Bender
Guest cast: Griffin Dunne (Leonid Lisenker), Ricky Gervais (Daniel Ryan), Nicholas

Hosking (Newscaster), Stana Katic (Flight Attendant), François Giroday (Capt. Verlot), David S. Lee (French Squad Cop), Ciaran Reilly (Swat Team Guy)

The CIA must pretend to be Covenant to gain the trust of bomber Daniel Ryan and stop him from detonating a second bomb.

"Façade" is an episode about revealing confidences, secrets, and oneself. Everyone on the show keeps up a façade of sorts (except maybe Marshall) as part of their job — and as part of their lives. Sydney, Vaughn, and Jack work as secret agents, but they carry their secrets into their personal lives as well, as does everyone around them.

This episode is fantastic, and casting funnyman Ricky Gervais in the serious role of a bomber was a stroke of genius. Gervais shows that he's more than a comedian, and he plays the dramatic scenes with the seriousness and sadness of someone who has suffered real trauma. The opening scene, where Weiss confronts Ryan and Sydney pretends to be Covenant, is brilliant, and it sets the pace for the rest of the episode. Sydney and the CIA try very hard to convince Ryan that they are Covenant (complete with a fake hotel room, elevator, and news broadcast) and then must convince him they're CIA. Either way, they want him to trust them, and it's no wonder that he stares at them with bewilderment when they make such a request. This episode is all about putting on a mask in front of people, getting found out, and having to regain their trust. It's something so many have done, and we've seen Jack try to regain Sydney's trust, Sydney try to regain Will's, and Sloane try to get everyone to believe that he's a changed man. In "Façade," the game is a lot clearer.

The CIA isn't the only player wearing a mask and pretending to be something it's not, and when it discovers Ryan's *real* plan, the consequences are devastating. Unfortunately, it's when Sydney drops her façade completely that she gets into serious trouble and puts Vaughn and everyone in the CIA rotunda in danger. Just as Ryan has been tricked into the CIA rotunda, Vaughn has been tricked into boarding a plane, and both sides will have to reach a compromise if they want to save lives.

The final scene of Ryan walking in slow motion across the rotunda while glaring at Sydney is amazing. Sydney has gained a new, formidable enemy — one we can only hope will resurface in a later episode. The many obstacles Sydney has faced this season are finally taking a toll on her, and she breaks down in the parking lot. She's lost Vaughn, and thought she was about to lose him permanently; she just escaped death (again); and now she's seen the emotional impact her murder of another man has had on his family. It's a wonder that she's held it together for as long as she has.

Highlight: Vaughn posing as Sark, complete with the accent.

Interesting Fact: J.J. Abrams is a huge fan of Ricky Gervais and had been asking him to appear on *Alias* for some time. "*The Office* is actually just as dramatic as it is comedic," Abrams told *Entertainment Weekly*. "Having said that, Ricky *did* have a blast on the set. In fact, there was probably more goofing off during the filming of this episode than any other. Ricky and Victor together were a particular [discipline] problem." Gervais admitted to having a great time on the episode. "The hardest part was keeping straight faced," he said. "Everybody around me was in black and cool and wearing Gucci and Armani and guns, there I was in a jumper looking like a country fisherman. I just pretended to be Jack Bauer from *24*."

Name That Guest Star: British comedian Ricky Gervais is best known for his portrayal of David Brent in the brilliant BBC series *The Office*. Gervais won the 2004 Golden Globe for Best Performance by an Actor in a Television Series — Musical or Comedy for the role, the night before he began filming "Façade."

Nitpicks: Why did Sydney feel the need to tell Ryan *everything*? It makes no sense that she reveals to him what her name was when she was Covenant — that she was kidnapped and brainwashed should be enough to get him onside without her having to disclose details that could get her into trouble. For a secret agent, sometimes she spills the beans a little too readily. Also, how was Vaughn able to use his cell phone on the plane without the flight attendant telling him to turn it off because it would interfere with the controls? And in a previous episode, when Sloane walks into the CIA, Dixon has all of the computer screens put on screensaver mode, yet Ryan walks in and you can see that many of the computer screens are still active. And finally, instead of going to such time and expense to re-create room 305 of the Commodore Hotel in Russia, why not just take Ryan there?

What Did He Say?: A bomb has gone off in a bank building in Belfast, Northern Ireland. The bomb was made by Daniel Ryan, formerly of the Royal Navy, who was dishonorably discharged. He wanted the Covenant to see how powerful his bomb was, so he set one in the bank and called in the bomb squad to show that they couldn't defuse it. If the Covenant doesn't agree to take one of his bombs, he'll detonate a second one in the U.S. to show other terrorist groups how powerful it is. He'll be in a pub and the CIA needs to meet with him and pose as the Covenant to gain his trust.

Locations: Belfast, Northern Ireland; Rome, Italy

Music/Bands: "All My Life" by Rosie Thomas (*Only with Laughter Can You Win*) plays when Sydney breaks down in the parking garage.

3.16 Taken

Original air date: March 21, 2004
Written by: J.R. Orci
Directed by: Lawrence Trilling
Guest cast: Raymond J. Barry (Senator George Reed), Jenny Gago (Erin), Patricia Wettig (Dr. Judy Barnett), Daniel E. Smith (Steven Dixon), Tristin Mays (Robin Dixon), Kevin Sutherland (Rotunda Agent), E.K. Butler (DSR Guard #4), Christian Boeving (DSR Guard #5)

The Covenant kidnaps Dixon's children and demands that the CIA release five Covenant prisoners in exchange for their safe return.

If there's one person in the CIA who has an emotional meltdown whenever he's under pressure, it's Marcus Dixon, and Lauren has done her homework when she tells the Covenant to target him for their latest caper. For Dixon, this job has proved more personal than it has to the others: he lost his wife when Sloane had her killed; he lost his faith in himself when he discovered he'd been working for a terrorist organization; and now his children are all he has left. It's understandable that he becomes frantic when he realizes they're gone. Because of what happened to Diane, and knowing what the Covenant are capable of, he fears he'll lose them, too. Thankfully, Dixon steps down momentarily, because there's no way he'd be able to think straight. It's human nature to want to save the person closest to you regardless of how many others may suffer as a result, and while Senator Reed is painted as a bit of a bastard for suggesting that they can't just hand over prisoners and give in to the demands of terrorists, he's right. If Dixon were to release the five Covenant prisoners immediately and retrieve Steven and Robin, they'd go missing again the following week when another terrorist organization decided to get some of their colleagues released as well. Dixon can't give in to these demands, no matter how much it's killing him not to.

Sydney has always been self-sacrificing, especially for Dixon, but in this episode she takes greater risks for the sake of Dixon's kids than she has before. She breaks into DSR, which not only puts her job in jeopardy but also could land her in prison. She withstands excruciating conditions waiting for Dixon to open the grate for her. And she continues to help him when doing so might put her life in jeopardy. Dixon might come off as cold by not interfering or suggesting that Sydney stop, but in the moment he is an emotionally fragile man and will do anything to save his daughter — even watch Sydney die. Jack, on the other hand, is Sydney's father and wants to save *his* daughter, and he argues that the undertaking is unfair. He worries that the Covenant's having the Rambaldi box could put Syd's life in danger, but Dixon won't listen. At the exchange, Syd once again steps in and puts Robin's life before her own. Sydney's reason for doing so is interesting — she explains that Robin didn't choose a life of danger. Therefore, Sydney argues that she herself should take the risk because she's more likely to escape from it. The thing is, we know that Sydney didn't choose this life, either. It seems like she did, but last year she discovered she'd been preprogrammed (by her father, no less) to become an agent and that she couldn't have become anything else. She's as innocent as Robin.

What Sydney recovers in the lab will drive the rest of the season. Why do the cameras go completely crazy when she gets in their way — do they recognize her as a Rambaldi "artifact"? How could a box fashioned centuries ago bear the inscription of her mother's name? Were Sydney's grandparents Rambaldi followers who knew their daughter would be part of the prophecy and therefore named her Irina? Or did Rambaldi know that the woman who would be responsible for the fulfillment of his prophecy would be named Irina? Either way, the Covenant now has the box; the CIA must get it back; and Sloane is in a CIA prison, where he will take on the role Derevko had last season. And on top of everything else, Jack thinks he knows who the mole is. "Taken" is a strong episode that sets us up for everything that will follow.

Highlight: The last line of the episode.

Name That Guest Star: Veteran theater and character actor Raymond J. Barry has appeared in dozens of television series and films, including *The X-Files* (where he again played a senator), *Dead Man Walking*, *Training Day*, and *Tulse Luper Suitcases*.

Did You Notice?: When we see the list of people who have been to the DSR in the last 24 hours, Maryann Brandon is listed above Dixon's name — she was the director of "After Six." Listed below Dixon is Meighan Offield, one of the show's producers.

Nitpicks: All the passengers on Sark's plane are frozen, indicating that he opened a door and jumped from a high altitude. Why weren't the passengers all sucked out of the plane, like Sydney was in "Phase One"? Also, the loop on the tape of the bunker in Nogales is so obvious that there's no way Marshall wouldn't have noticed it instantly. Finally, the scene in the lab is just creepy. Sydney dodges the cameras as if they are actively attacking her, and with the scene sped up slightly, it creates a jarring effect that's just weird. She acts like the cameras are about to shoot bullets or something.

What Did He Say?: Dixon reveals to Sydney only that the Covenant wants a Rambaldi artifact from Project Black Hole and that they know Dixon is the one with the access codes to get to it.

Locations: Chateaudun, France; Nogales, Arizona; Zurich, Switzerland; Nevada

Music/Bands: Quarashi's "Stick 'em Up" (*Jinx*) plays when Sydney is driving the dune buggy in the desert.

3.17 The Frame

Original air date: March 28, 2004
Written by: Crystal Nix Hines
Directed by: Max Mayer
Guest cast: Djimon Hounsou (Kazari Bomani), Peggy Lipton (Olivia Reed), Raymond J. Barry (Senator George Reed), Stephen Spinella (Kishell), Dmitri Boudrine (Lubo), Dmitri Diatchenko (Vilmos), Herman G. Sinitzyn (Petr Berezovsky), Kevin Sutherland (Rotunda Techie), James Sharpe (Technician)

Jack reveals his suspicions about the CIA mole to Senator Reed; Sark forces Lauren to make a difficult decision; Sydney and Vaughn search for the keys to open the latest Rambaldi artifact.

This episode sees Sydney and Vaughn enduring a roller coaster of emotions as Vaughn realizes that he loves Sydney and can't be with Lauren anymore and Lauren finds a way to force him to stay with her. Interestingly, if we step back from the action for a moment and look at things from Vaughn's point of view, his decision is an even more difficult one. He has no idea that Lauren is the mole and is working for the Covenant. As far as he's concerned, his wife has never given him a reason to leave her — she's never been unfaithful to him; she's never lied to him; and when she did turn Sydney in to NSC, she made up for it by helping get Sydney out of Camp Williams. The only reason he can't be with Lauren is Sydney. He loves Sydney as much as she loves him, and he knows that by being with Lauren and loving Sydney, he's being unfair to his wife and he can't do that to her. Little does he know that she *has* been unfaithful to him and lies to him every minute of every day.

Vaughn tells Sydney that he's made his decision, and while she displays a moving, "Oh, I'm so sorry" face, we know that this is the best news she's gotten since her return. Of course she doesn't want Vaughn to go through the pain of a divorce, but at the same time, she knows as well as he does that they are meant to be together, that they are soulmates, and not just on the emotional level — when they're in the field, they work together brilliantly. But just as Sydney's main weakness is her empathy for others, Vaughn's weakness is for people who lose their fathers. Just as he went back to Alice when her father died, he changes his mind about leaving Lauren when he hears the news about the senator. He can't escape the impact his father's death had on him as a young boy, and he empathizes with anyone going through a similar circumstance. Sydney understands but is crushed, and once again she has lost the love of her life.

The best part of the episode is when Lauren goes in to face her father. In other series, fathers tend to get a bad rap — on sitcoms they're usually clueless (at best they

ALBERT L. ORTEGA

Sydney gets some good news from Vaughn, but her smile is fleeting when a new twist occurs.

offer a snippet of advice before turning back to the ballgame), and on shows like *Buffy the Vampire Slayer* they're downright evil. But on *Alias* — as we've seen with Jack, Dixon, Vaughn's stories of his father, and now Senator Reed — fathers are caring and compassionate, and they will do anything to help their children. Senator Reed is a good person, but when faced with the news that his daughter might have betrayed him and his country, he wants to help her rather than punish her, and he wants to take on some of the blame himself. Lauren usually seems as cold as ice in situations like this one, but when faced with her father's desire to sacrifice himself to save her in the face of what she's planning on doing to him, she falters. What happens next is a huge shock, proving that in Lauren's case, the apple doesn't fall far from the tree.

Highlight: Sydney and Vaughn's escape from the Russian embassy, which is evocative of Luke Skywalker and Princess Leia.

Interesting Fact: Michael Vartan joked about the way Sydney and Vaughn get out of their situation in the underwater cave. "How many times have our lives been on the line, and how many times have we had Marshall's jacket, which turned into a parachute?" Michael asks with a laugh. "We are used to being in, 'This is the end of the line,' situations, and then, 'Oh my god, there is a paperclip — we're saved.'"

Name That Guest Star: Peggy Lipton played Julie Barnes, one of the original members of *The Mod Squad*, which aired from 1968 to 1973. In recent years she is best known from her role on the television series *Twin Peaks* as Norma Jennings.

Did You Notice?: This episode refers to several previous ones. The man Vaughn goes to speak with about the Irina box is Kishell from "Snowman," whose face and throat had been mangled by the Snowman. Lauren has Vaughn's watch fixed, but we know from his story in "Passage, Part 1" that his father had told him that a heart could be set by that watch, and the watch stopped the day he met Sydney. That it doesn't work has more significance to him than having it work. Sark reminds Lauren that after Vaughn had fallen in love with Sydney, his ex-girlfriend's father died and he went back to her out of pity, which is from "The Abduction" (it's unclear, however, how Sark would have this information). On her mission in Gaborone, Sydney must get the consulate general to say certain phonemes so she can get past his security system, something Sydney and Jack did with Sloane in "Almost Thirty Years." The map is a crystal that looks remarkably like the Sol D'Oro from "A Broken Heart."

Nitpicks: Kishell tells Vaughn that Stalin sent teams of archaeologists around the world looking for a way to open the box, and two men found the map to the keys in a deep hole in the desert. They fought to the death, the desert winds covered their tracks, and they were "never to be heard from again." If this is true, how does anyone know the story happened? There wasn't a third person in the cave who could have passed on the anecdote, and the only two who knew the map had been found were dead. Also, why do Sydney and Vaughn let go of the oxygen tank rather than try to get closer to the surface with it? It appears to be still propelling them when they just let it go and swim the rest of the way up.

Oops: When Vaughn opens the box to see his newly working watch, it says it's 3:00. That is one early-morning dinner they're having. Also, Sydney says the keys are located off the coast of Okinawa, but the screen before the location scene says "Sea of Japan," which is a different area.

What Did He Say?: Kishell tells Vaughn that legend has it Stalin tried to unlock the Rambaldi Irina box (which he believed contained a bioweapon), but despite sending teams of archaeologists around the world looking for the means to open it, he was unsuccessful. The Covenant now has the box, and it has footage proving that Bomani has found the map to the key. The Covenant calls the bioweapon "The Passenger." Bomani used Omnifam trucks to get the map, and when the CIA followed the transponder on the trucks, it tracked Bomani to an embassy in Gaborone. The consulate general there has strong Covenant ties, and it is believed Bomani and Sark are there now trying to read the map. Sydney must retrieve the map and bring it back. When seen through a kaleidoscope, the "map" points to an oceanographic site where the keys are located.

Locations: Mexico City, Mexico; Gaborone, Botswana; Sea of Japan

Marshall's Gadgets: A choker that contains a microphone, and when Sydney gets the consulate general to say certain words, Marshall can reconstruct the phrases used to get past the security system.

Music/Bands: John Mayer's "Clarity" (*Heavier Things*) plays while Vaughn and Weiss are jogging; "Closing Time" by Bobby Summerfield and Matt McGuire plays in the background of the restaurant where Vaughn tells Lauren he wants to separate.

3.18   Unveiled

Original air date: April 11, 2004
Written by: Monica Breen and Alison Schapker
Directed by: Jack Bender
Guest cast: Djimon Hounsou (Kazari Bomani), Geno Silva (Diego Muchaca), Vincent Riotta (Dr. Viadro), Morgan Weisser (Cypher), Jordi Caballero (Technician)

The CIA discovers that the Covenant is searching for a woman, and it suspects she has something to do with The Passenger; Jack suggests to Vaughn that Lauren may be lying to him; Sloane tells Jack about The Trust.

Until now, the parallels between Vaughn and Lauren's marriage and that of Jack and Irina have been hinted at, but in "Unveiled," Jack finally confronts Vaughn and outlines how his suspicions about Lauren match with what Derevko had done to him 20 years earlier. It's an amazing scene and we feel sympathy for Vaughn, who throws Jack's warning back in his face and tells him he's wrong. We know he'll soon be eating those words (and despite what he says, the seed has been planted, and Vaughn's suspicions will cause him to look at Lauren in a new way). But while Jack might think he's doing the right thing, Vaughn has a point when he implies that Jack is looking to exact revenge on Lauren because he was unable to do so with Derevko. For 20 years Jack's been regretting that he didn't act when he could have, that he didn't pick up on the warning signs, and that he let himself and Sydney be duped by a woman he thought loved him. Is he trying to help Vaughn, or does he see Lauren's possible duplicity as a way to make up for the past?

Sloane is now on death row and Dixon has informed him that his execution date has been set. While this may be a moment Sydney's been waiting for, Sloane is actually innocent of the charges laid against him, and the Covenant is framing him for its own dirty work. Sloane turns to the one person he thinks he can trust (despite what happened in "Crossings") and tells Jack to find proof of his innocence. However, when Dixon has a bit of news about Sloane's past that he passes on to Jack, Jack loses all sympathy for this "friend" of his, and his jealousy and desire for revenge take over once again. It's fitting that the organization Sloane claims to have belonged to is called The Trust — Sloane trusts that Jack will help him, and Jack refuses to do so because Sloane had betrayed his trust. Sloane is a walking reminder of Derevko's treachery, as is Lauren, and neither one will be getting Jack's sympathy any time soon. It's interesting that though Jack condemns anyone who reminds him of Irina and lives with the specter of his phony marriage hanging over him every day, he still keeps in touch with Derevko and tells her he misses her.

Meanwhile, the Rambaldi mystery deepens. The Irina box contains the di Regno heart (from "Countdown"), which powers *Il Dire* — all this time the Covenant has simply been reconstructing the device that Sloane had already put together in "The Telling." The Passenger is clearly a person, and Jack thinks it might be Irina. There are legions of people who have vowed to protect her, and when Sydney encounters one of them, he tries to kill her, shouting that she is destined to hurt the thing he's trying to protect. Who is The Passenger? And why would Sydney want to hurt her?

The ending of this episode fulfills Jack's own little prophecy about Lauren, and whether he likes it or not, Vaughn will have to face up to who his wife really is.

Highlight: Vaughn in Goth makeup.

Nitpicks: The screechy *Psycho*-like violins that accompany Lauren whenever she's being conniving are obviously being used as her recurring musical motif, but they've become really annoying. Also, when the doctor runs upstairs to what appears to be a panic room, Lauren steps in the way of the door as it's closing and it opens again. If it's a panic room that keeps out intruders, the door would slam shut regardless of what is in the way; it wouldn't open like an elevator door — what kind of security does that offer? Finally, how did Sark and Bomani put together *Il Dire* when we saw in "Taken" that most of the artifacts needed to build the machine are sitting at DSR?

What Did He Say?: Twelve hours previous, a cyberterrorist attack was launched, and servers in Europe and Asia were hit with a worm that is taking out hospital databases. The hacker is an online celebrity known as "Cypher," who is located in Berlin. Sydney and Vaughn need to go meet with him. When Sydney and Vaughn recover a partial program, Marshall determines that the Covenant is looking for an exact DNA match on a woman, and the organization has found 10, which means the woman must be using different identities. It's been targeting hospital databases looking for her whereabouts, and the databases are losing records, which is an unfortunate side effect of the worm, not its intent. Jack's contact for finding out more about The Trust mentions something called "Project Centigrade."

Locations: Florence, Italy; Berlin, Germany; Milan, Italy

Marshall's Gadgets: "Freshy-fresh" glasses that contain an electronic sniffer that seeks out Cypher, hacks into a computer, and sends him a message.

Music/Bands: Laibach's "Tanz Mit Laibach" (*Wat*) plays in the club in Berlin.

3.19 Hourglass

Original air date: April 18, 2004
Written by: Josh Appelbaum and André Nemec
Directed by: Ken Olin
Guest cast: Peggy Lipton (Olivia Reed), Glenn Morshower (Agent Marlon Bell), David Carradine (Conrad), Patricia Wettig (Dr. Judy Barnett), James D. Bridges (DOJ Agent), Rico McClinton (Doorguy)

Sydney discovers that The Passenger is her sister and there's a device that will lead Syd to her, but the device will only reveal The Passenger's whereabouts to her father.

"Hourglass" is one of those episodes that rewards the fans who don't read spoilers. If you had no idea how this episode was going to end, the lead-up to its conclusion likely left you breathless.

Many secrets are revealed in this episode: Sydney discovers that she has a sister;

ALBERT L. ORTEGA

Conrad (played by David Carradine) has a shocking revelation for Sydney, but he's unable to give her any details.

that Sloane is her sister's father; and, by extension, that Irina had been unfaithful to Jack while they were married (like *that* would come as a shock). This news just adds to Sydney's hatred of Sloane, and we get a parallel scene to one in "Unveiled." Just as Jack had walked in slow motion to Sloane's cell to confront him about the affair with his wife, now Sydney makes the same walk and shows a similar disdain toward him. Knowing what she does puts her relationship with Sloane in a different light, and she must realize that he's thought she was his daughter for a long time.

Vaughn is going through a range of emotions that are probably similar to what Jack felt when he discovered the truth about his marriage so long ago. In order to discover the Covenant's endgame, Jack insists that Vaughn pretend nothing has happened and turn the tables on Lauren — spy on her the same way she's been spying on him. Vaughn is a man of principles and values, and the thought that he's sleeping with someone who has been lying to him the entire time sickens him, and he just wants to kill Lauren. But he knows that if he's able to pull off the ruse and convince her that everything is fine, he might end up hurting her more by taking out the Covenant along with her. In the subsequent scenes the tension is palpable as Vaughn attempts to cloak his rage and play the part of the loving husband. As he sneaks through his mother-in-law's house, in much the same way Lauren must have sneaked through their apartment, the suspense is almost unbearable, but in the end he finds a way out of the situation, in exactly the same way Lauren must have done a million times. He appeals to her sense of nostalgia and talks about their wedding day. It's a brilliant tactic, and it shows that he's gone over their phony marriage in his head and has probably picked up a few pointers along the way.

Jack and Sydney butt heads when she discovers that he has evidence to exonerate Sloane and isn't using it. While she would like nothing better than to see Sloane dead, she has discovered that a Rambaldi device exists that will reveal The Passenger's location, but only to The Passenger's father, who is Sloane. The device's form, an hourglass, is important, because as Sydney rushes to retrieve it, she is in a race against time: she must return with the device before Sloane is executed. But unfortunately, it's too late. With several witnesses, Sloane is led into the chamber to receive death by lethal injection (also an apt form of punishment, considering what happens in "Blood Ties" and "Legacy"), and with astonishment, we watch as one of the main characters in the series is killed before our eyes. The look on Sydney's face when she returns speaks volumes, and she realizes that her only chance to find her sister is gone.

But we should never underestimate Jack. Earlier in the episode he goes to visit Sloane in his cell, almost taunting him with the news that he won't help him escape the execution. As they reminisce over a glass of wine, Jack utters the words that he's waited years to say: "What you have done to my daughter is nothing compared with what I will do when I find yours." With those words, Sloane goes to his death a haunted man, knowing that his daughter might be found some day, but when she is, she'll wish she hadn't been. Is Jack capable of such cruelty? Or is he able to say those words only because he knows they'll never come true? The truth is revealed at the end of the episode.

Highlight: Marshall acting jittery and nervous around Lauren, and her taking his behavior as perfectly normal.

Did You Notice?: Jack fakes Sloane's death in exactly the same way Sloane had faked Emily's. Also, Dixon tells Sloane that he prays Sloane's soul will find peace in the next life, a subtle suggestion that in Sloane's next life (which begins at the end of the episode) he'll find Rambaldi's endgame, which so far has only been revealed to him in the word *peace*.

Nitpicks: How did Sydney and Vaughn think they could "sneak" up on a convoy in the middle of the desert and *not* be seen in the rearview mirror? And for someone who keeps insisting she always acts professionally, Dr. Barnett has shown none of that professionalism in her dealings with Sloane. His revelation of the affair with Irina happened when they were on a date, not during a session, and she promised him everything he would tell her would be kept strictly confidential. Yet the notes she hands off to Dixon contain the very information she promised to suppress, and they claim that he told her his secret in a "session." Also, why is Sloane in chains when Dixon visits him but walking about freely when Jack shows up?

Oops: Sydney's bangs are gelled back in the briefing, and moments later, they are down when she's in Marshall's office for the op tech briefing. Also, Vaughn scans the Rambaldi pages horizontally in Olivia's study, but they come through vertically on Marshall's computer.

What Did He Say?: Dixon tells the agents that the Covenant has kidnapped someone (Conrad) who will lead them to The Passenger and they must intercept the convoy. Later, Weiss and Marshall explain that the Rambaldi manuscript, called *The Restoration*, reveals information about The Passenger and that the Covenant has the code, but the CIA has obtained the key through Project Black Hole. Vaughn must retrieve the manuscript from Olivia Reed's house, where it is being kept. The manuscript tells of another Rambaldi artifact, an hourglass that will reveal the whereabouts of The Passenger, but only to her father. The hourglass is owned by someone in the Yakuza, and it's in the basement of his art gallery.

Locations: Nepal; Thar Desert, India

Marshall's Gadgets: A sensor that Vaughn puts under a lightbulb in a lamp to tap into the power grid, which gives Marshall access to all the electricity-driven items in the house. Later, Sydney places a white strip on a door lock that sends a wireless signal to Marshall and allows him to open it.

Music/Bands: The Deftones' "Change (in the House of Flies)" (*White* Pony) plays as Sydney retrieves the hourglass and Sloane is executed.

3.20   Blood Ties

Original air date: April 25, 2004
Teleplay by: J.R. Orci
Story by: Monica Breen and Alison Schapker
Directed by: Jack Bender
Guest cast: Richard Roundtree (Brill), Mia Maestro (Nadia Santos), Glenn Morshower (Agent Marlon Bell), Erik Jensen (Phillip Terrance), Yun Choi (Carl)

Vaughn learns why his father died; Sydney finds The Passenger.

"Blood Ties" is about the bonds of family, whether it's Sloane and his daughter, Vaughn and his father, Sydney and her sister, or Lauren and her husband.

Vaughn discovers that his father was a Rambaldi follower, and at first he refuses to believe the source because to this point all Rambaldi followers seem to have evil designs. Was Vaughn's father as power hungry as the others? Was he protecting The Passenger for Derevko or for Sloane or because he hoped to reap the rewards of what she would reveal? Or was he actually shielding the little girl from the harm that might come to her at the hands of the Rambaldi zealots? Let's hope season 4 brings with it more insight into Vaughn's father and what he was doing during his final days.

Right after Vaughn learns this new information, he is kidnapped by Sark and faces

All in the Family

It seems like no one on this series works alone — there's always a parent or a sibling who's also in the business, even if they're not on the same side.

Sydney — She's a CIA agent; her father works for the CIA and was a double agent working against SD-6; her mother is KGB; and her sister works in Argentine Intelligence.

Vaughn — His father was CIA.

Sloane — He was head of the terrorist cell SD-6 and is now working independently. His daughter works in Argentine Intelligence and his wife briefly worked with the CIA, but only as an informant.

Sark — He is a Rambaldi follower who is bankrolling the Covenant and is co-head of the North American cell. His father was a Russian diplomat who was secretly working for the CIA, giving intel to Will.

Lauren — She works for the Covenant and is now co-head of the North American cell. Her father is a senator, and her mother also works for the Covenant.

Lauren for the first time since she found out that he knew she is Covenant. She seems to be concerned for his well-being, but her actions are calculated. Lauren sees a difference between Vaughn and her father, which is why she was sympathetic to one and not the other. Vaughn wants to condemn her for what she did, while her father was willing to forgive her and to try to help her. Both reactions have dictated the way she has treated their bearers.

Sydney finally comes face-to-face with her sister. She'd reassured Jack ahead of time that no matter what, she wouldn't become emotionally connected to her sister, but Jack knows what Sydney is like. Despite everything Derevko has done to both Syd and Jack, Sydney wanted a loving mother so much that during the course of season 2 she started to believe that Derevko really did care for her, and she found forgiveness

CHRISTINA RADISH

Jack worries that Sydney might become emotionally attached to Nadia, the way she did Irina.

for what Derevko had done. Now, when she finds her sister in a vulnerable state, she is overwhelmed with emotion, and the viewer can see the bond already forming between her and Nadia. The casting of Mia Maestro as Sydney's sister is brilliant — she looks a little like Jennifer Garner, a *lot* like Lena Olin, and when she cries, she has the same vein pop up on her forehead that Garner develops when she's playing an emotional scene. When Sydney later tells Jack that she's always wondered what it would be like to have a sibling, he knows that she's already attached to Nadia despite her protestations to the contrary.

Sloane (yes, he's still here) has been searching for his daughter for two years. He admitted to Jack in the previous episode that Omnifam might not be the big-hearted organization that he let on it was. In fact, he started up this charitable organization that does research into cancer and child poverty in order to get access to millions of patient records with the hope of finding his daughter. Now he expresses concern to both Jack and Sydney that if the Covenant finds The Passenger before he does, she'll be exposed to a green elixir that will force her to write out the secret to Rambaldi's endgame, and he can't bear to have that happen to her. Sloane seems to have the same concern for his daughter that he had for Emily, and as he strokes Nadia's hair in the CIA safehouse, we wonder if maybe Nadia could be his salvation. Unfortunately, moments later we realize that Sloane might be new to this whole father thing, but he's been a Rambaldi follower for 30 years. Old habits die hard.

Highlight: Sydney's hilarious pout to get into the Smithsonian vault.

Name That Guest Star: Argentinean-born Mia Maestro is best known to North American audiences from her work in *Frida*, *The Motorcycle Diaries*, and HBO's *For Love or Country: The Arturo Sandoval Story*.

Did You Notice?: When Brill and Vaughn are talking about The Passenger, there's a sign in the background that says, "This is not a passenger elevator." Also, when Jack tells Sydney that he did a DNA test to make sure he was her father, he says, "Our relationship is clear" but doesn't actually say he's her father. Finally, the way Sloane walks by Agent Bell is similar to the way Emily walked by Sloane and into the church in "Salvation."

Nitpicks: Why didn't Sloane get the retinal scans *before* Sydney went into the vault? She wasted valuable time just standing there waiting for Jack to uplink the scans when he could have scanned them, uplinked them, and then had her go into the Smithsonian to retrieve them. She could have taken the box and slipped out of the museum before the guy who was assisting her even noticed she was gone. The hourglass smash was a little too sci-fi — it looked like Flubber was going to emerge from the green goop. And until now, Marshall's stall tactics and stuttering have been amusing, but he's really annoying when he tries to go through each scene on the security cameras rather than cut to the chase and possibly save Vaughn's life. Finally, when Sark and Lauren get the call from Sloane informing them of where Nadia is, why aren't they completely shocked? The last they'd heard, Sloane was dead and Lauren had watched him die.

Oops: When Weiss finds Vaughn, Vaughn's face seems to be fine, yet in the hospital, there are cuts all around Vaughn's mouth and cheeks.

What Did He Say?: Vaughn, Sydney, and Sloane discuss the meaning of the hourglass. When Sloane smashes it, it creates a battery used to power a machine. Sydney needs to break into a vault in the Smithsonian where The Trust has created a five-way retinal scan security system, meaning it takes a retinal scan from each of them in order to open the vault. Inside the vault is the machine that the battery powers, and when it pumps out the brainwaves of a specific person, Sloane explains that there is a defense satellite network that reads brainwaves and can find out where that person is.

Locations: Washington, D.C.; Chechnya, Russia

3.21   Legacy

Original air date: May 2, 2004
Written by: Jesse Alexander
Directed by: Lawrence Trilling
Guest cast: Vivica A. Fox (Toni Cummings), Isabella Rossellini (Katya Derevko), Mia Maestro (Nadia Santos), Ric Young (Jong Lee), Mikhail Tank (Russian Guard), Ismail Abou-El-Kanater (Contact), Mio Dzakula (Groggy Russian Guard), Britney Espinoza (Young Nadia)

Toni Cummings (played by Vivica A. Fox) is one of the world's best security criminals — and is therefore an invaluable asset to the CIA.

Sloane subjects Nadia to the automatic writing that is her destiny; Jack works with Katya to try to find Nadia; Vaughn is furious that Lauren is still on the loose.

"Legacy" is one of the best episodes of the year and brings to a head everything that we've seen developing all season while bringing back a few old faces.

The main plot concerns Nadia and Sloane. He has tied her to a chair and is subjecting her to massive doses of the elixir that will force her to uncover Rambaldi's ultimate goal. The scenes of Nadia writing on the paper while Sloane pieces together a giant Rambaldi symbol on the wall are amazing. Sloane believes with all his heart that he is doing the right thing — so much so that he compares what he's doing to Nadia to the sacrifice Abraham was willing to make for God. Rambaldi is as much a religion to Sloane as Christianity or Judaism is to others, and he believes in sacrificing the one person who means the most to him for the greater good. Nadia, on the other hand, gives Sloane a brief insight into her childhood, and her story is sad and poignant, perhaps sparking the way Sloane acts later in the episode.

Vaughn is going through his own personal hell. As the reality of what Lauren did to him sets in, he becomes angrier and angrier, and his feelings of revenge deepen. He's livid that the CIA has continued to let Lauren go free, and where Dixon and Sydney are focused on finding Nadia, he believes the more important thing is to find Lauren. When he and Sydney face Jong Lee — the man who tortured Sydney, Will, and Marshall — Vaughn has a little torture scheme of his own up his sleeve, and Sydney is horrified by the man Vaughn is becoming. Jack senses Vaughn's vulnerability and swoops in to take advantage of it, but what he suggests Vaughn should do could destroy the man that Sydney has come to love.

Throughout season 3 the focus of the show has moved away from Sydney and onto other characters. We've watched Jack struggle with his ongoing feelings for Derevko; Sloane open up to Barnett and find his daughter; and Vaughn grapple with his feelings for Sydney and his loyalty to his wife only to find out that his wife has betrayed him. For the duration, despite still being the main character of every episode, Sydney has been put in a reactionary position rather than an instigating one. While she has admitted to her feelings for Vaughn, she's powerless to do anything about them because he's married, and now that he's realized Lauren has deceived him, she's watching him unravel and feels helpless to stop him from destroying himself. Although she became Sloane's handler earlier in the season, we only saw her acting as such once, and since then he's been out of her control. By the end of this episode, Vaughn will have turned his back on her when she needs him in the field, and he will have put his hatred for Lauren above his love of Sydney. Even Nadia, whom Sydney has vowed to protect, tells Sydney that she believes Sloane was trying to protect her and it will be useless for Sydney to try to convince her otherwise. Sydney's pleas to Jack fall on deaf ears, Vaughn ignores her offer to help save him from himself, and Nadia seems to believe Sloane wants what's best for her. No wonder Sydney feels completely helpless.

Highlight: The two "come on" scenes: Katya telling Jack she finds him sexy, to which he responds with nary a bat of an eyelash, and Toni saying to Marshall "I want you," stopping him dead in his tracks.

Interesting Fact: Jennifer Garner ended up with a nasty cold after filming the scenes coming out of the water in Cuba (which was actually the Pacific Ocean on a very chilly day).

Did You Notice?: Jack must have told Sydney about Katya's helping him in North Korea, because Sydney calls her "Katya" and Jack had called her by her full birth name, which was the only one he knew from Derevko's files.

Nitpicks: In "After Six" we see Sloane heat up the elixir on a spoon as if it were heroin, but here he draws it directly from the bottle. In the briefing, Sydney explains that Sloane has taken Nadia, yet no one seems to be shocked that Sloane is still alive. You'd think Jack would have to face severe repercussions for faking the death of an enemy of the state and then letting him free, especially when Dixon relished Sloane's death as much as he did. Also, Katya's story about Nadia's birth seems to throw everything we know into chaos and doesn't make much sense in the show's chronology. She says that Irina left the U.S. by faking her death and returned to Russia, where she gave birth to Nadia. First of all, if this were the case, how could Sloane have ever thought Sydney was his daughter if Sydney was about six at the time of his affair with Derevko?

Second, Brill said that Irina had William Vaughn killed because he kidnapped The Passenger when she was a little girl, presumably aged five or six. Yet in the first season we found out that Irina killed William Vaughn before she disappeared (he died when Vaughn was eight years old, which would have been 1976, and she "died" in 1981), and if Nadia wasn't taken until about 1986, then he couldn't possibly have kidnapped her if he'd already been dead for almost 10 years.

Oops: Toni Cummings complains that she can't get lipstick in prison, yet she has a fancy manicure. Also, Lauren hooks up Nadia to the I.V., and she, Sark, and Sloane are all standing on the side of the chair closest to the door. When Sydney and Vaughn come in seconds later, Lauren is suddenly standing on Nadia's other side, facing the door.

What Did He Say?: The CIA believes Sloane boarded a plane with Nadia in Grozny, but they don't know where he took her. Nadia was recruited by Argentine Intelligence six years ago, and Chechnya was her first field assignment. She grew up in an orphanage in Buenos Aires, and Sydney believes that Sloane will kill her to find the answer to the Rambaldi puzzle. When Sydney and Vaughn travel to Novgorod to try to recover some of the elixir, they find a video of a young Nadia being subjected to the writing, and Jong Lee, until now known as Suit & Glasses, is the scientist heading up the experiment. He's in Cuba and Sydney and Vaughn need to find him. Lee tells them that the coordinates Nadia was writing when she was a child reveal the location of Rambaldi. Marshall explains that the elixir works on the memory and causes a person to do things from stored memory. Nadia is able to write out Rambaldi's formula because somehow she already knows his endgame, but it's been stored deep in her memory and the elixir is bringing it out.

Locations: Kyoto, Japan; Novgorod, Russia; St. Petersburg, Russia; Cienfuegos, Cuba

Music/Bands: Osnel Odit Bavastro's "Curu Curu" plays on the radio when the two men are playing cards on the beach in Cuba and Sydney runs up to them.

3.22   Resurrection

Original air date: May 23, 2004
Written by: Jeff Pinkner
Directed by: Ken Olin
Guest cast: Isabella Rossellini (Katya Derevko), Mia Maestro (Nadia Santos), Cotter Smith (Agent Hank Foster), Ed Brigadier (Reynard Kaufman), Burt Bulos (Safe House Agent), Jordi Caballero (The Plumber), Cosimo Canale (Covenant Foreman), Kendall

Clement (Hospital Guard #1), Rolando De La Maza (ER Director), Eddie Diaz (Hospital Guard #2), Michael Guarnera (Agent), Andrea Lwin (EMT)

Vaughn finally faces Lauren; Sydney discovers the location of the most important Rambaldi artifact and travels there. In the final moments of the episode, Sydney makes a horrible discovery.

If there's one thing *Alias* writers do better than any other team of television writers, it's developing nail-biting season finales that resolve some of the plotlines of the season while creating a slew of questions for viewers to ponder while they await the next season. "Resurrection" is no exception.

Vaughn has taken Jack's advice, and when he comes face-to-face with Lauren, we see a side of Vaughn that doesn't seem possible. He's so full of

Jennifer Garner might be smiling in this photo, but we wonder if Sydney will ever find true happiness.

anger that he can barely speak, and his emotions have been pushed to the breaking point. He's prepared to torture Lauren to within an inch of her life but says that he'll spare her because he loves Sydney (however, while Sydney said she didn't want him to go to a dark place by killing Lauren, she probably wouldn't look too kindly on him pouring hydrochloric acid on her, either). Michael Vartan is amazing in this scene, playing the opposite of the cool, calm person we're used to. When Sydney realizes what Vaughn is about to do, she begs him to rethink things, but he doesn't listen.

Jack isn't willing to listen to her, either. Jack's actions toward Vaughn are questionable, as he seems to take advantage of Vaughn when Vaughn is most vulnerable. As mentioned earlier, he is using Vaughn to make up for the actions he didn't take years earlier (and Sydney calls him on it in this episode), hoping to live vicariously through him. Sydney asked a very important question in the previous episode, one that may take years to answer: Will Vaughn have to live with Lauren's betrayal the way Jack did? Will it eat him up in the same way? Jack seems to think that if Vaughn gets his revenge it will be healthier for him, but Sydney knows the kind of man Vaughn is and that he'll hate himself if he takes things too far.

Throughout this complex and exhilarating episode, people switch sides, revelations come when we least expect them to, and true loyalties are shown. Katya proves that deceit is inherent to the Derevko name; Sloane urges Nadia to join him in his search for the final Rambaldi artifact; Lauren admits to Sydney that she knows a secret Sydney doesn't and that nothing in Sydney's life has happened by chance; and the end of the episode provides a shocker that casts Jack in a whole new light.

As the strong third season draws to a close, it's clear the writers still have reams of stories to write and countless storylines to pursue. The search for Rambaldi has been developing at a gradual pace that keeps us interested and aware of past episodes. We've seen so many twists and turns of loyalty that we expect people to become turncoats, and so far the only true bond that has been unwavering is the one between Sydney and Vaughn. As we await the fourth season, the writers have created myriad questions for us to turn over, many of which will no doubt be answered in the season premiere:

- Will Sydney be able to convince the CIA she didn't blow up the rotunda, that it was Lauren in disguise?
- What is Project 47? Is Sydney herself an experiment of some kind? Has Jack been lying to her this whole time? Is he, in fact, a Rambaldi follower?
- Is Marshall going to be OK?
- How did Lauren know about vault number 1062 in Wittenberg?
- What is the Sphere of Life? Can Rambaldi be brought back to life somehow? If he can, who will play him in the series?
- Will Nadia become Sydney's nemesis?
- Does Sydney have any other siblings we don't know about? Sark, maybe?
- What is Katya's interest in all this?
- Is Sydney really the Chosen One, or is her mother?
- Will Irina Derevko ever return in person?

The only thing we know for sure is that the answers to these questions will be what we least expect, creating an even deeper spiral of complexity as we continue to travel down the rabbit hole with Sydney.

Highlight: OK, we're all worried about how Vaughn's gone off the deep end, yadda yadda, but him whacking Lauren with a crowbar and saying, "Hi honey" is a brilliant moment.

Interesting Fact: J.J. Abrams has always written the season premieres and season finales of *Alias*; this episode marks the first time someone else has written one.

Did You Notice?: Nadia's altering the sequence and sending both the CIA and

Covenant to the wrong place is like *Raiders of the Lost Ark*, when they are digging in the wrong spot.

Nitpicks: Sloane says there are guards in Nadia's safehouse, and we see them by the end of the episode shouting that they're ordering Chinese food. When Sydney drops by the safehouse to deliver a sandwich to Nadia, which she tells Hank Foster, why doesn't he just call the guards to confirm her story? He tells her bluntly that she needs an alibi, but she'd have several at the safehouse. Also, the disguises that Sydney and Lauren both wear are completely over the top. Sydney is probably six inches taller than Lauren (watch when Lauren comes into the jail cell to talk to Sark: her face is just above one of the horizontal bars, yet when the mask is removed Sydney's head is much further above it), their jaw structures are completely different, and it's just far too implausible — CIA issue or not. And if Sydney pulled a clip out of a gun, why wouldn't Katya notice that it was a lot lighter when Sydney handed it back to her?

Oops: Vaughn seems to get to Palermo in a couple of hours, which would have been impossible, and with him escaping the hospital in the way he does, the chances of him being able to board a plane would have been slim.

What Did He Say?: The technician that Lauren goes to see says he's found the latitude and longitude of the final Rambaldi artifact, and Sydney goes to Sark to get the coordinates from him so she can travel there and get the artifact before the Covenant does. Unfortunately, Nadia was able to alter the code enough to send them all to the wrong place.

Locations: Palermo, Italy; Wittenberg [actually spelled Wittenburg], Germany

The Story So Far . . .

Still confused? A lot has happened on *Alias*, and since each episode might seem to get a little bogged down in the mission of the week, here's a quick primer that focuses on the two major storylines that have been carried through the seasons: Sydney and Rambaldi.

Sydney

Sydney Anne Bristow was born in 1975 to Jack and Laura Bristow. Jack was a CIA agent. Laura died in 1981 in a car accident. Shortly afterward, Jack began instructing Sydney using Project Christmas, a program designed to train small children how to speak various languages, fight, assemble weaponry, and become agents. He then wiped her memory clean, but she was fated to become an agent because of her stored knowledge.

In 1994 Sydney was recruited to work for SD-6, a covert section of the CIA. In 2001 she discovered not only that SD-6 wasn't a CIA division, but that it was a cell of The Alliance, a terrorist network. SD stands for *Section Disparu*, or "The Section That Does Not Exist." She became a double agent for the CIA and found out her father was one as well. She also discovered the truth about her mother: her real name is Irina Derevko, she was an agent for the KGB, and she deceived Sydney's father by stealing secrets from the CIA while she was married to him (she's also a Rambaldi follower). She faked her death when Sydney was six years old and reappeared in Sydney's life in 2002. Irina killed William Vaughn, the father of Sydney's CIA handler (and lover), Michael Vaughn.

Sydney's likeness appears on page 47 of the Rambaldi journal (see below) and the Rambaldi followers believe that she is the Chosen One, someone who will bring forth Rambaldi's ultimate design. In early 2003, Sydney's work helped the CIA take down SD-6 and the other Alliance cells, rendering the group useless. Only afterward did she discover that Arvin Sloane, the head of SD-6, had known for a long time that she was acting as a double agent and had been feeding her information to help her bring down SD-6 so he could work independently toward his endgame: finding out the truth about Milo Rambaldi's creations.

In 2003 Sydney discovered that her friend Francie had been killed and replaced with an exact double, Allison Doren. Doren fought Sydney, but Sydney shot her. Sydney's death was faked, she was kidnapped by the Covenant (made up of Rambaldi worshipers), and brainwashed into believing she was Julia Thorne. She killed a man to prove she believed her new life was real, but nine months after being kidnapped, she called the director of the CIA and told him what had happened. He insisted that she stay in the Covenant and act as a double agent, which she did. She was ordered to kill Andrian Lazarey, a Russian diplomat, but she informed him of the plan ahead of time and together, they faked his death. The Covenant had taken some of her eggs in order to fertilize them with the DNA of Rambaldi, and to prevent that from happening, she and Lazarey found the DNA in a cube, took it, and hid it in Graz, Austria. She then voluntarily had her memory wiped, and woke up in Hong Kong with absolutely no recollection of the previous two years.

Sydney spent much of 2005 and 2006 (if we push the calendar year ahead by two years) trying to piece together what had happened, and she eventually discovered what had transpired. She found out that Sloane had had an affair with her mother and the result was Nadia, a sister she never knew she had. Irina had gone back to Russia after faking her death and gave birth to Nadia, but Nadia was soon kidnapped, and Irina has been searching for her ever since. Nadia is believed to be The Passenger, the person who will lead Rambaldi's followers to his endgame. After rescuing Nadia from Sloane's clutches, Sydney finds documents that reveal the existence of Project SAB 47; she herself is the experiment's subject, and the project initiation date is the same as the day she was born. It appears her entire life has been an experiment of some kind, and her father, Jack Bristow (also the project manager), has a lot of explaining to do.

Rambaldi

Milo Rambaldi (1444–1496), a genius who lived in the 15th century, was an artist and an inventor. He created devices that were far ahead of their time, including a gadget similar to a transistor radio and plans for an instrument resembling a cell phone. Today Rambaldi's followers belong to the Magnific Order of Rambaldi, and they bear the <o> symbol on their hands. The group is entrusted with safeguarding Rambaldi's creations, but several terrorist organizations have infiltrated and tarnished the order. Arvin Sloane became a Rambaldi worshiper sometime in the 1970s, and hence many of Sydney's assignments while at SD-6 involved her retrieving Rambaldi devices. The one most significant in relation to Sydney is the Rambaldi journal, which has a picture of a woman who looks remarkably like her on page 47. The journal says this woman is the Chosen One and will possess "unseen marks" and "render the greatest power unto utter desolation."

After finding several Rambaldi artifacts (one leads to the next, which leads to the next), Sloane put together a machine called *Il Dire*, or "The Telling," which was supposed to reveal Rambaldi's meaning. It simply gave him one word — "Peace" — but he found an ancient Greek derivation of that word that means "irine," or "Irina." Rambaldi wrote a second manuscript, *The Restoration*, which Conrad keeps in his monastery in Nepal. Conrad was the one who sent Sloane on a quest 30 years earlier, and in 2003 he revealed to Sloane that Sloane has a daughter, who is known as The Passenger in Rambaldi's works. *The Restoration* is a notebook that explains how to find The Passenger and what she will do. When Sloane recovered his daughter, Nadia, he began injecting a green elixir into her arm (the formula for which is in *The Restoration*), and she performed automatic writing from a stored memory that revealed the coordinates of the Sphere of Life.

Rambaldi's main focus was on finding immortality — Sydney found a 500-year-old flower that lived without any food or light. Sloane believes that if he can find Rambaldi's endgame, he'll find the secret to immortality and save the life of his wife, Emily. Rambaldi's own DNA and tissue was recovered in season 3, and the Covenant tried to fertilize Sydney's eggs with it to bring forth Rambaldi's legacy. At the end of season 3, Sloane and Nadia set out to find the Sphere of Life, what we're told is Rambaldi himself. Sydney was also warned that in Rambaldi's prophecy, he says the Chosen One shall fight The Passenger, and neither one will survive.

Rambaldi 101

Parity
The SD-6 agents find out who Rambaldi was, and they need to find two **pages of machine code**. SD-6 has one; Sydney must retrieve the second, which is **in a box**.①
She recovers the box, but SD-6 can't open it.

A Broken Heart
Anna has the key and Sydney has the box, so they open it together and the machine code is revealed. The code discloses **coordinates** for a church, in which the **Sol D'Oro** ② is hidden. Sydney retrieves it.

Reckoning
SD-6 finds birthday cards with little songs in them, and within the songs are codes that point to the whereabouts of FTL, a criminal organization. However, it also finds within the codes the possible position of a Rambaldi artifact in Tunisia.③

Time Will Tell
Syd retrieves a **clock** from Oxford University④ that was built by Donato, a clock-maker used by Rambaldi (who is still alive, apparently, lending credence to what Sloane later reveals about Rambaldi's work). The clock, when set to a certain time and with the **Sol D'Oro** inserted into it, reveals a star chart for a particular place and date, and Syd travels to that place to get the next puzzle piece.

Mea Culpa
The coordinates from the clock reveal the location of **Rambaldi's journal**,⑤ which is stolen by K-Directorate.

The Box, Part II
McKenas Cole tries to steal a **vial of liquid**⑥ from SD-6's vault, and the CIA gets it instead.

The Coup
Sark steals a Rambaldi artifact from FTL⑦ and meets with K-Directorate to discuss sharing Rambaldi info.

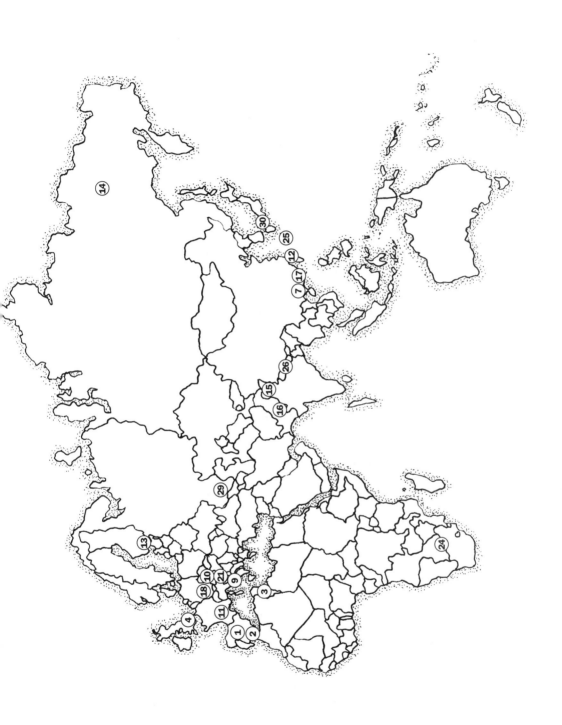

Page 47

Syd retrieves **Rambaldi's journal** ⑧ and the CIA uses the **vial of liquid** on the empty **page 47**, discovering what appears to be a portrait of Sydney.

The Prophecy

Sydney and Vaughn break into the Vatican and find a **portrait of Pope Alexander VI** ⑨ that Rambaldi painted, and in the frame they discover the key code that explains how to read page 47.

Masquerade

Khasinau has two computers ⑩ that are capable of taking the present Rambaldi artifacts, putting them together, and filling in the pieces to figure out what the big picture is.

Rendezvous

Khasinau has a **Rambaldi document** ⑪ that is blank and needs the vial of liquid to reveal what is on the page. Sydney steals it for the CIA.

Almost Thirty Years

Syd steals the page back from the CIA and uncovers **The Circumference,** ⑫ the object she found in the season-1 opener, which is a type of battery. She has to hand over the page to Sark in exchange for Will.

Cipher

Syd steals a **camera** ⑬ in previous episode that turns out to be a prototype for one that will be used in a satellite. The satellite detects the Rambaldi sign in the Siberian snow, which points to the location of a **music box.** ⑭

Dead Drop

The song that the music box played contains the equation for Rambaldi's formula for **zero-point energy**.

Passage, Part 2

In Part 1, six nuclear warheads were stolen and taken to Kashmir. ⑮ In Part 2, Jack discovers one of them contains Rambaldi's **proof of endless life**. Inside the core is a **flower** that was part of Rambaldi's research into **self-sustaining cell regeneration**, and Vaughn tells Sydney the flower is 400–600 years old.

A Free Agent

Sloane kidnaps Neil Caplan, a mathematician from California, and forces him to use the **Rambaldi journal** and figure out a way to piece the Rambaldi artifacts together to create something, which we later discover is a 16th-century **neutron bomb**.

Firebomb

Sloane meets with and tries to convince Ahmad Kabir to work with him, and he comments on a Buddhist statue in Kabir's home. Out of gratitude for Sloane's work, Kabir gives him the statue. Sloane breaks it and finds a **Rambaldi document** inside. ⑯

A Dark Turn
Jack and Derevko steal a **notebook** (17) that belonged to Rambaldi that contains his notes on his **study of the human heart**.

Truth Takes Time
Sark and Derevko steal a disk (18) that has data containing the DNA of millions of citizens on it, which they will use in a Rambaldi device that Sloane is building.

Countdown
Marshall has a copy of the Rambaldi notebook from "A Dark Turn," and he discovers on the corner of each page a DNA string matching that of Proteo di Regno, a man living in Italy. He is dead by the time Syd and Dixon get to him, but they discover that he's been living without his **heart**, which is later discovered to be a device of some sort that they find in a shipyard. (19)

The Telling
Sloane takes all the components that have been collected so far and constructs *Il Dire*, (20) which means "The Telling."

The Nemesis
Allison Doren reveals that in **Rambaldi's journal** there was a formula for a medication that helped her stay alive after the attack in "The Telling."

Remnants
Sydney recovers a cube in Graz, Austria, that contains **human tissue** (21) and is marked "Milo Rambaldi."

Full Disclosure
We find out the cube was originally recovered in Fish River Gorge, Namibia. Sydney and Lazarey had used **12 keys** to open the vault containing the cube. Sydney's eggs were extracted and the Covenant had planned on combining them with **Rambaldi's DNA** (22) to create a child, as they believe Sydney is the Chosen One.

Taken
Sydney recovers a **box engraved with the name "Irina"** (23) from the Department of Special Research.

The Frame
Sydney and Vaughn find a **map** (24) in the form of a crystal, and the map leads them to **the keys** (25) that will open the Irina box.

Hourglass
Sark retrieves a Rambaldi manuscript called *The Restoration*, (26) which reveals who The Passenger is and mentions an hourglass that will divulge The Passenger's whereabouts, but only if it is used by The Passenger's father. The CIA has the **code key** (27) in its possession already, which allows its agents to read the manuscript. Sydney retrieves **the Hourglass** (28) from an art gallery.

Blood Ties

When Sloane smashes the hourglass it creates a **battery** to be used in a **Rambaldi machine** that prints out the brainwaves of The Passenger. When Sloane, Sydney, and Jack track the brainwaves, they find **The Passenger.**㉙

Legacy

The Passenger, when injected with a **green elixir** (the formula for which is in the **Rambaldi manuscript**), writes out a **formula** ㉚ that explains Rambaldi's endgame.

Resurrection

The formula can be broken down to degrees of latitude and longitude that point to the **Sphere of Life**, the essence of Rambaldi himself.

Writers

J.J. Abrams
Truth Be Told; So It Begins; Spirit (with Vanessa Taylor); The Confession (with Daniel Arkin); Page 47 (with Jeff Pinkner); Q & A; Almost Thirty Years; The Enemy Walks In; Phase One; The Telling; The Two

Jesse Alexander
Reckoning; The Box, Parts 1 and 2 (with John Eisendrath); Snowman (with Jeff Pinkner); Dead Drop; A Dark Turn; Repercussions; Full Disclosure; Legacy

Josh Appelbaum and André Nemec
Conscious; Crossings; Hourglass

Laurence Andries
Blowback

Daniel Arkin
Doppelgänger; The Confession (with J.J. Abrams)

Monica Breen and Alison Schapker
A Missing Link; After Six; Unveiled; Blood Ties (story)

John Eisendrath
The Box, Parts 1 and 2 (with Jesse Alexander); The Prophecy; The Solution; Trust Me; The Counteragent; A Higher Echelon; Firebomb

Debra J. Fisher and Erica Messer
Mea Culpa; Rendezvous; Passage, Part 1

Breen Frazier
Second Double (story); Breaking Point

R.P. Gaborno
Countdown (story); Façade (with Christopher Hollier)

Sean Gerace
Endgame

Crystal Nix Hines
Passage, Part 2; Second Double (teleplay); The Nemesis; The Frame

Christopher Hollier
Façade (with R.P. Gaborno)

Alex Kurtzman-Counter and Roberto Orci
Parity; Color-Blind; The Coup; Masquerade; Cipher; Salvation; The Abduction; Double Agent; A Free Agent; Succession

J.R. Orci
Truth Takes Time; Prelude; Taken; Blood Ties (teleplay)

Jeff Pinkner
Time Will Tell; Page 47 (with J.J. Abrams); Snowman (with Jesse Alexander); The Indicator; The Getaway; Countdown (teleplay); Reunion; Remnants; Resurrection

Vanessa Taylor
A Broken Heart; Spirit (with J.J. Abrams)

Directors

J.J. Abrams
Truth Be Told; Almost Thirty Years; The Telling

Daniel Attias
Reckoning; The Solution; Cipher; The Counteragent; Succession; Breaking Point

Guy Norman Bee
Dead Drop; A Higher Echelon

Jack Bender
Color-Blind; Spirit; The Box, Parts 1 and 2; Phase One; Reunion; Prelude; Remnants; Façade; Unveiled; Blood Ties

Maryann Brandon
After Six

David Guggenheim
The Prophecy

Barnet Kellman
Snowman

Alex Kurtzman-Counter
A Free Agent

Perry Lang
Time Will Tell; Salvation; Endgame

Max Mayer
The Frame

Nelson McCormick
The Abduction; Truth Takes Time

Ken Olin
So It Begins; Doppelgänger; Mea Culpa; Page 47; Q & A; Rendezvous; The Enemy Walks In; The Indicator; Passage, Parts 1 and 2; Double Agent; A Dark Turn; Second Double; The Two; Repercussions; Conscious; Crossings; Hourglass; Resurrection

Mikael Salomon
Parity

Lawrence Trilling
The Getaway; Countdown; A Missing Link; The Nemesis; Full Disclosure; Blowback; Taken; Legacy

Harry Winer
A Broken Heart; The Confession

Tom Wright
The Coup

Craig Zisk
Masquerade; Trust Me; Firebomb

So, You Want to Join the CIA
(CIA Trivia Answers)

CIA History: True or False (10 points)

1. True. President Roosevelt asked William J. Donovan to draft a plan to create a new intelligence service, and Donovan was appointed the Coordinator of Information (COI) in July 1941. It was Donovan's job to be the director for the U.S.A.'s first peacetime, nondepartmental intelligence group.

2. False. The initial group created in 1942 was the Office of Strategic Services (OSS), as a consequence of World War II. The goal of the OSS was to take information obtained by the Joint Chiefs of Staff and analyze it. With that information, the OSS would conduct special operations that were unrelated to other agencies. The organization was run by Donovan. The Central Intelligence Agency was created in 1947.

3. True. The OSS was dissolved by Donovan's civil and military rivals for fear he would create a peacetime intelligence organization based on the OSS. President Harry S. Truman stated that there was no need for the OSS after the war. The group disbanded in October 1945 and its functions and information were transferred to the State and War Departments.

4. False. The three groups supported the idea and advised the President of the need for a centralized intelligence organization. The CIG was created in January 1946. Its two main functions were to provide strategic warning as well as to conduct "clandestine" missions.

5. True. The CIG was actually under the direction of the National Intelligence Authority, which had the following representatives: a presidential rep, and the Secretaries of State, War, and the Navy.

6. True. Navy Rear Admiral Sidney W. Souers, USNR, went from being the Deputy Chief of Naval Intelligence to the Director of Central Intelligence.

7. True. Twenty months following the creation of the CIG, the National Security

Act of 1947 led to its dissolution. In its place, the National Security Council (NSC) and the Central Intelligence Agency (CIA) were born.

8. True. The CIA's purpose was to coordinate the country's intelligence activities and then organize, evaluate, and disseminate the intelligence that would affect national security. It was to carry out its responsibilities in accordance with various instructions and directives stated by the President and the National Security Council.

9. True. The CIA was permitted to obtain funds from the budgets of other departments, disregarding the restrictions placed on the initial budgetary breakdown. This allowance helped to keep the CIA's true budget a secret.

10. False. Former President George Bush was the CIA Director from January 30, 1976, to January 20, 1977. On October 20, 1998, the Intelligence Authorization Act for 1999 (fiscal year) stated, among other things, that the Headquarters section of the CIA in Langley, Virginia, was to become the George Bush Center for Intelligence.

CIA Statues and Memorials (8 points)

1. d.

2. d. Only 34 of the stars are for anonymous members.

3. b. The book is handbound in Moroccan goat skin, and the CIA seal is only embossed in gold on the front. While the 46 members who could be named are listed in the book, the other 34 members are also recognized with gold stars.

4. d. The OSS Memorial was dedicated in 1992, 50 years after the organization was established.

5. a. The monument is near the southwest entrance and points north-south in an attempt to mirror the original wall. It has been placed in the middle of a path so it is impossible to miss. There is also a bench-height wall on both sides of the memorial, allowing for individuals to sit and contemplate. A bronze plaque explains that the pieces of the wall were located close to Checkpoint Charlie and that the monument is a reminder to never allow such a situation to occur again.

6. c. The seal is made of granite, is 16 feet in diameter, and became the official seal on February 17, 1950.

7. b. While there is no actual portrait of Nathan Hale, the life-sized sculpture is based on the written description of him. His last words were: "I regret that I have but one life to lose for my country."

8. c. The wood, granite, and copper statue was created with Native American materials and has around 2,000 letters on the copper screen. The "Kryptos" code has four parts, and to this date, no one has cracked the full code.

CIA Employment: True or False (15 points)

1. False. U.S. citizenship is a requirement.
2. True. Potential employees are also studied for any potential to be coerced and their ability to follow the rules. They are also checked out for possible conflicts with previous allegiances.
3. False. There are many internal opportunities to learn new languages, however.
4. False. Only a minimum cumulative 3.0 GPA is required.
5. True. Students selected are also provided with a salary and up to $18,000 per school year for expenses, tuition, supplies, etc. They work at the CIA during the summer.
6. True. There are many options under each of these headings.
7. False. The most common reason for denial of security clearance is a history of drug abuse.
8. False. There are many positions available at the CIA, and there are no course requirements in order to apply, although knowing a second language is a bonus.
9. True. The CIA Recruitment Center will ignore you if you live abroad. You have to be a permanent U.S. resident in order to apply.
10. False. It is highly recommended, but life experience is also noted. For some overseas positions an undergraduate degree is required, and in some cases even a more advanced degree is mandatory.
11. False. They are actually recommended through the university campus co-op programs.
12. True. You have to finish your term with whatever military branch you are a part of before applying to the CIA.
13. True.
14. False. It actually stands for "Family Advisory Board," which is designed for spouses of agency employees. It provides information to spouses about the CIA and grants scholarships annually to different dependents of CIA employees.
15. True. George J. Tenet, a New York native, has an extensive intelligence background, a BSFS from Georgetown University School of Foreign Service, and an MIA from Columbia University's School of International Affairs.

Spies in the Movies (11 points)

1. Diana Rigg, Honor Blackman, and Joanna Lumley.
2. His hand was detachable, and he could attach other gadgets to it.
3. The Dutch.
4. Alan Cummings, Steve Buscemi, and Sylvester Stallone.
5. The cat was never given a name, although Mike Myers spoofed it in the *Austin Powers* films and named the cat "Mr. Bigglesworth."
6. It sends them to Russia as decoys, while the real spies sneak in.
7. *The Ipcress File.*
8. Matthew Archer.
9. Eliza Dushku.
10. Her secret notebook.

Bonus: Michelle Trachtenberg.

Sources

The Anatomy of *Alias*

Abbie Bernstein, "If Looks Could Kill," *Alias*, November/December 2003.

—, "The Music Man," *Alias*, March/April 2004.

—, "The Spy Master," *Alias*, November/December 2003.

—, "The Telling," *Alias*, January/February 2004.

—, "The World is Not Enough," *Alias*, January/February 2004.

"ABC Goes Over the Top with Innovative '*Alias* Underground' Game," ABC press release, 12 September 2002.

"Abrams Hints *Alias*' Future," *Sci Fi Wire* (online), 16 January 2004.

"*Alias* Adds Mama Lena!" *Entertainment Tonight*, 30 October 2002.

"*Alias* brings back Evil Francie and Will," *The Edge* (online), November 2003.

"*Alias* Creator Abrams Stays at Touchstone," Zap2it.com, 4 February 2004.

"*Alias* in Family Way," *Sci Fi Wire* (online), 5 August 2002.

"*Alias* into Home Stretch," *Sci Fi Wire* (online), 22 April 2004.

"*Alias* gets a 'super' broadcast and *The Practice* moves to a new day & time, as ABC announces scheduling changes for midseason," ABCmedianet.com, 12 December 2002.

"*Alias* Gets More Complex," *Sci Fi Wire* (online), 19 July 2002.

"*Alias*' Michael Vartan and Bradley Cooper Come to Chat!" *Chat with Wanda* (E! online), 15 October 2001.

"*Alias* Outwits Its Ratings," Zap2it.com, 26 November 2002.

"*Alias* Producer Thrilled Over Pick Up," Zap2it.com, 24 October 2001.

"*Alias*' Sark Cuts It Short," *Sci Fi Wire* (online), 12 September 2003.

Amy Amatangelo, "Agent Anders: *Alias* star discovers he's a teen idol," *Boston Herald*, 16 January 2004.

Andrew Wallenstein, "TNT Uncovers Low Fee for *Alias*," HollywoodReporter.com, 2 March 2004.

Bill Brioux, "Warrior Babe," *Toronto Sun*, 10 December 2001.

Brad Cook, "You Spy: Become a Double Agent in *Alias*: Underground," ABCmedia-net.com, January 2003.

Brian Lowry, "And they're also known as jokesters," *Los Angeles Times*, 27 October 2002.

Brian Stenberg, "The Pitch: ABC's Latest Mission? Hyping *Alias* to Crowds," *Dow Jones Newswire*, 11 January 2003.

Brill Bundy, "*Alias* Star Gets into Her Role," Zap2it.com, 23 July 2001.

Chris Maxwell, "She Who Dares/*Alias* Revealed," *SKY*, March 2003.

Dan Snierson, "*Alias* — Spy Anxiety," *Entertainment Weekly*, 13 September 2002.

—, *Entertainment Weekly*, 15 June 2001.

—, "Returning Shows: *Alias*," *Entertainment Weekly*, 12 September 2003.

—, "Secrets & Spies," *Entertainment Weekly*, 8 March 2002.

—, "Spy Jinx?" *Entertainment Weekly*, 7 February 2003.

Dana Calvo, "Is *Alias* A.K.A. a Trend?," *LA Times* (online), 28 July 2001.

Danny Spiegel, "Classified Information — We've Blown their Cover: *Alias* Revealed," *TV Guide*, 25 January 2003.

Don Kaplan, "The Girl Who Killed *X-Files*," *New York Post*, 22 January 2002.

Doug Young, "ABC to Air *Alias* Debut Commercial-Free," Reuters, 22 July 2001.

"Drama's New Wave," *Daily Variety* (Emmy Commemorative Issue).

Edward Gross, "Action and Stunts," *Cinefantastique*, October 2002.

—, "Agent Provocateur," *Cinefantastique*, October/November 2003.

—, "*Alias* Special Effects," *Cinefantastique*, October 2002.

—, "*Alias*: Turning the Spy Genre and Television on Its Head, a College Student Turned Secret Agent Takes No Prisoners," *Cinefantastique*, October 2002.

—, "Hi, Hi Miss American Spy," *SFX UK*, March 2003.

—, "Quick Change," *Cinefantastique*, October/November 2003.

—, "Techno Thriller *Alias* composer Michael Giacchino's driving beats are one of the show's key creative components," *Cinefantastique*, October/November 2003.

—, "Wiggin' Out *Alias*' Emmy-nominated hairstylist, Michael Reitz, reveals the secrets behind Syd's wild looks," *Cinefantastique*, November/December 2003.

Eric Mink, "Spin Doctor, Heal Thyself," *Daily News*, 31 July 2001.

Frazier Moore, "Garner of *Alias* Is a Can-Do Woman," Associated Press, 29 November 2001.

Gregg Kilday, "Kryptonite Web reviews drub *Superman*," *Hollywood Reporter*, 4 October 2002.

Gregory M. Lamb, "TV's higher threshold of pain," *Christian Science Monitor*, 23 August 2002.

Heidi Vogt, "Very cool *Alias* getting the chills. Expectations were high but numbers are faltering," *Media Life*, 18 October 2002.

Ian Spelling, "Double Crossed," *Xpose*, July 2003.

—, "Marcus Out of Ten," *Cult Times*, June 2003.

"It Jennifer Garner Enhancer: Laura Goldsmith," *Entertainment Weekly*, June 28/July 5, 2002.

"It's All New on *Alias*," Sci Fi Wire (online), 4 February 2003.

J.D. Biersdorfer, "Hollywood's Gadget Factories," *New York Times*, 27 September 2002.

James Poniewozik, "The Upfronts: Of Regis-cide and the Prodigal Buffy," *Time TV*, 16 May 2001.

Jeffrey Abrams, "Letter from J.J. Abrams to Critics," 20 September 2002.

—, "Truth Be Told," *Alias* pilot episode, aired 30 September 2001.

"Jennifer's *Alias* Kiss," *Entertainment Tonight*, 10 September 2003.

Jenny Cooney Carrillo, "Dangerous Liaisons," *Dreamwatch Issue #115*, 2004.

Jesse Alexander, "*Alias* Chat Transcript," 29 September 2002.

Jill Feiwell, "Morning Glory for Emmy Nominees," *Variety*, 19 July 2002.

John Krogh, "Behind the Scenes of ABC's *Alias*," *Keyboard*, July 2002.

—, "Q&A with *Alias* creator J. J. Abrams," *Keyboard*, July 2002.

Josef Adalian, "*Alias*' creator packs a punch while reinventing the spy game," *Daily Variety*, 30 August 2002.

Joyce C. Abano, "Victor Garber *Alias* Jack Bristow: Good guy, bad guy," *Philippine Daily Inquirer*, 26 November 2003.

Judy Hevrdejs, "Spies invade TV realm," *Chicago Tribune*, May 2002.

Kate O'Hare, "*Alias* Creator Offers 'Full Disclosure,'" Zap2it.com, 31 December 2003.

—, "*Alias* exile returns with new look," Zap2it.com, 6 December 2003.

—, "*Alias* Gets Ready to Ramp Up," Zap2it.com, 5 April 2002.

—, "*Alias*: Just Another Family Affair," Zap2it.com, 4 November 2002.

—, "The Secret Life of Eric Weiss on *Alias*," Zap2it.com, March 2004.

Kathie Huddleston, "Happy Returns: *Alias* leads the charge with dark new missions as returning friends launch new seasons," *Sci Fi*, October 2003.

Ken Tucker, "New Shows: Best New Drama," *Entertainment Weekly*, 7 September 2001.

Kevin Williamson, "Making a name for itself," *Calgary Sun*, 14 December 2001.

—, "Spy stakes It's do-or-die for *Alias*' secret agent — on and off screen," *Calgary Sun*, 5 October 2002.

Lindsay Arent, "Unmasking *Alias*," *Tech Live*, 13 November 2002.

Lynette Rice and Dan Snierson, "Sensitive Material — The new spy shows — In the wake of the attack find out what's now in store for spy-themed shows," *Entertainment Weekly*, September 2001.

Mark Cotta Vaz, *Alias: Declassified*, Bantam Books, 2002.

Marla Lehner, "Fans Take TV to the Web," foxnews.com, 30 September 2003.

Matt Roush, "Roush Room: Ask Matt," *TV Guide* (online), 3 November 2003.

"Meet the Real-Life Marshalls of *Alias*," Zap2it.com, 13 November 2002.

Melissa George/Henry, "Interview with Melissa George," Melissa George — The Authorized Web site, www.melissageorge.com, 3 November 2003.

Michael Ausiello, "An *Alias* Movie? Secret Plot Exposed!" *TV Guide* (online), 27 January 2003.

—, "I Spy Super *Alias* Spoilers!" *TV Guide*, 24 January 2003.

Michael Szymanski, "Garner Says *Alias* a Go for Season Four," Zap2it.com, 3 April 2004.

Mike Hughes, "CIA goes undercover with *Alias*," Gannett News Service, 13 September 2001.

Mumtaj Begum, "Role to relish — Victor Garber talks about his double agent role and his co-stars in the highly entertaining series *Alias*," *The Star Online*, 4 November 2003.

Nancy Mills, "*Alias* star spies new identity for show," *New York Daily News*, 3 September 2003.

Neal Justin, "On TV, hot shows go in for hot tunes," *Minneapolis–St. Paul Star Tribune*, 2002.

Noah Robischon, "Secret Agent Fan," *Entertainment Weekly*, 19 October 2001.

"Olin Hopes For *Alias* Return," *Sci Fi Wire* (online), 10 June 2003.

"The 100 Most Creative People in Entertainment It Television: It Multitasker," *Entertainment Weekly*.

Paul Farhi, "ABC Promoters, Feverishly Forging an *Alias* Identity: Publicity Strategy for Spy Series Is Anything but a Hush-Hush Operation," *Washington Post*, 23 September 2001.

Paul Spragg, "Also Known As . . ." *Cult Times*, May 2002.

—, "Entertaining Mr. Sloane," *Cult Times*, August 2003.

Paul Terry, "Renaissance Woman," *Alias*, January/February 2004.

Paula Bernstein, "Hardest-Working Actor of the Season: the C.I.A.," *New York Times*, 2 September 2001.

Peter Rubin, "Why Jennifer Garner Might Like to Kick Your A**," *GQ*, March 2003.

Rick Porter, "*Alias, Blue* Go Rerun-Free Next Season," Zap2it.com, 17 May 2004.

—, "*Alias* Creator Explains Why SD-6 Had to Go," Zap2it.com, 19 February 2003.

Robert Levine, "The Episode: Cracking the Code of *Alias*," *New York Times*, 25 April 2004.

Ron Rifkin, "On *Alias: Declassified* (DVD)," Bantam Books, 2002.

Sarah Kuhn, "*Alias* Season Two," *Cinescape*, Fall 2002.

Shawna Malcolm, "Spy Games," *TV Guide*, 21 September 2002.

—, "With *Alias*, Lena Olin takes a wicked turn," *TV Guide*, 21 September 2002.

"Sister Act!," *Alias*, March/April 2004.

Steve Murray, "*Alias* blurb," Cox News Service, 15 January 2004.

—, "The bod squad: TV's powerful, take-charge heroines give viewers cheesecake, positive role models," *Atlanta Journal-Constitution*, 29 November 2002.

Terry Morrow, Scripps Howard News Service, 2002.

Thomas McLean, "Jennifer Garner: Female Star of Tomorrow," Variety.com, 23 March 2004.

Vanessa Sibbald, "Fall Spy Shows Will Still Make It to Air," Zap2it.com, 20 September 2001.

Vicki Vasilopoulos, "What Makes Jennifer Garner TV's Sexiest Spy . . . Baby Powder and a Rubber Dress," *New York Post*, 12 March 2003.

Watch with Kristin (E! online), 21 July 2003.

Watch with Kristin, "We Fan the Burning Embers of *Alias* Anticipation," (E! online), 29 August 2003.

"Who's That Girl?" *play #1*, 2004.

William Keck, "For 13 rollout, 'cute' sums it up," *USA Today*, 15 April 2004.

"You Spy: Become a Double Agent in *Alias*: Underground For Your Eyes Only: Inside the World of *Alias* Q&A with J.J. Abrams," Apple.com, January 2003.

The Cast of *Alias*
Jennifer Garner

Abbie Bernstein, "The Confession," *Alias*, November/December 2003.

—, "The Spy Master," *Alias*, November/December 2003.

"Actress Jennifer Garner Gives Speech," Associated Press, 6 October 2002.

Ann Wycoff, "Secret Agent," *Seventeen*, March 2002.

Bari Nan Cohen, "Stand aside, stunt double!" *Self*, January 2002.

Barry Koltnow, "*Alias* Elektra — Jennifer Garner departs from her TV role to bring the *Daredevil* character to the big screen," *Orange County Register*, 14 February 2003.

Bill Muller, "Partners in Pain — Jennifer Garner relished playing opposite Affleck in *Daredevil*," *Herald Dispatch*, 16 February 2003.

Bob Strauss, "*Alias* star Jennifer Garner continues the action stuff in *Daredevil*," *Los Angeles Daily News* (online edition), 14 February 2003.

Brendan Vaughan, "Women We Love," *Esquire*, 6 January 2002.

Christopher Heard, "Garnering Raves," *Toronto Fashion*, June 2003.

"Countdown," *Alias*, January/February 2004.

Dan Snierson, "Secrets & Spies," *Entertainment Weekly*, 8 March 2002.

David Keeps, "Jennifer Garner Kicks Butt," *Teen People*, March 2003.

David Martindale, "The Hit Girl: *Alias*' Jennifer Garner," *Biography*, December 2002.

Edward Gross, "Hi, Hi Miss American Spy," SFX UK, March 2003.

—, "Jennifer Garner," *Cinefantastique*, October 2002.

—, "Jennifer on Their Minds," *Femme Fatale*, March/April 2003.

"50 Most Beautiful People — Jennifer Garner," *People*, 13 May 2002.

"The 50 Most Beautiful People — Jennifer Garner," *People*, 12 May 2003.

"Garner Gets Personal," *The Age*, 13 October 2003.

"Garner Going on 30," *Sci Fi Wire* (online), 3 February 2003.

"Garner Visits W.V. Hometown," Associated Press (online), 2 May 2003.

"Intelligence Gathering," *Allure*, September 2002.

James Brady, "In Step with Jennifer Garner," *Parade*, 30 September 2001.

"Jennifer Garner's Secret Life," *ET* (online), 3 September 2001.

"Jennifer's Marriage Heartache," *In Touch*, 21 April 2003.

Jill Feiwell, "Morning Glory for Emmy Nominees," *Variety*, 19 July 2002.

John Griffiths, "Catch Her If You Can," *Premiere*, November 2002.

—, "Jennifer Garner's Dos & Don'ts," *Glamour*, February 2003.

Josh Grossberg, "Garner on Assignment for CIA?" *E!* (online), 28 August 2003.

Laura Brown, "Jennifer's prime time — Real-life superhero Jennifer Garner proves that nice girls finish first," *W*, November 2003.

Lia Haberman, "Double agent by day, newlywed by night," *E!* (online), 1 September 2001.

Mark Binelli, "Spy Girl," *Rolling Stone*, 14 February 2002.

Mark Cotta Vaz, *Alias: Declassified*, Bantam Books, 2002.

Mary A. Fischer, "I, Spy," *Allure*, September 2002.

Mary Wade Burnside, "City Native on Cover of *Rolling Stone*," *Charleston Daily Mail*, 26 January 2002.

Michael A. Lipton, "Agent Provocateur," *People*, 11 March 2002.

Michael Fleming, "Lass Action Hero," *Fade In*, December 2002.

Michael Hamersly, "*Alias* agent takes no prisoners," *Miami Herald*, 8 January 2002.

Michael Hogan, "Action Attraction," *Vanity Fair*, January 2003

Michael Moses, "Hype: people, places & things in the spotlight — Jennifer Garner," *Movieline* (online), 4 April 2001.

P.J. Tarasuk and Angela Ryan, "Secret Agent Girl," *FW*, December 2001.

Quote from *The Tonight Show with Jay Leno*, 13 December 2002.

Robert Bianco, "TV: Garner goes undercover in *Alias*," *Lansing State Journal* (online edition), 8 February 2002.

Ryan J. Downey, "Affleck, Garner Open Up about *Daredevil*," MTV (online), 24 June 2002.

—, "Jennifer Garner, Ben Affleck Suit Up for *Daredevil*," MTV (online), 3 June 2002.

Sean Daly, "Heroine Chic," *Toronto Star*, 8 February 2003.

"Senior spy," nzoom.com.

Shawna Malcolm, "Spy Games," *TV Guide*, 21 September 2002.

"The Spy Next Door," ABC News (online), 6 March 2002.

Todd Gold, "Star Rising," *US Weekly*, 19 November 2001.

Victor Garber

Abbie Bernstein, "Truth Be Told," *Alias*, November/December 2003.

"*Alias* Stars Ante Up," *Watch with Wanda* (E! online), 18 October 2002.

Dan Snierson, "*Alias* — Spy Anxiety," *Entertainment Weekly*, 13 September 2002.

Dana Gee, "Garber Loves His Musicals," *Province*, 16 February 2003.

Fred R. Conrad and Frank Moher, "Stephen Sondheim: A long haul," *National Post*, 13 March 2000.

Helen Branswell, "VG wants to see cure for the tyranny of diabetes in his lifetime," CJAD 800 AM/Canadian Press, 11 November 2003.

Jamie Portman, "Sunken ship buoyed Garber's career: Role in *Titanic* led to better offers for Canadian actor," Southam Newspapers, 8 August 2001.

Jenelle Riley, "Variously Victor," *Backstage*, 3 September 2003.

John Ryan, Direct quote, 2004.

Mark Magill, "Alfred Molina and Victor Garber," *Bomb*, Spring 1998.

Michael Buckley, "A Hell of a Guy," *Theater Week*, 6 June 1994.

Mumtaj Begum, "Role to relish: Victor Garber talks about his double agent role and his co-stars in the highly entertaining series *Alias*," *The Star Online*, 4 November 2003.

Rachel Sklar, "Garber gets bad guys, good ratings," Canadian Press, May 2002.

Roy Harris, "In That One Specific Moment — Victor Garber, Part I," in *Conversations in the Wings Talking About Acting*, Heinemann, 1994.

—. "In That One Specific Moment — Victor Garber, Part II," in *Conversations in the Wings Talking About Acting*, Heinemann, 1994.

Sam Whitehead, "Victor victorious," *TimeOut NY*, 19 February 1998.

"Senior Spy," nzoom.com.

Sheryl Flatow, "Mr. Garber's Profession," *Theater Week*, 28 November 1988.

Transcript of Garber and Rifkin on *Canada AM*.

Transcript of Victor Garber's appearance on *The Wayne Brady Show*.

Victor Garber and Fulton King, "Great Escapes: Oh, the siren call of Sag Harbor on Long Island," *Toronto Star*, November 2000.

"Victor Garber Unites with Juvenile Diabetes Research Foundation in PSA Campaign," Juvenile Diabetes Research Foundation (online).

Michael Vartan

Abbie Bernstein, "Married to the Job," *Alias*, January/February 2004.

Adriana Leshko, "Cameo: Michael Vartan," *Premiere*, January 2002.

B. Kokkinos, "Michael Vartan Interview: I am the target of hysterical fans!" *Star Club*, November 2002.

Barry Mann, "The Next Best Thing," *New Weekly*, March 2000.

"Boys of Summer," *Cosmopolitan*, Summer 1998.

Dina Sansing, "Hot for Teacher," *Seventeen*, August 1999.

Josef Adalian, "Vartan Spies ABC *Alias*," *Variety*, 28 February 2001.

Lesley Goober, "Hunk of the Month: We're Mad for Michael Vartan," *Cosmopolitan*, March 2002.

Louis B. Hobson, "Pool Career Scratched," *Calgary Sun*, 5 April 1999.

Marilyn Beck and Stacy Jenel Smith, "Michael Vartan Didn't Want to Shovel Manure," *The Hollywood Exclusive*, 2002.

Mark Cotta Vaz, *Alias: Declassified*, Bantam Books, 2002.

"Michael Vartan," *Stuff for Men*, 2001.

"Michael Vartan," *Venice*, May 1996.

"No Holds Barred," *Philadelphia Inquirer* (online edition), 29 August 2000.

"Our show-biz know-it-all has the answers," *Ask Marilyn Beck* (E! online), 7 April 2000.

Pia Chikiamco, "The Spy Who Loved Me," *Guide* (The Philippines), September 2003.

Ray Pride, "Straight Man," *New City Chicago*, 14 April 1999.

"Running Man," *Arena UK*, October 2002.

Sophie de Rakoff, "Franco-American Fox," *Paper*, September 1997.

Suzan Colon, "Michael Vartan," *Jane*, December 1997.

Tom Johnson, "Meet the Rising Stars You'll Be Talking About All Year," *E!* (online), 1999.

"Top 30 Bachelors," *People*, 24 June 2002.

William Keck, "*Alias*' date has a fishy end," *USA Today*, 27 August 2003.

"Work is Play for *Alias* Actor," nzoom.com, 1 October 2001.

Carl Lumbly

Carl Lumbly, "Jamaica has made me a happy man," *Jamaica Gleaner*, 2001.

Ian Spelling, "Marcus out of Ten," *Cult Times*, June 2003.

Kate O'Hare, "*Alias*: Just Another Family Affair," Zap2it.com, 4 November 2002.

Mark Cotta Vaz, *Alias: Declassified*, Bantam Books, 2002.

Neal Justin, "Minneapolis actor Carl Lumbly has managed to keep his cool," *Minneapolis Star Tribune*, 18 January 2003.

Rob Kendt, "What's up with . . . Carl Lumbly," *Back Stage West*, BPI Entertainment News Wire Feature, 22 January 2003.

Sharon Gless, Direct quote, 2004.

Susan Young, "Just another TV secret agent at Home Depot," *Alameda Times Star*, 6 May 2003.

Kevin Weisman

Abbie Bernstein, "Masquerade," *Alias*, January/February 2004.

"*Alias* Stars Ante Up," *Watch with Wanda* (E! online), 18 October 2002.

Amy Eslinger, "Technically Speaking," *On Sat*, 27 June 2002.

Bryan Cairns, "Marshalling the Troops," *Cult Times*, December 2003.

Daniel Roberts, "Q&A with Kevin Weisman," *TV Guide*, 24 November 2003.

John Crook, "Checking in with Kevin Weisman," Tribune Media Services (online), December 2003.

Kenneth Andrew Wert, "*Alias* — Mr. Wizard," *Soap Opera Weekly*, 2002.

Kevin Weisman, "Theater Section," Kevin Weisman's Official Web site, www.kevin-weisman.com.

Mark Cotta Vaz, *Alias: Declassified*, Bantam Books, 2002.

Tim Clodfelter, "ON TRACK: Actor goes on trip with Trainwreck," *Journal Now*, 25 July 2003.

Tom Provenzano, "Not in My House," *Stage and Screen*, 25 May 2000.

Greg Grunberg

"Amy Jo Johnson & Greg Grunberg: transcript," E!Online.com, 8 May 2000.

"Countdown," *Alias*, January/February 2004.

Dana Meltzer, "A Hanukkah Feast Entertain 10 to 12 guests," *Washington Post*, 30 November 2003.

"Greg Grunberg Chat Transcript," *Talk City* (ET online), 1 August 2000.

"Greg Grunberg Interview," Greg Grunberg — A Fan Site, www.cybamall.com/greg-grunberg/greg.html.

"Greg Grunberg: Transcripts," *TV Guide* (online edition), 17 May 2000.

"Grill, gossip & gripe," *Watch with Wanda* (E! online), 20 May 2002.

"Interview with Greg Grunberg," www.aliasboards.com.

Lisa Kincaid, "One Weiss Man," *Cult Times*, 9 December 2003.

Vanessa Sibbald, "*Felicity*'s Grunberg Moonlights on *Alias*," Zap2it.com TV News, 10 October 2001.

Watch with Kristin, (E! online), 21 July 2003.

Merrin Dungey

"Abrams Answers," *Alias*, January/February 2004.

Bruce Fretts, "Dungey Jumping," *Entertainment Weekly*, 16 November 2001.

"Doing Two Shows Is Twice As Nice," *New York Vue (Sunday Daily News)*, 30 November 2003.

Eric Moro, "Return of the Francinator," *Alias*, March/April 2004.

"Lookin' good, sisters!" *Rosie*, June 2002.

Mark Cotta Vaz, *Alias: Declassified*, Bantam Books, 2002.

"Meet *Alias*'s New Bad Girl," *TV Guide*, 31 January 2003.

Mike McLaren, "Pride of the Lions President Shines for His Daughters," *Fair Oaks Guardian*, January 1998.

Regina, "The Bradley Cooper Interview," *Television without Pity* (online).

Bradley Cooper

FW Magazine #34.

"Grill, gossip & gripe," *Watch with Kristin* (E! online), 27 October 2003.

"Grill, gossip & gripe: *Alias*' Michael Vartan and Bradley Cooper Come to Chat!" *Chat with Wanda!* (E! online), 15 October 2001.

Heather Rush, "Bradley Cooper: *Alias* Star on Comfy Clothes and Suspenders," *Platinum*, September 2002.

"Hunk of the Month," *Cosmopolitan*, September 2002.

Kate O'Hare, "Will to Live on ABC's *Alias*," Zap2it.com.

Mark Cotta Vaz, *Alias: Declassified*, Bantam Books, 2002.

Nicole Vecchiarelli, "Spy Fame: Success hasn't ruined *Alias*' Bradley Cooper . . . yet," *Teen Vogue*, February/March 2003.

Regina, "The Bradley Cooper Interview," *Television without Pity* (online).

—, "The Bradley Cooper Interview Part Deux," *Television without Pity* (online).

Vanessa Sibbald, "In Defense of *Alias*' Will," Zap2it.com TV News, 4 March 2002.

Watch with Kristin (E! online), 3 October 2003.

Watch with Kristin (E! online), 17 October 2003.

"What Sex Feels Like for a Man . . . In a *Sex and the City* love scene with Carrie," *Glamour*, February 2003.

Ron RifkFin

"*Alias* Stars Ante Up," *Watch with Wanda* (E! online), 18 October 2002.

Emmanuelle Soichet, "Moving Into America's Living Rooms," *LA Times* (online edition), 16 September 2001.

Mark Cotta Vaz, *Alias: Declassified*, Bantam Books, 2002.

Paul Spragg, "Entertaining Mr. Sloane," *Cult Times*, August 2003.

"Ron Rifkin not like *Alias* spy he plays," Associated Press, 29 October 2002.

Stan Schwartz, "The Substance of Ron Rifkin — Talks with Ron Rifkin," *Urban Desires*, January/February 1997.

Télé Star, 27 September 2003.

Transcript of Victor Garber and Ron Rifkin on *Canada AM*.

Transcript of Victor Garber on *Open Mike with Mike Bullard*.

Lena Olin

Amy Longsdorf, "Lena Olin acts her age in *Hollywood Homicide*," *Courier Post* (online edition), 13 June 2003.

Barrett Hooper, "What would Bergman have to say about it? Actress Lena Olin is still acutely aware of her mentor's sensibilities," *National Post*, 12 June 2003.

Dan Snierson, "*Alias* — Spy Anxiety," *Entertainment Weekly*, 13 September 2002.

Geoffrey Macnab, "Desperately Seeking Obscurity," *Independent*, 16 February 2001.

Hilary de Vries, "A Night Out with Lena Olin," *New York Times*, 1 December 2002.

Hillary J. Johnson, "World's Sexiest Soccer Mom," *In Style*, August 1999.

J. Rentilly, "Lena Olin, finding TV dangerous," *Audience*, Summer 2003.

Jim Slotek, "Lena Olin: *Alias* Irina, Bad-Girl Mom," *Toronto Sun Television Listings*, 27 July 2003.

Kate Coyne, "Her Secret Weapon," *Good Housekeeping*, August 2003.

"Lena Olin: Redefining an Image," Amazon.com, 2000.

Margy Rochlin, "Ultra Swede," *Elle*, 1993.

Marshall Fine, "Movienotes: Reluctant Guy Notes," *Journal News* (online edition), 19 June 2003.

Merle Ginsberg, "The Swedish Confection: Lena Olin and Lasse Hallström," *WWD*, 2 January 2001.

Steve Vineberg, "An Action Heroine Is Given a Worthy Adversary: Mom," *New York Times*, 29 September 2002.

"With *Alias*, Lena Olin takes a wicked turn," *TV Guide*, 21 September 2002.

David Anders

Abbie Bernstein, "The Spy Master," *Alias*, November/December 2003.

Bartie Lancaster, "Local actor appears on TV's *Alias*," *Grants Pass Daily Courier*, 23 February 2002.

—, "Local Actor Gets Recurring TV Role," *Grants Pass Daily Courier*, 30 July 2002.

David Anders, "Interview with David #1," Official Web site of David Anders, www.davidanders.com, 10 April 2003.

Jessica Su, "Star Profile: David Anders," *Teen Scene*, 14 October 2003.

Kate O'Hare, "Sark Attack," Zap2it.com, 25 April 2003.

Kristi Turnquist, "Sinister Sark on *Alias* an Oregon 'dude,'" *Oregonian*, 3 May 2003.

"Sark! The Herald Angels Sing!" *Watch with Kristin* (E! online), 15 August 2003.

Tara DiLullo, "Sark of the Covenant," *Alias*, March/April 2004.

Melissa George

Brian J. Robb, "The Enemy Walks In," *Alias*, January/February 2004.

Di Stanley, "Melissa George Inc.," *TV Week*, 24 August 1996.

"Get the Scoop on *Alias* Direct from Cast and Crew," *Watch with Kristin* (E! online), 19 September 2003.

Glen Williams, "Melissa's Short Cut to Success," *TV Week*, 2 November 1996.

Lawrie Masterson, "Angel in the city of angels," *Woman's Day*, 31 August 1998.

—, "Melissa is still an Angel in Waiting," *Sydney Telegraph*, 14 January 2001.

Matt Hall, "18 Questions," *Playboy*, August 1996.

"Melissa George Bio," Melissa George — The Authorized Web site, www.melissageorge.com.

Melissa George/Henry, "Interview with Melissa George," Melissa George — The Authorized Web site, www.melissageorge.com, 3 November 2003.

"Melissa George," Special Events Transcripts (online), 25 January 2001.

"Melissa George's *Alias* Is the Other Woman," Zap2it.com, 6 December 2003.

Steve Baltin, "MELISSA GEORGE ALIAS: Hollywood Star on the Rise," *Venice*, November 2003.

Susan King, "Thieves: Stolen Moments," *LA Times*, 16 September 2001.

Alias Episode Guide

Alias — The Complete First Season (DVD), Buena Vista Home Entertainment.

Alias — The Complete Second Season (DVD), Buena Vista Home Entertainment.

Alias, Season Three, ABC.

"Behind the Scenes as Jennifer Gets Wet and Wild," *Entertainment Tonight*, 4 March 2004.

Bill Keveney, "Bond, James Bond Will Make an *Alias* Appearance," USA *Today*, 8 February 2002.